CW00673825

Tea and empire

Manchester University Press

Tea and empire

James Taylor in Victorian Ceylon

ANGELA MCCARTHY AND T.M. DEVINE

For Rosemary,

Hope you enjoy this!

Best wishes

Angela McCarthy.

Manchester University Press

Published by Manchester University Press
Altrincham Street, Manchester M1 7JA

www.manchesteruniversitypress.co.uk

British Library Cataloguing-in-Publication Data
A catalogue record for this book is available from the British Library

ISBN 978 1 5261 1905 6 hardback

First published 2017

Typeset by
Servis Filmsetting Ltd, Stockport, Cheshire
Printed in Great Britain by
TJ International Ltd, Padstow

Contents

Figures and tables

Figures

Table

Abbreviations

CO	*Ceylon Observer*
COO	*Colombo Overland Observer*
ICS	Institute of Commonwealth Studies
NLS	National Library of Scotland
NMS	National Museums Scotland
OCO	*Overland Ceylon Observer*
TA	*Tropical Agriculturalist*
WCO	*Weekly Ceylon Observer*

Editorial notes

Reproduction of the spelling and grammar contained in the original Taylor letters remains unaltered, although sentence breaks have been incorporated for ease of reading. Editorial excisions have been kept to a minimum but are as follows:

Clarifications:	misfortin [misfortune]
Authentic oddities:	untill; in *in*
Illegible words:	[*word illegible*]
Illegible words with suggestions:	[*?favour*]
Elements lost through mutilation:	marr[ied]
Words deleted or omitted:	[*erased:* success] [*omitted:* to]

Errors in other sources are indicated with [sic].

The spelling of Loolecondera, the estate upon which Taylor worked, is rendered in many diverse ways. We use Loolecondera consistently throughout, but have retained alternative spellings where these have appeared in original documents quoted.

Acknowledgements

Around early 2012, Graham McGregor, a Scot living in Dunedin, New Zealand, visited Angela's office to speak about Sri Lanka's Scottish legacy. During several subsequent meetings Graham mentioned the activities of several important Scots in Ceylon (as Sri Lanka was previously known), including James Taylor. On a trip to Edinburgh Angela consulted several Scottish migrant letters from Ceylon, including those of Taylor. Thus began research into Taylor's life, including transcription of all his letters, both private and those published in the press, the latter having never before been examined. Graham also kindly put us in contact with a number of Scots currently living in Sri Lanka.

Numerous folk in the Mearns area of Aberdeenshire have shared this journey into Taylor's life. Marion Robson invited us to participate in Scotland's first tea festival in 2014 and, together with her husband, Mike, has continued to provide wonderful hospitality during visits to Laurencekirk. At nearby Auchenblae, Taylor's home village, we were fortunate to draw upon the expertise and interest of local historian Jenny Thomson. Jenny, her husband, Jimmy, and daughter Margo Titmuss have been most welcoming. Jenny also kindly provided two photographs for reproduction in this book. Every attempt has been made to trace the copyright owners of these two images, but without success. Tom, Anne, Jane, and Katie Lawson, who now live at in the restored Taylor home at Mosspark, were wonderful hosts and helped track down research leads and answer queries. Revd Michael Turner, Revd Douglas Lamb, June McB Melvin, and Malcolm McCoig, also proved most supportive. To the many other folk in the Mearns who similarly offered advice and support, we are deeply grateful.

Others in Scotland who proved generous with their time include Anne and Iain Fraser, Sheena Blackhall, and Revd John and Patricia Purves. We are deeply appreciative to David Forsyth, Stuart Allan, and Elaine Edwards at National Museums Scotland for making Taylor's tea service and photograph album available to view on several occasions and to Maggie Wilson for assisting with photographic reproductions. Elaine Phillips and Craig Steven at the University of Edinburgh helped in scanning Tom Barron's collection of Taylor photographs, some of which appear in this book. Frances Humphries, the great-granddaughter of Taylor's sister Margaret, managed to solve one of the mysteries about Taylor – where his tea service had been deposited. Margaret Begbie very kindly typed Tom's longhand script. We thank you all.

Across the border in England, Catriona Warner, the daughter of Roy Cameron, a former superintendent on Loolecondera, where Taylor worked, and Catriona's aunt, Elizabeth Baxter, generously shared memories and photographs of their time on the estate. Ian McCorquodale and Byrony Brind provided a memorable lunch and delightful guided tour of Camfield, the home of the late Barbara Cartland. The renowned romance novelist included Taylor as a character in her novel set in Ceylon, *Moon Over Eden*. During a trip to Dunedin Dr Sujit Sivasundaram of the University of Cambridge kindly took time out from his busy schedule to discuss Sri Lankan history.

In Sri Lanka, Anselm Perera, owner of the Mlesna tea company, has been continuously supportive of this research. Anselm has done more than anyone to keep James Taylor's legacy alive, having built a thirteen-foot monument and Scottish baronial tea castle at Talawakelle in memory of the Scot. Anselm also funded two miniature replica statues of Taylor and shipped them to Scotland to commemorate the 2017 Sri Lankan tea anniversary. We are deeply grateful to Anselm for his generosity and warm hospitality during visits to Sri Lanka and for putting us in touch with several tea experts who provided advice, contacts, and hospitality. We therefore thank for all their support: Lalith Abeykoon, Anil Cooke, Sunil de Alwis, Avi De-Silva, Malik Fernando, Malin Goonetileke, Suresh Ganeshan, H.M.S.D. Hunugala, Vige Bede Johnpillai, Dickie Juriansz, Heniantha Kahatapitiya, Inderkumar Kithnasami, Ishan Rajasuriya, Reggie Rajiah, Nihal Rodrigo, M.S. Sunderaj, the late Andrew Taylor, Russell Tennekoon, I.P. Vitharanage, and Upali Wijeyesekera. We are indebted to several archivists for their assistance, especially Michael Anthonisz at the Scots Kirk in Colombo and Dr Asoka Senarath, Municipal Council, Kandy. Padamina Gridley kindly shared her family history. Charles Carmichael, caretaker of the Garrison cemetery, Kandy, was an informative guide.

Many Scots and those of Scottish descent living and working in Sri Lanka also shared their experiences and hospitality. We would like to thank the Revd Norman and Elizabeth Hutcheson, Gordon and Michelle Kenny, Kenneth McAlpine, and Elizabeth Moir. Former High Commissioner to Sri Lanka John Rankin was a most generous host. Peter Hooper, an English planter, also kindly shared his memories. Leelananda De Silva and Martin Straus gave of their time to share their insights. We are deeply obliged to our expert driver, Kapila Ranathunga, who carefully navigated Sri Lanka's roads, acted as an interpreter on many tea estates, and shared many adventures during the course of this research. Whether in stopping the car suddenly when spotting a cobra at Loolecondera, displaying utmost patience during efforts to pinpoint locations from old estate photographs, and sharing his extensive knowledge of Sri Lanka, Kapila gave us exceptional support.

In the online world, others have come to the rescue with suggestions to help answer many questions. David Air (editor of KoiHai), Larry Brown, Rex Naug, and Eileen Hewson were most helpful in attempts to trace details of Taylor's brother, William, who died in India. Anne Tischlinger and Herb Alexander kindly shared much of their research on the Moir family. Colin A. Milne assisted with information about gravestones. Dr Nicholas J. Evans at the University of Hull was a huge help with genealogical sources.

In Dunedin, several colleagues provided tips and research leads. Thanks to Judy Bennett, Rosi Crane, Jacqui Leckie, Jane McCabe, Angela Wanhalla, and Erika Wolf. As well as recommending Kapila as a driver and providing travel tips for Sri Lanka, Mark Seymour spoke on the significance of the emotions in scholarly research in a Works in Progress session in the Department of History and Art History. This influenced us to consider the emotional dimension of Taylor's life. Marie Nissanka provided helpful advice about history textbooks in Sri Lankan schools. The exceptional library staff at Otago must also be thanked, particularly Charlotte Brown, who organised a trial of the Asian newspapers online which proved so vital to this study.

This book would not have appeared without the assistance of staff at numerous archives. In the UK we would like to thank the following institutions: the British Library; the Centre of South Asian Studies and the Rare Books Room at the University of Cambridge; the Bodleian Library at the University of Oxford; the Highland Council Archive; the Institute of Commonwealth Studies at the University of London; the Mitchell Library, Glasgow; National Records Scotland; the Public Record Office of Northern Ireland; the Royal Botanic Gardens at Kew; Special Collections and Archives at the University of Aberdeen; and the University of St Andrews Special Collections. We are indebted to Dr Maria Castrillo and Yvonne Shand at the National Library of Scotland (NLS), who greatly facilitated research on the Taylor materials held there, and to Sally Harrower, who assisted with images of Taylor. Dr Ralph McLean, also of the NLS, very kindly alerted us to the Fettercairn Estate Papers, where we found two gems of information. Craig Brough at the Royal Botanic Gardens Kew Archive aided with photographs held there. In Sri Lanka, we thank staff at the Ceylon Tea Museum Archives, the Planters' Association of Ceylon, and the Sri Lanka Tea Board.

Visits to Sri Lanka and the UK were assisted by University of Otago Research grants and the Royal Society of Edinburgh. We acknowledge the support of the University's Humanities Research Grant for funding towards reproduction fees for many of the images that appear throughout the book and for the two maps expertly drawn by Les O'Neill. That grant also supported the indexing of the book, proficiently undertaken by Dr Lisa Marr.

Dr Tom Barron, formerly of the University of Edinburgh, who wrote about Taylor in a couple of unpublished papers, deserves special thanks. Tom has shown ongoing interest in the research, answered many questions, and read this entire manuscript in draft. We are deeply grateful for his eagle eye, corrections, and suggestions. Tom also very generously gave permission for us to reproduce in this book several Taylor photos in his possession.

We also want to pay utmost thanks to the superb Emma Brennan and her wonderful team at Manchester University Press. They wholeheartedly supported the book from the outset and worked quickly to ensure its publication in 2017, the 150th anniversary of Ceylon tea and the 125th anniversary of Taylor's death.

Angela McCarthy and Tom Devine

Maps

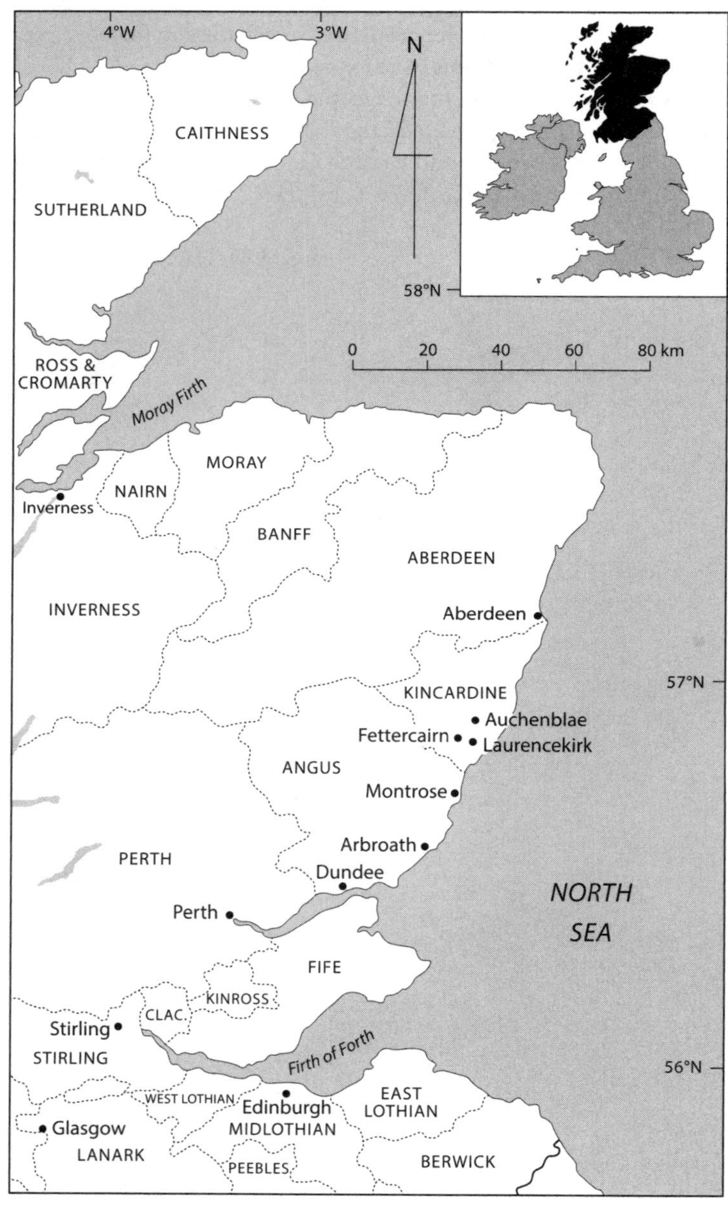

Map of Scotland

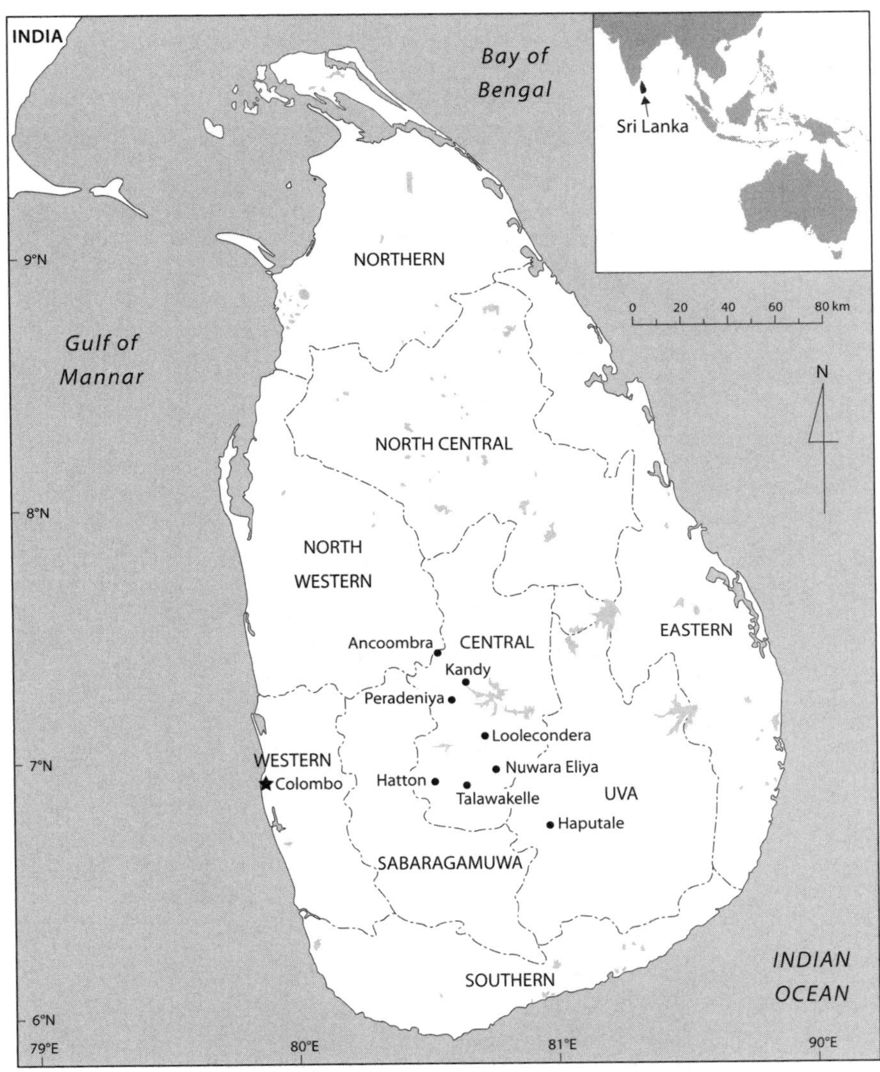

Map of Sri Lanka

James Taylor, 'father of the Ceylon tea enterprise', 1835–1892.

Introduction

In 1891 the Planters' Association of Ceylon publicly celebrated the seminal achievements of a Scotsman, James Taylor, who had successfully pioneered what had become by then the vast new tea economy of the colony. As the Association's Chairman put it: 'There was no denying the fact that he [Taylor] originally proved in this Island that Ceylon could make good tea.'[1] A mere six months after this public accolade, Taylor was dead, and his reputation sullied beforehand. He had been dismissed in disgrace from the post of superintendent at the estate that he had served for more than forty years and where he had carried out his famous and successful experiments in the cultivation of tea.

This book, set in its contemporary context, examines the remarkable life story of James Taylor from his upbringing in north-east Scotland until his death in 1892 in Ceylon (known as Sri Lanka since 1972). He was born in 1835 near the village of Auchenblae in Kincardineshire and, after leaving there at the age of sixteen, spent the rest of his days working on the island colony in coffee, cinchona, and tea cultivation. In a sense he was fairly typical of the countless number of young Scots who sought their fortunes in the British Empire and beyond throughout the nineteenth century. Yet, for the reasons given below, his particular career merits special attention.

Taylor was a key progenitor of what became a global trade in Ceylon tea. As late as the early 1860s little was cultivated on the island, but by 1900 150 million pounds of tea were exported and the land devoted to its cultivation had expanded to 384,000 acres. As one commentator retrospectively put it in the 1930s, this '"rush into tea" on the part of Ceylon planters, with a corresponding growth of exports constitutes one of the most remarkable instances of rapid development in the history of the tea trade'.[2] Today, Sri Lanka is the world's fourth-largest producer of tea, and second-biggest when measured by its share of global tea exports. Taylor's early efforts in Victorian times therefore helped to create the foundations for the transformation of the country's economy and, in the process, helped to shape the world's drinking habits.

In addition, while biographies of the imperial great and good are commonplace, the individual lives of the hundreds of thousands of Britons from more humble backgrounds are either ignored or considered only in the mass as part of broader examinations of migration patterns.[3] James Taylor belonged to that social class of the skilled and the semi-skilled which was vital to the imperial project but whose private lives have mainly fallen below the historical radar. He came from artisan stock in north-east Scotland and his father was a wright (carpenter) of modest means. Taylor himself always remained an employee of larger concerns in Ceylon and never rose above the rank of plantation manager throughout his life. As he put it in 1874, 'Some how or other I was born apparently to do good for others without much benefitting myself.'[4] He did not achieve wealth and, though earning a high reputation and generous acclaim among his peers in the cinchona and tea economies of Ceylon before he died, never received recognition in the land of his birth. To this day, his name stirs little or no resonance in Scotland, although he is a national figure in Sri Lanka. Taylor has never been recorded among the pantheon of 'Great Scots' whose remarkable deeds in far-off lands aroused such pride across the nation during the heyday of empire.[5] Indeed, but for the chance survival of his voluminous correspondence, Taylor's name, outside Sri Lanka at least, might well have been lost to history. It is the long and detailed series of letters which he wrote to his family at home – together with his photographs and published correspondence – which have made this 'subaltern biography' possible.

Between 1851 in London, where he awaited passage to Asia, and 1891, just before his death, Taylor corresponded regularly, mainly with his father, but also with his sister, brother-in-law, and maternal grandfather in Scotland.[6] There is only one significant gap in the sequence, between 1861 and 1868, when his letters home do not seem to have survived.[7] The bulk of his correspondence, some 83,000 words in all, is preserved in the National Library of Scotland in Edinburgh. To the best of our knowledge, the correspondence is unique to one of Taylor's social class and function in the published history of empire. To this, we can add his two photograph albums and his many published letters in the press and in the Proceedings of the Planters' Association, the island's representative body for the planting community.[8] Extending over four decades, these collective sources are by far the richest archive we have come across for a nineteenth-century migrant of humble origin from Scotland. As John MacKenzie, the esteemed historian of the British Empire, has put it, 'In the annals of imperial correspondence, the forty-year consistency of the Taylor letters to his family is exceptionally unusual for someone from his social background. They therefore constitute an unrivalled source for the origins of tea production in Ceylon (Sri Lanka).'[9] So too does this correspondence illuminate forty years of distinct transformations in Ceylon's history.

The late Denys Forrest, the first to make some use of the Taylor letters, recognised their importance in containing 'perhaps the most complete account in existence of a young planter's experiences and feelings'.[10] The archive is indeed a fascinating mine of information on a range of subjects, including little known details on the coffee, cinchona, and tea economies of Ceylon; Taylor's own pioneering efforts which eventually resulted in a virtual tea monoculture on the island by the end of the nineteenth century; the life of a planter in the high noon of the Victorian empire; the labour force in coffee, cinchona, and tea; cross-cultural relationships; the ties of an emigrant with family at home; and much else. Taylor's acclaim as the 'father of the Ceylon tea enterprise' has overshadowed his other achievements, but these are given due acknowledgement here.

Taylor's writings and photographs can be supplemented by a number of other important sources, including the private and published papers of fellow planters (among them his relatives Henry Stiven and Peter Moir), the proceedings of their professional associations, and the Ceylon press. A particularly valuable source on tea and other commodities in Ceylon and beyond the island's borders is the *Tropical Agriculturalist*, the brainchild of a Highland Scot, John Ferguson. Ferguson's own personal archive, the botanical archives at Kew, and records from official tea repositories in Sri Lanka have also been employed to amplify and extend the story. We have drawn too upon crucial genealogical sources, both manuscript and digitised.

Material from archives and libraries is central to the book, but we have gone further by following in Taylor's footsteps, both in Scotland and in Sri Lanka. Several visits have been made to his birthplace at Auchenblae and the surrounding district where he grew to manhood. In Sri Lanka, we travelled to Loolecondera, the estate that he managed for forty years, visited his grave just outside Kandy, and traced the commemorations of his legacy, including the imposing 13-foot bust at the Mlesna Tea Castle at Talawakelle and artefacts that supposedly belonged to him and which are now lodged in the Ceylon Tea Museum at Hantana.

What emerges is, we believe, the first serious academic study of a British planter in nineteenth-century Asia at a time when plantation economies were prominent throughout India, Borneo, Ceylon, Burma, Malaysia, and elsewhere in the age of empire. Throughout, we quote at length from Taylor's letters in order to understand the public and private man in his own terms, the language he used, and his personality and mindset.

The book, then, is the first large-scale study of James Taylor and is the only one to use his extant correspondence from beginning to end.[11] While several scholars have drawn on personal letters in the analysis of other ethnicities to examine their migrations over time,[12] never before has a long series of correspondence on this scale been considered to project the life and work of a migrant from Scotland.[13] Given the long history of Scottish emigration, dating back to medieval times, this in itself is a remarkable fact. The focus on Ceylon and Asia also serves to offer a fresh perspective on the study of the

Scottish diaspora, which to date has mainly focused on the Atlantic world and the settlement colonies of Australasia and South Africa.[14]

The richness and diversity of the source material permits the detailed consideration of a number of themes and questions emerging from historiographical issues in imperial, Asian, diaspora, and Scottish history. They include the nature of colonisation, cross-cultural contact, identities, the emerging field of emotions, and study of the global trade in new consumer commodities. Thus, although Taylor's life is a key concern, we are in full agreement with the contention of one distinguished biographer that 'to have explanatory power, biography needs to be embedded in a wider history of social and political forces which shape the individual and his … scope for action'.[15] Some biographies often do not take account of the forces that help to shape the life of an individual or provide scope for the impact he or she made and which both mould and constrain that effect.[16] That, we suggest, is a myopic approach. Therefore, we have tried throughout to set Taylor's character, behaviour, aspirations, and emotions within the context of the social, economic, cultural, and political history of his times. This also explains why the book is structured as a thematic biography, which allows scope for analytical depth and breadth rather than a chronological narrative of the life of one individual.

By making ethnicity a core theme throughout the book, we also try to connect with ongoing debates within the history of the British world by challenging the view that tends to portray migrants as an undifferentiated mass. This approach has the potential to obscure the profoundly important influence of the different cultures of the homeland on the formation of mindset and personal identity among those who left for the new lands.[17] As one scholar has put it, the 'ethnic mix from the United Kingdom … [is] the great hidden story of imperial rule'.[18] The value of adopting this approach has been argued recently by one of us in a global overview of Scottish migration: 'individual nations of Britain still do merit special consideration in their own right as part of the broader British dynamic. This is true in terms of the nature of their emigration, migrant identities and global impact because of the distinctive nature of their own economic, social and intellectual structures.'[19] This book therefore examines the special Scottish contribution to Ceylon, and in doing so engages with Gary Magee and Andrew Thompson's view of 'culture as the matrix in which economic life occurs'.[20] It will be clear from the pages that follow that in order to understand James Taylor it is also necessary to comprehend the distinctive cultural, religious, social, and economic milieu that shaped his early years in his native land.

Our sense is that this particular intellectual battle has now been won. Some, however, may well wish to refine 'the nation' further in the direction of the region and locality and so to a sub-national experience. That aspiration is perhaps predictable, given the concentric nature of human identity that can encompass nation, country, region, locality, town, parish, and family. To uncouple these, distinctions may or may not be of value depending on the particular circumstances and the questions under consideration. At least in the case of James Taylor, who hailed from a village in the north-east of Scotland, it is not immediately apparent that his local experience complicated or altered his central identity as a Scot. It did, however, provide him with skillsets that would facilitate his achievements abroad.

The 150th anniversary of Ceylon tea is commemorated in 2017. This is, then, an appropriate time to recover the life of a significant figure in the history of Sri Lanka and in the story of Scottish emigration to Asia in the nineteenth century.

Notes

1 'Proposed testimonial to Mr James Taylor, pioneer tea planter', *Proceedings of the Planters' Association of Ceylon for year ending 17th February, 1891* (Colombo, 1891), p. 38.

2 William H. Ukers, *All About Tea*, vol. 2 (New York, 1935), p. 132.

3 Recent biographical work includes Clare Anderson, *Subaltern Lives: Biographies of Colonialism in the Indian Ocean World, 1790–1820* (Cambridge, 2012); David Lambert and Alan Lester (eds), *Colonial Lives Across the British Empire: Imperial Careering in the Long Nineteenth Century* (Cambridge, 2006); and Emma Rothschild, *The Inner Life of Empires: An Eighteenth-Century History* (Princeton, 2011).

4 Taylor letters, 25 January 1873, in NLS, Papers of James Taylor, planter in Ceylon, MS 15908. See Appendix 1 for list of letters.

5 See, for example, David Nasaw, *Andrew Carnegie* (New York, 2006); Claire Harman, *Robert Louis Stevenson: A Biography* (London, 2005); Michael Gardiner, *At the Edge of Empire: The Life of Thomas Blake Glover* (Edinburgh, 2008).

6 The collection also includes six letters sent to Taylor from his maternal grandfather, one from his father, one from his brother Robert, and four from the Planters' Association of Ceylon. Two letters from fellow planter C.E. Bonner were sent to Taylor's relatives after Taylor's death. See Appendix 1.

7 Denys Forrest speculates that these letters may have been borrowed by one of the Fergusons 'when compiling their biographies of the planting pioneers; indeed, John Ferguson quotes at least one phrase from a Taylor letter which is not in the correspondence as we have it'. See D.M. Forrest, *A Hundred Years of Ceylon Tea, 1867–1967* (London, 1967), pp. xi-xii. Forrest does not cite the phrase but presumably means the following extracts from the *TA*, 2 July 1894, p. 2: 'That he had trials for some time in his new sphere as in his native land we learn from a letter written home some years afterwards, in which he says:- "The first two years in Ceylon were the most uncomfortable in my life." Another time he sends his respects to all old schoolfellows, adding: "We were a noble lot, and how well many of us have got on, especially John Ross, now Rector of Arbroath Academy."' Neither of these phrases appear in any of the Taylor letters held at the NLS, though the latter may be paraphrased.

8 Two of Taylor's photograph albums are held at the NLS. Further photographs are held at the NMS in a volume titled *Views of Ceylon*. The book features a number of renowned images of Sri Lanka including the Kandy Lake and Temple of the Tooth. Blank pages at the back of the volume contain smaller images that Taylor acquired during his brief trip to Darjeeling in Assam (see 6.1). It also features two images of cinchona with captions, both taken from Alistair Ferguson's *Abbotsford Album*, which showcased twenty photographs of coffee, tea, and cinchona plantations at Dimbula in the mid-1870s taken by W.L.H. Skeen. See *The Abbotsford Album: A Series of Twenty Views on and from a Mountain Plantation in the District of Dimbula, Ceylon, Illustrative of the Culture of Coffee, Tea, and Cinchona* (Colombo, c.1875). Thanks to James Webb for alerting us that the album is held at the Archives of the Royal Botanic Gardens at Kew. Several smaller loose photographs in the Taylor file at NMS include his portrait, a view of his famous first 20 acres of tea planting beneath Loolecondera rock, his early bungalow and factory, his grave at Mahiayawa, near Kandy, and Sir William Gregory, Governor of Ceylon between 1872 and 1877.

9 John MacKenzie email to Angela McCarthy, 29 August 2016.

10 Forrest, *A Hundred Years of Ceylon Tea*, p. 63.

11 Taylor features fleetingly in such works as Forrest, *A Hundred Years of Ceylon Tea*; James Webb, *Tropical Pioneers: Human Agency and Ecological Change in the Highlands of Sri Lanka, 1800–1900* (Athens, 2002); James Duncan, *In the Shadows of the Tropics: Climate, Race and Biopower in Nineteenth Century Ceylon* (Aldershot, 2007); John Weatherstone, *The Early British Tea and Coffee Planters and their Way of Life, 1825–1900: The Pioneers* (London, 1986); Royston Ellis, *The Growing Years: History of the Ceylon Planters' Association* (Colombo, 2014); and Maxwell Fernando, *The Story of Ceylon Tea* (Colombo, 2000). Extracts from Taylor's letters also appear in two unpublished pieces that Tom Barron kindly provided to us: 'British coffee planters in 19th century Ceylon', presented to the postgraduate seminar at the Institute of Commonwealth Studies, University of London, 1973, and 'Sir James Emerson Tennent and the planting pioneers', presented to the Ceylon Studies seminar series, 1970/72.

12 See, for instance, works on the letters of Irish migrants in David Fitzpatrick, *Oceans of Consolation: Personal Accounts of Irish Migration to Australia* (Cork, 1995); Angela McCarthy, *Irish Migrants in New Zealand, 1840–1937: 'The Desired Haven'* (Woodbridge, 2005); Kerby A. Miller, *Emigrants and Exiles: Ireland and the Irish Exodus to North America* (New York, 1984); and Patrick O'Farrell, *Letters from Irish Australia, 1825–1929* (Kensington, 1984).

13 The potential for this is evident in Angela McCarthy (ed.), *A Global Clan: Scottish Migrant Networks and Identities since the Eighteenth Century* (London and New York, 2006).

14 Marjory Harper, *Adventurers and Exiles: The Great Scottish Exodus* (London, 2003); Angela McCarthy, *Personal Narratives of Irish and Scottish Migration, 1921–65: 'For Spirit and Adventure'* (Manchester, 2007); John M. MacKenzie with Nigel R. Dalziel, *The Scots in South Africa: Ethnicity, Identity, Gender and Race, 1772–1914* (Manchester, 2005). A recent exception is T.M. Devine and Angela McCarthy

(eds), *The Scottish Experience in Asia, c.1700 to the Present: Settlers and Sojourners* (Cham, 2017).

15 Ian Kershaw, 'Personality and power: The individual's role in the history of twentieth-century Europe', *Historian*, 83 (2004), p. 15.

16 Ibid., p. 18.

17 This elision of ethnicity is evident most recently in James Belich, *Replenishing the Earth: The Settler Revolution and the Rise of the Anglo-World, 1783–1939* (Oxford, 2009). See also Antoinette Burton, 'Who needs the nation? Interrogating "British" history', *Journal of Historical Sociology*, 10:3 (1997), pp. 227–248.

18 John M. MacKenzie, *Empires of Nature and the Nature of Empires: Imperialism, Scotland and the Environment* (East Linton, 1997), pp. 64–65.

19 T.M. Devine, *To the Ends of the Earth: Scotland's Global Diaspora, 1750–2010* (London, 2011), p. xvi.

20 Gary B. Magee and Andrew S. Thompson, *Empire and Globalisation: Networks of People, Goods and Capital in the British World, c.1850–1914* (Cambridge, 2010), p. 14.

1

Before Ceylon

James Taylor, aged sixteen, left his home and family in Scotland and boarded ship in London for Ceylon on 23 October 1851. He was accompanied on the voyage by his kinsman, the equally young Henry Stiven, and would never see his native land again. Taylor wrote briefly to his father from the ship *Sydney*: 'We are now afloat.' The boys spent the first night at anchor in the river and Taylor slept well. The second day, with no wind, the *Sydney* had to depend on a steam tug to reach the Downs. Writing on a slate on his knees, Taylor expressed satisfaction with his surroundings: 'We are very comfortable here and have plenty of room and too much meat if we like.'[1]

During the voyage, Taylor kept a meticulous shipboard journal which is now archived with his letters from Ceylon. It records in a table the date, day, number of days out of London, the course sailed, the distances covered, latitude, longitude and prevailing wind, and temperature. Brief comments accompanied the lists. He recounted catching albatrosses, sighting porpoise, sharks, and sperm whales, and signalling other ships (including the *Glenbervie* bound from London to Sydney, the *Mary Carson* from Liverpool to Calcutta, the *Tamerlane* from Liverpool to Calcutta, and the *Hannah Salkeld* from Liverpool to Calcutta). The crossing was far from smooth, the *Sydney* encountering strong winds and a 'Violent gale very heavy sea thunder and rain'. His mind occasionally turned to home and, on 22 November, after about a month at sea, he noted wistfully, 'Martinmas market day ... I can know something of what is doing at home to-day.'

As well as these specific comments, Taylor usually provided some general remarks for each day of the week while at sea. The day's routine included rising at 7am, coffee at 8am, dinner at noon, and tea at 6pm. Pork and pea soup, beef and rice, beef and barley, and tea and coffee were the staple foods and drinks. Each passenger received a gallon of water every afternoon at 4pm and took sugar weekly. Treats were rare: 'We had no allowance of spirits but we sometimes got a glass and sometimes when Mr Lamert got drunk or when the captain had rather much and on Christmas and New Years day they would have us into the Cabin for a spree as it was called which was very good as it cost us nothing.' Here we see early signs of Taylor's financial astuteness. He slept, read, worked, and walked on deck. Beds and clothing in his trunk had to be aired regularly because of the prevailing dampness on board.[2]

After a 'very pleasant but somewhat tedious passage' of 122 days, the *Sydney* anchored in Colombo Bay on Friday, 20 February 1852. Taylor's first sight of Ceylon was 'a mass of precipitous mountains of very irregular heights. Six canoes with natives came to us with fruit and jewelry to sell. The canoes look savage like made out of a tree with an outrigger to keep them from upsetting.' When he stepped ashore the following day he stayed initially at 'Mackwoods bungalow', presumably Captain William Mackwood whose mercantile firm, established in 1841, still exists to this day.[3] Henry Stiven's letter to his laird, Sir John Hepburn Stuart Forbes of the Fettercairn estate, further fleshes out their short stay in Colombo: 'We had a drive round the suburbs and through the Native town which is large and much scattered. The streets are narrow but clean and almost every house is a shop.' Stiven further told how 'I attended Divine Service in the English Chapel which is a neat commodious building holding from three to four hundred. It has a good organ and the music I thought nothing inferior to some of the smaller Chapels in London. There is a Presbyterian kirk and Roman Catholic Chapel within the Fort. Also a large Mormon Church in the native town. They are a strong party here.'[4] Taylor similarly noted attending Episcopal chapel on Sunday, stopping at a hotel on Monday, and on Tuesday morning travelling by coach to 'Candy', his luggage having been sent ahead by bullock carts. After an eleven-hour journey, comprising 'a fine ride through some fearful scenery', they arrived at Kandy.[5] Stiven described the exhilarating environment, which still captivates to this day:

> Mountain rise above mountain as far as the eye can reach. Some of them are much peaked and wooded to the summitts with here and there a huge barren rock looking out among the trees. There is little appearance of cultivation except the hollows where the natives cultivate rice. The scenery is the most beautiful one could imagine and from the great number of Huts at the roadside a stranger would think it a very thickly populated country, which is not the case – the road having drawn them there.[6]

The following day Stiven and Taylor went their separate ways.[7] Both were to work as assistants on George Pride's coffee estates. Taylor went to the Hewaheta district, south of Kandy, and Stiven to Amcoombra, north of the town. Thus began a lifetime's work for Taylor on the coffee, cinchona, and tea estates of the colony. To understand what shaped his personality during those decades we return to his early years in north-east Scotland, his schooling, and his family relationships there.

Early years

James Taylor, also called Jamie, was born on 29 March 1835 in the small house of Mosspark (Figure 1.1). The croft sat on seventeen acres within the Monboddo estate in the historical county of Kincardineshire.[8] His father, Michael Taylor, usually referred to as a wright (carpenter), was reputedly 'a respectable hard-working man'.[9] In this, Michael seems to have been typical of the parish of Fordoun more broadly, where the inhabitants were deemed in the *Statistical Account of Scotland* a 'highly respectable class'. The tidy, picturesque countryside mirrored its inhabitants, for it was said to possess 'a rich and highly cultivated appearance'.[10] Today, Mosspark is an enlarged and restored private house and lies in a rolling expanse of field. It is reached by car in about two minutes, or ten minutes by foot as the crow flies, from the nearby village of Auchenblae, which in Gaelic means 'Field of Flowers'. Many of the attractive village houses around, such as Lilac Cottage, Rose Cottage, and Beechvilla, echo this botanical allusion.[11]

Auchenblae is now located in Aberdeenshire. To the modern eye, the village has a pleasing ambience of picturesque rural tranquillity. In the mid-1840s, however, as a bustling community of around 550 people, it was one of Fordoun parish's main settlements. In this 'clean and thriving place', dominated by its flax-spinning mill and three meal mills, the people worked as artisans, farmers, farm servants, and linen manufacturers.[12] Towards the end of the century,

1.1 Believed to be James Taylor's birthplace at Mosspark, Auchenblae, Kincardineshire, c.1863.

1.2 '[E]xceptionally clean, comfortable, and prosperous': Auchenblae village.

Auchenblae continued to be praised for its 'exceptionally clean, comfortable, and prosperous appearance'[13] (Figure 1.2). At that time, too, the 'romantic village' was hailed as a health resort that helped to 'restore nervous vigour'.[14] Visitors took walks in the countryside and visited the renowned Drumtochty Glen. Auchenblae's popularity endured into the late 1960s, and only with the closing of the railway and advent of cheap air travel for overseas holidays did the village lose its appeal to visitors.

Various local histories, land records, and family history sources indicate that numerous Taylor families lived in Fordoun parish. As well as at Mosspark, where James Taylor was born and reared, Taylors resided at Culback, Coulie, and Cushnie. Michael Taylor, James's father, born in 1810, was the son of William Taylor and Marjory (May) Spark. They had married in 1805 and Michael had at least two older siblings, William and Mary. Two William Taylors lived in Fordoun parish. One was a 'worthy tenant' known as 'Auld Fordoun', who was most likely the resident of Kirktown of Fordoun (where the parish church today is located) and who had married Ann Thom.[15] His threshing mill drew power from the Luther Water and, according to one account, was on the estate of Lord Monboddo, the principal landowner in the district.[16] The other William Taylor was most likely Michael Taylor's father and James Taylor's grandfather. He had 'an industrial residence at a small farm on the estate of Monboddo' and was known in the locality as 'Old Fanners' because he pioneered the making of farm fans, which 'were well-compacted machines, in good demand in their day'.[17] These cylindrical wooden devices contained an internal manually operated fan and were used to separate the wheat from the chaff during harvest time.[18]

On 28 April 1833, three months after his mother's death at Culback, Michael Taylor (Figure 1.3) married Margaret Moir, a daughter of Robert Moir and Margaret Stiven of Laurencekirk. Michael's new wife, Margaret, likewise came from an artisan-class background, for she, as with her cousin Henry Stiven, shared a grandfather in Charles Stiven. Born at Glenbervie in 1753, Charles Stiven, the son of a 'gryte Jacobite', was named after Charles Edward Stuart,

1.3 '[A] respectable hard-working man': Michael Taylor, James Taylor's father.

the Young Pretender.[19] Stiven found fame in his time as an expert snuff-box maker and was encouraged by the local landholder, Lord Gardenstone, to transfer his box-making manufacture from Glenbervie to Laurencekirk, a larger town renowned for its handloom weaving and the making of 'Mearns linen'.[20]

Taylor's other great-grandfather, John Moir of Bank Head, lived close to Taylor's paternal grandfather, William, who died in July 1848, aged eighty, at Monboddo.[21] Many of these Taylors are memorialised in stone in Auchenblae's Presbyterian churchyard, while two Stiven graves can be found at the Laurencekirk Presbyterian cemetery. Unlike the Presbyterian Taylors, however, the Moirs were Episcopalian. Robert Moir's brother David would even go on to become bishop of Brechin in the Episcopal Church of Scotland.

Michael and Margaret Taylor had three further children after James, their eldest: May Spark (born November 1836), Margaret (born January 1839), and Robert Moir (born June 1842).[22] We know little about their childhood years, although they were hit by tragedy at an early age when their mother died in April 1844 aged only thirty-three. Her passing was for the nine-year-old Taylor 'a bitter sorrow and irretrievable loss'.[23] Whether Michael Taylor was similarly stricken is unknown, but three years later he found another partner in Isobel Anderson. That union produced a further two children: Elisabeth Gregor (b. 1849) and William (b. 1855). Later accounts about Taylor attest that after Michael's remarriage, 'home life became almost unbearable to the young lad who was no favorite with his stepmother'.[24] That retrospective report also conveys something of James Taylor's character and physique. According to his church minister, John Philip, Taylor was 'a quiet steady-going lad with prominent eyes and eyebrows, and a heavy but thoughtful expression'. Another neighbour described him as 'a big-headed, large-chested burly lad'.[25]

Taylor would initially have worshipped with his family at the Church of Scotland in Auchenblae until the Great Disruption split Scottish Presbyterianism in 1843. In September of that year the famous Dr Thomas Chalmers, leader of the new Free Church, visited the village and opened a new place of worship for his followers in the area, among them the Taylor family.[26] The fracturing of the Presbyterian community at Auchenblae, as elsewhere in Scotland, lasted until the early twentieth century. Subsequently converted into a cinema, the United Free Church building became a garage in the 1940s and remained as such until it closed in 2001.[27]

Today, Auchenblae's Presbyterian community worships in a church built around 1828 on the site of St Palladius' chapel.[28] The Burnetts, one of the local landowning families, and from whom Taylor's father rented his land, are commemorated within the walls. The acclaimed philosopher James Burnett, Lord Monboddo (1714–1799), is the family's most famous figure. A further renowned individual with ties to the area is the great Scottish bard, Robert

1.4 Monboddo House, Auchenblae.

Burns. His father had been a crofter on the Monboddo estate, while Burns' great-grandparents were buried at the nearby Glenbervie cemetery.[29] Indeed, Burns was said in 1779 to have visited the Mearns, as Kincardineshire is known, in search of his ancestral roots and there are claims that he spent the night at the Inn of Fordoun.[30] During subsequent visits he may have encountered Monboddo's daughter, Eliza, whom he praised in two poems.[31] The Monboddo estate eventually passed to another daughter, Helen, and, upon her death in 1833, to her son James Burnett Burnett (1792–1864), considered a 'most philanthropic gentleman, active in all deeds of charity and benevolence'.[32] He remained the Monboddo laird until his death in 1864, aged seventy-two, and was succeeded by his son, James Cumine Burnett (born 1835), who had served for ten years in the Madras Cavalry in India, from 1857 until 1867.[33] As we discuss later, Taylor showed considerable interest in the Burnetts when he wrote home from Ceylon.

Schooling

Before the Disruption of 1843, James Taylor probably received his early education at one of the schools in Auchenblae.[34] The earliest was a room in the house of schoolmaster Alexander Spencer, but by 1815 a new school was erected 'in the north-west corner of the churchyard'.[35] After 1843 it is likely that Taylor, 'under the surveillance of the new ecclesiastical denomination',[36] attended the new 'thoroughly equipped' Free Church school where he was taught reading, writing, arithmetic, Latin, and Greek by the master, David

Souter.[37] Not all elementary schools in Scotland taught the classical languages, so the young Taylor did have the benefit of an academically demanding education at a tender age. The building still survives in Auchenblae, although it is now the privately owned Beechvilla.[38]

In later years in Ceylon, Taylor proudly recalled his schooling and warmly remembered his contemporaries. Among them were John Brebner and John Ross, both of whom had initially been pupils at John Edward's School of Paldy Fair in the north of Fordoun parish, also known as 'Tipperty School'.[39] Brebner's memoir features an illuminating account of their schooldays. The subjects taught included reading and spelling, writing (learned by imitation from the master), arithmetic, and some grammar and geography. Pupils were required to memorise the shorter catechism and repeat it every Saturday. Before they joined Souter's class, Brebner and another contemporary, Robert Thom, were taught by two schoolmasters, David Milner and Mr Wood, at Laurencekirk.[40] According to Taylor's later recollections, Thom went on to study at Montrose Academy and 'gave us a sort of veneration for learning which took effect on all those who had any inclination in that way'.[41] Brebner, he noted fondly, was 'one of the best fellows' Taylor had known. Following his education at Aberdeen and ordination into the Free Church, Brebner had emigrated to South Africa where he set up the Orange Free State education service and became its first Inspector of Education.[42] Brebner also wrote history, which he termed 'the biography of the human race'. He reckoned the best way to teach the subject was through a series of biographies: 'All the great actions of an epoch group themselves round some eminent individual, who may serve as a type of the age in which he lived.'[43]

John Ross, meanwhile, had begun his career as a pupil teacher of Souter's but then went on to study at the University of Edinburgh. It was likely his winning of the Miller Scholarship there that impressed Taylor in 1857: 'Tell John Ross I'm most happy to hear of his success but I always knew he would be successful. He is a most clever little fellow "little knoitty" as we used to call him.'[44] Ross was later appointed rector of the Free Church Institution, first at Inverness and then at Arbroath.[45] Reflecting on his contemporaries, Taylor reckoned them a 'noble pack' and their successes sparked 'others of their acquaintance from envy [to] set to it too'.[46] While Taylor was unusual in his family in achieving scholarly success, it is plain from these recollections that he was indeed part of a group that had excelled academically. Although often a modest, self-effacing man, Taylor, here and elsewhere in his correspondence, recognised his abilities and the need to use these talents to good effect. This concern for advancement through learning is one aspect of his early life that would continue to influence his later career in Ceylon.

It is relevant at this point to underline the importance of Scotland's educational system in the nineteenth century. Although not free before 1872, education was open to all regardless of class and offered an enviable breadth of curriculum.[47] The evidence suggests that north-east Scotland, in particular, had the best literacy rates and schooling in the country during this period. While the quality of education varied and attendance sometimes fell, especially during some of the winter months, there remained notable differences from England and most other parts of Europe. These variations included a national system of schools, the professional status and high regard in which schoolmasters were held, and a deep-rooted cultural demand for education which ran through Scottish society.[48] It hardly surprises, then, that the products of Scottish schooling, equipped with key numerical, surveying, and writing skills, were sought after as planters and managers in Ceylon, as they were throughout the bureaucracies and counting houses of the wider Victorian empire.[49] One description of another migrant to Ceylon, Alexander Campbell, stated that 'he had the privilege of being fitted for his work in life with that useful practical education for which the Parish Schools of Scotland … have been specially famous'.[50] In this way, those Scots who became planters in Ceylon were typical of their fellow countrymen who made successful careers throughout the British Empire.[51] Scottish penetration of empire was not simply due to 'limited opportunities at home but it was facilitated by the training Scots had received in basic numeracy, literacy and often in an impressively wide range of vocational skills'.[52]

There is, however, no evidence to suggest that Taylor himself was pushed towards education in order to pursue an imperial career. On the contrary, his love of learning likely arose not just from his own aptitudes but because of dissatisfaction with 'the drudgery of farm-life' at Mosspark. In two terse letters sent to his father from Ceylon, he reflected on this and the preference of his parent that he should concentrate on routine domestic tasks.[53] In the first of these missives, out of sequence in the archive, Taylor declared that 'the mucking of the byre was of too much importance with you'. He further claimed that his father considered his education 'a lazy sort of existence and of little importance compared to work'. This prompted Taylor 'to feel qualms that I should not succeed in the world so well as if I had been learning a trade [and] made me feel less respect for my education which I was engaged in and so less interest in it and less spirit in pushing it'.[54] His frank remarks clearly offended his father, for in his next letter Taylor explained:

> I dont know what I could say that I should be sure would not offend you. You seem to consider things in such a different manner from what I do that I cannot be sure that you will not think I am angry or abusing you in anything I could say. I'll say first that I neither was angry nor meant to vex or abuse you in the letter you complain so much of nor did I expect you would have been vexed about it.

He went on to justify his earlier comments in more detail, claiming that his father took 'little notice of us or what I was doing in learning. I was left to myself … [and] had not spirit to exert myself.' Taylor alleged that his father only paid him attention when he had

> not been attending properly to my duty in cleaning the byre or back hole and I know I did not exert myself like a man as you say. You took notice of my failings in that way and sent me off to it with some remark about my laziness or with a scolding … [which induced me] to be sulky and dissatisfied. I had no pleasure being about the house and no notice taken of me except as far as I was wanted to clean the byre or back hole or do some other job.[55]

Taylor emerges as a disgruntled and sullen teenager who had been rebuked for failing to reach his father's high standards in carrying out humdrum manual labour. We also see here the first signs of Taylor's desire to be acknowledged for his chores, and his sensitivity to criticism. As a consequence of being given routine tasks, such as cleaning the cow shed, Taylor queried whether it was any surprise that he was

> dissatisfied with learning especially after a while when for want of spirit and perseverance in it I found I had been falling behind my fellows? Is it surprising I should have wished to be at something else and not having the courage to say so and why I wished it. I dont think it astonishing that I should have formed the idea of running away to be a soldier which was the culminating point of my dissatisfaction … Now I think I have given you what was the substance, and meaning of my writing on the subject before. I wrote it not because I was angry nor to vex you but to inform you of circumstances that you did not think of and when you had the success of those who were then my fellows before you I took the opportunity to remind you of … the little estimation in which you held it [*learning*]. And I said it was perhaps lucky for me I got a good job in another way than in learning for in that I might have fallen behind.[56]

Here was clear recognition of his annoyance at not being able to attain the academic success of his classmates, while at the same time disclosing that family obligations and the attitudes of his father held him back. This mix of frustration but acceptance of his lot would continue throughout his life. The language of this extended extract also suggests, on the one hand, Taylor's deference to his father and a tendency to tread gingerly, but at the same time a willingness to stand up for himself. These feelings would continue to shape their correspondence, for Michael Taylor was a tough, uncompromising man, sensitive to perceived offence. His sole surviving letter in the archive also shows him to be a semi-literate individual whom his son had to treat with some compassion. As Taylor once placated him, 'I find no faults with your misspelling and bad writing which is very good with a few words misspelled and altogether far more legible to me than I fear you will find mine.'[57] The reality was quite different. Taylor's script was infinitely more legible and grammatically correct than that of his father.

James Taylor's correspondence is not the only source to demonstrate Michael Taylor's attitude to his son's schooling. A remembrance from 'an Edinburgh correspondent', after Taylor's death, similarly observed that 'his father had no sympathy with his son's eager pursuit after all kinds of solid and useful learning'.[58] Michael Taylor was equally unhappy about his daughter May's decision to become a teacher:

> May is to go to School to quilefy herself for a teacher. I do not think her constitution will stand hard study. I think she spoild hir health sitting up late and writing ... I think a Nurse Maids place in [*word illegible*] family whare she [*?c*]ould get plenty of exersise in open air is the place best fitting for her.[59]

James Taylor grew to manhood at a time when parts of the north-east of Scotland had become renowned as centres of excellence for agriculture, not simply nationally but further afield. Agrarian 'improvement' in Scotland since the 1760s had resulted in better land use, more efficient organisation of labour, deployment of more capital resources, and dissemination of commercial expertise.[60] The thinking of the Scottish Enlightenment was influential in this transformation of Lowland Scotland through rational, systematic and planned intervention.[61] Managed by the proprietors and their factors, all this 'demanded a practical versatility'.[62] Scots ploughmen and other farm servants were important in this respect because landlords and tenant farmers generally regarded them as a 'compliant labour force'.[63] This revolution of Scottish agriculture from a semi-subsistence base to a condition of advanced capitalism between c.1760 and c.1830 saw it become ever more 'precise and progressive'.[64] As a result of this great leap forward, the Scottish agricultural system attracted international attention for its excellence and was widely copied elsewhere.[65]

The agricultural revolution did not simply lead to the spread of farming skills, but also triggered an expansion of trades associated with agriculture. Very relevant in this respect was the broader industrial revolution in Scotland which generated 'a labour force which had already developed skills in engineering, mining and textiles and, crucially, had become accustomed to more rigorous time and work disciplines of industrial capitalism'.[66] Taylor, as noted, was primarily interested in his early years in the development of his academic education, but he would also have been aware of the skills of his father's trade as a wright. Proficiency and knowledge may in this way have been transferred through the generations within the families of rural tradesmen.[67] Taylor could also have appreciated how the Luther river provided the water power for Auchenblae's mills, knowledge that he would later put to good use in Ceylon.[68] Indeed, at one time Auchenblae was reckoned to have had one of the best water systems in the country.[69] As the *History of Kincardine* put it in 1795, 'the banks of the rivers and streams furnish numberless commodious situations for erecting mills for grinding corn'.[70]

James Taylor was, however, determined to reject a job in either farming or manufacturing in Scotland. Instead, in April 1849, at the age of fourteen, he entered upon a career path to which he seemed well suited: as a pupil-teacher at the Free Church School of Fordoun under the schoolmaster, David Souter. It was three years since the government had introduced the pupil-teacher system whereby pupils would 'serve a five-year apprenticeship, during which they were taught full-time and studied after school'.[71] Taylor was licensed to teach by the Free Church of Scotland, and his indenture was signed by himself, his father, Souter, and Joseph Henderson, Francis Legg, and James Henry, managers of the Free Church School.

According to the terms of the indenture, he would 'conduct himself with honesty, sobriety and temperance, and not be guilty of any profane or lewd conversation or conduct, or of gambling or any other immorality, but shall dillegently and obediently assist in the instruction and discipline of the scholars of the said Fourdon Free Church school'. In addition, he was expected to 'regularly attend divine service on Sunday'. Souter in return would provide Taylor with the opportunity 'of observing and practising the art of teaching', supply lodging, food, and medical attendance, and instruct him for at least one and a half hours every school day before or after hours in 'the several branches of useful learning usually taught in the said school'.[72]

In later years Taylor reflected on his time as a pupil-teacher. He felt it 'an unlucky thing for me for I was able to stand two or three years of its requirements when first passed and had nothing to do but amuse myself' because Souter had no system for training. His mentor, he recalled, was 'a good man but a slow and far from able man'.[73] Had he stayed the course, Taylor would probably have taken annual exams, received a Queen's Scholarship and stipend, and been certified as a trained teacher.[74] He might also, like John Ross and John and James Brebner, have gone on to university.[75] Although not his eventual lifetime work, these years equipped him with skills and values that would prove vital in Ceylon.

It is within this context of concerns about his chosen profession and the troubled relationship with his stepmother that Taylor made the decision to go to Ceylon, although another more personal factor has to be borne in mind. It appears from his letters that he was expected to marry a local Fordoun girl, Janet or 'Jessie' Ross. As he wrote with relief during his first decade in Ceylon, 'I'm glad to hear that "My Jessie" as you call her is likely to get married. I shall then be clear of her instead of feeling as if I had wronged her and were still doing so by not courting faster.'[76] These varied influences in James Taylor's personal decision to leave Scotland remind us that we cannot simply attribute the motives for the migration of an individual to any single overarching cause.

The broader context of Scottish emigration also has to be remembered. For centuries the Scots had been a nomadic people, first in England and across

Europe, then, from the seventeenth century, to the north of Ireland, across the Atlantic, Asia, and beyond. One is reminded of the medieval French proverb: 'Rats, lice and Scotchmen: you find them the whole world over.'[77] By the second half of the nineteenth century, only Ireland and Norway, among European countries, had a higher rate of per capita out-migration than Scotland.[78] For many generations, young Scots in their thousands had left home to seek a better life in foreign lands, and so the culture into which James Taylor had been born had few of the social constraints on mobility which had long persisted in many parts of Europe. For him, like so many other young Scots, leaving home and the place of his birth was almost an expected rite of passage to adulthood.[79]

Scots in Ceylon

The use of family networks, in the Scottish emigrant tradition, was crucial to Taylor's decision to opt for Ceylon rather than other potential destinations.[80] His mother's cousin, Peter Moir, was employed by coffee agencies on the island, having previously toiled as a gardener on the Fettercairn estate.[81] Taylor clearly acknowledged in 1872: 'Peter got me out here.'[82] Hugh Blacklaw of Laurencekirk, a town close to Auchenblae, confirmed that Peter Moir's influence was fundamental in facilitating the movement of several young men from the north-east of Scotland to Ceylon:

> The late Mr Peter Moir, who came from the same place as I did, had come out to Ceylon in 1843. He was manager of Messrs Hadden's properties out here, and enticed a lot of young people from our small town to come out. It was through his influence that my brothers and I came to Ceylon. It is a very small town, ours. It is St Laurencekirk, Kincardineshire, with a population of about 2,000 souls, yet at one time there were as many as fourteen St Laurencekirk men in Ceylon. There were my four brothers and I, the four Moirs, James Taylor of Golconda, pioneer of tea and cinchona, Robertson, father of Robertson of the G.P.O., Petrie, the two Bissets and Stiven of Ancoombra, Matale West, who afterwards went to Kandanuwara and died at the Galle Face Hotel[.][83]

The list of names reveals a group of men from neighbouring areas, several of whom were connected by blood and marriage. The four Moirs and Henry Stiven, for instance, were cousins to Taylor's mother (see Appendix 1), while Peter and James Moir were also in charge of the Ceylon properties of cousins Frederick and Charles Hadden from Aberdeen. According to testimony about Peter and James Moir in the late nineteenth century, 'Two more sensible, honest, and hard-working Scotchmen never landed in Ceylon. Under their charge the estates continued to flourish.' Moir's reputation was clearly that of an upright citizen: 'Succeeding generations of planters came to hear of Peter Moir as the man whose word was as good as his bodn [sic].'[84] Laurencekirk also had existing ties to India through Henry Shank, who had previously obtained East India Company appointments for many young men in the district.[85]

The Moirs, Stiven, and Taylor all made their journeys to Ceylon through kin networks. Other ethnic groups also commonly deployed networking, but the considerable and early scale of chain migration from north-east Scotland to the eastern empire did much to help the success of these young men in Ceylon. The connections proved vital, as migrants there could not take advantage of assisted passages as in some other imperial territories.[86] Neighbourhood ties continued to be important even as the nature of migration to Ceylon changed in the later nineteenth century (see chapter 9).

Another key link in the movement from north-east Scotland to Ceylon was Robert Boyd Tytler (1819–1882) from Inverurie. He had learned much about tropical agriculture while he was in Jamaica,

> having previously received some little knowledge of practical gardening, and of agriculture, such as it then was, in this country. For three years he remained in Jamaica in the employment of Mr. Charles Anderson, an Aberdeenshire man. Thereafter he proceeded to Ceylon, having been engaged to take a part in the active management of estates in that island belonging to Messrs. Ackland, Boyd, & Company, the second partner in the firm being a relative of his own on the mother's side.[87]

Once in Ceylon, Tytler took over the management of the Pallikelle estate and ran the only profitable sugar estate in the island. In his account of a Ceylon dinner in Aberdeen in 1875, the Aberdeenshire-born Arthur Sinclair, who had trained as a gardener in Scotland, described Tytler's life in the following way:

> Some forty years ago a shrewd Scotchman, during a sojourn in the island, discovered that the land was good – not exactly a land flowing with milk and honey, but a land that would grow excellent coffee. He returned home, secured the hardest-headed young Aberdonian that he could find, and quietly shipped him off to Jamaica, where, after learning all that was necessary, his valuable services were transferred to Ceylon. Here he introduced systematic cultivation. The coffee grew, and from that day Ceylon prospered.[88]

Tytler had acquired knowledge from planting manuals in the West Indies, but he undoubtedly learned also from other Scots, who were then over-represented among sugar plantation managers and overseers in Jamaica before slave emancipation in 1833.[89] The early north-east Scottish presence in Ceylon, discussed further in chapter 9, likewise owed much to connections forged earlier in the eighteenth century with India, where Scottish migrants were increasingly conspicuous in the administration, military, and trading cadres of the East India Company.[90]

Leaving home

Taylor's kin ties to Ceylon meant that it was an obvious destination for him. Moreover, he did not go alone in 1851. His mother's cousin Henry Stiven (Figure 1.5) accompanied him on the mail train to London in October of that year. For Taylor, London was 'a nasty, smoky hole', where 'all the beautiful buildings are black with it which greatly spoils their look'. His three surviving letters penned there show the sixteen-year-old as astute, well organised, and determined. This was especially notable in his dealings with the agents of George Pride's coffee estates in Ceylon.[91] George and James Hadden, whom Taylor described as one 'an old man and the other a young man', were

1.5 Taylor's relative Henry Stiven, who would work on Ancoombra estate.

relatives of Frederick and Charles Hadden, James Moir's employers.[92] On the surface, they seem to fit the well-known model of 'gentlemanly capitalism', where English financial and commercial elites based in the capital became key influences on the expansion of empire.[93] The Scottish Haddens, however, were not members of a business aristocracy, nor were they English. George Hadden had been born in Aberdeen and the family followed in a long line of Scottish mercantile émigrés who settled in the metropolis but who continued to maintain strong commercial and personal ties in the 'periphery'.[94]

Taylor's consultation of his contract shows him to be capable and assured, with an attention to detail, for he spotted that the length of his indenture had been omitted. After insisting on changes to his contract, Taylor agreed on an initial engagement of three years at a salary of £100 per annum. This was a considerable sum at the time, for a decade later the yearly wage for an agricultural labourer in his native Kincardine was about a quarter of what Taylor had been offered.[95] With deductions for his passage, which cost £20, and clothing, Taylor eventually received £50 for his first year.[96] The Haddens provided the boys with a list of items to purchase, including a mattress, blankets, pillow cases, towels, lamp, 'Looking Glass', and shaving utensils. Taylor used his advance to cover his expenses in London and to buy sheets, a pillow, brushes for shoes, and cloths, cabin lamp, and lamp box.[97] He learned that the vessel, the *Sydney* from Glasgow, would sail on Saturday 18 October, although the crew reckoned that date to be unlikely. Taylor went to see the ship and found it 'a dwarf beside some of the enormous vessels beside her'.[98]

While in London, Taylor called on some acquaintances from the north-east, including Charles Trail, probably a relative, who found Taylor and Stiven lodgings at a coffee house.[99] They shared the accommodation – which was meant for only one person – for five shillings, an early sign of Taylor's fundamental concern with thrift, which would preoccupy him throughout his adult life. But he reassured his father that 'we both make out very well except that we are like to tumble out of the bed in the night. I got a good start last night with that when I awoke I was falling out but managed to keep up my head and was not hurt.' The widowed landlady provided 'coffee a small loaf and butter a rasher of bacon for sixpence each' but not many potatoes: 'When we ask for a plate of potatoes here we just get 3 on a little plate for a penny.' The food in London caused Taylor to suffer a stomach complaint that led to an 'inclination to vomiting'. He blamed the problem on either 'the change of meat living almost wholly on flesh' or the consumption of apples.[100]

The water was also bad, so 'that nobody drinks it and as I cannot get a right drink of anything else I have been perishing with thirst since I came here. Every person wonders to see me drinking water. We are like to drink all the water we get to wash with.' He wore 'the same dress I came away in' and had only one other shirt 'and two dickies' to hand, as the remainder of his clothing was packed in his trunk at the docks.

Like many visitors to the city, Taylor still managed to do some sightseeing at the Chelsea Hospital, the Royal Military asylum (where he observed soldiers' children in training), St James' Park, Hyde Park, and Buckingham Palace 'with the foot and horse guards parading about'. He claimed, 'We have not seen her Majesty yet but may easily do so. I think the people here would almost worship her.' Unable to find a Presbyterian church, he 'went into a Puseyite chapel and heard service there' before attending divine service at Westminster Abbey,

> one of the grandest concerns I ever saw. The great organ thundered through among the vaults and rows of pillars with arches between very sublime. We did not hear a word they said nor saw any person speaking but only heard a small sound in the direction of the speaker except during the sermon when we were beside the pulpit. It is ornamented with an enormous quantity of sculpture and has some beautiful painted windows. The service was conducted only in a part of the Abbey.[101]

He was captivated by his surroundings, and the contrast with his earlier religious experiences in plain Presbyterian churches could not have been starker.

London, during Taylor's time there, played host to the Great Exhibition of the Works of Industry of all Nations held at the Crystal Palace in Hyde Park from 1 May to 11 October 1851. It was the first in a series of world fairs, and all nations were invited to provide exhibitions. A 'spectacle of commodities', the Exhibition highlighted the work of skilled artisans, among them the Stivens, represented by Alexander Stiven, Henry's brother.[102] Their snuff-boxes, or 'Scotch boxes', were among 13,000 exhibits on display, many of which were of local manufacture, including Sheffield wares.[103] Under Class 29, Miscellaneous Manufactures and Small Ware, Charles Stiven and Sons of Laurencekirk exhibited other items, including an array of chests and boxes featuring Scottish scenes such as Balmoral, Melrose Abbey, and Scone Palace, and patterns including Murray, Royal Stuart, and Hunting Stuart tartans.[104] Renowned for their perfect hinges and fitted covers, their Scottish snuffboxes were considered 'ingenious productions', made originally at Laurencekirk by Stiven, 'whose son and successor is present by his works in the Great Exhibition'. The Stiven snuffbox received favourable notice.[105] The Exhibition was not simply about trade, industry, and labour, but encompassed important aesthetic aspects as well.[106]

Taylor did not visit the Exhibition, but had he done so he would have seen the machinery, buildings, and implements associated with Ceylon's coffee plantations of the time.[107] Little could he have known that a mere three decades later his Ceylon tea would feature in imperial exhibitions. Even so, the crowds and carriages were so numerous that Taylor wrote to his father two days after the Exhibition ended, showing signs of impatience and excuses, traits that would forever be with him: 'I have not time nor patience to say anything of the Exhibition for if I were to begin I would never get done. Henry's Brother went out on Friday to go some where and he along with many more stood at the side of a street for about two hours and could not get across the street for carriages and so had to come home again.'[108] Returning with the Stivens 'to help them to get out their boxes and the case out of the Exhibition', Taylor observed, 'I never saw any business going on so quick as the removal of the goods. There is just a great crowd of people and waggons and cabs &c about it and a continual drove of them going away in all directions laden with things.'[109] Other comments at the time echoed Taylor's depictions: 'to cross the streets was a hazardous and bewildering task for the pedestrian'.[110] He quickly grew tired of London and its noise, such 'that if you go into the street you can scarcely here any person speaking unless they cry into your ear and we can scarcely know what the people here say which makes us look somewhat awkward'.[111]

The experience provoked in him sensitive inner feelings, for he reflected on the sorrow of leaving home but at the same time looked forward to a reunion at some point in the future:

> I hope you are quite happy and pleased that I am now on my way from home to a good place for it would make me much happier to know that you were so. … I hope you will not trouble yourself concerning my absence Dear Father but let these feelings die away and wait till I come back to see you again then the meeting which I hope through Providence we shall yet have will amply repay our parting. … I find a person is more free to express their mind in a letter than any other way.[112]

Writing could have provided an easier and 'distancing' means for Taylor to express his inner feelings than experiencing the challenge of a face-to-face encounter. His father's reply must have pleased the sixteen-year-old, for he later recorded 'how much I value this letter', and continued in similar vein:

> Every thing has gone middling well yet but it is a heavy thought going away so far from home and all my friends but I cannot tell how this letter has relieved me … My Dear Father I shall never forget our parting and if we should never meet here again I hope we shall meet where parting is unknown and if every thing goes right a few years will soon pass away and a meeting then would fully repay our parting. I find it is a pleasure to be writing to you.[113]

Here Taylor put aside previous disagreements, recollections of which, however, would surface in his later correspondence from Ceylon.

The depth of feeling arising from the separation of families is, of course, a familiar aspect of the migration experience. Yet in a Scottish context, it is usually the departure of Highlanders that is represented in emotive terms, rather than that of those like Taylor who left in even greater numbers from Lowland society. Famous paintings, such as Thomas Faed's *Last of the Clan*, depicted the emigration of the Gael as one of sorrow and exile, as did much of the canon of nineteenth-century Gaelic verse and song. Some Scottish migrants, whatever their regional origins, surely did see themselves as exiles. But current historical thinking tends to see those who left from Lowland rural society as being primarily influenced by a search for opportunity rather than by the result of direct coercive pressures.[114] Taylor's heartfelt comments, however, are a reminder that the pain of separation could still torment those who emigrated for personal advancement or in the eager anticipation of adventure.

Nevertheless, Taylor's mood seems to have brightened after he took ship and the long sea voyage to Ceylon actually began. When he finally arrived in Colombo there was initially little time for further wistful reflections of the kind that had afflicted him while in London. A mere two days after he set foot on the island he was already on his way to his first posting and a new life in the coffee plantations of the hill country around Kandy.

Notes

1 Taylor letters, 23 October 1851, 24 October 1851.

2 Taylor letters, Notes from Voyage.

3 Taylor letters, 13 March 1852.

4 NLS, Fettercairn Estate Papers, Acc 4796, No. 54, Letters to Sir John Stuart Forbes, 1833–1852, Henry Stiven (Ancoombra) to Sir John Stuart Forbes (Fettercairn), 5 April 1852.

5 Taylor letters, 13 March 1852. Stiven, in his letter to Forbes, 5 April 1852, noted that, had they travelled by bullocks, the journey would have taken twelve to fourteen days.

6 Stiven to Forbes, 5 April 1852.

7 Taylor letters, 13 March 1852.

8 See the rental details in NLS, Monboddo Estate Accounts (1861–3), MS 24608. Details for 1858 are on p. 88. Michael Taylor is also noted in the following records of the Monboddo Estate Papers: Notebook of James B. Burnett (1834–8), MS 24627; Accounts (1862–3).

9 'Pioneers of the planting enterprise in Ceylon: James Taylor', *TA*, July 1894, p. 1. As well as holdings at the British Library, the *TA* can be browsed online at: www.biodiversitylibrary.org/item/185639 (for the years 1881–1912).

10 *The New Statistical Account of Scotland: Vol. 11. Forfar, Kincardine* (Edinburgh and London, 1845), p. 68.

11 A. Gove, *The History of Auchenblae* (unpublished booklet entered in the Village History book competition under the auspices of the Scottish Women's Rural Institutes, 1967, held at NLS).

12 *The New Statistical Account of Scotland: Vol. 11. Forfar, Kincardine*, p. 103; Gove, *History of Auchenblae*.

13 Charles A. Mollyson, *The Parish of Fordoun: Chapters in its History, or Reminiscences of Place and Character* (Aberdeen, 1893), p. 89. A searchable version is available

online at https://archive.org/stream/parishfordounch00mollgoog/parishfordounch00mollgoog_djvu.txt

14 Mollyson, *The Parish of Fordoun*, pp. 333–334.

15 It was further stated that 'Auld Fordoun' would intervene when local schoolchildren as a prank would descend 'into the dark cavern where his threshing mill wheel performed its revolutions'. See Mollyson, *The Parish of Fordoun*, p. 44.

16 Arthur Bruce, *Laurencekirk: Days Gone By* (Laurencekirk, 2004), p. 40.

17 Mollyson, *The Parish of Fordoun*, p. 154.

18 We are grateful to Tom Lawson for details about the farm fans.

19 William Ruxton Fraser, *History of the Parish and Burgh of Laurencekirk* (Edinburgh and London, 1880), pp. 8, 204–205; Bruce, *Laurencekirk*, p. 9.

20 Details about Charles Stiven can be found in Fraser, *History of the Parish*, pp. 204–210. See also Bruce, *Laurencekirk*, p. 9. Family history records show that Charles Stiven married Margaret Burnett, a daughter of James Burnet and Anne Burness. He died in 1821 aged 68. See *The Edinburgh Magazine*, 9 (July–December 1821), p. 295. The spelling of Burnett and Burnet varies over time.

21 Taylor letters, 3 September 1859.

22 The family is listed as resident at Black Knaps in the 1841 Census, with May listed as 'Mary' and Michael returned as a 'wright'. In 1851, Michael held 17 acres at Mosspark. By 1861, he held 24 acres and ten years later 15 acres.

23 'Pioneers of the planting enterprise in Ceylon', p. 1.

24 Ibid., p. 1.

25 Ibid., p. 1; D.M. Forrest, *A Hundred Years of Ceylon Tea, 1867–1967* (London, 1967), p. 63.

26 *Memoir of the Life and Work of Rev. John Brebner, MA., LL.D, late Superintendent of Education in the Orange Free State, South Africa* (Edinburgh, 1903), p. 14. Chalmers was invited to Auchenblae by the landowner, Captain Burnett.

27 Information from Jenny Thomson, Auchenblae.

28 Information from the Auchenblae Heritage Walk leaflet.

29 E.L. Cloyd, *James Burnett: Lord Monboddo* (Oxford, 1972), p. 56. See also Sheila M. Spiers, *The Kirkyard of Glenbervie* (Aberdeen, 1996), p. 12. Burns' great-grandparents were James Burnes and Margaret Falconer of Bralinmuir.

30 Bruce, *Laurencekirk*, p. 50; Gove, *History of Auchenblae*.

31 The first poem, from 1786, is his 'Address to Edinburgh' in which Burns acclaims Eliza as 'the Fair Burnet', who 'strikes th' adoring eye'. He wrote to William Chalmers that same year deeming her 'heavenly Miss Burnet, daughter to lord Monbodo, at whose house I have had the honor to be more than once'. See Burns to William Chalmers, 27 December 1786, in James A. Mackay (ed.), *The Complete Letters of Robert Burns* (Alloway, 1987), p. 219. The second poem was his 'Elegy on the Late Miss Burnet, of Monboddo', written following her death of consumption in 1791 at just 24 years of age. Burns wrote that she was 'lovely from her native skies' and puzzled whether 'Thy form and mind, sweet maid, can I forget?' Other individuals, while acknowledging Eliza's beauty, noted her decayed and discoloured teeth and 'thick Clumsy Ancles'. See Cloyd, *James Burnett*, p. 129, and footnote 2.

32 Mollyson, *The Parish of Fordoun*, p. 224. James Burnett Burnett's correspondence shows that he spent time in England in the 1830s and wrote regularly to Monboddo remitting funds to improve his property and keep up the 'garden & grounds, offices, farm steadings on the Property, Drainings & other improvements the making of roads'. See NLS, Monboddo Papers, Notebook of James B. Burnett, MS 24604, Ashton to Arthur letter, 19 January 1836, p. 34.
33 Mollyson, *The Parish of Fordoun*, p. 226.
34 'Pioneers of the planting enterprise in Ceylon', p. 1.
35 Mollyson, *The Parish of Fordoun*, p. 43.
36 Ibid., p. 63.
37 These subjects were all taught at the school in 1831, at which time the parish had six schools. See *New Statistical Account of Scotland*, p. 105.
38 Our thanks to Jenny Thomson, local historian at Auchenblae, for this information. Our discussion with the current owner of Beechvilla revealed that the school was on the ground floor of the building and entered through the current front door. The master's house on the second floor was reached from the rear of the house. Additional school recreational land was donated by Burnett at a later date.
39 Mollyson, *The Parish of Fordoun*, p. 59. See also W. Cramond, *The Annals of Fordoun* (Montrose, 1894), p. 106.
40 *Memoir of the Life and Work of Rev. John Brebner*, pp. 8–10, 15.
41 Taylor letters, 17 September 1857. Information about Robert Riach Thom is in Cramond, *The Annals of Fordoun*, p. 108. He later became a minister of the Free Church.
42 See John M. MacKenzie with Nigel R. Dalziel, *The Scots in South Africa: Ethnicity, Identity, Gender and Race, 1772–1914* (Manchester, 2005), p. 187, and *Memoir of the Life and Work of Rev John Brebner*.
43 *Memoir of the Life and Work of Rev John Brebner*, pp. 116–120.
44 Taylor letters, 17 September 1857.
45 Cramond, *The Annals of Fordoun*, pp. 106–107.
46 Taylor letters, undated, c.1858.
47 Lindsay Paterson, 'Traditions of Scottish education', in Heather Holmes (ed.), *Scottish Life and Society: Institutions of Scotland: Education* (East Linton, 2000), p. 23.
48 R.D. Anderson, *Education and the Scottish People, 1750–1918* (Oxford, 1995), p. 23.
49 Ranald C. Michie, 'Aberdeen and Ceylon: Economic links in the nineteenth century', *Northern Scotland*, 4 (1981), p. 69; Angela McCarthy, 'The importance of Scottish origins in the nineteenth century: James Taylor and Ceylon tea', in Angela McCarthy and John M. MacKenzie (eds), *Global Migrations: The Scottish Diaspora since 1600* (Edinburgh, 2016), pp. 121–123.
50 *TA*, February 1897, p. 513.
51 Douglas J. Hamilton, *Scotland, the Caribbean and the Atlantic World, 1750–1820* (Manchester, 2005), pp. 4, 18.
52 T.M. Devine, *The Scottish Nation, 1700–2000* (London, 2000), pp. 99–100.
53 'Pioneers of the planting enterprise in Ceylon', p. 1.
54 Taylor letters, undated letter, c.1858.
55 Ibid., 21 February 1859.

56 Ibid.
57 Ibid., 17 September 1857.
58 'Pioneers of the planting enterprise in Ceylon', p. 2.
59 Taylor letters, 23 December 1859.
60 T.M. Devine, *The Transformation of Rural Scotland: Social Change and the Agrarian Economy, 1660–1815* (Edinburgh, 1994), p. 165.
61 Ibid., p. 65.
62 Laurance James Saunders, *Scottish Democracy, 1815–1840: The Social and Intellectual Background* (Edinburgh, 1950), p. 17.
63 Alastair Orr, 'Farm servants and farm labour in the Forth Valley and south-east lowlands', in T.M. Devine (ed.), *Farm Servants and Labour in Lowland Scotland, 1770–1914* (Edinburgh, 1984), p. 29.
64 Saunders, *Scottish Democracy,* p. 38.
65 T.M. Devine, 'Scottish farm service in the agricultural revolution', in T.M. Devine (ed.), *Farm Servants and Labour in Lowland Scotland, 1770–1914* (Edinburgh, 1984), pp. 1, 4.
66 T.M. Devine, 'Industrialisation', in T.M. Devine, Clive Lee and George Peden (eds), *The Transformation of Scotland: The Economy since 1700* (Edinburgh, 2005), pp. 41, 58.
67 Gavin Sprott, 'The country tradesman', in T.M. Devine (ed.), *Farm Servants and Labour in Lowland Scotland, 1700–1914* (Edinburgh, 1984), pp. 143–155, at p. 144.
68 Mollyson, *The Parish of Fordoun*, pp. 154, 149.
69 Gove, *History of Auchenblae*, n.p.
70 James Donaldson, *General View of the Agriculture of the County of Kincardine; Or, The Mearns: With Observations on the Means of its Improvement* (London, 1795), p. 10.
71 Willis B. Marker, 'Scottish teachers', in Heather Holmes (ed.), *Scottish Life and Society: Institutions of Scotland: Education* (East Linton, 2000), p. 274.
72 Teaching indenture, 1 April 1849, in NLS, Papers of James Taylor, planter in Ceylon, MS 15908. Taylor's original signed indenture, together with that of John Ross, was discovered in 2016 by Jenny Thomson. Jenny also found a letter from John Philip (Free Manse, Fordoun) to the Secretary, Committtee of Council on Education, 13 December 1849, which stated that schools were closed in September and October for the harvest, which meant that Inspectors needed to rearrange their visits to 'hear the pupil teachers examine a class'.
73 Taylor letters, 17 September 1857. Souter's name is also rendered 'Soutar'.
74 Marker, 'Scottish teachers', pp. 274–276, and Taylor's indenture.
75 Cramond, *Annals of Fordoun*, pp. 94, 106–107.
76 Taylor letters, undated, c.1858.
77 Cited in David Armitage, 'The Scottish diaspora', in Jenny Wormald (ed.), *Scotland: A History* (Oxford, 2005), p. 272.
78 Dudley Baines, *Emigration from Europe, 1815–1930* (London, 1991), p. 10.
79 See T.M. Devine, *To the Ends of the Earth: Scotland's Global Diaspora, 1750–2010* (London, 2011).
80 Angela McCarthy (ed.), *A Global Clan: Scottish Migrant Networks and Identities since the Eighteenth Century* (London and New York, 2006).

81 See, for instance, references to Moir in NLS, Fettercairn Estate Papers, Acc 4796, No. 149, Factor's letters, 1837–1859, especially 1837 and 1838.

82 Taylor letters, 18 March 1872.

83 Blacklaw's quote is cited in Forrest, *A Hundred Years of Ceylon Tea*, p. 61. Some accounts refer to Moir as Taylor's cousin, but that he was a cousin to Taylor's mother is evident from reconstruction of the family tree (see Appendix 2). Another account from 1895, presumably by Blacklaw, further notes the Laurencekirk contingent: 'Peter Moir led the way, and 13 of us followed – Jamie Moir, David Moir, Charlie Moir, H. and W. Stiven, Jamie Taylor, Sandy Robertson, J. Oliphant, five Blacklaws, and the Bissets from close by.' See *OCO*, South Asian newspapers online, dated 1 August 1895, p. 11.

84 *TA*, 1 April 1898, p. 662.

85 Fraser, *History of the Parish and Burgh of Laurencekirk*, p. 167. Arthur Bruce mistakes this as causing the presence of Laurencekirk men in Ceylon, p. 48.

86 Marjory Harper, *Emigration from North-East Scotland: Volume One. Willing Exiles* (Aberdeen, 1988), p. 330.

87 'R.B. Tytler: In memoriam', *WCO*, 18 July 1882, p. 592. This obituary gives his birthplace as Peterhead. In the 1861 UK census, on the other hand, Tytler gives his place of birth as Inverurie. See also Beryl T. Mitchell, *Tea, Tytlers and Tribes: An Australian Woman's Memories of Tea Planting in Ceylon* (Henley Beach, 1996).

88 *TA*, 1 May 1900, pp. 723–730.

89 T.M. Devine, 'History, Scotland and slavery', in T.M. Devine (ed.), *Recovering Scotland's Slavery Past: The Caribbean Connection* (Edinburgh, 2015), p. 250.

90 Michie, 'Aberdeen and Ceylon', p. 70; Andrew Mackillop, 'Locality, nation, and empire: Scots and the empire in Asia, c.1695–c.1813', in John M. MacKenzie and T.M. Devine (eds), *Scotland and the British Empire* (Oxford, 2012), pp. 66, 70. See also T.J. Barron, 'Scots and the coffee industry in nineteenth century Ceylon', in T.M. Devine and Angela McCarthy (eds), *The Scottish Experience in Asia, c.1700 to the Present: Settlers and Sojourners* (Cham, 2017), pp. 163–185.

91 Taylor letters, 18 October 1851. It is said that Taylor and Stiven conferred at Fettercairn, where Stiven was an 18-year-old gardener to Sir John Stuart Forbes and resided with fellow servants at Fettercairn House. See *TA*, 2 July 1894, p. 2, and 1851 Scotland Census for Fettercairn, online at ancestry.co.uk.

92 Taylor letters, 16 October 1851; George Hadden was born in Aberdeen in 1775, and in 1805 became a merchant in London, where he died in 1859. James Alexander was his third son (the others dying as infants), born in London in 1822 and died in 1871. See William Johnston, *A Genealogical Account of the Descendants of James Young, Merchant Burgess of Aberdeen and Rachel Cruickshank his wife, 1697–1893* (Aberdeen, 1894), p. 83, https://archive.org/stream/agenealogicalac00johngoog#page/n60/mode/2up. These Haddens are related to the cousins Frederick and Charles Hadden who went to Ceylon in 1840, leaving Peter Moir in charge of their estates with his brother James to assist. See Taylor's letter and *TA*, 1 April 1898, p. 663.

93 P.J. Cain and A.G. Hopkins, *British Imperialism: Innovation and Expansion, 1688–1914* (London and New York, 1993).

94 For further comment on this thesis see John M. MacKenzie and T.M. Devine, 'Introduction', in John M. MacKenzie and T.M. Devine (eds), *Scotland and the British Empire* (Oxford, 2011), pp. 24–25.

95 The annual wage for an agricultural labourer in Kincardine was £27 6s. See Frederick Purdy, 'On the earnings of agricultural labourers in Scotland and Ireland', *Journal of the Statistical Society*, 25:4 (1862), Table IV, p. 470.

96 Taylor letters, 18 October 1851.

97 Ibid., 13 October 1851, 16 October 1851.

98 Ibid., 16 October 1851.

99 Ibid., 13 October 1851. Taylor's grandfather Robert Moir refers in a letter to his sister Jean, who was married to a James Trail, 1 August 1859.

100 Ibid., 13 October 1851, 18 October 1851.

101 Ibid., 13 October 1851.

102 The phrase is from Peter H. Hoffenberg, *An Empire on Display: English, Indian, and Australian Exhibitions from the Crystal Palace to the Great War* (Berkeley and Los Angeles, 2001), p. 23, referring to work by Thomas Richards (1990). See also Paul Greenhalgh, *Ephemeral Vistas: The* Expositions Universelles, *Great Exhibitions and World's Fairs, 1851–1939* (Manchester, 1988), p. 54.

103 Lara Kriegel, *Grand Designs: Labor, Empire, and the Museum in Victorian Culture* (Durham and London, 2007), p. 99.

104 *Great Exhibition of the Works of Industry of All Nations, 1851, Official Descriptive and Illustrated Catalogue*, vol. 2 (London, 1851), p. 791.

105 J.G. Strutt (ed.), *Tallis's Description of the Crystal Palace, and the Exhibition of the World's Industry in 1851*, vol. 2 (London and New York, 1851), p. 254; *Exhibition of the Works of Industry of All Nations, 1851: Reports by the Juries on the Subjects in the Thirty Classes into which the Exhibition was Divided* (London, 1852), p. 675. Henry and Alexander were the children of Alexander Stiven, son of Charles. Henry's brother may therefore have been in London exhibiting with his father. The *Reports by the Juries* further notes that the manufacture of the boxes soon spread to Old Cumnock and Mauchline in Ayrshire.

106 Kriegel, *Grand Designs*, p. 10.

107 John Tallis, *Tallis's History and Description of the Crystal Palace and the Exhibition of the World's Industry in 1851*, vol. 1 (London and New York, 1852), p. 49.

108 Taylor letters, 13 October 1851.

109 Ibid., 16 October 1851.

110 Tallis, *Tallis's History and Description of the Crystal Palace*, vol. 1, p. 20. Tallis estimated that six million people visited the exhibition and London's population increased ten-fold as a result. This was facilitated by admission fees which enabled all but the low working classes to attend. See Greenhalgh, *Ephemeral Vistas*, p. 30.

111 Taylor letters, 18 October 1851.

112 Ibid., 13 October 1851.

113 Ibid., 18 October 1851.

114 Devine, *To the Ends of the Earth*. See also Marjory Harper, *Adventurers and Exiles: The Great Scottish Exodus* (London, 2003).

2

The rise and fall of 'King Coffee'

James Taylor was first placed on the Naranghena estate in the Hewaheta district, but after six weeks was instructed to move to the neighbouring property of Loolecondera. During the next few years he worked between the two of them and also managed Wal Oya. Very quickly, therefore, having just turned seventeen years of age after his arrival in Ceylon, he had been given some responsibility over several estates which stretched for many miles. Taylor estimated that these three of George Pride's estates were between four and five miles long. Loolecondera, with which he would come to be mainly associated, was 110 acres; Naranghena comprised 200 acres of old coffee and a new field of 42 acres; and Wal Oya was around 200 acres. With four additional estates, Taylor estimated that 'Mr Pride has about 1000 acres of coffee now and I suppose nearly as much more forest.'[1]

James Taylor's eventual fame undeniably came from his achievements as a tea planter. Yet, for several years, cultivating coffee, the main enterprise in Ceylon during his early years on the island, was his prime responsibility. The first sections of this chapter therefore describe the broad context of the coffee industry, before focusing on Taylor's role within it.

Britain took possession of Ceylon, lying to the south-east of its Indian Empire, in two stages during the early decades of the nineteenth century. First, the island became a British Crown Colony in 1802 after it was won from Dutch control. Second, between 1815 and 1818, the British achieved, where other colonial powers before them had failed, the conquest of the Kingdom of Kandy, in the centre of the country. This was of crucial importance to the subsequent expansion of the coffee economy in Ceylon. These lands of higher altitude were much more suited to the cultivation of coffee plants on a large scale than were the coastal areas previously occupied by the Dutch. Their earlier experimentation with the introduction of coffee growing in the maritime districts of the west of the island did not prove a success. Anyway, for the Dutch the main economic prize in Ceylon had been control of cinnamon production and trade, together with other spices such as pepper and cardamoms.[2]

The coffee plant was not indigenous to Ceylon, with Arabs or Persians having probably introduced it in earlier times.[3] By the early nineteenth century it was cultivated on a modest scale by some Sinhalese in the highlands of Kandy as part of their general mode of subsistence husbandry, while they sold some surplus berries to itinerant merchants.[4] Several British writers, both then and later, were wont to dismiss early Sinhalese coffee cultivation, arguing that only with the coming of the imperial power was there any. According to Sir James Emerson Tennent, for example, writing in 1859, 'although the plant had existed from time immemorial on the island ... the natives were ignorant of the value of its berries and only used its leaves to flavour their curries, and its flowers to decorate their temples'.[5] Yet, often overlooked is that the first British coffee exports from Ceylon were in fact the result of Sinhalese cultivation.[6]

From such small beginnings there eventually came a massive growth in plantation coffee production in Ceylon. The transformation did not occur immediately after the imposition of British rule, but by the 1830s a cycle of ongoing development was already becoming apparent. In 1834, the export weight of coffee was a mere 26,000 hundredweight. By the early 1850s, this had climbed to 344,000 hundredweight, and in the peak years of the late 1860s Ceylon exported 939,000 hundredweight. In the meantime, the area planted in coffee had risen from 23,000 acres between 1840 and 1844 to 310,000 in the years 1875–1879.[7] By the mid-1860s an estimated eight hundred coffee estates were in operation.[8] The colonial export economy of Ceylon was transformed into a coffee monoculture between the 1830s and 1860s. The industry had also demonstrated its intrinsic resilience. Between 1847 and 1849, coffee prices collapsed due to financial crises in the British and European economies, overproduction, and increasing international competition. Numerous coffee estates went bankrupt and were sold off.[9] Nonetheless, this disaster resulted mainly in the culling of marginal and less-profitable plantations. The core of the coffee economy survived and expanded to even greater levels of cultivation and production after c.1850. Ceylon coffee became a prestigious international brand. A veritable 'coffee mania' was triggered on the island, and by 1870, 85 per cent of the total export value of Ceylon consisted of this single commodity.[10]

The origins of 'King Coffee'

By 1860, Ceylon had become, with Brazil and Indonesia, one of the three leading coffee-producing countries in the world. Its rise to prominence from the 1830s can be considered as a South Asian example of the transoceanic revolution in international commerce which linked the modernising economies of Europe and the United States to the primary producing countries of the southern hemisphere.[11] Rising population, industrialisation, urbanisation, and increases in per capita incomes in the North all combined to generate a massively enhanced demand for raw materials and foods from the agrarian societies of the South. Wool, raw cotton, sugar, tea, and coffee were just some of the commodities that underwent unprecedented expansion in markets during the second half of the nineteenth century. In return, the richer North provided investment funds, capital goods, and financial services to the poorer South. The entire mechanism of commerce was lubricated by a series of path-breaking innovations in global communications in the form of faster sailing ships, the introduction of steam navigation, and the worldwide expansion of railway networks.

Nevertheless, how far individual countries or regions were able to exploit these new opportunities depended, in the final analysis, on their comparative advantages in particular economic sectors or distinctive strengths in commodity specialisations. Before the 1820s, Ceylon lacked the necessary infrastructure to excel in coffee cultivation and marketing in competition with more favoured locations. After that period, however, prospects rapidly improved.

In this respect, the influence of the colonial government was often crucial, especially in establishing the initial preconditions for coffee development. For the first time after the British annexation of Kandy in 1818, a single authority governed the whole of Ceylon. This guaranteed the political stability essential to sustained investment from outside the island in plantations, roads, bridges, and harbours.[12] It was important too that, unlike the coastlands of the west, the hill country of Kandy was ideally suited to the cultivation of the coffee crop. The first plantation in that region had been established in 1827.

But the role of the colonial administration went further and deeper than that. It was always susceptible to the demands of the planter community, because government revenues soon began to depend on coffee exports.[13] Moreover, to a quite remarkable degree, both British civil servants and military men became involved as planters in the coffee economy. Indeed, this process, until reforms were implemented in 1845, was aided and abetted from London to an extent unparalleled in any of the other tropical colonies. In 1829, the Colonial Office dispatched a special Commission to Ceylon to assess the administration of the island.[14] Its far-reaching recommendations had a transformative impact on the economy. For instance, the Commission reduced the salaries of administrators, limited promotion prospects, and curtailed several of their financial privileges. At the same time, both civil servants and army officers were encouraged to exploit the potential of the plantation economy for profit. This strategy was so successful that it soon became evident that servants of the state were neglecting their official duties in the search for profit in the agricultural economy. This was the case until 1844–1845, when further civil service reforms were implemented.[15]

But the report of the Colebrooke-Cameron Commission had even more fundamental effects. It advocated a free-market economy in the colony, recommending the adoption of *laissez-faire* policies throughout government and the abolition of controls on land sales. As a result, Ceylon was likely to become a capitalist's paradise and the drive to a coffee monoculture now accelerated. By 1833, Crown lands were being sold by auction and a free market in land was in place. Seven years later, the Crown Lands Encroachment Ordinance introduced a new security of land title in law that at a stroke removed many of the traditional rights of the peasantry.[16] The core of the coffee economy in Kandy was in a region less densely populated than in other areas of the island, but the relentless expansion of the plantations may have resulted in some loss of land. There is no scholarly consensus on this controversial issue but one perspective has it that dispossession helped to stoke the social anxieties that led to disturbances in the Kandyan provinces of Matale and Kurunegala in 1848. Opposition to new taxes is, however, a more likely explanation. Whatever their origins, the rebellion was soon crushed by British military force.[17] The conversion of vast tracts of forest land to plantations eventually eased the pressure on peasant holdings, but lingering tensions prompted by the coffee boom never entirely vanished. In 1894, for instance, natives claimed forest land at Rajawelle. Even so, the agent took 'possession, built a hut on the land, and put two watchmen in charge. The natives story is that the land was sold by a Mr Gavin to a party who sold it to them.'[18]

The colonial government also had a significant influence on the development of the transport infrastructure which was so vital to the success of the plantation economy. Communications were primitive in the hill country of Kandy, while the harvested berries had to come overland to the port of Colombo rather than along the traditional sea routes by the coasts. The colonial administration completed the Kandy–Colombo road in 1830, ostensibly for political and military reasons, but the road was also likely to have substantial economic benefits in the long term. Planters then pressed for further investment as the coffee cultivation increased in scale. In the following decades, therefore, a new road network was constructed throughout the central highlands. Finally, in 1867, the first railway on the island was completed when the Colombo–Kandy line was opened. After that, road building had the subsidiary purpose of providing feeders from remote plantations to the railway lines.[19]

The momentum of expansion depended on four other factors: investment funds, enterprise, availability of labour, and, by no means least, the problems of competitor Caribbean coffee production after slave emancipation in 1833. Slave emancipation not only undermined the West Indian coffee economy in the short term but also encouraged the movement of some sugar and coffee planters in the Caribbean islands to seek fresh opportunities in Ceylon. This represented the transfer of both cultivation skills and experience, refined over generations in the West Indies, together with the capital realised from plantation sales and the financial benefits of the huge compensation payments paid from 1833 to former slave-owners for the loss of their 'property' after emancipation.[20] One of the most influential émigrés of the time from the Caribbean was the Scot Robert Boyd Tytler, who, as shown in chapter 1, encouraged many of his compatriots to settle in Ceylon. From the outset of his migration to Jamaica at fifteen years of age, it was intended that he would at some point transfer his knowledge to Ceylon, where 'a shrewd Scotchman' had discovered the land 'would grow excellent coffee'. In 1837, after three years in Jamaica in the employ of an Aberdonian, Charles Anderson, Tytler took up a post in Ceylon as a manager on the estates of Ackland and Boyd and Company.[21] He is credited both with introducing more advanced cultivation techniques in the coffee economy and with providing an essential point of contact through which several kinsmen and associates from north-east Scotland eventually followed in his footsteps.[22]

Tytler's migration from Jamaica to Ceylon has generated a convincing argument that Ceylon's coffee enterprise was shaped initially by previous experience in the West Indies. Tom Barron, for instance, observed that 'the first generation of planters were the inheritors of nearly 200 years of planting experience' in the Caribbean. It was reckoned that 'the West India method of cultivation', and especially the processing of coffee, produced a better-quality product.[23] Before 1830 the first British planters in Ceylon had in general followed the traditional methods of the natives. However, the new approach that originated in the Caribbean led to a step-change in methods. These were founded partly on long experience of coffee planting in the West Indies, but a highly influential planting guide, *The Coffee Planter of Saint Domingo*, published in 1798 by a French West Indian planter, P.J. Labourie, was also crucial. Labourie's advice had been designed to pass on the secrets of French high-quality coffee cultivation in exchange for British support of France during the famous slave rebellion led by Toussaint L'Ouverture in Saint Domingo.[24] Even so, planters had to adapt their techniques to Ceylon conditions.

Enterprise and investment came from a range of sources. Most British colonial governors at the time were scions of the landed classes at home who had served as senior army officers or imperial administrators in the empire earlier in their careers. They came from a social class in the metropole that was long accustomed to seeking higher returns from landed assets through agricultural improvement. It was not a coincidence, then, that Sir Edward Barnes, Governor of Ceylon from 1824 to 1831, was one of the first to spot the potential of coffee planting in the Kandyan Highlands.[25] As seen above, his example was eventually followed by a stream of army officers and civil servants when the 'coffee rush' achieved momentum from the later 1830s when West Indian coffee output fell after the abolition of slavery. The new opportunities also triggered an inward movement of small planters, adventurers, and speculators from India and Britain. The initial capital costs of setting up a coffee plantation were relatively modest, and land during that period was virtually given away at the nominal price of five shillings an acre.[26]

Contemporaries likened the scale of activity at the time to a gold rush. By the early 1850s, more than 60,000 acres of land from the Crown were cultivated in coffee.[27] The fevered speculation drew in financial support from agency houses, long dominant in the trade throughout India. Small planters, in particular, needed short-term credit, as it took nearly a year from the harvesting of the crop for returns to come through from sales in London. In addition, there was a considerable risk during the period of cultivation. Annual crops were dependent on the weather, and unseasonable heavy rains could prove disastrous. Banks were also established to provide credit to cover the time-lag between initial planting and final sales. The Bank of Ceylon, for instance, first opened its doors in 1841. Many made profits in these years, but the whole system, based as it was on small, under-capitalised plantations and bank lending on a lavish scale, was nonetheless potentially precarious.[28]

The supply of labour

A fundamental precondition for the emergence of the coffee economy on a large scale was the availability of workers for the essential tasks of planting, pruning, and harvesting. While in the early years small-scale coffee production depended on recruiting labour from the local Sinhalese, by the 1830s and 1840s the rapid growth of the plantations had soon outstripped this supply. The mass of the native population were not easily attracted by low-wage labour under strict regulation and intensity of production, as they lived within a subsistence system of agriculture where the produce of vegetable gardens and paddy fields met most of their needs. As the plantations began to absorb some peasant lands and to threaten others, antagonism between planters and people may also have caused some alienation from the new economic system.[29] Some have suggested there were deeper reasons within the culture of the Sinhalese people for opposition to wage labour. One contemporary commentator noted that the Kandyan had 'such a reverence for his patrimonial lands, that were his gain to be quadrupled, he would not abandon their culture'. He went on to assert that working for hire was regarded 'as almost slavery … being obliged to obey orders, and to do just what they are commanded in [sic] galling to them'.[30] But the evidence suggests that these early views are somewhat overstated. As shown below, the Sinhalese did work on the estates, not to any extent as field labour, pruning the bushes and harvesting the crops, but, rather, in specific, higher-paid tasks.

In a highly labour-intensive plantation economy, owners and overseers had soon to look beyond Ceylon, and especially to the neighbouring, densely populated, and impoverished regions of south-east India, for a cheaper labour force.

These Tamils took work on the estates that Sinhalese were reluctant to undertake. As James Taylor indicated when he first arrived in Ceylon:

> I was only employed for about a month and a half on the old estate. After that I was employed with the Cingalese natives from what we call the village a pretty level place in the bottom of the Glen where the natives live and cultivate Rice. These are employed chasing up that is cutting the branches off the trees and so forth and making them in heaps and burning them. The trees were all cut down before and burned as much as they would without heaping. The Cingalese are employed at this as it is too hard work for the coolies who work the estates. They all come over from the continent or Malabar coast just beside us. They are a set of poor things but the Cingalese are a hardy active strong race compared to coolies though not [*erased:* to] perhaps to some other half civilized races ... these new coolies are such a pest for running away. It is not every one we can trust. About a hundred of our new coolies have run away this last 2 or 3 weeks. We have always to keep sending Kanganys to the coast to bring more.[31]

This extract is important in two respects. First, Taylor's recognition of the different ethnicities in his labour force is in conflict with those views that suggest planters used the term 'coolie' to describe all those working on the plantations, whether they were Sinhalese, Ceylon Tamils, or Tamil migrants from India.[32] Instead, he made clear distinctions between them, and on occasion used the term 'natives' without any qualification to refer to the Sinhalese. His comment also casts doubt on claims that planters made little effort to recruit Sinhalese workers to the estates. Taylor's reference to the different languages spoken by his estate workers suggest the same conclusion: 'I can scarcely talk a word to the Cingalese and when I speak to coolies they are so childishly superstitious that I cannot make anything of them.'[33] Like tea planters in India, he explicitly acknowledged the significance of ethnic differences in the work-force.[34]

The second point of interest is Taylor's comments on the migratory character of his labourers. Some scholars point to an ongoing circular migration between India and south-east Asia, including Ceylon, until the 1930s, based on the kangany system of recruitment. Through this process, Tamil foremen on Ceylon estates returned to India to enlist further workers.[35] By 1882, some claimed that no fewer than 2,700,000 Tamils had arrived in Ceylon from South India since 1843.[36] This meant that Ceylon was one of the three most important destinations for migrants from India, with around eight million moving there up to 1940.[37] However, determining what percentage of this huge number worked on the plantations is difficult. As Patrick Peebles argues, 'the records never refer unambiguously to the immigrant population' and do not record the Tamil estate population as 'temporary', 'seasonal', or 'circulatory'. Instead, he suggests that this circular mobility is not relevant to Tamil estate workers, as arrivals and departures did not coincide with the coffee season. In addition, he points out that planters tried to maintain a year-round labour force.[38] Even so, critics highlight that his statistics show a seasonal pattern of migration.[39]

What light does the evidence consulted for this book throw on this issue? Certainly, Taylor's letters show unequivocally that some of his Tamil workers did come from India rather than from elsewhere in Ceylon. As well as stating in 1852 that they originated from the continent and Malabar coast, in 1874, after he visited Darjeeling, he described a particular area in India from where they migrated: 'I went ashore at Negapatam as some of the people here come from there.'[40] This human traffic from India crossed the Palk Strait and then trekked 150 miles over a week to reach the coffee estates.[41] Taylor's correspondence also reveals that he considered some of his Tamils, at least during his first decade in Ceylon, to be seasonal labourers who went back to India after the harvest. In September 1857, during a time of labour shortage caused by the Indian 'Mutiny' and a cholera outbreak, he wrote: 'You mistake our "Co." It is not coal shipping but cooly shipping bringing over our coolies and taking them back again.'[42] This comment probably concerns an attempt made in 1856 to establish a scheme to transport migrants to Ceylon and which was subsequently legislated on in the Immigration Ordinance of 1858.

Taylor's relative Peter Moir was also inclined to view Tamils as a circulatory population. In 1869 he noted that Gampola was 'on the main route of coolies to and from their country' and added that 'Ceylon is not an unknown country to the coolies: they have been coming and going for the last 30 years, and they go and come of their own accord' with no lengthy engagements and two weeks' notice.[43] Henry Byrde similarly described a fluctuating population of 75,000 Tamil coolies who came annually to the plantations in June, July, and August. They were, however, joining around 300,000 Tamil plantations workers who he estimated had become settlers in Ceylon.[44] In conceptualising Tamil migrants this way, planters also drew similarities between them and Irish and Scottish migrants. One report, for instance, likened Tamil migrants to 'the exodus of the Irish to England, during the Harvest time, and in both cases the Emigrant leaves his country with the same object, viz., to obtain a temporary subsistence'.[45] John Ferguson, publisher of the *Ceylon Observer* and *Tropical Agriculturalist*, compared them with the reputation garnered by Scottish settlers: they 'have been called "the Scotchmen of the East," from their enterprise in migrating and colonising'.[46] Bishop Caldwell similarly saw similarities between the Tamils and Scots: 'wherever money is to be made, wherever a more apathetic people is waiting to be pushed aside, thither swain the Tamilians, the Greeks, or the Scotch of the East, the least superstitious and the most enterprising and persevering race of Hindus'.[47] There is, then, certainly evidence confirming seasonal Tamil migration to Ceylon for plantation work (primarily picking), but also evidence that this annual movement co-existed with a settled population on the estates due to the year-round demand for a range of estate duties.[48]

A further aspect of Peebles' deconstruction of the 'myth of seasonal labour' is that the considerable movement of workers *between* plantations may have been one reason for the official perception that all plantation Tamils were sojourning migrants rather than permanent workers in Ceylon.[49] Certainly, mobility *within* Ceylon was a characteristic of the labour force. Taylor, for instance, was angered in 1857 at attempts to 'take some of my coolies to another estate trying to induce them to run away'.[50] A constant problem, this 'floating unsettled labour'[51] often arose due to an inability of some planters to pay regular wages. As he reported in 1879: 'On many places the people have not been paid for eight or nine months and on some all the coolies have gone off as they could get no pay nor anything to eat; leaving their wages unpaid.'[52] Almost ten years later, two of Taylor's workers who 'seduced two of the labourers working on the estate ... to go away to another estate' appeared in court. Taylor's kangany, however, could not provide contractual details and the case was dismissed.[53] On other occasions, superintendents themselves were responsible for Tamil plantation mobility between estates: 'I have had about 1/3 of the men ill of chicken pox during just exactly the time I most wanted them. I helped two estates whose crops ripen earlier than mine to pick their crops by sending part of my men there and I got 76 men for three weeks to help me from Stiven and another, Scott at Gampola.'[54] The transitory nature of the work-force created uncertainties: 'we've already sent for coolies for crop without knowing what crop we may have to employ them with and how many we will want'.[55]

Another explanation for the construction of the 'sojourner thesis' might be that estate Tamils, even after living for several generations in Ceylon, still saw themselves as natives of India. The 1881 Census reported, for instance, that 'coolies born in Ceylon and who have never been out of it shew an invincible repugnance to entering an estate or a Ceylon district as their place of birth and almost invariably give the village in Southern India to which their family belongs'.[56] This ongoing sense of Indian identity among some plantation Tamils may have helped to shape and complicate the debates surrounding their 'belonging' and time of residence in Ceylon.

With the upward spiral in labour requirements, planters started to provide the kanganies with cash advances to finance the future journeys of labourers to the coffee estates. As a result, the migrants fell into debt before they had even started work in the fields around Kandy. In addition, through the impact of debt, labourers often found themselves in informal bondage with the kanganies, which often prevented their freedom of movement from one employer to another. Worse, the recruiters tried to keep migrant travel and food costs to a minimum, and so to pocket some of these payments for themselves. This also contributed to high mortality rates during the journey to the plantations. According to one historian, 'Contemporaries estimated that the *kanganies* did not spend even a third of the coast advance and that therefore hundreds of immigrants died of starvation – their bodies being thrown into the sea or left behind on the roadside.'[57] Clearly, not everyone gained from Ceylon's great coffee boom.

Depression, recovery, and the end of 'King Coffee'

In 1844 Britain lifted its protectionist duty on British colonial coffee as the free-trade school of thought became dominant in political circles. Oversupply in the British market was an immediate consequence which was then exacerbated by the financial crisis in Europe between 1847 and 1849, leading to a reduction in demand for coffee. At this point the intrinsic weaknesses in the Ceylonese plantation economy were exposed. Precious few of those who had become planters in the boom period had much previous agricultural expertise or experience. As one commentator put it, only 'the merest fraction of our planters ever were slave-holders or slave-drivers in the West Indies'.[58] Instead, those who entered the planting enterprise were army officers, ardent speculators, small capitalists, and adventurers from England and India who were supplemented by judges and civil servants who rarely took into account the need for maintenance of quality soil or improving methods of cultivation. Their aims were more limited: to make money in order to supplement their official salaries by speculating in land and coffee until the practice was declared illegal in the mid-1840s.[59] Reflecting back on that earlier period in 1857, James Taylor likewise reckoned most of the superintendents to be 'sailors and soldiers'.[60] They were motivated above all else by the opportunities for making a quick fortune.[61] Unscientific estate management, neglect of systematic weeding, poor methods of storage, and inadequate plantation superintendents all aggravated the malaise.[62] Soon many of the smaller and indebted planters were ruined as credit dried up and coffee prices collapsed. Around one-tenth of Ceylon plantations were abandoned and a further third were sold off at nominal rates.[63]

Yet the crisis proved to be temporary, and recovery from the depression became evident from the early 1850s. Indeed, the industry seems to have emerged stronger than before. By 1875 there were 1,215 plantations in Ceylon, with an estimated extent of 270,000 acres. Seven hundred and fifty British managers and some 200,000 Indian Tamils and their families were employed across the industry, which was capitalised at around £11 million sterling. If anything, coffee monoculture now intensified on the island, with a mere 560 acres devoted to tea and 300 to cinchona (a source of quinine).[64] The work of the plantations became underpinned by a more professional system of management and scientific methods of good husbandry, including better drainage, manuring, weeding, and irrigation.[65] Investors at this time sought those with relevant background skills to tend the estates and scientific methods of cultivation were introduced.[66] This was the period when James Taylor and many other young Scots of his generation with artisan and agricultural skills found employment as superintendents and managers in Ceylon. They were termed by one commentator 'Knights of the Coffee Bean'.[67] The 1840s crisis had virtually eliminated the smaller, less-profitable, under-capitalised plantations, which were now absorbed by larger and more robustly financed concerns.

With finances in place, the opening up of new estates or new areas of old estates involved many tasks. An early commentator, the planter William Boyd, explained the cycle of preparation. In September the ground was cleared for nurseries that included coffee seeds and young plants. Once trenched and lined, plants were sown every six to eight inches. It was then, he noted, that the 'cutting down of the forest began in real earnest'. In October the trees were 'mercilessly laid low' by a 'ceaseless clatter of axes' (Figure 2.1). Branches were then lopped and laid on the ground for burning in the drier months of March and April.[68] Indeed, in April 1852, just after he arrived in Ceylon, Taylor put local Sinhalese to work cutting branches from the trees and preparing them for burning.[69] For Boyd, the burning 'was one mass of seething scorching flame' which leapt and flashed while the 'burning timber crackled and hissed and occasionally exploded'. After tasks such as tree felling, Boyd noted, the Sinhalese went back to their villages, as

> They have, as a general rule, their own paddy fields, their own cows, bullocks, and buffaloes, their own fruit gardens; and the tending and managing of these occupy all their attention. Their wants are few and easily supplied, and, unless when they wish to present their wives with a new cloth, or to procure a gun or powder and shot for themselves, they have really no inducement to work on the coffee plantations.[70]

At this point, the Tamil workers were employed to undertake 'lining' of the estate, that is, to stake out the clearing using ropes as guidelines to show where the coffee trees were to be planted. By the middle of June the holes were dug. For Taylor's workers this involved each of them digging twenty-five holes of eighteen-inch depth every day.[71] Plants were then acquired from the nurseries and put into the ground. The holes were filled with surface soil and ashes from the burnings.[72] Although the coffee trees would normally grow to between ten and twelve feet tall, pruning kept them below four feet.[73]

These seasonal rhythms continued after the crop had come to fruition, although they varied from estate to estate. As Taylor observed, the routine at Loolecondera differed because the crop there took around eight months to ripen, as compared with 'places when it all ripens in three months'.[74] On the established estate of Naranghena, when he first arrived in March 1852, Taylor

2.1 An image of forest being felled by Sinhalese from A.M. Ferguson's *Abbotsford Album*.

2.2 Tamil workers at morning muster from A.M. Ferguson's *Abbotsford Album*.

supervised a hundred labourers who were weeding and gathering the crop.[75] Meanwhile, at Loolecondera in December 1857 he had two hundred labourers picking the coffee berries, 'about the size and shape of cherries at home and of a purple colour'. His workers had to cover twelve to seventeen acres about eight to ten times over a time-frame of four to five months, with December and January the key period. Taylor quizzed his father on how this routine compared to work at home: 'What do you think of that for crop operations? It is a greater push than your harvest work.'[76] Henry Stiven, writing in April 1852, likewise noted the labour variations: 'There are at present about 120 labourers employed but at crop time it requires 600.'[77] In early years, Taylor sometimes received a 'scolding' and admitted that, had his employer 'not coolies that understood better than I do I could not do at all'.[78] Despite this inauspicious beginning, over time Taylor sharpened many of the qualities that would contribute to his later acclaim.

To contemporaries, the period from the 1850s to the early 1870s was seen as one of 'coffee mania' as banks, agency houses, and joint-stock companies poured investment into the plantations.[79] From 1865 to 1869 Ceylon exported an annual average of 939,000 hundredweight of coffee. The export peak came in 1870, when more than one million hundredweight were shipped to the London market.[80] No one could have guessed, however, that less than two decades later the entire Ceylonese coffee industry would have vanished.

Taylor's correspondence charts the fluctuating fortunes of Loolecondera's coffee crop during this period. An 'unfavourable season' in the mid-1850s produced 'good merchantable coffee' but it barely covered the estate's costs.[81] In other words, he suggested, quality 'does not nearly make up for the loss of quantity'.[82] By 1857, Taylor considered coffee 'a splendid investment' as it sold in England for between £3 and £5 a hundredweight but only cost £2 a hundredweight to transport to market.[83] He enthusiastically predicted that his year's crop of 2,500 hundredweight would yield '£4500 of clear profit to the proprietors'. The following crop, by contrast, would be more than 3,000 hundredweight 'or about 150 tons so I myself raise coffee enough to supply a country side. But enough of coffee. I never drink any of it.'[84] There was, however, a snag. Despite the buoyant market, many planters had to borrow their capital on credit.[85] According to Taylor in 1858, 'Ceylon is not fit to stand much for as prosperous as it is. Few or none are working on their own money, all is borrowed and then they have all been going ahead planting more land as fast as money could be got, and have no capital on hand.'[86]

Nevertheless, he was naturally optimistic during the prosperous times: 'Fine fun for proprietors but there has been what were called bad times not that they need have been so but because people were too indolent to manage affairs.'[87] Other planters similarly recorded the volatility associated with coffee crops. This meant that they were prepared for disappointing seasons. In presenting bad news to owners, however, they would usually emphasise that other estates were worse off.[88] Despite some dips in coffee consumption in Britain during the 1860s, between 1868 and 1870 the prosperity of the industry reached a peak, generally fetching a profit of £7 10s an acre, or 20–25 per cent on the capital invested.[89]

The value of coffee estates similarly fluctuated over the course of the nineteenth century. After Taylor's manager, George Pride, died in February 1856, his estates were sold. According to Taylor, the prices fetched were: Ancoombra £15,000; Naranghena £8,500; Loolecondera £6,500; and Wal Oya £2,500. He pronounced the purchases 'a bargain' and predicted that the places would sell in two years for 'nearly three times as much as it has now sold for'. The new owners, estate agents Keir Dundas and Co, one of the top two leading agency houses in Kandy, already managed nearly one third of Ceylon's coffee estates. Taylor, however, evaluated its partners, George Hamilton Dundas and Simon Keir, as 'real close cut & dry business people not over agreeable to deal with but all infernal lazy'.[90] His judgements of them in this manner suggest that he valued, by contrast, hard work and courtesy.

In charting the ups and downs of the coffee enterprise in Ceylon, Taylor's letters set forth a range of factors that affected crop production for the worse. Issues relating to his work-force were one aspect and included both their health and availability. When illnesses hit his workers, such as chicken pox in 1857, or when crops ripened early, estates sent workers to assist other plantations.[91] Labour circulated at other times in order to reduce costs such as travelling expenses, postage, salary, horse deliverance, weeding, pruning, manuring, picking, roads and bridges, and cattle.[92] Workers were not always available in sufficient numbers, as in 1857 when 'nearly every estate in Ceylon has lost crop this year for want of sufficient number of coolies to pick it. There never was such an ado about want of coolies.'[93]

Even more challenging were changing climatic conditions. Very heavy rains caused acute problems in 1857, while at Naranghena that same year Taylor sombrely noted 'pulped and cured coffee hanging black, rotten and dried on the trees'. Dried berries had fallen to the ground and he feared that they would not be collected before the rains began again. He wryly reported, 'This will show you what a precarious job it is.'[94] Drought was another threat. In 1860 there was little blossom, while some berries turned white, and others 'yellow and red evidently spoiled. Half of the leaves have fallen off the trees … This will be greatly against the crops growing and ripening well.'[95] Other planters reported back to Scotland that drought tended to produce inferior berries by preventing the proper manuring of the crop.[96]

Strong winds posed other dangers, especially the south-west monsoon, which Taylor estimated resulted in a third of the crop every year being lost. In even windier parts of the estate 'the coffee is so blasted that the trees are stunted, not over half their natural size, and so never form a proper crop. In some places the trees cant grow, and are actually killed out by the wind.' In the adjacent estate, by contrast, 'there is never in any part of it so much wind as would take off one's hat I may say unless in some swirling whirlwind sort of gust.'[97] George Thwaites, superintendent of the botanical gardens at Peradeniya, noted the wind's detrimental influence on innumerable spores which were propagated in a short time-frame and 'are light enough to be conveyed long distances by the wind'.[98] Taylor, meanwhile, drew attention to the climate which 'is getting undoubtedly drier owing to the felling of the forests'. These problems prompted him to speculate, 'If I had a naturally fine place to manage then I would give crops that would bring me a name.'[99]

While external comment recognised the 'great evils' of 'soil sourness, and underground fungi' to the coffee tree, the greatest enemy was 'the grubs which feed on the roots and the external fungus which destroys the leaves of the plant'. Nature, then, rather than methods of cultivation, was held responsible for any deterioration.[100] Taylor observed the conditions in 1860, noting that an insect 'attacks the trees and destroys the young berries in dry times' in the recently planted fields, while the older coffee crops were largely unharmed. The last dry year he experienced caused the destruction of one third of the Loolecondera crop.[101] During the following decade his tribulations became more acute as the estate began to suffer from the first signs of coffee disease.

The end of coffee

Coffee leaf disease, or *Hemileia vastatrix*, was first observed in Ceylon in 1869. It may have been brought from Africa by humans, perhaps British soldiers, or by the monsoon winds carrying the spores across the island.[102] It soon spread with alarming speed in the 1870s and had infected almost all the coffee estates by the end of that decade.[103] The conditions for rapid infestation were all present: a system of plant monoculture, the concentration of the plantations in a relatively small part of the country in the Kandyan Highlands, and the density of the coffee estates, situated close to each other.[104] No scientific explanation of cause, nor effective remedy, was available at the time.

But the disaster which finally overwhelmed the coffee economy came about in fits and starts between the early 1870s and the final collapse of the mid-1880s. It was not an inevitable cycle of decline in the yield of the plants. Bad years were sometimes followed by short periods of recovery. Only after c.1880 did the total victory of the disease become certain. Moreover, the plantation owners and superintendents tried to fight back. The increased use of fertiliser came to be regarded as a possible remedial treatment. Imports of fertiliser to Ceylon rose in three years from 612,560 rupees in 1874 to 2,610,000 rupees in 1877.[105]

In addition, although coffee exports from the plantations fell from a peak of 886,000 hundredweight in 1870 to 249,000 hundredweight by 1883, there were two countervailing factors that helped to shield the industry from complete collapse for a time. Bad coffee harvests in Brazil and Java, together with the opening up of the USA market to Ceylon coffee, resulted in substantial increases in prices before they fell back again.[106] The continued expansion of the transport network serving the coffee-growing region was also a source of short-term resilience. A landmark development was the completion of the railway from Colombo to Kandy in 1867. Investment in roads also grew apace. On one estimate all this reduced transport costs for coffee from the plantations to the docks at Colombo by 60–75 per cent.[107] Taylor noted Ceylon's strengths in these respects, observing that if Indian planters had 'our advantages of roads and convenience for shipping' they could beat Ceylon.[108] But the price rises and a fall in costs provided but a short stay of execution. From 1879 onwards the leaf disease became even more rampant and caused a continuous collapse in coffee exports. The industry was doomed: 'By 1886 the Ceylon coffee industry was, for all practical purposes, dead.'[109]

In his letters Taylor provides an illuminating insight into the end of the coffee economy. He was well placed to do so, not simply because of his own responsibilities but also due to his appointment to a committee that was 'to collect every possible information on leaf disease, and to consult some eminent scientific men on the best remedy for the disease'.[110] In 1873 he anxiously wrote, 'The coffee leaf disease which ruined our coffee crops last year has again done a fearful amount of harm this year. My crops are again short. Last year they were a total failure. One place had I may say no crop at all, another a quarter of a crop and this place not quite half its usual crop. Well, this year I estimate the crops to be smaller than usual again and they are turning out a good deal smaller even than I estimated.' Prices remained high, however, and prevented ruin in the short term. But the onset of the disease prompted Taylor's mounting concern:

> This leaf disease only appeared here two years ago and was never known in Ceylon, nor anywhere else I believe, till about a year or two years, before that. It weakens the tree as well as destroys the crop and I see no good prospect of crops next year here. It is beginning to come on now again for the third time and if it is severe what the result will be goodness knows. I think however it seems of a milder and more chronic character spreading much faster in the place but as yet very mild everywhere, instead of beginning virulently at the bottom and gradually walking up to the top. I believe we shall never get rid of it any more than the potatoe disease has been got rid of. It is a disease of the same nature. It has not yet been so severe in new coffee districts when the trees are all young, and at a high elevation, higher than this coffee but in a drier climate during blossoming season. However it was in a rather low new district and a dry one where it first appeared. It is a sort of thing that may possibly annihilate coffee cultivation

> in Ceylon altogether, though I fancy the way will be that it will reduce crops only but possibly to such an extent as to ruin many of the present proprietors of coffee who are in debt. It may become chronic and mild and do little harm after the first year or two.[111]

Three years later, the disease had reduced crops by half. To prevent the trees from 'dying out', extensive manuring was required at 'enormous cost'. Again, however, coffee prices increased. Had they not, Taylor reckoned, 'we should have all been ruined, except a few places in some districts with unusually fine soil. Thus the bulk of proprietors are rather in a shaky condition though some are making fortunes who have such good soil as not to suffer much from the leaf disease and so get good crops and high prices.'[112] By 1879, unable to suppress his anxieties, he ominously predicted, 'nothing but ruin is in store for most of the present proprietors of coffee estates. Some few estates in favored places do well yet. But most estates are worked at a loss and have been for long and only get worse & worse.'[113]

Efforts to counteract the decimation of the crop included the planting of cinchona and tea on coffee areas and in jungle land. Taylor's predictions, however, remained dire, for he feared 'things are in too bad a way to be brought round. On many places the people have not been paid for eight or nine months and on some all the coolies have gone off as they could get no pay nor anything to eat; leaving their wages unpaid.' Some superintendents also suffered and now received only enough in wages to buy their food. Fortunately for Taylor, he continued to receive his whole salary. He did, however, feel the strain and contemplated giving up his post: 'we are terribly bullied to keep down expenditure on the estates. Such irritating letters as I get from the old proprietor is enough to make me give up charge if it were not that I know he must be driven to desperation by circumstances: and places are scarcely to be got.'[114] The situation remained precarious, with Taylor predicting in 1882 'the most miserable coffee crop coming season we have ever seen'. With the price of coffee in the market having dropped to lower figures than seen for many years, 'you may guess how anxious we feel'.[115]

By 1882, the sheer scale of the disaster was there for all to see: 'We have sold off our cattle and abandoned the grass fields. So there will be no more manuring. This means that the coffee is hopeless and will not pay to keep up any longer. We have abandoned a lot of bad land in the cinchona fields, and all expenditure is cut down in every way to less than we can probably do the work expected for.' Superintendents' salaries fell, while other planters were unemployed, including one of Taylor's assistants, and they left either for home 'or to some other colony'. The Oriental Bank sought to dispose of two of Taylor's places: 'It seems clear that the Bank would not mind ruining the estates and leaving them abandoned if they could see their way to get their money out of them.' Credit from the UK dried up; no longer were banks or agency houses willing 'to lend money or invest in property here'. Yet, despite all the omens, he did not panic, but remained resilient: 'if we can hold on for some years we'll come round again. Many places will pay on new products from now almost.' With an air of optimism, he forecast that 'Next year the country will give a coffee crop of some quantity again and that will make matters easier for one season.'[116]

No correspondence from Taylor during 1883 survives in the archive, but in 1884 the picture did indeed look rosier: 'I have got a very good crop of coffee this year, as crops go now-a-days. It looks like being nearly twice as much as was expected.'[117] But these hopes proved false. By the end of the decade, 400 of a total of 1,700 European planters had gone from Ceylon, while those who remained were forced to abandon the cultivation of coffee for tea and cinchona.[118] Many went to Fiji, the Straits settlements, and North Borneo, where they were 'pioneering and building up a planting enterprize'. Because of the number who left for southern India, the planting districts there 'may be said to be off-shoot settlements from Ceylon'.[119] Overall, coffee yields had fallen by a staggering 80 per cent due to

2.3 Mr. David Reid is compelled to abandon his coffee.

the lethal effects of the disease.[120] The financial losses were reckoned to be in the region of £12–15 million.[121] The blight then spread to South India, Africa, Java, Fiji, and Queensland.[122] As a former coffee planter, Arthur Sinclair, strikingly put it towards the end of the nineteenth century, 'no such calamity has befallen Scotch colonists since the Darien disaster'.[123] Through the ups and downs, however, Taylor remained steadfast and determined.

Taylor and coffee

While James Taylor is widely recognised and heralded for his key role in Ceylon's tea economy, his role in the coffee enterprise is little known. Overlooked, in particular, is the contribution he made to debates on pruning and manuring the coffee plant, as well as insights into micro-climates and soil varieties. In this, he was like other planters who experimented and debated their findings. He also won recognition for his engineering talents during the coffee period. His efforts show that the cultivation of coffee varied throughout the island and generated a range of experimental practices.[124]

When Taylor first arrived in Ceylon he noted the use of cattle in the manuring of the coffee crop. This procedure was important, as the felling of the forests put pressure on the soils, particularly erosion from rainfall, while burning off the forests reduced the soil acidity.[125] With the onset of the coffee leaf disease, the application of manure was thought to aid the shrub, and Taylor reported on its usage in 1876: 'to get even moderate crops and keep the trees from dying out we have to manure very extensively at enormous cost'.[126] The advantages of cattle manure applied to each tree had been extolled by George Wall almost two decades earlier when he suggested that the benefits could last for two to four years.[127] Coffee trees were said to have produced increased crops as a result of its application.[128] Yet sourcing manure was difficult. The poor-quality grasses on estates meant livestock failed to produce significant quantities and when they did, grubs were attracted which then attacked the plants.[129] Some planters even resorted to collecting human excrement from their labourers to apply to the coffee bushes.[130]

Despite the use of cattle manure, only those districts 'with unusually fine soil' initially coped well during the years after the leaf disease struck.[131] Loolecondera's soil, Taylor felt, was 'inferior on the average'.[132] Consequently, he experimented with the application of ashes. His report to his managers on the results and six samples of branches with berries and leaves from trees planted in both good and bad soil on Loolecondera and Wal Oya were sent to Dr Augustus Voelcker, consulting chemist to the Royal Agricultural Society of England. Taylor explained that the exhausted soil was from a clearing that had been felled and burned and he sought guidance on the impact of the ashes on the soil. From his experience, he considered coffee grew better when planted after the forest was burned, and speculated that the alkali of the ashes destroyed the acids in the soil.[133] Further samples were taken from land that had not been manured. In seeking to know what proportion of organic matter each sample contained, he believed, 'In all I see of artificial manuring leads me to doubt if mineral matter be as yet wanted for our Coffee.' He summed up that 'exhaustion of organic matter in the soil' did not seem to be the answer in many cases for the decline of coffee.[134]

Voelcker considered one of the Loolecondera samples that had not been manured to be 'very superior to the majority of Ceylon Coffee-soils, which have been brought under my notice from time to time'. It was rich in organic matter and contained more phosphoric acid than many other soils, which benefited it. Voelcker pronounced that it would be fertile without manure but did recommend occasional manuring to prevent its exhaustion. A poorer sample, in contrast, needed to be manured with phosphate of lime and potash in order to grow good coffee. He concluded, though, that 'Although rich soils contain frequently much organic matter, there is not necessarily a close and invariable connection between the amount of organic matter in different soils and their relative fertility.'[135] This prompted one comment that 'Dr. Voelcker, the man of science, attaches far less importance to organic matter than does the merely practical planter, Mr. Taylor.'[136]

These developments in Ceylon had repercussions in Scotland. In 1885, former planters returning to take up farming in the east of Scotland applied the knowledge they had gained on the coffee estates of Ceylon and India in 'the vexed question of manuring'. The writer supposed that the leaf disease was not all to blame for coffee's failure and that artificial manures 'applied to coffee bushes did more harm than good by forcing the trees to undue bearing only to make them collapse afterwards and made them less able to withstand any disease'. Replicating the use of artificial manures in Scotland, the writer claimed, produced unsatisfactory results. Instead, he recommended 'bulky manure'.[137]

Taylor's most influential intervention in the coffee economy came in 1865 when he distinguished between micro-climates by writing about cultivation on high estates. He judged that manure had little impact and that pruning 'is the evil'. Developing his thoughts further, he argued that early pruning, except on low estates or during dry seasons, resulted in a crop below expectations.[138] Taylor's letter provoked a robust engagement in the press. Some fellow planters reckoned that he was 'mistaken in his conclusions … we *must* prune very considerably' to produce new wood 'for each successive blossom'.[139] Another commentator, presumably William Sabonadière, discussed below, argued that light pruning weakened the tree and reduced the crop. For him, 'not to prune properly is to my mind as injurious as to ignore the necessity of weeding or manuring'.[140] Others, however, agreed with Taylor that pruning ought to be delayed: 'As long as I am a planter I never intend pruning heavily again.' The writer declared, however, that Taylor's system was better for estates at medium elevation because late pruning means 'the young wood that shoots out after that work is finished, cannot possibly be ready to bear when the next year's blossoming time comes round'. In a sharp twist, the writer concluded, 'I do not wish to make an insinuation, but J. Taylor's system reads like a learned apology made by a Superintendent to his visiting Agent, for being found behind in his pruning.' Still others thanked Taylor for provoking a discussion: 'It is profoundly to be regretted that planters are either too selfish or too lazy, mutually to communicate the individual results of their experience for each other's benefit.'[141]

In response to the criticisms, Taylor claimed that he had been misunderstood. He did not advocate, he argued, a complete absence of pruning but, rather, that annual pruning should occur immediately after blossom. To add weight to his claims he stated that 'the principle I have tried to explain is well understood amongst scientific gardeners at Home apparently, though it has not been recognised, I believe, in the treatment of Coffee trees'.[142] The Planters' Association thought his contribution significant enough to publish his article on pruning coffee in its proceedings.[143]

In private, in later years, Taylor noted the part played by William Sabonadière, who attracted acclaim due to an influential book he wrote on coffee pruning:

> He wrote strongly against me when I wrote my essays on Pruning. He wrote a book on Coffee-Planting soon after and in it quoted several of the letters written in the newspapers against me but did not quote any of my writing. He was asked by one of our agents why he was so unfair and he replied that he would not endanger coffee planting by publishing or reproducing my ideas. From what I saw and have noticed of his place for several years I know I should take very much larger crops and have very much finer coffee. In fact I would expect to double his crops almost and would not be surprised if I did so fully. I see the place looking gradually worse and worse every year and yet giving miserable crops. Last crop time in a note to me about coolies he wrote that 'he would be sure to require lots for this coming crop, for if they did not have good crops this coming time Ceylon had better shut up shop'. These have been seasons his place should have done well being not too dry nor too wet. Well, this coming crop of his from what I saw the other day I fancy will be still smaller than before.[144]

Competition, as well as collaboration, was at the heart of the enterprise and Taylor was not above taking satisfaction at having achieved more than a rival.

Despite Taylor encountering challenges in his own lifetime, his influence on coffee cultivation received recognition the year after his death. Contemporaries considered him 'a great authority on coffee pruning, doing a great deal to check the excessively heavy cutting so much in vogue years ago, and which no doubt did a lot towards shortening the life of the coffee tree'.[145]

Taylor's contributions to the coffee economy extended to talents in building, engineering, and surveying skills. This was critical, for, as the planter William Boyd reported, there were no professional architects in Ceylon and 'every manager of an estate had to follow the devices and desires of his own mind, so far as the plants and erection of these buildings were concerned'. This meant collecting materials and issuing work directions to those who 'had never seen a brick made in their lives, who had never seen a lime kiln'.[146] Again, Taylor excelled, drawing on prior knowledge from home. Taylor told his father, 'I have commenced sawing the timber for the Loole Condera store. I am to have a crack store at all events with a machine to dry the coffee in rainy weather so that we shall be before the common. I'd have been better to have been a Wright now.'[147] He was not shy at boasting about his achievements. Putting up his own machinery on Loolecondera and Wal Oya, he noted in 1857, saved about £60, the cost of an engineer to do the same work. The machinery on Loolecondera, he surmised, 'is the best going set of its kind I've seen in Ceylon', while his alterations to the Wal Oya store and pulping house made them 'the neatest and most convenient I see'.[148] The two pulpers were 'driven by a nice Iron water-wheel on the other side of these trees. The water is conducted over a ravine in a great wooden spout.'[149] Indeed, Tom Barron has observed that the design of machinery and buildings was Britain's vital contribution to the coffee industry. John Brown, William Clerihew, and John Walker were all important in this regard.[150]

Taylor's measuring of the land also saved on the cost of a surveyor.[151] His skills in this area, he evaluated, gained praise from others and he even thought about entering the surveying profession.[152] He spent just five shillings for a cross drain on the roads 'and they were now in better order than the roads on about any place newly sorted. It is the same with all my work it lasts for ever.'[153] A further innovation involved drawing water from streams to irrigate Loolecondera. He noted that most was 'brought from the big stream nearly ¾ of a mile and to get it out which is done by a spout and carried in spouts or iron pins about 100 feet along the face of a perpendicular rock and then through to a cutting between two rocks about 20 feet deep (was an exercise for my inventive faculties)'.[154] These techniques caused some anxiety among one of the estate's agents. George Hamilton Dundas, of Keir, Dundas and Co., was 'frightened at the expence I was going to in sorting the main road through the estate' by blasting out blocks of rock. Taylor, though, was dissatisfied that Dundas did not appreciate all his efforts.[155] In contrast, he impressed his other proprietor. John Gavin, the firm's senior partner and Taylor's agent, later recalled his 'ingenious arrangements of a water duct ... [which] showed considerable engineering skill'.[156]

Having been brought up on the Monboddo estate in Scotland, Taylor would have been familiar with the improved drainage practices, which were widely introduced throughout the country in the 1840s. His cross-drains, based on the Scottish model, are still visible at Loolecondera to this day. John Gavin, 'one of the most influential men in Ceylon', noted that drains should be regularly cleared out in order to ensure roads remained in good repair. It was a practice 'common in the Highlands of Scotland, which can boast of the best roads in the world'.[157] These practices also proved vital in the development of tea, the subject of the following chapter.

Notes

1 Taylor letters, 9 March 1854.

2 Roland Wenzlhuemer, *From Coffee to Tea Cultivation in Ceylon, 1880–1900* (Leiden and Boston, 2008), pp. 28–30, 54; Michael Roberts and L.A. Wickremeratne, 'Export agriculture in the nineteenth century', pp. 92–94, and Vijaya Samaraweera, 'Economic and social development under the British, 1796–1832', pp. 48–65, in K.M. de Silva (ed.), *University of Ceylon History of Ceylon, vol. 3: From the Beginning of the Nineteenth Century to 1948* (Peradeniya, 1973).

3 William Sabonadière, *The Coffee Planter of Ceylon* (Guernsey, 1866), p. 1.

4 Roberts and Wickremeratne, 'Export agriculture', pp. 91–92.

5 Sir James Emerson Tennent, *Ceylon: An Account of the Island, Physical, Historical and Topographical* (London, 1859), II, p. 39.

6 Roberts and Wickremeratne, 'Export agriculture', p. 92.

7 Donald R. Snodgrass, *Ceylon: An Export Economy in Transition* (Homewood, IL, 1966), Table 2–1, p. 20.

8 Sabonadière, *The Coffee Planter of Ceylon*, p. 3.

9 Wenzlhuemer, *From Coffee to Tea Cultivation*, pp. 2, 60–1.

10 Ibid., pp. 2–3.

11 Recent works on this revolution include John Darwin, *The Empire Project: The Rise and Fall of the British World-System 1830–1970* (Cambridge, 2009) and James Belich, *Replenishing the Earth: The Settler Revolution and the Rise of the Anglo-World, 1783–1939* (Oxford, 2009).

12 K.M. de Silva, *A History of Sri Lanka* (Colombo, 2005 edition), pp. 325–337.

13 Wenzlhuemer, *From Coffee to Tea Cultivation*, p. 104.

14 G.C. Mendis (ed.), *The Colebrooke-Cameron Papers*, 2 vols (Oxford, 1959), *passim.*

15 de Silva, *History of Sri Lanka*, pp. 346, 351.

16 Asoka Bandarage, *Colonialism in Sri Lanka: The Political Economy of the Kandyan Highlands 1833–1886* (New York, 1983), pp. 93–94.

17 K.M. de Silva, 'Nineteenth century origins of nationalism in Ceylon', in de Silva (ed.), *University of Ceylon History of Ceylon, vol. 3*, p. 252.

18 University of Aberdeen Special Collections, Moir family of Stoneywood and Scotstown, Aberdeenshire: Papers, MS 2736/6, Box 1, Robert Brown to Peter Moir, 7 November 1894.

19 L.A. Wickremeratne, 'The development of transportation in Ceylon c.1800–1947',

in de Silva (ed.), *University of Ceylon History of Ceylon, vol. 3*, pp. 303–310; Patrick Peebles, *Sri Lanka: A Handbook of Historical Statistics* (Boston, 1982), pp. 169–170.

20 Catherine Hall et al., *Legacies of British Slave-Ownership: Colonial Slavery and the Formation of Victorian Britain* (Cambridge, 2014).

21 'R.B. Tytler: In memoriam', *WCO*, 18 July 1882, pp. 592–593. One of the partners in the firm was a relative of Tytler's mother.

22 'Pioneers of the planting enterprise in Ceylon from the 1830s onwards', *TA*, 2 October 1893, pp. 217–222.

23 T.J. Barron, 'Sir James Emerson Tennent and the planting pioneers', unpublished paper presented to the Ceylon Studies seminar series 1970/72, p. 13; T.J. Barron, 'Science and the nineteenth-century Ceylon coffee planters', *Journal of Imperial and Commonwealth History*, 16:1 (1987), p. 13.

24 P.J. Labourie, *The Coffee Planter of Saint Domingo* (London, 1798); T.J. Barron, 'Scots and the coffee industry in nineteenth century Ceylon', in T.M. Devine and Angela McCarthy (eds), *The Scottish Experience in Asia, c.1700 to the Present: Settlers and Sojourners* (Cham, 2017), p. 164.

25 Wenzlhuemer, *From Coffee to Tea Cultivation*, p. 54.

26 Ibid., pp. 56–57.

27 'Report of the Sub-Committee of the Planters' Association appointed to consider and report on the difficulty of obtaining Crown land for cultivation', 1 June 1854, *Report of the Proceedings of the Planters' Association of Kandy with an Appendix* (Colombo, 1855), p. 8.

28 de Silva, *History of Ceylon*, pp. 347, 349.

29 Wenzlhuemer, *From Coffee to Tea Cultivation*, pp. 104, 111, 113.

30 C.R. Rigg, 'On coffee planting in Ceylon', *Journal of Indian Archipelago and Eastern Asia*, 6 (1852), p. 125.

31 Taylor letters, 23 June 1852. A kanganay was a recruiter and supervisor of estate labour. See Patrick Peebles, *Plantation Tamils of Ceylon* (London and New York, 2001), pp. 34–38.

32 Ibid., p. 9.

33 Taylor letters, 12 December 1852.

34 Jayeeta Sharma, '"Lazy" natives, coolie labour, and the Assam tea industry', *Modern Asian Studies*, 43:6 (2009), p. 1288.

35 Sunil S. Amrith, *Migration and Diaspora in Modern Asia* (Cambridge, 2011), pp. 32–37.

36 *Proceedings of the Planters Association, Kandy, for the year ending 17th February 1882* (Colombo, 1882), p. 185.

37 Amrith, *Migration and Diaspora*, p. 32.

38 Peebles, *Plantation Tamils*, pp. 3, 82–84.

39 Wenzlhuemer, *From Coffee to Tea Cultivation*, p. 80.

40 Taylor letters, 11 April 1875. Other areas of origin include Malabar, Madura, Trichinopoly, Tanjore, Salem, Coimbatore, Tinnevelly, and Ramnad. See I.H. vanden Driesen, *The Long Walk: Indian Plantation Labour in Sri Lanka in the Nineteenth Century* (New Delhi, 1997), p. 18, and Raj Sekhar Basu, *Nandanar's*

Children: The Paraiyans' Tryst with Destiny, Tamil Nadu, 1850–1956 (New Delhi, 2011), p. 116.

41 vanden Driesen, *The Long Walk*, p. 19; James S. Duncan, *In the Shadows of the Tropics: Climate, Race and Biopower in Nineteenth Century Ceylon* (Aldershot, 2007), pp. 73–74.

42 Taylor letters, 17 September 1857; M.W. Roberts, 'Indian estate labour in Ceylon during the coffee period (1830–1880)', Part I, *Indian Economic and Social History Review*, 3:1 (1966), p. 17.

43 Peter Moir, 10 November 1869, *Proceedings of the Planters Association, Kandy, for the year ending 17th February 1870* (Colombo, 1870), pp. 93–95.

44 H. Byrde to Directors, Bank of Madras, 1 March 1871, *Proceedings of the Planters Association, Kandy, for the year ending February 17, 1871* (Colombo, 1871), p. 114.

45 C. Shand and Co., 5 February 1862, *Proceedings of the Planters Association, Kandy, for the year ending 17th February 1862* (Colombo, 1862), pp. 45–46.

46 John Ferguson, *Ceylon in the 'Jubilee Year'* (Colombo, 1887), p. 46.

47 Quoted in P. Arunachalam, 'Population: The island's race, religions, languages, caste, and customs', in Arnold Wright (ed.), *Twentieth Century Impressions of Ceylon: Its History, People, Commerce, Industries and Resources* (New Delhi, 1999), p. 340.

48 Nira Wickramasinghe, *Sri Lanka in the Modern Age: A History of Contested Identities* (London, 2006), p. 34.

49 Peebles, *Plantation Tamils*, p. 15.

50 Taylor letters, 3 December 1857.

51 T. Skinner (Colombo), 27 June 1862, *Proceedings of the Planters Association, Kandy, for the year ending 17th February 1863* (Colombo, 1863), p. 50.

52 Taylor letters, 1 November 1879.

53 *OCO*, 2 February 1888, p. 110.

54 Taylor letters, 27 January 1857.

55 Ibid., 18 June 1860.

56 *WCO*, 2 December 1881, p. 1105.

57 Wenzlhuemer, *From Coffee to Tea Cultivation*, p. 248.

58 'Maritius and the Cape', *COO*, 15 January 1866, p. 10.

59 Margaret Jones, '"Permanent boarders": The British in Ceylon, 1815–1960', in Robert Bickers (ed.) *Settlers and Expatriates: Britons over the Seas* (Oxford, 2010), p. 210.

60 Taylor letters, 17 September 1857.

61 T.J. Barron, 'Science and the nineteenth-century Ceylon coffee planters', *Journal of Imperial and Commonwealth History*, 16:1 (1987), p. 11.

62 Lennox A. Mills, *Ceylon under British Rule 1795–1932* (London, 1933), pp. 229–230, 236.

63 Ibid, pp. 235–236.

64 Ranald C. Michie, 'Aberdeen and Ceylon: Economic links in the nineteenth century', *Northern Scotland*, 4 (1981), p. 73.

65 Ibid., p. 73.

66 Mills, *Ceylon under British Rule*, 238.

67 *Jubilee of the Planters' Association of Ceylon, 1854–1904: Illustrated Souvenir of the 'Times of Ceylon'* (Colombo, 1904), p. 7.
68 William Boyd, 'Ceylon and its pioneers', *Ceylon Literary Register*, 10 February 1888, pp. 234–235. See also James Webb, *Tropical Pioneers: Human Agency and Ecological Change in the Highlands of Sri Lanka, 1800–1900* (Athens, 2002), pp. 77–78.
69 Taylor letters, 23 June 1852.
70 William Boyd, 'Ceylon and its pioneers', *Ceylon Literary Register*, 24 February 1888, p. 251.
71 Taylor letters, 13 March 1852, 23 June 1852.
72 William Boyd, 'Ceylon and its pioneers', 24 February 1888, pp. 251–252.
73 Sabonadière, *The Coffee Planter of Ceylon*, pp. 43, 38–39.
74 Taylor letters, 18 June 1860.
75 Ibid., 13 March 1852.
76 Ibid., 3 December 1857.
77 NLS, Fettercairn estate papers, Acc 4796, No. 54, Letters to Sir John Stuart Forbes, 1833–1852, Henry Stiven (Ancoombra) to Sir John Stuart Forbes (Fettercairn), 5 April 1852.
78 Taylor letters, 11 April 1852.
79 Wenzlhuemer, *From Coffee to Tea Cultivation*, p. 57.
80 Snodgrass, *Ceylon*, Table 2.1, p. 20; vanden Driesen, *The Long Walk*, p. 168; Peebles, *Sri Lanka*, p. 207.
81 Taylor letters, 13 June 1856.
82 Ibid., 27 January 1857.
83 Ibid., 17 September 1857.
84 Ibid., 3 December 1857.
85 Ibid., 17 September 1857.
86 Ibid., 23 January 1858.
87 Ibid., 17 September 1857.
88 See letters dated 16 April 1862, 16 May 1862, and 17 June 1862, in NLS, Seton and Bremner Papers, Letters concerning Hannagalla estate, MS 19228.
89 John Ferguson, *Ceylon in the 'Jubilee Year'* (Colombo, 1887), pp. 62–63.
90 Taylor letters, 27 January 1857.
91 Ibid.
92 NLS, Seton and Bremner Papers, Walter Agar, 30 November 1861, MS 19228; NLS, Seton and Bremner Papers, Account book of Hannagalla estate, 1863–5, MS 19230.
93 Taylor letters, 3 December 1857.
94 Ibid., 27 January 1857, 3 December 1857.
95 Ibid., 18 June 1860.
96 NLS, Seton and Bremner Papers, Letters concerning Hannagalla estate, 30 March 1861, MS 1922/46–61.
97 Taylor letters, undated.
98 G.H.K. Thwaites, 'Leaf disease', *Proceedings of the Planters Association, Kandy, for the year ending 17th February 1872* (Colombo, 1882), pp. 82–3.

99 Taylor letters, undated.
100 *OCO*, 13 January 1880, p. 43.
101 Taylor letters, 18 June 1860.
102 Duncan, *In the Shadows of the Tropics*, p. 170.
103 Wenzlhuemer, *From Coffee to Tea Cultivation*, p. 64.
104 S. Rajaratnum, 'Growth of plantation agriculture in Ceylon, 1886–1931', *Ceylon Journal of Historical and Social Studies*, 4:1 (1961), p. 1.
105 Ibid., p. 2.
106 vanden Driesen, *Long Walk*, pp. 168–169.
107 Wenzlhuemer, *From Coffee to Tea Cultivation*, p. 68.
108 Taylor letters, 17 September 1857.
109 Snodgrass quoted in Wenzlhuemer, *From Coffee to Tea Cultivation*, p. 65.
110 *Proceedings of the Planters' Association of Ceylon for year ending February 17th, 1875* (Liverpool, 1875), p. 28. Other committee members were George Wall, A. Brown, W. Bowden Smith, W. Cameron, A.G.K. Borron, W.X. Buchanan, J. Murdoch, G. Maitland, W. Rollo, W. Sabonadiere, Dr Shipton, and J.F. Wingate.
111 Taylor letters, 25 January 1873.
112 Ibid., 5 November 1876.
113 Ibid., 1 November 1879.
114 Ibid.
115 Ibid., 27 March 1882.
116 Ibid., 2 September 1882.
117 Ibid., 15 December 1884.
118 Mills, *Ceylon Under British Rule*, pp. 246–50.
119 *Ceylon Observer New Year Supplement*, 31 December 1883, p. 1.
120 Webb, *Tropical Pioneers*, p. 112.
121 Duncan, *In the Shadows of the Tropics*, p. 175.
122 Webb, *Tropical Pioneers*, p. 116.
123 Arthur Sinclair, *In Tropical Lands: Recent Travels to the Sources of the Amazon, the West Indian Islands, and Ceylon* (Aberdeen, 1895), p. 165.
124 Webb, *Tropical Pioneers*, p. 80.
125 Ibid., p. 81.
126 Taylor letters, 5 November 1876; Webb, *Tropical Pioneers*, p. 112.
127 George Wall cited in E.C.P. Hull, *Coffee Planting in Southern India and Ceylon* (London, 1877), pp. 246–247.
128 Hull, *Coffee Planting*, p. 248.
129 Webb, *Tropical Pioneers*, p. 83.
130 Ibid., p. 83.
131 Taylor letters, 5 November 1876; Webb, *Tropical Pioneers*, p. 112.
132 Taylor letters, undated.
133 'Report on Ceylon coffee soils', *Proceedings of the Planters' Association, Kandy, for the year ending February 17, 1871* (Colombo, 1871), pp. 136–137.
134 Ibid, p. 139.
135 Ibid., pp. 144–145.
136 'Fertilizing substances for Ceylon coffee lands', *OCO*, 14 December 1871, p. 444.

137 'Coffee planting and Scotch farming', *TA*, 1 May 1885, p. 806.
138 James Taylor 'On the pruning of coffee on high estates', *OCO*, 29 May 1865, p. 127 (his letter is dated 17 May 1865).
139 'Pruning: Reply of a planter to Mr J. Taylor', from 'A. Planter', *CO*, 5 June 1865, p. 2. The letter is dated 31 May 1865.
140 W.S., 'A few remarks on the pruning of coffee trees', 10 June 1861, in *Proceedings of the Planters' Association, Kandy, for the year ending 17th February 1862* (Colombo, 1862), p. 202.
141 'Another planter on Mr. J. Taylor's system of pruning', from P.T.P.H.I., *COO*, 12 June 1865.
142 'J. Taylor's answer to "A Planter," or a supplement to his letter on pruning high estate coffee', *COO*, 15 June 1865, p. 140.
143 James Taylor, 'On the pruning of coffee with especial reference to high and wet estates', *Proceedings of the Planters Association, Kandy, for the year ending 16th February 1868* (Colombo, 1868), pp. 64–81.
144 Taylor letters, undated. William Sabonadière's book was *The Coffee Planter of Ceylon*.
145 'Planting pioneers and the T.A.', *OCO*, 24 July 1893, p. 827
146 William Boyd, 'Ceylon and its pioneers', *Ceylon Literary Register*, 2 March 1888, p. 258.
147 Taylor letters, 9 March 1854.
148 Ibid., 17 September 1857.
149 Ibid., 9 January 1853.
150 Barron, 'Science and the nineteenth-century Ceylon coffee planters', pp. 14–15.
151 Taylor letters, 17 September 1857.
152 Ibid., 9 March 1854, 13 June 1856.
153 Ibid., 9 September 1860.
154 Ibid., 13 June 1856.
155 Ibid., 9 September 1860.
156 *Ceylon Mail or Weekly Independent*, 21 October 1891, p. 11, in NLS, Papers of James Taylor, planter in Ceylon, MS 15908.
157 Taylor letters, 17 September 1857; John Gavin, 31 July 1862, in *Proceedings of the Planters Association, Kandy, for the year ending 17th February 1863* (Colombo, 1863), p. 62. Gavin became the managing partner in the leading agency house of Keir, Dundas and Co. in 1856. He sold the firm in 1862 to G.D.B. Harrison and W.M. Leake. See *TA*, 2 April 1894, pp. 647–650.

3

Transition to tea

Tea entered European consumption as one of the exotic foods, stimulants, and beverages like tobacco, sugar, coffee, and chocolate which were the fruits of colonial expansion across the globe from the fifteenth century. In the long run, the rise in tea consumption was not uniform across Europe. In France, the German states, and Spain, tea-drinking did spread but not to any significant extent. In Britain, however, by the early nineteenth century tea had become a national addiction.[1] Before 1700 it remained a luxury item, drunk mainly by the social élites, but in the eighteenth century tea-drinking was democratised with a great surge in consumption taking place from the 1730s. Rising imports and falling costs when the direct clipper trade from China was introduced were important factors, along with rising affluence. By the later eighteenth century contemporary opinion was unanimous that all social classes were now drinking tea, often on a daily basis.[2]

But this was just the beginning. According to one estimate, annual per capita consumption of tea in Britain rose more than 300 per cent between the 1830s and the 1880s, from 1.48 pounds in 1836 to 5 pounds in 1885.[3] Tea-drinking was even coming to be seen as a distinctive mark of British identity. Of Victoria's reign it was said, 'tea did not merely remain everybody's drink: it became everybody's drink, all of the time'.[4] In 1863 the father of the founder of Typhoo Tea could proclaim that 'the great Anglo-Saxon race are essentially a tea-drinking people'.[5] There were, of course, other drinks that could be produced by infusing parts of a plant in water, such as chocolate and coffee. Coffee did well in polite circles in the seventeenth and eighteenth centuries but its relatively high caffeine content meant that as a mass drink taken on a regular basis it could not easily replace either water or beer and porter, the favoured drinks of the urban poor.[6] Tea, on the other hand, was weaker than coffee and, unlike beer, was not an intoxicant. The qualities that made it an irresistible world conqueror were several:

> True tea, made from the *Camellia sinensis* plant, ... can be produced cheaply. The plant which yields it is very productive, giving new leaf every six weeks or so.

> It grows over quite a range of climatic zones, from central China to East Africa. Just a few leaves are needed to make a good pot of tea and they can be re-used. Dry tea is very light and stores well. It is easily prepared for drinking ... It is extremely safe to drink and indeed many believe it has special health benefits. It is attractive because it makes the drinker feel stimulated and relaxed, optimistic and focused. It is mild enough to be drunk throughout the day without any harmful side effects.[7]

The coming of the worker's tea-break in Britain made the drudgery of long hours in factories or offices more bearable. When it was drunk with sugar and milk in the British way, men and women returned to their labours reinvigorated. Tea also became both a symbol and a weapon of the great temperance movement of Victorian times in the campaigns against the abuses of alcohol.[8]

Ceylon was a latecomer to the global trade in tea. When James Taylor began his experimental attempts at planting in the later 1860s the two dominant suppliers to the international market were China, which had long monopolised the commerce to Europe, and, to a lesser extent, Assam in India, which started to emerge as a potential threat to absolute Chinese hegemony in the second half of the nineteenth century. Even Taylor's pioneering efforts did not at first lead to much in the way of a significant increase in commercial tea planting or marketing in Ceylon. Indeed, Taylor, from the mid-1860s, was mainly concerned with the cultivation of cinchona rather than tea. The establishment of a vast new tea economy did not really start to develop in Ceylon until after 1880.[9] Although the first recorded consignment of Ceylon tea was shipped abroad in 1873, this was something of a false dawn, as the rate of growth in sales remained modest for the rest of that decade.[10] Indeed, it was not until 1885 that the area planted in tea exceeded 100,000 acres, while exports remained limited until the following year.[11]

Ironically, the most significant constraint on tea expansion in Ceylon was the coffee industry. Coffee remained prosperous throughout the 1870s since, as seen in chapter 2, the really devastating impact of the leaf disease did not become apparent until the early 1880s. In essence, before that joint plantation cultivation of both coffee and tea on any substantial scale was impossible. Interplanting could not succeed, as the tea bushes needed space to allow their roots to spread as well as sufficient light and air for the growth process to mature. As a result, when the tea plant was around eighteen months old, surrounding coffee bushes had to be uprooted to allow growth to continue. Manifestly, this was an unlikely possibility while returns from coffee remained attractive. In addition, unlike coffee, the set-up costs of tea plantations were considerable, with new factory-style production facilities required for final processing.[12] Inevitably, also, there was a natural reluctance to risk investment in a relatively untried crop when the global market for tea was still dominated, as it had been for centuries, by China.

Cultivation of cinchona

More attractive at first, before the devastation of the coffee disease, was cinchona, from which the drug quinine, widely used in the treatment of malaria, could be extracted. As European migration to the tropics grew, endemic diseases such as malaria in mosquito-infested regions became ever more a lethal threat to the lives of white settlers. The cinchona tree was native only to the forests of South America but consignments of young plants had reached India and Ceylon by the 1860s. Growing them in the east was considered more economic than purchasing quinine from South America.[13] G.H.K. Thwaites, superintendent of the botanical gardens at Peradeniya, received 'a parcel of seeds' in 1861 and passed them on to Mr MacNicoll at Hakgala Gardens, who successfully grew eight hundred plants from them.[14] In 1864 he supplied around 130,000 cinchona plants to thirty-nine purchasers on the island. Seventy-five per cent of them were the red bark *succirubra* rather than the yellow *officinalis*.[15] Among the recipients were Loolecondera's owners, Martin Leake and G.D.B. Harrison of the firm Keir and Dundas, who had been encouraging Taylor's experimentations there with cinchona since the early 1860s.[16] Taylor had also explored the possibilities of 'the cocoa & chocolate plant' but found that 'the climate is too cold for it up here'.[17] Loolecondera specialised initially in producing the *succirubra* red bark, with the first small batch, peeled in July 1867, reaching the London market in April 1868. An 'extensive peeling' of bark in April 1870 was sent to London and sold well. In recognition of its superiority over cinchona from other countries, eventually all Hakgala *officinalis* plants, around 300,000, were sent to Loolecondera for free 'as there was no demand for cinchona by anyone else' at that time.[18]

On the London market prices for quinine between 1870 and 1885 were at a healthy average of around twelve shillings per ounce.[19] Initially, however, Loolecondera did not achieve such returns, as the firm had specialised in *officinalis* whereas 'demand was mostly for succirubra plants, of which we had taken none'.[20] Nevertheless, Loolecondera did eventually benefit financially. James Taylor noted that in 1872 cinchona 'pays enormously: something like five or six times the whole cost in as many years'.[21] The press were effusive in their praise: 'we heartily congratulate the proprietors and the manager of Loolcondra and Stellenberg. We believe we saw some of the trees from which the bark has been gathered just as Mr. James Taylor was putting them out from the nursery into his field.'[22] This was around the time when Taylor sent a photograph to his father of Loolecondera rock with the 'cinchona trees we were amongst in the foreground',[23] possibly the photograph in Figure 3.1.

As he had done with coffee, Taylor made what turned out to be realistic predictions about cinchona. His reservations were astute in 1872:

3.1 Loolecondera Rock showing Taylor's cinchona harvest and the first twenty acres of tea, c.1870s. The figure in front of the cabin might be Taylor.

> We are now planting on a larger scale but not going in extensively for cinchona as no doubt the price of bark & quinine will fall immensely when it becomes generally known that it can be grown so profitably. The price of quinine fell greatly as soon as it was known that cinchona could be [*erased:* success] grown in India so as to produce quinine at all. Being only used for medicine the market would soon be swamped with large supplies of Cinchona.[24]

Towards the end of the decade, however, he was planning to invest to a greater extent in cinchona cultivation but downplayed it to his father: 'You must not bother me about my place as you call it. My share in it is not yet fixed as I objected to the terms of partnership. I am supposed to have a share and have the supervision of it. It is about 28, or 29, miles from here. It is a small affair and not of my choosing.' Taylor had, instead, attempted to invest in other land but had been 'defeated … in every attempt to get land of my own choosing. The land I have now to deal with belongs to our Colombo agents. They and I were to hold it but when the proprietors of this place heard of it at home they wanted a share also.'[25] By November 1879 he had invested in shares in a cinchona estate called Lover's Leap near Nuwara Eliya with Jardine, Campbell, and Whittall and Co. As he told his father:

> it is the proprietor of these places and Ceylon Agents who have shares with me in the Cinchona estate at Nuwara Eliya and who advance the money for my share of the working expenses. I paid them for my share of the land. If they become bankrupt the estate has to be sold by auction. Perhaps I could get some other firm to back me in buying it up.[26]

According to Ferguson's directories, Taylor never owned the land but managed it with A.C. Aaron. It comprised ninety-six acres of cinchona.[27] By 1883/4 Taylor was no longer involved and the land was said to have been taken over by mortgagees.[28] He perhaps took a chance at investing, having missed out on previous opportunities, including the prospect of acquiring coffee land near Ancoombra. 'Stiven is to manage it and I am to help in the funds',[29] he predicted. So too had he contemplated acquiring land in India on the 'Neilgherries in the Madras' that 'promises well'.[30] Neither eventuated. With a degree of resigned acceptance at these missed prospects, he wrote in 1879:

> Cinchona is a good spec just now and there is a great rush to plant it in Ceylon. But as it is only a medicine, though the most extensively used one, the supply will soon bring down its price. We were the first to find out its value here and to start planting it extensively. We have 250, acres of it well on towards maturity and will no doubt get the good prices for that. If I had money to buy land and plant that some years ago I should have made a fortune.[31]

Cinchona initially had two key advantages in the Ceylon setting. First, little capital was needed to buy and grow the trees and, second, crucially, they could be easily inter-planted with coffee.[32] Thus, from 1873 to 1876 around 3.6 million cinchona plants were sold to planters, while exports climbed from 1.3 million pounds in 1881 to 13.7 million by 1885. Demand for cinchona was rigid, however, because quinine was mainly confined to single use as a medicine and increased cultivation could easily threaten to saturate the market.[33] As prices dropped in the 1880s some planters responded by increasing production even further by selling younger and inferior bark.[34] Thus, while exports rose from 3 million in 1882 to 15 million in 1886, prices fell.[35] This policy predictably hastened the ruin of the industry. By the late 1880s the end of cinchona cultivation was in sight in Ceylon.

In yet another example of progress and regression, Taylor occasionally charted the fluctuations of cinchona cultivation in his correspondence. He recognised that its production could not be a satisfactory replacement in the long term for the ailing coffee economy. In 1884 'Cinchona seems doing as well as expected, too, except that prices for bark are now so low that there is little to be made out of that product. We made fine lots of money out of it at first and till 2, or 3, years ago.'[36] Five years later, reporting on tea, Taylor observed, 'It was the same with Cinchona. When we began sending home bark we were getting 6, or 7, shillings a lb. for it and now the same "barks" would only sell for as many pence. Manufacturers of quinoa are selling it at a mere fraction of their former prices and yet I understand the druggists at home charge just as high for it as ever.'[37]

Despite the long-term failure of cinchona, Taylor earned plaudits from the press for his system of 'sowing and seedling', though it would not be widely adopted:[38]

> Some years ago Mr. James Taylor wrote to us stating his conviction that cinchona would be a sown crop and that the cost of planting might be dispensed with. He came to his conclusion after taking crop from the experimental patches. After all his further experience he states that if he could get plenty of good seed he would never plant a cinchona clearing again. He has tried sowing the seed at various seasons and in various modes, and always successfully. … The rooting out process is that which prevails in British Sikkim, but neither there nor on the Nilgiris were seedlings ever allowed to grow amongst the old trees. Plants from cuttings are chiefly in favour. Mr. Taylor may claim to be the inventor of the sowing and seedling system.[39]

He made a further contribution by recommending 'deep subsoil draining' to cultivate cinchona of the finer varieties and to 'prune away the branch of *C. officinalis* on which blossom comes prematurely'.[40] Encouraged by this recognition, Taylor later assessed his contribution to cinchona cultivation in the following way: 'we were not the first to plant a few trees or even a small patch but we were the first to regularly cultivate a few acres and to test the value of the bark in the market and then to start the cultivation on a large scale. Our experiences as to raising seedlings in field nurseries and that the bark of diseased trees if taken in time was valuable, and so on, must have been useful to others who planted later.'[41] Indeed, Ceylon, for a short time, dominated the world market of cinchona. While Taylor did become well known for his contribution to that success it was to be his pioneering contributions to the tea economy which really made his name.[42]

Early developments in tea

The eventual disappointment in cinchona cultivation and the demise of the coffee industry ensured that only tea could eventually become the bedrock of the Ceylon economy. Yet its early history gave little indication that it would prove the economic saviour of the island after the end of coffee. Indeed, the future success story of tea planting in Ceylon was far from inevitable. Early tea trials had taken place from the later eighteenth century but all had failed. Two promising experiments then occurred around 1840. First were the efforts of two Germans, Gabriel and Maurice Worms, to plant imported China tea on the Rothschild estate in Pusellawa and on the Condegalla estate (now a division of Labookellie) in Ramboda. The experiments were abandoned, however, due to the costs involved (said to be £5 for each pound of manufactured leaf) and the competitive profitability of coffee sales at the time.[43] A relative of the two Worms', by contrast, attributed the failure to objections surrounding imported Chinese labour and the Sinhalese inexperience in making tea.[44] Looking back on this period, Taylor was keen to dismiss these earlier endeavours: 'I do not admit the Messrs. Worms' old tea experiments into the matter, as they were failures; and long ago given up when we began.'[45] Another attempt was made by Mr Llewellyn of Calcutta, who owned the Penylan estate at Dolosbage.[46] These and numerous other efforts to introduce tea were deemed 'unsuccessful in permanent and profitable cultivation'.[47] It is in large part because of this background of successive failure in large-scale, commercial tea planting that James Taylor is recognised to this day as a figure of such importance in the history of Sri Lanka. John Ferguson put it simply and succinctly when he declared that Taylor was the 'first to make good tea on an appreciable scale'.[48] But on what basis does this claim rest?

The assessment of Taylor's development of Ceylon tea which is considered here relies primarily on his letters home, a published recollection of 1890 together with an earlier and unused account written by him from 1878, documents from the Ceylon Association in London, and the memoirs of contemporary planters. These accounts reveal that Taylor first experimented with making China tea 'from old bushes in the garden and from roadside plan[*t*]ing' on the estate.[49] He cheerfully admitted to his father that the result of his early experiments 'was pretty nearly rank poison'.[50] But he was also aware that he was on to something, realising that 'Some of what I made then was fairly good tea though I could not believe it was right because it did not taste like the China tea of the shops.'[51] More expert figures in the cultivation of tea, however, did recognise its potential. They included a London broker who thought 'highly' of an early sample of Taylor's tea made 'from the ordinary China Bohea Tea'.[52]

In 1865, some years after Taylor's original experimentations on the roadside plantings, G.D.B. Harrison, one of Loolecondera's proprietors, ordered him to obtain tea seeds from Peradeniya Botanical Gardens. Tea plants were planted on the estate's roadsides the following year.[53] The outlook seemed bright and Taylor applied for a job as a commissioner to report on tea plantations in India. He was, however, overlooked in favour of Arthur Morice from the neighbouring Mooloya estate, who had taken an interest in Taylor's experiments.[54] In 1866 Morice travelled to India to report on 'the cultivation and preparation of tea' there. William Martin Leake, Harrison's business partner and also Secretary of the Planters' Association at the time, was among those who 'took an active part in promoting the mission of Mr. Arthur Morice'.[55] Leake later recollected that he had acquired a consignment of Assam hybrid tea seed (a combination of China and Assam varieties) from Calcutta following Morice's trip:

> That mission, if it had no other result, caused me in the following year on behalf of my firm to order from Calcutta a consignment of seed of the hybrid Assam plant, and these seeds committed to the care of that ever watchful nurse, Mr. James Taylor (who had already by his success with cinchona, and more recently with China tea earned the complete confidence of his employers for experimental work), formed the beginning of the now famous Loolcondura estate. In due course (I think in 1872) I found myself selling in Kandy to all-comers the produce of our little garden.[56]

Perhaps being overlooked for the mission made Taylor determined to succeed when entrusted with these seeds. At the end of 1867, when he was thirty-two years of age, he cleared twenty acres of land in Loolecondera, and planted them in early 1868. The initial outlook, however, was far from favourable as they 'completely failed to grow'.[57] More seeds arrived in January 1869 and young plants raised from them were sown later that year. The cultivation of this crop on the twenty acres of Field no. 7 at Loolecondera became Taylor's first success at commercial tea clearing and planting. The achievement effectively sealed his reputation and five acres of it remains to this day on the estate, the oldest tea field in Sri Lanka under continuous cultivation.[58]

In tracing these early developments, however, it is important to recognise the parallel activity of the Ceylon Company. That firm, which had purchased the Worms' estates in 1862, 'found a small extent of tea on Kondegala on the Ramboda Pass, to which they soon began to pay attention'. They employed W.J. Jenkins from Assam, imported Bengali labourers, and tried to cultivate the crop, but 'the experiment did not turn out well, and although a succession of planters with Indian experience was employed, this Company made so little success that for a long time, Ceylon planters were prevented from going into tea in consequence'. Like Taylor, they planted hybrid Assam seeds in 1869 on land they had prepared a year earlier.[59] Taylor, in his later published recollection of those events, recalled their efforts:

> Our clearing was mentioned in the *Kandy Herald*, at the time it was felled. The Ceylon Company felled small pieces on several of their places the year after, perhaps as much, or may be more, acreage than our clearing altogether. However, our first year's importation of seed from Assam completely failed to grow. We got our second importation of seed next year at the same time as the Ceylon Company got their first and both grew. So that they and we both began the actual planting out of *hybrid* tea at the same time, or same season.[60]

Here, Taylor was clearly staking his claim as the pioneer of tea, based on the earlier clearing of land for tea planting at Loolecondera in 1867, a year before the initiative of the Ceylon Company. Recollections to his family, composed closer to the time these events took place, were consistent with his later testimony: 'We felled and meant to plant a year before the Ceylon Company thought of it, but our first year's seed all failed so we had to wait a year to get more from Assam, and they then got a supply at the same time.'[61] He elaborated in another account: 'We were the first to start tea-planting here, too. It had been tried many years before but failed as they could not make tea. We started it successfully at once and in quality of tea as well as planting it we have beaten another company who started it immediately after us though they got an Englishman who had been some thirty-five years tea planting in Assam to manage it.'[62]

Two conclusions emerge from this evidence. While Taylor was indeed first to produce a commercially viable crop of tea, he was soon followed by similar success on the part of others. The possibilities of tea were clearly on the agenda of some Ceylon planters and it was perhaps likely that the challenges of cultivating it properly would soon be overcome. Moreover, it is also plain that Taylor did not function in a technical vacuum, disassociated from what his fellow planters were doing. He was only too willing to honestly admit the support he received from them:

> I knew pretty fairly how to make it before. I had a lot of road sides bordered with it years before we made the field; and a Tea Planter who was here for a few hours at breakfast one day showed me a part of the process a good number of years ago. The rest I learned from reading books and essays on it and by experimenting. The first I made long ago was pretty nearly rank poison. It is a complicated and difficult matter to make the Tea really good or as good as it may be and the methods are constantly being improved upon. I really understand it but little yet and green tea I have not yet attempted to make.[63]

He similarly reiterated a few years later: 'I had no help nor information about it except what I could pick up from books and papers and one or two tea planters I met. I learned a good deal from this old Assam tea planter and how it is we have so beaten him in quality of tea I don't know.'[64]

The 'old Assam tea planter' who aided Taylor's early experiments on China tea was W.J. Jenkins, who worked for the Ceylon Company. He had visited Taylor to 'see how my Tea was growing, and so on, and showed me how to manufacture it'.[65] As Taylor warmly acknowledged, 'Before Mr. Jenkins gave me confidence that the tea was correct, I spoiled large lots of it experimenting, trying to make it taste like the tea I bought in Kandy from shops.'[66] His early experiments on China tea also benefited from Mr. Noble, an 'Indian tea planter from Cachar', who showed Taylor how 'to pluck and wither and roll tea with a little leaf growing on some old tea bushes in my bungalow garden. It was all rolled by hand then. He told me about fermenting and panning and the rest of the process as then in vogue.'[67] Taylor's reference to books and essays demonstrates his academic approach to planting and highlights the printed materials which were available, primarily from the Planters' Association and the press. His generosity towards the influence of others, however, was matched by recognition of his own achievements and their significance. Perhaps having never managed to purchase land or obtain financial riches in the plantation economies, Taylor was at pains to ensure appropriate recognition of his experiments.

The evidence surrounding these developments of Ceylon tea contradicts claims made by some that Taylor made tea only after a visit to India. He did undertake a trip to the Darjeeling tea district but not until 1874, the only time he left the island.[68] He described visiting 'a number of tea gardens' and a cinchona plantation near Darjeeling, probably Mungpoo, before intending to investigate tea at Cachar. He planned to visit Assam but 'I find it takes too long a time to get to Assam, three weeks steaming up the Burhampooter and two weeks coming down; so I have given up the intention of going there.'[69] The trip was inevitably short as the leading partner of the London firm which owned Loolecondera had arrived in Ceylon and 'was anxious that I should be back before he went home again' within two months.[70]

In all, Taylor stayed ten days in the Darjeeling tea district, stopped at Madras for a couple of days, and 'then went across by rail to the Neilgherries going up to Ootacamund to see Cinchona there. Then went down to Beypore and took steamer to Ceylon again.' He travelled by rail at night 'in order to be cool'.[71] There is no indication in his correspondence that he travelled with other planters, though in 1891 John Ferguson stated that 'Mr. Crüwell accompanied Mr. Taylor on his trip to Darjiling and wrote a very interesting account of the Sanitarium and the tea estates for the *Observer*. Mr. Taylor's experience of actual tea cultivation and manufacture at Darjiling must have been of great value to him.'[72] Certainly, Taylor did acknowledge learning from his Darjeeling experience, although he mistook the year: 'I also saw light pruning and heavy cutting down of Hybrid tea in the Darjeeling Terrai in 1871 just before their plucking season commenced.'[73]

Quite apart from being the first to produce a large-scale commercial tea crop, Taylor contributed in other significant ways to the development of the Ceylon tea enterprise, sometimes with the help of other planters. He developed the renowned fine plucking of two leaves and a bud from the tea plant. Before that, they had been picked coarsely. He had learned from a fellow planter, William Cameron, who practised fine and regular plucking.[74] When a memorial fund for Cameron was set up in 1883, Taylor subscribed and offered heartfelt gratitude towards the deceased: 'I wish I had had the chance of learning more from him, but am thankful for what I have seen of his style of working, and feel that I, as well as, I should think, most others engaged in tea-planting in Ceylon have been indebted to him.'[75] Initially, however, his method was not universally accepted, for 'fine plucking as defined by Mr. Taylor ... is decidedly more trying to the bush than medium plucking as the shoots are removed before the bush benefits by them'. Critics also argued that Taylor's approach was twice as expensive as medium plucking.[76]

However, as a result of Taylor's fine plucking of less tea, greater profit per acre was realised, as compared to producing double the amount with coarse plucking: 'he does not distress his bushes and he tops the market'.[77] Another observer described how 'Taylor informed me, that the old tea on Loole Condera yielded over 380lb per acre for many years; this was with *fine* plucking, without which, he said, he could not produce teas of the quality for which that estate was renowned before the present competition prevailed.'[78] Yet another recalled how 'Mr. Taylor was unremitting in his endeavors to perfect himself in the preparation of the leaf. And to such good purpose did he work that in 1872 he was able at once to produce a tea of such quality as not only to ensure the ready sale in Ceylon of all his produce, but also to secure the approbation of the leading London brokers.'[79] Persistent dedication in experimentation was perhaps Taylor's chief hallmark. Taylor himself remembered that when he began to pluck more finely he 'began to top the sale lists ... That finer plucking largely increased the selling prices of my tea and still more largely the profit per acre.'[80] Taylor also drew inspiration from Cameron and Baker's method of heavy pruning, even though Cameron was criticised by several planters for an 'over-severe system of pruning and plucking'.[81]

After plucking, the tea leaf was withered in order to reduce the moisture of the leaf before processing. Here again Taylor's methods attracted attention and he was one of sixteen 'practical planters' who responded to an enquiry in 1886 about tea preparation. He declared that he favoured hard withering 'to allow the rolling to be properly done ... With under-withering, rolling will also be imperfect ... Besides a lot of water must be evaporated from the leaf in withering or else juice will drop from the machine during rolling.' Taylor usually spent up to three hours on the first roll of the day: 'I spread loosely to ferment in flat trays about two or three inches deep for two hours, turning it at the end of one hour; at the end of two hours I put it into a deep basket, still loosely, to ferment the rest of the time. It gets a little warm during the process, but my turning of it is to let air get more evenly at it and to break small umps [sic].'[82]

Encouraged by these methods, Taylor helped to develop the mechanisation of tea processing in Ceylon. His efforts were witnessed by many, including his kinsman Peter Moir who 'visited his old protégé, Mr. Taylor on Loolecondura, and found him busy erecting new machinery with which he expects to turn out even finer teas'.[83] Taylor's early tea production, in contrast, had been carried out on the veranda of his bungalow and in godowns. One planter who visited Taylor told how the early factory 'was in the bungalow. The leaf was rolled on the veranda by hand, *i.e.*, from wrists to elbow, while the firing was done in *chulas*, or clay stoves, over charcoal fires, with wire trays to hold the leaf.'[84]

In 1872, however, Taylor had designed a tea-rolling machine, made to crush the leaves, which would release the juice and enzymes which provided the tea flavour:

> I have a machine of my own invention being made in Kandy for rolling the Tea which I think will be successful. If so we cannot help making a profit on Tea if it grows of fair quality in this country. The picking or gathering the leaves and the rolling are the greatest expenses in the production; and rolling costs nearly as much as gathering. So if we can do the rolling by a machine we will save immensely in the cost of production. This has often been tried in India but without success I believe. However I think my machine will do it. I tried various ways to do it by a machine without success before I hit on my present idea.[85]

With a blend of patience, keen anticipation, and a healthy dose of realism, he divulged a year later:

> I have a machine of my own invention for rolling the Tea being made in Kandy, but it is a year since I sent in the plans and ordered it. If it should be a success it will reduce the expense of making the Tea very greatly. Tea rolling machines have been invented in Assam & Cachar and perhaps elsewhere but none of them I have yet heard of are thoroughly successful so as to dispense altogether with hand rolling. Mine may do so, but it is hard to say till we see it at work. I suppose the chances are all against it. It is entirely different in everything from any of the machines I have yet heard of.[86]

Taylor's experiments with tea rolling have to be seen in the context of a substantial history of machine and building design in Ceylon which can be traced back to the early nineteenth century but which became much more relevant with the more heavily mechanised tea economy.[87] This technological expertise, which 'gave the Ceylon planters a world-wide reputation in the nineteenth century', is considered by one authority to be the most 'outstanding omission' in studies of agricultural enterprise in the island.[88] As a writer in the late 1880s reckoned, 'The character of Ceylon Tea owes much to its soil and climate, but also a great deal to the skill and improved machinery which the energy of the planters has introduced into the manufacture.'[89] Another contemporary reiterated this, stating that apart from knowing the native language colloquially, the Ceylon planter 'must become partly an engineer, so many were the constructive and mechanical works he had to supervise'.[90] A further report from the later nineteenth century amplified and expanded upon these desired planter attributes:

> A young man properly graduating as a planter in Ceylon is bound to acquire much practical knowledge respecting the best treatment of the plant and soil on which he is engaged; in regard to the proper management of coloured labour – (and nowhere are labourers treated more kindly) – including the learning to speak the coolies' language colloquially; he is expected to understand not only the mysteries of seed nurseries, of planting, draining, and road making; but to be able to design and superintend buildings, whether in wattle and daub for coolly lines, or in brick and stone for his own bungalow and factory, and the more he is, or becomes, of a practical engineer, land surveyor, and even physician for his coolies, the better. To know something of chemistry and geology, of soil constituents and manorial applications is no drawback, but the reverse to such colonists.[91]

Machinery innovation gave Ceylon a decisive advantage over the hand processing that was still dominant in the production of Chinese tea: 'Whereas in China all operations are carried out by hand, hand labour on a Ceylonese tea estate ceases almost entirely with the plucking of the leaves. Every after operation is carried out automatically, and thus security from all possible taint is secured.'[92]

What happened to Taylor's tea rolling machine, however, is uncertain. Denys Forrest claims that it was in operation in 1873.[93] Certainly, an early Kinmond tea roller was said to have been in existence in Ceylon in 1870 in which 'Only the upper rolling-surface of it moved'. What we do know for sure is that by the later 1870s William Jackson had invented a machine in India which became known as the Loolecondera Standard, 'the first Standard machine introduced into Ceylon'.[94]

Coinciding with Taylor's machinery experimentations was the construction of a tea house initially situated just below his bungalow (Figure 3.2).[95] In January 1873 he reported that 'The Tea house is finished and I have been making Tea in it for a month nearly now.'[96] Made of rockstone, wattle and daub, Taylor wrote that 'It is all my own contrivance but is very much thought of by Mr Jenkins and another Tea Planter I had a visit of the other day from Cachar.'[97] Taylor proudly judged it 'an excellent one about 70, feet by 35 ft

3.2 The site at Loolecondera of Taylor's tea factory and bungalow, c.1870s.

from eave to eave and fitted for an acreage of about 50, or 60, acres of Tea in full bearing but I believe it might do for more'.[98] So highly did Jenkins think of the tea house that he established one at Condegalla which Taylor found 'was a copy in all its working parts and arrangements of the one I had built which was according to a plan of my own and different from the style of Indian tea houses, and Mr. Jenkins did not like it when he first saw it'.[99]

Not surprisingly, Taylor's technical skills were soon admired by others. The 'ingenious arrangement of a water duct' that he built 'showed considerable engineering skills' which he carried out in a 'quiet, unobtrusive persevering way'.[100] This was presumably the waterwheel built to power the roller.[101] One report mentioned that 'a more intelligent, practical planter does not exist', while his employer Martin Leake stated, 'He is a man who, of all whom I have known, is the most entirely devoted to his work. Self-advancement has been, I believe as nothing in his eyes.'[102] Here was clear, external recognition of several of Taylor's key attributes including his creativity, competence, determination, industriousness, modesty, and selflessness.

Despite the acclaim, Taylor was again quick to draw attention to the input of others, including Sir William Henry Gregory, the Irish Governor of Ceylon in the 1870s. Gregory had visited Loolecondera and Taylor showed him his tea and cinchona experiments: 'They seemed immensely pleased with these places and the Governor was greatly taken with our Tea & Cinchona cultivation ... and is to help all he can to further Tea growing in Ceylon and hopes to have the hill tops too high for coffee utilised for Tea & Cinchona.'[103] Taylor also acknowledged his employers and proprietors, who 'allowed me to plant cinchona ordered me to plant tea, and it was they who paid for these things, and stood the risk of failure'.[104] Despite these attempts to downplay his own role, Leake had little doubt about Taylor's achievement, stressing that he and his business partner, Harrison, had merely provided the first seeds and then 'entrusted the tea experiment' to Taylor.[105]

It is undeniable, then, that Taylor led the way in many developments within the Ceylon tea economy. But it should also be remembered that the transformation of Ceylon's economy from coffee to cinchona and then tea was set within a knowledge economy of practical agricultural innovation. As John Ferguson put it, 'Our planters vie with each other in observation, experiment, and interchange of ideas. Many of them are practical engineers, some are well read in scientific agriculture, while there are local working engineers.'[106] Planters were clearly eager to experiment with a 'constant interchange of ideas, experiments and criticism in our island'.[107] This prompted the view that 'the practical knowledge of planters is much more valuable than any information agricultural science can give'.[108] Taylor took part in this planter culture of knowledge exchange, albeit infrequently, telling his family in 1873, 'I might have sent you lots of newspapers with my name and writings and doings figuring in them for

3.3 A view of tea and cinchona nurseries and coffee bushes in A.M. Ferguson's *Abbotsford Album*.

many years past, with discussions and writing praising and condemning me, and so forth. I keep as much out of the way of that as convenient generally but get frequently hauled in for all that, and very often by means of some letter to the Planters' Association or some such thing, never intended for a newspaper. That counts for little here.'[109]

Even after his success with tea became publicly known, Taylor continued to experiment with a range of crops in Ceylon. He reported lengthily on these efforts in 1876:

> We are now trying Cardamoms and Cinnamon. Of course Cinnamon is an old Ceylon product and was first supplied from the jungles. We have it wild in our jungle here of a coarse kind but the cultivation of it has been confined to the low country near the sea. I do not expect to make much by it and am only using it to plant up poor sandy soil and windy ridges where coffee won't pay to keep up. We may make money by Cardamoms. I am raising spectacular plants, too, but they grow so slowly it will take a terrible time before we do much in that line. There is a new kind of coffee being introduced from Liberia but it won't grow up here. It seems as if it might do in the low country. Cotton growing is being tried a little in the low country also. Our climate up here is far too wet for cotton, and soil not suitable. Chocolate is being tried on some low lying coffee estates. I tried chocolate here many years ago but it would not do up here. I tried a few plants of nutmegs, cloves, and vanilla plants but none of them would do here. They are now being thought of in the low country. By & by we may have lots of cultivation in Ceylon beyond the old coffee and the coco-nuts & cinnamon on the sea coast. I am planting timber and ornamental trees here also great numbers now[.][110]

Ultimately, however, it was Taylor's successful commercial cultivation of tea which proved a lifeline for Ceylon in the aftermath of the economic devastation unleashed by the failure of the coffee enterprise which has been described in the previous chapter. We turn now to consider the global context within which Ceylon tea eventually became a favourite across the world.

Notes

1 Markman Ellis, Richard Coulton and Matthew Mauger, *Empire of Tea: The Asian Leaf that Conquered the World* (London, 2015).
2 Alan Macfarlane and Iris Macfarlane, *Green Gold: The Empire of Tea* (London, 2003), pp. 69, 72–73, 179.
3 Ellis, Coulton and Mauger, *Empire of Tea*, p. 221.
4 Ibid.
5 Ibid., p. 222.
6 Macfarlane and Macfarlane, *Green Gold*, p. 38.
7 Ibid., p. 39.
8 Ibid., pp. 87–88

9 'The Ceylon tea industry', *OCO*, 8 June 1892, p. 625.
10 It is stated that the first recorded export of Ceylon tea was 23 pounds in 1873. See 'Days of old in Ceylon: The early period of the planting enterprise and its progress in the fifty years since 1837', *OCO*, 1 March 1892, p. 246.
11 'The Ceylon tea industry', p. 625. See also the table in Sir Percival Griffiths, *The History of the Indian Tea Industry* (London, 1967), p. 125, which provides statistics for UK imports of Indian, China, and Ceylon tea between 1866 and 1889.
12 Roland Wenzlhuemer, *From Coffee to Tea Cultivation in Ceylon 1880–1900* (Leiden and Boston, 2008), pp. 76–79
13 James L.A. Webb, *Tropical Pioneers: Human Agency and Ecological Change in the Highlands of Sri Lanka* (Athens, Ohio, 2002), p. 117.
14 Archives of the Royal Botanic Gardens at Kew, MR 285, Miscellaneous Reports Ceylon, 1861–90, Royal Botanic Garden report 1861, p. 209.
15 Ibid., Royal Botanic Garden report 1865, p. 134; Webb, *Tropical Pioneers*, p. 118.
16 'The tea industry of Ceylon', *TA*, 1 March 1888, p. 601. Leake's biography can be found in *TA*, 1 October 1897, pp. 223–227.
17 Taylor letters, 1 November 1879.
18 Taylor stated in 1878 that the small batch peeled in 1867 was mentioned by the quinologist John Eliot Howard as the first instalment from the Ceylon plantations to reach London. See James Taylor letter dated 16 February 1878 in 'Tea and cinchona in Ceylon', *TA*, 1 August 1890, p. 78. The first private experiment of cinchona was said to be at Loolecondera in 1868–69 with a quarter of a million plants. See 'Nuwara Eliya cinchona and tea district', A.M. and J. Ferguson, *Planting Directory for India and Ceylon* (Colombo, 1878), p. 58. Howard is mentioned in the planter biography for Taylor in *TA*, 2 July 1894, p. 3. See also Webb, *Tropical Pioneers*, pp. 118–119.
19 Wenzlhuemer, *From Coffee to Tea Cultivation*, p. 73, Table 5.6.
20 'Tea and cinchona in Ceylon', p. 78. *Succirubra* required more shelter and could be grown with coffee but provided less quinine. *Officinalis*, by contrast, could withstand wind and be grown at a higher elevation. See Archives of the Royal Botanic Gardens at Kew, MR 285, Miscellaneous Reports, Ceylon, 1861–90, Royal Botanic Garden Report, 1862–3, pp. 137–138.
21 Taylor letters, 18 March 1872.
22 'Large and satisfactory sale of Ceylon cinchona bark', *OCO*, 15 August 1873, p. 565.
23 Taylor letters, 25 January 1873.
24 Ibid., 18 March 1872.
25 Ibid., undated, c.1879.
26 Ibid., 1 November 1879.
27 A.M. and J. Ferguson, *The Ceylon Directory; Calendar, and Compendium of Useful Information (edition of 1880–81)* (Colombo, 1881), p. 675. Press reports, by contrast, reveal that Taylor had a share of Lover's Leap with a Mr Scott. Scott's first name is not provided but it may have been A.L. Scott or John Scott, both of whom learned from Taylor. See *OCO*, 26 September 1879, p. 802, and S.N. Breckenridge, *The Hills of Paradise: British Enterprise and the Story of Plantation Growth in Sri*

Lanka (Colombo, 2012), p. 113. The *TA*, by contrast, states that Taylor's co-proprietor was John Duncan. See 'Pioneers of the planting enterprise in Ceylon', *TA*, 2 July 1894, p. 4.

28 A.M. and J. Ferguson, *The Ceylon Directory; Calendar, and Compendium of Useful Information (edition of 1883–84)* (Colombo, 1884), p. 689; 'Pioneers of the planting enterprise in Ceylon', *TA*, p. 4.
29 Taylor letters, 27 January 1857.
30 Ibid., 17 September 1857.
31 Ibid., 5 November 1876.
32 Wenzlhuemer, *From Coffee to Tea Cultivation*, p. 71.
33 Ibid., p. 74.
34 Ibid.
35 'Centenary of the Botanic Gardens, Hakgala, 1861–1961', *TA*, 117 (1961), p. 199.
36 Taylor letters, 15 December 1884.
37 Ibid., 18 July 1889.
38 Webb, *Tropical Pioneers*, p. 200, note 45.
39 'The great sale of Ceylon cinchona, and cinchona culture in Ceylon', *OCO*, 13 September 1878, p. 642.
40 'On the hills in September', *OCO*, 21 September 1875, p. 300.
41 'The Taylor testimonial', *TA*, 2 November 1891, p. 340. Jno Atwell claimed in 1883 to be the first cinchona planter in Ceylon, having purchased with G.B. Carson five acres of plants from McNicol in October or November 1862. See 'First cinchonas planted out in Ceylon', *TA*, 2 April 1883, p. 777.
42 Webb, *Tropical Pioneers*, pp. 125, 127.
43 'The tea-planting enterprize in Ceylon', *OCO*, 20 June 1890, p. 643.
44 George de Worms, letter 19 August 1886, quoted in D.M. Forrest, *A Hundred Years of Ceylon Tea, 1867–1967* (London, 1967), p. 52.
45 'Tea and cinchona in Ceylon', p. 78.
46 Forrest, *A Hundred Years*, p. 54.
47 'S.B.' in 'Days of old in Ceylon: The early period of the planting enterprise and its progress in the fifty years since 1837', *OCO*, 1 March 1892, p. 246. For other accounts of Ceylon tea's early developments see William H. Ukers, *All About Tea*, vol. 1 (New York, 1935), p. 178; John Ferguson, *Ceylon in 1893* (London, 1893), pp. 73–74, 262; Frederick Lewis, *Sixty-Four Years in Ceylon: Reminiscences of Life and Adventure* (Colombo, 1926), p. 126; Roy Moxham, *A Brief History of Tea: The Extraordinary Story of the World's Favourite Drink* (London, 2009), ch. 5; Thomas Lister Villiers (ed.), *Recollections Personal and Official of James Steuart, 1817–1866* (Colombo, c.1935), pp. 64–65; M. Kelway Bamber, 'The tea industry', in Arnold Wright (ed.), *Twentieth Century Impressions of Ceylon: Its History, People, Commerce, Industries and Resources* (New Delhi, 1999), p. 248.
48 'Notes and comments', *OCO*, 16 June 1890, p. 624.
49 'Tea and cinchona in Ceylon', p. 78. The reproduced letter is dated 16 February 1878. It was also retrospectively published in the *OCO*, 23 June 1890, p. 651.
50 Taylor letters, 25 January 1873.
51 'Tea and cinchona in Ceylon', *TA*, p. 78.

52 British Library, C531, *Administration Reports Ceylon 1867* (Colombo, 1868), p. 316.

53 'Tea and cinchona in Ceylon', p. 78. See also 'Nuwara Eliya cinchona and tea district', p. 50. Leake endorsed this account, noting that Taylor began experimenting with 'leaves growing on bushes in the gardens of Loolecondura and Waloya bungalows'. See Archives of the Royal Botanic Gardens at Kew, MR 293, Miscellaneous Reports – Cultural Products, 1863–1916, Taylor testimonial, p. 226.

54 'The tea industry of Ceylon', p. 602.

55 'The tea enterprize in Ceylon', *WCO*, 21 July 1885, p. 593; 'The oldest regularly cropped tea in Ceylon still thoroughly vigorous', *OCO*, 16 May 1890, p. 503. Morice's report was published in 1867. Taylor applied for the appointment that Morice received but was not shortlisted. See Forrest, *A Hundred Years*, p. 68.

56 'The tea enterprise in Ceylon', *TA*, 1 September 1885, p. 153. See also William Martin Leake, 'Events of eleven years: 1863–1873', in *Jubilee of the Planters' Association of Ceylon, 1854–1904: Illustrated Souvenir of the 'Times of Ceylon'* (Colombo, 1904), p. 25. The consignment was ordered from Messrs Weinholt Brothers of Calcutta.

57 'Tea and cinchona in Ceylon', p. 78. Taylor's evidence for this is reference to an article in the *Kandy Herald* which mentioned the felling at Loolecondera.

58 See 'Pioneers of the planting enterprise in Ceylon', *TA*, 2 July 1894, pp. 3–4.

59 'The tea-planting enterprize in Ceylon', *OCO*, 20 June 1890, p. 643. The date of 1862 for the purchase of the Worms' estates is from Rothschild Archive London, Victor Gray and Ismeth Raheem, 'Cousins in Ceylon', www.rothschildarchive.org/materials/ar2004ceylon.pdf.

60 'Tea and cinchona in Ceylon', p. 78. William Martin Leake also noted that in the early days only two estates were producing tea – Loolecondera and the Ceylon Company. See 'The tea industry of Ceylon', p. 602.

61 Taylor letters, 25 January 1873.

62 Ibid., 5 November 1876.

63 Ibid., 25 January 1873.

64 Ibid., 5 November 1876.

65 James Taylor (Loolecondera) to the Secretary, Planters' Association (Kandy), 28 September 1891, reproduced in *Ceylon Mail*, 21 October 1891, NLS, Papers of James Taylor, planter in Ceylon, MS 15908.

66 'Tea and cinchona in Ceylon', *OCO*, 23 June 1890, p. 651.

67 James Taylor (Loolecondera) to the Secretary, Planters' Association (Kandy), 28 September 1891, reproduced in *Ceylon Mail*, 21 October 1891. NLS, Papers of James Taylor, planter in Ceylon, MS 15908.

68 Taylor wrote to his father from Darjeeling in March 1874 and reflected again on his visit in a letter from Loolecondera dated 11 April 1875.

69 Taylor letters, 29 March 1874.

70 Ibid., 29 March 1874, 11 April 1875.

71 Ibid., 11 April 1875.

72 'Mr James Taylor's reminiscences of the tea and cinchona enterprise', *TA*, 2 November 1891, p. 339.

73 'The Taylor testimonial', *TA*, 2 November 1891, p. 340. The letter was dated 28 September 1891.
74 Ibid. Also see the letter of September 1891, reproduced in *Ceylon Mail*, 21 October 1891, NLS, Papers of James Taylor, planter in Ceylon, MS 15908.
75 'Cameron memorial fund', *WCO*, 13 June 1883, p. 534. Mr Cameron's surname was often said to be Campbell. See 'The tea-planting enterprize in Ceylon', p. 643.
76 'Tea preparation in Ceylon', *WCO*, 25 May 1886, pp. 481–482.
77 'Ceylon as a field for the investment of capital and energy', *WCO*, 19 January 1885, p. 49.
78 'Ceylon tea industry', *TA*, 1 August 1892, pp. 107–108.
79 'Testimonial to Mr. James Taylor', *Proceedings of the Planters' Association of Ceylon for year ending 17th February, 1891* (Colombo, 1891), p. clxx.
80 'The Taylor testimonial', *TA*, 2 November 1891, p. 340.
81 'Mr Hay on the tea enterprise in Ceylon', *TA*, 1 November 1883, p. 320.
82 'Tea preparation in Ceylon', *WCO*, 25 May 1886, pp. 481–482.
83 'A veteran on Ceylon planting prospects', *TA*, 1 August 1888, p. 109.
84 Ukers, *All About Tea*, vol. 1, p. 197.
85 Taylor letters, 18 March 1872.
86 Ibid., 25 January 1873.
87 T.J. Barron, 'Science and the nineteenth-century Ceylon coffee planters', *Journal of Imperial and Commonwealth History*, 16:1 (1987), p. 14.
88 T.J. Barron, 'Sir James Emerson Tennent and the planting pioneers', presented to the Ceylon Studies seminar series 1970/72, p. 13.
89 Letter from John Hughes to 'The Standard', *TA*, 1 November 1888, p. 307.
90 'Notes from our London letter', *TA*, 1 September 1892, p. 213.
91 'Ceylon as best field for tropical planter', *TA*, 1 November 1892, p. 337.
92 *TA*, 1 October 1887, p. 230
93 Forrest, *A Hundred Years*, p. 72. Forrest confuses the machine with the tea house.
94 'The tea roller case', *WCO*, 24 October 1885, p. 914. See also 'The tea roller patent case', *TA*, 1 March 1892, pp. 654–674.
95 Forrest identified this as the dhoby's house which was situated just below the Loolcondera assistant superintendent's bungalow. See Forrest, *A Hundred Years*, p. 72. When we visited in 2014 the dhoby's house had been destroyed and the land was cultivated in crops.
96 Taylor letters, 25 January 1873.
97 Breckenridge, *The Hills of Paradise*, p. 113; Taylor letters, 25 January 1873.
98 Taylor letters, 25 January 1873.
99 'The Taylor testimonial', p. 340.
100 *Ceylon Mail or Weekly Independent*, 21 October 1891, in NLS, Papers of James Taylor, planter in Ceylon, MS 15908.
101 Breckenridge, *The Hills of Paradise*, p. 113.
102 'The tea industry of Ceylon', p. 602.
103 Taylor letters, 18 March 1872.

104 James Taylor (Loolecondera) to the Secretary, Planters' Association (Kandy), 28 September 1891, reproduced in *Ceylon Mail*, 21 October 1891, NLS, Papers of James Taylor, planter in Ceylon, MS 15908.
105 Forrest, *A Hundred Years*, pp. 66, 70.
106 'The Ceylon tea industry', *TA*, 1 July 1892, p. 44.
107 'Ceylon as best field for tropical planter', *TA*, 1 November 1892, p. 337.
108 'Science in planting', *TA*, 1 May 1893, p. 694.
109 Taylor letters, 25 January 1873.
110 Ibid., 5 November 1876.

4

Globalising Ceylon tea

In 1872 James Taylor and W.J. Jenkins from the Ceylon Company's Condegalla estate provided samples of Loolecondera tea to brokers in Calcutta for the first time. Jenkins' batch fetched 2s 9d to 2s 10d a pound while Taylor's was set at 2s 2d to 2s 7d per pound. As one journalistic commentator remarked, these values were reputedly 'higher than those usually obtained for tea exported from Calcutta. This is most encouraging and there can be little doubt that tea will yet be amongst our Ceylon staples.'[1] According to Taylor's recollections almost twenty years later, 'Mr. Jenkins' sample was valued a little higher that [sic] any of mine, but mine were also pronounced good, except one indifferent and one spoiled. With these exceptions both Jenkins' sample and the rest of mine were said to be better than the most of the Indian teas that were being sold in Calcutta at the time.'[2] In July the following year this positive response was repeated: 'the specimens of tea grown and cured in the Island by Mr Jenkins of the Ceylon Company, and by Mr. Taylor of Lúlkandrua, have been pronounced, both here and in England, to be of excellent quality.'[3] Later testimonials stated that Taylor 'was able at once to produce a Tea of such quality as not only to ensure the ready sale in Ceylon of all his produce but also to secure the approbation of the leading London Brokers'.[4]

Other contemporary comments about the flavour were also supportive. According to John Loudoun Shand, Taylor 'turned out tea which secured local appreciation and favourable comment in the London market'.[5] Some even hailed it as the 'best tea going in the local market' and complained of difficulties sourcing it.[6] It was said that 'Tea at Loolecundura contrasts favourably with any I have seen at Darjeeling or Kurseong.'[7] Loolecondera tea may also have been in the mind of the former Governor of Ceylon Sir William Gregory when he 'formally stated that so highly was Ceylon tea thought of that it was impossible to meet anything like the demand for it'.[8] Indeed, Gregory's supply often came direct from Taylor, who was instructed to despatch 'a first rate sample of his making'. George Thwaites of the Royal Botanical Gardens at Peradeniya was the go-between and reckoned that 'Very good tea is being produced now in the island, but the L. Condera is still A.1. in my estimation.'[9] Ceylon tea was deemed preferable to China and Indian teas because 'it combines the two in flavour and strength, and does away with blending China and Indian'.[10] A key difference was the presence of one-third more *theine* than in China leaf.[11]

Initially, however, the market for Ceylon tea was confined to the island itself and there was little need to sell it abroad. Taylor made the reasons for this clear: 'It pays on this place very well just now as we sell it all in Ceylon for well on to twice the price we would get for it in London and save the expense of sending it home.'[12] In another letter, undated, he wrote, 'Our Tea pays us handsomely, too; selling it for use in Ceylon as we do, It will pay us I believe very fairly when we have to send it home for sale.'[13] His boss, William Martin Leake, emphasised the 'rattling good prices' that the two companies producing Ceylon tea in the early 1870s achieved.[14] This pattern continued into the later years of that decade, with Taylor noting in 1879 that others were now benefiting from the resort to the new crops. Although the Ceylon economy 'is all a mess', he stated, 'It is our new products Cinchona & Tea no doubt that keeps the planting interests from ruin.'[15]

Some commentators, however, pointed to other factors to explain why Ceylon tea was initially restricted to the home market, including the different taste of Indian and Ceylonese teas. Some in the UK found Ceylon tea 'deficient in strength and flavour' and reckoned time was required before it could compete in the UK with Indian tea. Part of the problem, the critics contended, was that although it was fresh on arrival in London, the tea soon became 'flat and lost flavour rapidly'. This 'created a prejudice against Ceylon tea'.[16] A further problem lay in marketing, with Loolecondera tea marked as 'Assam tea of strength'. Allegations were made that 'People don't seem to care about buying Ceylon tea, and I think its being packed in tins is against it.' The same observer noted that 'it is only in Scotland that I have heard of your tea growth being properly appreciated, and yet, whenever I have been able to have samples tried at the family tea table, I have never heard anything but praise of it'. He recommended that the tea had to become more effectively established on the London market, advice that was soon taken up in earnest.[17]

Within six years, however, Ceylon tea was being considered in some quarters as preferable to China and Indian brands because 'it combines in flavour and strength, and *does away with blending China and Indian*'.[18] Tea on the island could also be profitably grown at higher and lower elevations than coffee, with a consequent overall increase in acreage and output. The first signs of the boom which was to follow were now starting to emerge. Few, however, could have predicted the remarkable scale of the export success which was eventually achieved. By 1882, around 20,000 acres of tea were planted and 700,000 pounds exported; at the end of 1886, nine hundred estates were growing tea in Ceylon. By 1907, 380,000 acres were planted and 170 million pounds exported. The maximum acreage for coffee planting, in contrast, had been 272,000 in

1877, with 103 million pounds exported. The 1,600 tea plantations in 1907 employed 400,000 Tamil workers and the overall investment in the industry was estimated to be £9 million. In light of these figures, John Ferguson waxed lyrical: 'Never in the history of agriculture has there been a more extraordinary supersession and development than that of tea taking the place of coffee, and spreading far beyond its limits, in Ceylon.'[19] Three years later, Westland's Ceylon Tea Agency at Aberdeen could also proudly proclaim that 'the popularity of Ceylon Tea has increased immensely, till it is now recognised as the Leading Tea of the Day'.[20]

These developments saw Ceylon and India effectively challenge the dominance of China tea. In the early nineteenth century, for instance, nearly four-fifths of the tea sold in the London market came from China, as it had done since the British first developed a taste for it.[21] In 1885, China still provided 62 per cent of the tea consumed in the UK.[22] Two years later, however, the turning point came as tea imports to Britain from Ceylon and India surpassed those of China.[23] By 1895, the Chinese share of the market had fallen to little more than 14 per cent.[24] The following year, 1896, Ceylon's share, in contrast, had reached 35 per cent.[25] A decade later, 93 per cent of tea came from India and Ceylon and only 7 per cent from China.[26] Ceylon and India were now the dominant suppliers to the world's biggest market for tea.[27] The Chinese had lost their virtual monopoly thanks to the competitive edge developed by Ceylon and Indian tea planters.

The key stimulus of this massive growth was increasing tea consumption per capita in Britain. The figure stood at 1.22 pounds per capita in 1840, but by 1880 it had trebled to 4.57 pounds, and it rose to 6.2 pounds by the end of the century.[28] Indeed, in the mid-1880s Britain consumed almost half of the tea cultivated in the world.[29] But that pattern of demand does not in itself explain the remarkable transformation of the Ceylon tea economy. The island's advantages in tea cultivation have also to be understood and, crucially, reasons given why Ceylon was able to compete so effectively alongside India against the traditional hegemony of China in the British tea market.

After the collapse of coffee on the island, land became available in abundance for alternative uses. Coffee bushes were uprooted throughout the plantations and burned as firewood. The same estates which had grown coffee for so long soon began to show an interest in cultivating tea, while infrastructure which had developed under coffee now became available to underpin the radical expansion in tea production. This included roads, railways, drains, bungalows, and stores.[30] To these, new harbour improvements in the capital, Colombo, were added. The opening of the Suez Canal in 1869, together with the steamship revolution of the second half of the nineteenth century, had a decisive impact on the reduction of transportation costs from Ceylon to the markets in Europe. The island also had some important natural advantages in tea cultivation. In contrast to coffee, tea bushes needed considerable moisture and the ample rainfall of the Kandy highlands shortened the period between planting of crops and the first harvest to around three years, or five years on estates above 5,000 feet. Tea flourished more in areas too wet for coffee and could also grow more profitably at altitudes higher and lower than for coffee cultivation.[31] It also fared better than coffee in poor soil.[32] All this helped to give Ceylon tea producers a distinct advantage over Assam and Chinese competitors.[33]

The British masses soon began to show a preference for the black teas of Ceylon and India over the weaker green teas from China. Black tea was said to have a more stimulating effect and the cost per cup was lower than for the green variety.[34] But the victory in the global market was also won by the systematic application of more efficient business methods, cultivation techniques, and new technologies. Chinese peasants simply could not compete with the cost advantages which came from these innovations which were rapidly introduced within the plantations of India and Ceylon. It has been rightly said that in this period the tropical plantation became 'an extended factory roofed only by the shade of trees'.[35] Within it an 'unlimited supply' of full-time labour, who were paid minimal wages, were carefully regulated and managed.[36] The tea economy also benefited from efficient machinery for preparing the leaf.[37] Technology was applied to the leaves after picking, with machines for rolling and drying powered by steam or water and with little human input to the process. This meant that South Asian tea came to be regarded as less tainted and of more even quality than Chinese.[38] In 1872 the cost of production of plantation tea was 11d a pound, which was roughly in line with Chinese levels, but by the first decade of the twentieth century improved machinery had cut it to 3d a pound.[39] Even impoverished Chinese coolies could not compete with this dramatic fall in cost triggered by the industrialisation of cheap tea and its efficient delivery to market by railway and steamship. Greater expertise in tea planting and treatment also led to higher outputs, with yields per acre increasing dramatically from 158 pounds in 1880–1881 to 750 pounds in 1890–1891.[40]

At this time too, the marketing of the product overseas became more dynamic and sophisticated. Presence at international exhibitions was especially important in raising the profile of Ceylon tea throughout the world, at Melbourne (1880–1881), London (1886), Glasgow (1888), Dunedin (1889), and Paris (1889). Of great importance for Loolecondera and James Taylor was the Melbourne International Exhibition, which ran from October 1880 until April 1881 and attracted almost 1.5 million visitors.[41] Various Ceylon teas competed for prizes, with Loolecondera winning first Order of Merit for its orange and flowery pekoes, Souchong, Pekoe Souchong, and Broken Pekoes. Indeed, Keir, Dundas and Co., the owners of the estate, received most prizes, almost one-third of the thirty-six awards given for Ceylon tea out of seventy-eight exhibits of tea. This prompted the remark that it 'must be gratifying to those immediately interested, especially to him who may be regarded as almost the pioneer of tea growing and tea manufacture in Ceylon, – Mr. James Taylor.'[42] Even an under-fermented tea sample of Taylor's was declared 'as near perfection as possible. Such a judgment and indeed the rank generally assigned to the teas prepared by Mr. Taylor are very creditable to him, considering that, with the exception of a visit to Darjeeling, his experience has been all gained in Ceylon.'[43]

The following year, in the afterglow of this success, the *Tropical Agriculturalist* announced that 'The reputation of Loolecondera is fully established.'[44] Such was the ongoing impact of Taylor's tea that even in 1883 no other had yet excelled the samples sent to the Melbourne exhibition.[45] Taylor himself admitted that he had made 'fancy lots for the Melbourne Exhibitions (and for Sydney) that have never been beaten, I believe'.[46] Even so, Ceylon tea itself had not yet established a ready market in Australia as the public could not easily obtain it in the shops.[47] Eventually, however, the country came to be considered a great tea-drinking nation. British settlement increased and the immigrants brought the tea-drinking habits of the mother country to the Antipodes. These new Australians showed a special preference for Ceylon teas. Tea consumption in Australia – averaging more than 7½ pounds per person each year – became linked in the eyes of some with the notion that its citizens were among the healthiest people in the world.[48]

Loolecondera samples were also supplied to exhibitions in the UK and Ceylon tea went from strength to strength. John Loudoun Shand reported from the Liverpool exhibition in 1883 that 'We are selling three cups of Ceylon tea for every cup of Indian tea that is sold in the exhibition, and many people who had never heard of Ceylon tea before are loud in its praises.'[49] At the Colonial and Indian Exhibition of 1886, held in London from May to October, which an estimated 5.5 million or more people visited, a Ceylon tea house featured, with the 'Sinhalese attendants of course adding much to its popularity.' The promotional activities paid off, as 'There was more Ceylon than Indian tea sold in cups during the Exhibition at the Commission tea rooms.' Some predicted that the Exhibition would give 'a great stimulus to the consumption of Ceylon tea'.[50]

In 1886 the Ceylon Tea Syndicate was formed to market the product globally, while two years later the Ceylon Tea Fund was established with similar objectives. More than six hundred estates and donors provided support for the scheme.[51] The Glasgow International Exhibition of Industry, Science and Arts ran from May to November and included the formation of a 'Ceylon Court' as well as 'Ceylon Tea House'. Ceylon tea received a major boost when Queen Victoria visited the Exhibition and accepted a cup of Ceylon tea.[52] The event succeeded beyond expectation, with sales there averaging around six thousand cups a week.[53] All told, more than 4.5 million passed through the displays and 'Tea was talked about all over Scotland.'[54] Indeed one observer informed that 'the little Ceylon Tea-house was crowded with people, while the larger and certainly better appointed Indian House was almost empty'.[55] The attraction was maintained at the Melbourne Centennial Exhibition of August 1888 to January 1889, when the kiosk was 'thronged all the afternoon', with the tea being 'a great novelty'.[56] Demand for Ceylon tea in Australia after the Exhibition increased from 292,671 pounds shipped in August 1888 to almost 700,000 pounds by August 1889.[57]

Ceylon producers were now able to diversify their markets throughout the empire as the upward volume of emigration from Britain inevitably spread the tea-drinking habit across the globe. Another exhibition was held in 1889–1890 in Dunedin, New Zealand. Advertised as the New Zealand and South Seas Exhibition, it attracted fewer crowds than elsewhere – just 625,000 – but still made a profit. According to the *Otago Daily Times*, 'The Ceylon Tea Kiosk is one of the most attractive features in the Exhibition, and its popularity is attested by crowds who throng it.'[58] This success prompted the formation of a local company and the opening of a shop to sell both wholesale and retail Ceylon tea. William Watson, previously with the Oriental Bank Corporation in Ceylon, was instrumental in this regard. Support, however, was not easily forthcoming as some competitors 'depicted Ceylon tea as injurious, and sickly to the taste, and even pictorial cartoons were resorted to in the hope of bluffing us out of the market'. Nevertheless, Watson estimated there was potentially strong demand, particularly among the 'working farmer and the artisan'.[59] Indeed, the exhibitions would eventually lead to the creation of tea shops and trigger enhanced tea sales as the exhibitions demonstrated the ability to trade in Ceylon tea globally.[60] These activities were all part of broader imperial propaganda activities from the later nineteenth century onwards.[61]

Various agencies ensured the distribution of the increasingly attractive Ceylon tea. The oldest in Britain may have been Westland's Ceylon Tea Agency, which opened in 1879 in Aberdeen.[62] Supposedly, however, specialist firms established to market Ceylon produce would not be very successful. The *Tropical Agriculturist* argued that 'The tea must find its way into the recognized channel – the grocers. At present grocers cannot get it.'[63] A swift transition soon occurred. By 1887 reports suggested that 'A few years ago Ceylon tea was absolutely unknown, and even in 1885 not a grocer in the place kept it. I was told by the largest grocer here that there was now more Ceylon tea sold in the County of Kinross than all other kinds put together.'[64]

At this time, also, tea blenders were trying to find teas suitable for 'the peculiar tastes of the district in which it is to be consumed.'[65] In Glasgow, tea blends in the late 1870s were generally made from two-thirds Chinese and one-third Indian teas, while over time Indian tea was used more freely.[66] By contrast, Ceylon tea was pushed in the early 1880s as being better, stronger, refreshing, more richly flavoured, and more economical. Newspaper reports contended that the 'delicious taste, and agreeable flavour of Pure Ceylon tea are fast gaining for it universal favour'. The press further added that 'Ceylon tea is sold absolutely pure, because, unlike China tea, it requires no admixture to give it strength; and unlike Indian tea, it requires no addition of China tea to correct harshness and make it palatable.'[67] Indeed, by 1883 China teas were considered 'unsatisfactory', while Indian teas 'for consumption alone ... are not yet quite adapted to Scotch taste'.[68] Only six years later claims were made that 'Ceylon produces some of the finest Teas we have ever handled, combining the strength of the finest Indian with some of the delicacy of the best China Tea.'[69]

Just as diverse ethnicities were identified in Ceylon, as discussed later in this book, commentators also recognised divergence within the UK in preferring different types of tea:

> For instance, Darjeelings are largely consumed in the North of Ireland and in Scotland, while broken Pekoes of the finest kinds are drunk pure by the lower classes in Ireland. Strong and rather burnt liquoring Assam teas are also popular in Ireland. Pale pungent teas are in great request in the midland counties of England, and in other districts, where the public taste had been accustomed to the China scented caper tea.[70]

It was at this point that the colourful figure of Thomas Lipton entered the business of marketing Ceylon tea in Britain through his chain of grocery stores. The future Sir Thomas Lipton (1838–1931) was born in Glasgow to Irish parents. He had achieved initial success in the UK through the general provision trade, in which he cut out the middleman to make his products less costly to the consumer and also to give himself more profit. Tea, in Lipton's words, soon became 'an adjunct' to his other activities. He bypassed the wholesale tea merchants for whom his shops had previously been regarded as the ideal retail distribution centres for their product. Instead, Lipton became his own wholesaler. He himself began blending tea and developed a product that 'created a sensation' in the market.[71] An important key to his success was Lipton's awareness that the taste of tea varied across the country according to the water it was brewed in because of the chemical properties of different water supplies.[72] As such, his tea-tasters in London took samples of water from various towns throughout Britain and suitable blends were then carefully prepared for each district. As Lipton explained: 'The tea I was selling in Edinburgh was quite a different blend from that retailed in Glasgow, while the London tea, specially blended to suit the water, was a different article altogether to the hard-water tea sent from my headquarters to Manchester.'[73] James Taylor had an alternative explanation for the popularity of blending: 'Pure Ceylon is dear and they cannot make the profit they want by selling it.'[74] In this way, then, tea was adjusted for the diversity of the British palate just as other British beverages, like whisky, had to be adapted for colonial tastes.[75]

Lipton recalled that after a year in the tea trade he was approached by the London bankers of a group of Ceylon estates. As a result, he took ship in 1889 for Ceylon to inspect these properties. Lipton initially made a low offer of purchase for them but eventually settled on £21,000 for the Downall estates of Dambetenne, Monerakande, and Laymostotte in the Haputale region.[76] Shortly afterwards, he took over the Pooprassie estate at Pussellawa and left instructions for others to be acquired as they became available. Lipton recalled that he had decided to spend in the region of £100,000 within a fortnight on Ceylon plantations.[77] Eventually, around three thousand workers were thought to be employed on his estates.[78] 'From the tea garden to the tea pot' became his famous slogan. By his eliminating the middleman, his tea became recognised for its highly competitive prices.[79]

Lipton's Ceylon tea also made a major impact because of his imaginative marketing techniques. He, more than any other, promoted it alongside an image of Ceylon estates as ordered and civilised, in both an environmental and a social sense.[80] He deployed several stock images of the work associated with the estates, such as plucking, the manufacturing process embodied through the estate factories, and the transportation of the product by rail and ship. Tamil female workers were depicted as 'decorative, exotic and submissive'.[81] That image would endure and is still used in advertisements for Ceylon tea to this day, but it bore little relationship to the realities of life on the plantations. Another of Lipton's advertising ploys was to deck out a group of men to parade in Glasgow streets 'in white suits, red turbans, red and yellow umbrellas, and a commander on horseback with his face coloured to match his turban'.[82] He also organised full-scale public processions with 'Cart-loads of tea chests' accompanied by brass bands.[83]

Since output from his own Ceylon estates could not satisfy rising demand, Lipton blended his own tea with other varieties bought at the Colombo market.[84] This generated claims that although 'pure' when leaving Ceylon, his tea was 'not when it reaches the tea-pot'. Some asserted that he did not produce 'strong, dark, bitter Teas' but 'mild and refreshing' ones. The flavour was deemed to possess an 'exquisite aroma and delicious flavour'.[85] When his name was suggested to promote Ceylon tea in the United States, critics stated that he would have to promote 'pure Ceylon tea, unblended and unmixed, with any other'. The detractors charged that Lipton 'is interested in our tea, no doubt, but only as it serves his own personal profit, in the shape of a blend; such are not the men to help in extending the use of pure Ceylon tea'.[86] Lipton's response to these attempts to discredit him was immediate and direct. He sourced a sample of his finest gold-tipped tea grown at Haputale and auctioned it at Mincing Lane in London. When it fetched a record price, he proclaimed, 'After this there was no further attempt to decry Lipton's tea.'[87]

Other rumours, however, had circulated earlier and even concerned the tea of Loolecondera. In 1875 the press reckoned that 'The popular belief is that the best-flavoured tea made in Ceylon is the result of a mixture of leaf from the China plants with that from the true hybrids.'[88] Two years later, Loolecondera's 'delicate flavour' was attributed to a mixture of China and Assam hybrid leaf.[89] John Ferguson, however, thought this was mistaken: 'The fact is that Loolecondura has not many China bushes, and these are scattered along the roads. The leaf is plucked and prepared, despatched and sold separately and generally fetches 1d to 2d the lb. below the Assam-Hybrid tea.'[90] It was, nevertheless, recognised that between 1873 and 1874 'a good many plants of both the Assam hybrid and the China variety were distributed from the Peradeniya and Hakgala gardens; later on, the chief means of supply was through the importation of large quantities of Assam seed from Calcutta'.[91]

Irrespective of how Ceylon tea tasted, it soon became obvious that it was not always guaranteed to produce a profit. In the early 1880s, James Taylor noted that the new cultivations of cinchona and tea 'have kept us going by raising hopes of great profits from them. But loss rather than profit is turning out to be the case in very many instances. They have been extensively planted in unsuitable land and although in some cases they are doing splendidly in many they are turning out failures, I believe; and I can see a good deal of such', although his own places were 'profitably carried on'.[92] That same year, 1882, there were claims in the press 'that the pioneer of tea among Ceylon planters – Mr. Taylor of Loolcondera – has not made the cultivation a profitable one; but we are in a position to state on the best authority that this is a mistake for the tea-plantation in question is giving "a very fair return."'[93] Some properties such as Culloden, Dunedin, and Ruanwella did experience low prices but Loolecondera topped the market with its reputation 'fully established'.[94] Part of the problem for many of the estates was that their gardens were young and the production of poor-quality tea in them was caused by ignorance or carelessness. By contrast, older estates such as 'Loolecondera, Blackstone and Galboda have continued to be held up in the Brokers' reports as models of what ought to be followed in the preparation of Ceylon teas'.[95] This recognition produced a sense of relief, as 'it must be reassuring to find the oldest estate in the island holding out in quality as it does, and though giving no very large yield per acre maintaining its quality so well'.[96] The distinctions, however, highlighted the problems of growing tea at low altitudes that produced a stronger but less refined brew. Most Ceylon tea today blends the produce from high- and low-grown estates.

In 1883 some boasted 'that tea-planters in Ceylon can beat their brethren in either Northern or Southern India – in Assam or in the Nilgeries – in producing as good a tea at a lower cost'.[97] Indeed, Loolecondera's tea the following year fetched two shillings a pound, 'far higher than almost any estate'.[98] Yet, prices from 1884 until 1907 began to drop, partly the result of declining consumption in the UK due to economic difficulties and rising unemployment towards the end of that period. At the same time, imports of Ceylon tea in the UK increased from around 4 million pounds in 1885 to 96 million pounds in 1897.[99] The Oriental Bank Corporation also failed at this time and investment money in planting was scarce. To this was added the cost and shortage of tea seeds.[100] Perhaps troubled by remembering the problems that had afflicted coffee and cinchona in the past, Taylor wrote forlornly in 1889:

> We have swamped the market with Tea and it is now selling at such low prices as hardly to pay expenses. We over do everything apparently as soon as Ceylon goes in for it. A few years ago I was making £15, English money, of profit an acre a year on the Tea here and one much better place than this was said to have made £37, an acre profit one year. That is the crack tea estate in Ceylon and heavily manured.

He feared what the 'price will be when all is in full cropping' and drew similarities with cinchona: 'I suspect it is the same to a large extent with Tea. We get little more than half the price for it in London which we got a few years ago.' As he noted, 'my tea which was selling for two shillings average a lb. in bond in London some years ago now sells for one shilling & twopence average'.[101] Indeed, between 1884 and 1889 the price of Ceylon tea fell by 45 per cent.[102]

For Taylor, the future continued to seem somewhat bleak. In 1890 he dejectedly reported, 'Our tea has been selling generally a little lighter than it was some time ago but for very much less than it used to years ago when the Company was formed, and I fear they will be more cantankerous and unreasonable than ever presently.' Part of the problem, as he found with cinchona, was that only half the cultivated land on the estate provided a crop. 'Were the cultivated land all in full cropping things would be vastly different', he explained. 'It takes years after planting before the things we grow come into cropping and years more before they are in full cropping but they have to be cultivated and money spent on them all that time.' Nevertheless, the directors of the company in London seem to have had little sympathy with his problems. Taylor warned that same year, 'Most of the Tea, or all of it except our old original fields, is still only young and small bushes giving only a little crop and that will give, say, half a crop coming year.'[103] Little had changed by 1891: 'Ceylon seems in a precarious way again. We are making more tea than all the wives at home can drink and so we get very small prices for it now. There seems a probability that by & by inferior estates will not be able to pay.'[104]

In contrast with Taylor's anxieties, however, Ceylon's tea industry – at least for its owners – remained generally prosperous until 1897, aided partly by the depreciation of the rupee against sterling.[105] This meant that expenses could be paid in rupees but profits accrued in sterling. Production costs had also fallen by about a third.[106] Yet, after 1897 the profit margin threatened to disappear, due to over-production as a result of coarse plucking which made inferior tea.[107]

As the twentieth century dawned, however, many planters began to adopt Taylor's system of fine plucking which was the key to producing quality teas.[108]

Good news also came from reports on Taylor's initial twenty acres of tea planting. John Ferguson, of the *Ceylon Observer* and *Tropical Agriculturalist*, regularly corresponded with Taylor about the condition of his original tea fields. According to Ferguson, Taylor in 1888 considered the bushes 'very vigorous' and in 1891 he wrote to Ferguson, 'The field is as good as ever, giving about the same crops; it was manured once only with castor cake in the beginning of 1885.' Ferguson then remarked, 'though there is, perhaps, no other case in the island so old and so reliable in its information, yet there is abundant evidence to show that there is nothing in the appearance of our tea fields generally, or in the yield of crop – I shall come to quality – to justify doubts as to the stability of the Ceylon tea-planting industry.'[109] These enquiries continued even after Taylor's death, with G.F. Deane writing that the twenty acres of Assam Hybrid at Loolecondera are 'full of vigour shewing no signs of decay' while the China tea planted along the roadsides in 1866 'is also flourishing and yielding well. And we infer that very little manure, and that only at intervals, has been given to this good old tea.'[110] Today, more than a century after these comments were made, five acres of Taylor's first commercial tea crop in Ceylon remain in cultivation. Unlike coffee and cinchona, tea had indeed become the saviour over the long term of the economy of Ceylon.

Notes

1 'Ceylon tea', *OCO*, 20 September 1872, p. 392.
2 'The Taylor testimonial', *TA*, 2 November 1891, p. 340.
3 'Tea', *OCO*, 30 July 1873, p. 14.
4 Archives of the Royal Botanic Gardens at Kew, MR 293, Miscellaneous Reports, 'Ceylon Association in London, testimonial to James Taylor', 17 July 1890, p. 226.
5 'The tea industry of Ceylon', *TA*, 1 March 1888, p. 596.
6 *OCO*, 21 December 1876, p. 696.
7 *WCO*, 15 March 1880, p. 262.
8 'Tea in Ceylon', *OCO*, 30 May 1878, p. 375.
9 Bodleian Library at the Weston Library, University of Oxford, Dep. d. 979, W.H. Gregory Papers, General correspondence concerning Ceylon, Aug. 1877–Dec. 1878, G.H.K. Thwaites (Peradeniya) to Sir William Gregory, 27 September 1878.
10 'The progress of tea cultivation and manufacture in Ceylon', *WCO*, 23 June 1885, p. 510.
11 John Capper, *Handbook Ceylon Products and Industries with a Catalogue of the Exhibits in the Ceylon Court* (Edinburgh, 1888), p. 34.
12 Taylor letters, 5 November 1876.
13 Ibid., undated, c. mid-1870s.
14 'The tea industry of Ceylon', p. 602.

15 Taylor letters, 1 November 1879.
16 'Ceylon tea in the north of Scotland', *TA*, 1 October 1889, p. 283.
17 *OCO*, 24 December 1879, p. 1147.
18 'The progress of tea cultivation and manufacture in Ceylon', *WCO*, 23 June 1885, p. 510.
19 John Ferguson, *The Rise of the Planting Enterprise and Trade in Ceylon Tea* (c.1907), pp. 1–3; *TA*, 1 October 1887, p. 278.
20 Advertisement, *TA*, 1 September 1890.
21 Roland Wenzlhuemer, *From Coffee to Tea Cultivation in Ceylon 1880–1900* (Leiden and Boston, 2008), pp. 81–2.
22 J. Dyer Ball, *Things Chinese* (1903; reprinted Singapore, 1989); D.M. Forrest, *A Hundred Years of Ceylon Tea, 1867–1967* (London, 1967), p. 189.
23 John Weatherstone, *The Pioneers, 1825–1900: The Early British Tea and Coffee Planters and their Way of Life* (London, 1986), p. 29. If considering statistics for India and Ceylon alone, however, China still had the edge. See the table in Sir Percival Griffiths, *The History of the Indian Tea Industry* (London, 1967), p. 125.
24 Ball, *Things Chinese*; Forrest, *A Hundred Years of Ceylon Tea*, p. 189.
25 S. Rajaratnam, 'The Ceylon tea industry 1886–1931', *Ceylon Journal of Historical and Social Studies*, 4:2 (1961), p. 171.
26 Andrew Thompson, *The Empire Strikes Back: The Impact of Imperialism on Britain from the Mid-Nineteenth Century* (Abingdon, 2014), p. 48.
27 K.M. de Silva, *A History of Sri Lanka* (Colombo, 2005), p. 369.
28 Rajaratnam, 'The Ceylon tea industry', p. 174.
29 Wenzlhuemer, *From Coffee to Tea Cultivation*, p. 84, fn. 65.
30 *TA*, 1 June 1885, p. 877.
31 Rajaratnam, 'The Ceylon tea industry', p. 172; 'Tea in Ceylon', p. 375.
32 Lennox A. Mills, *Ceylon Under British Rule, 1795–1932* (London, 1933), pp. 246–250.
33 Ibid., p. 174.
34 Wenzlheumer, *From Coffee to Tea Cultivation*, p. 81.
35 Alan Macfarlane and Iris Macfarlane, *Green Gold: The Empire of Tea* (London, 2003), p. 195.
36 *TA*, 1 September 1892, p. 214.
37 Ibid.
38 *TA*, 1 October 1887, p. 230.
39 Macfarlane and Macfarlane, *Green Gold*, p. 196.
40 Wenzlhuemer, *From Coffee to Tea Cultivation* p. 83.
41 John Parris and A.G.L. Shaw, 'The Melbourne International Exhibition 1880–1881', *Victorian Historical Journal*, 51:4 (1980), p. 245.
42 *TA*, 1 June 1881, pp. 6–8. It was further reckoned that Keir Dundas and Co would have won a further First Class award, had an additional sample not been lost – see p. 11.
43 'Ceylon tea in the Australian colonies', *WCO*, 20 December 1880, p. 1192.
44 *TA*, 1 December 1882, p. 480.
45 Ibid., 1 September 1883, p. 185.

46 Taylor letters, 15 December 1884.
47 'Ceylon tea in Australia', *TA*, 1 March 1888, p. 585.
48 John Ferguson, *The Rise of the Planting Enterprise and Trade in Ceylon Tea* (c.1907), pp. 4–5.
49 *TA*, 1 September 1887, p. 171.
50 'Report on the colonial and Indian exhibition', *Proceedings of the Planters Association, Kandy, for the year ending 17th February 1887* (Colombo, 1887), pp. cii–ciii.
51 'Ceylon tea fund: Glasgow, Melbourne, and Brussels exhibitions, &c', *Proceedings of the Planters' Association of Ceylon for year ending February 17th, 1888* (Colombo, 1888), p. xxviii
52 *Proceedings of the Planters' Association of Ceylon for year ending 16th February, 1889* (Colombo, 1889), p. 88.
53 Ibid., p. ccxiv.
54 'Tea fund and what it has done', *Proceedings of the Planters' Association of Ceylon for year ending 16th February, 1890* (Colombo, 1890), p. 74.
55 Letter from John Hughes, *TA*, 1 November 1888, p. 307.
56 *Proceedings of the Planters' Association of Ceylon for year ending 16th February, 1889* (Colombo, 1889), p. 90.
57 'Tea fund and what it has done', p. 75.
58 'Exhibits', *Proceedings of the Planters' Association of Ceylon for year ending 16th February, 1890*, p. ccviii.
59 'Ceylon tea in Australia and New Zealand', *TA*, 1 February 1894, p. 519.
60 Joanna De Groot, 'Metropolitan desires and colonial connections: Reflections on consumption and empire', in Catherine Hall and Sonya Rose (eds), *At Home with Empire: Metropolitan Culture and the Imperial World* (Cambridge, 2006), p. 184; Peter H. Hoffenberg, *An Empire on Display: English, Indian, and Australian Exhibitions from the Crystal Palace to the Great War* (Berkeley and Los Angeles, 2001), p. 118.
61 John M. MacKenzie, *Propaganda and Empire: The Manipulation of British Public Opinion, 1880–1960* (Manchester, 1984).
62 Advertisement, *TA*, 1 September 1890.
63 'Ceylon tea agencies in Britain', *TA*, 1 October 1881, p. 359.
64 *TA*, 1 October 1887, p. 277.
65 'Direct tea shipments from Calcutta to Glasgow', *TA*, 1 July 1887, p. 33.
66 'Ceylon vs China and Indian teas in Glasgow', *TA*, 1 October 1888, p. 228.
67 *WCO*, 21 February 1882, p. 167.
68 Ibid., 24 January 1883, p. 8
69 'Ceylon tea in the north of Scotland', *TA*, 1 October 1889, p. 283.
70 *The Overland*, 23 January 1880, p. 85.
71 Sir Thomas J. Lipton, *Leaves from the Lipton Logs* (London, n.d.), pp. 165–168. The most recent biography of Lipton is Alex Waugh, *The Lipton Story: A Centennial Biography* (London, 2013).
72 *TA*, 1 March 1892, p. 863.
73 Lipton, *Leaves from the Lipton Logs*, pp. 170–171.
74 Taylor letters, 12 June 1890. The *TA* also reported in 1887 that 'Ceylon teas are

somewhat higher in price, but they can be relied on for purity ... For flavour they are incomparable.' *TA*, 1 October 1887, p. 230.

75 Gary B. Magee and Andrew S. Thompson, *Empire and Globalisation: Networks of People, Goods and Capital in the British World, c.1850–1914* (Cambridge, 2010), p. 156.
76 *TA*, 1 July 1890, p. 37; Lipton, *Leaves from the Lipton Log*, pp. 174–175.
77 Lipton, *Leaves from the Lipton Log*, pp. 175–176.
78 *TA*, 1 September 1890, p. 235.
79 Ibid., 1 February 1892, p. 589.
80 Anandi Ramamurthy, *Imperial Persuaders: Images of Africa and Asia in British Advertising* (Manchester, 2003), p. 109.
81 Ibid., p. 123.
82 *TA*, 1 September 1890, p. 187.
83 'Ceylon upcountry farming report by Peppercorn', *TA*, 1 March 1890, p. 640.
84 Rajaratnam, 'The Ceylon tea industry', p. 186.
85 *TA*, 1 September 1890, pp. 187, 235.
86 Ibid., 1 February 1892, p. 589.
87 Lipton, *Leaves from the Lipton Log*, p. 179.
88 'On the hills in September', *OCO*, 21 September 1875, p. 300.
89 *OCO*, 20 August 1879, p. 662.
90 'A veteran on Ceylon planting prospects', *TA*, 1 August 1888, p. 109.
91 'The tea-planting enterprize in Ceylon', *OCO*, 20 June 1890, p. 643.
92 Taylor letters, 27 March 1882.
93 'The tea enterprize in Ceylon: Especially with reference to the redemption of unprofitable or abandoned coffee land', *WCO*, 18 July 1882, p. 592.
94 'The tea controversy', *WCO*, 4 November 1882, p. 956.
95 'Ceylon teas from & old young estates: and alleged deterioration' [sic], *TA*, 1 June 1886, p. 809.
96 'Ceylon tea statistics: Prices and grouping of districts', *TA*, 1 July 1887, p. 5
97 'Our planting industries', *WCO*, 17 April 1883, p. 318.
98 Taylor letters, 15 December 1884.
99 Rajaratnam, 'The Ceylon tea industry', p. 175.
100 Wenzlhuemer, *From Coffee to Tea Cultivation*, p. 84.
101 Taylor letters, 18 July 1889.
102 Rajaratnam, 'The Ceylon tea industry', p. 180.
103 Taylor letters, 23 October 1890.
104 Ibid., 28 July 1891.
105 Rajaratnam, 'The Ceylon tea industry', pp. 175–176.
106 Wenzlhuemer, *From Coffee to Tea Cultivation*, p. 88.
107 Rajaratnam, 'The Ceylon tea industry', pp. 179–180; Wenzlhuemer, *From Coffee to Tea Cultivation*, p. 88.
108 Rajaratnam, 'The Ceylon tea industry', p. 183.
109 'The Ceylon tea industry', *TA*, 1 July 1892, p. 43.
110 'Some of the oldest tea in Ceylon: Loole-Condura fields', *TA*, 1 September 1893, p. 244.

5

A planter's life

Ceylon's natural environment underwent huge changes during the nineteenth century due to the importation of new crops, above all the coffee tree from Ethiopia, cinchona from the Andes, and tea from the Himalayas.[1] These all presented challenges of adjustment for the planter class. Here, we examine the responses to such transformations through the prism of James Taylor's contemporary correspondence. While other planters also wrote about their lives in Ceylon, the surviving material is predominantly found in their retrospective memoirs and does not always convey a sense of change over time. The range of topics and depth of detail in Taylor's letters also allow us to go beyond existing academic studies of plantation life, such as James Webb's *Tropical Pioneers*, which largely focuses on environmental issues, and James Duncan's exploration of 'race' in Ceylon in the context of tropical degeneration.[2] What changes and continuities are evident in planting life in Ceylon during the mid-to-late nineteenth century? While several aspects of 'a planter's life' feature throughout other chapters in this book, four key themes are considered below: environment; health; living conditions; and social relations.

A new environment

When he arrived at Naranghena in 1852, Taylor confronted strikingly different natural surroundings to those he had left in Scotland. They made a big impression on him, so much so that his early letters are crammed with evocative descriptions of the strange, new environment in which he found himself. One of the first tasks given him was the clearance of jungle on the estate. At Loolecondera, for which he would be largely responsible, this meant the removal of around three hundred acres of forest before any planting could begin. He described it as an 'impenetrable mass with underwood and climbing plants with prickles and poisonous or useless fruit'.[3] He added in awe, 'There are enormous trees of 10 and 11 feet circumference of very hard wood red coloured like Mahogany. Others are yellow tinged. We have no trees of the fir or pine kinds here.' The name Loolecondera itself, Taylor claimed, meant in the Sinhalese language 'the destruction of good timber', and, 'were the timber that is lying rotting here in Scotland it would be of very great value'.[4] He may have had in mind the historic deforestation of Britain that created massive demand at home for imported timber, not least in Scotland, which had long suffered from a paucity of natural woodland.[5]

Taylor was concerned that his first boss, George Pride, wanted the forest felled in its entirety without confirming whether it would all be planted. Indeed, that task, Taylor reckoned, 'would have frightened every coolie from the place to have seen that Jungle coming down and think that they had it all to plant'.[6] Here, Taylor showed some concern for their feelings and his own need to secure an adequate labour force. The Sinhalese, on the other hand, were already adept foresters as they 'cut down a lot of the jungle for a kind of grain they raise and so spoiled it for coffee which requires virgin soil to be planted in'.[7] The scope of the work was so daunting that he predicted, 'I suppose we'll be clearing the top of Loole Condera Rock in a few years more.'[8] Taylor also soon recognised the ecological side-effects of these interventions: 'The climate of the coffee districts is getting undoubtedly drier owing to the felling of the forests.'[9]

Here was striking evidence of the impact on the natural environments of the development of the plantation economy. It has been said that imperialism was 'inseparable from the history of global environmental change',[10] and the 'tropical pioneers' in Ceylon, as James Webb describes them, carried out the most extensive removal of rainforests and the conversion of vast areas for planting on a scale which was greater than in any other region in the British Empire.[11] This widespread deforestation took place largely between 1840 and 1870, due to the huge expansion in the cultivation of coffee, and resulted in significant ecological change.[12] In particular, the transformation was responsible for the massive loss of topsoil in the middle and upper highlands, which limited the options for later alternative land use.[13] But Webb notes that planter practices followed on from the *chena* cultivation of the Kandyans, who were the 'only settled farmers in Asia to make extensive use of slash-and-burn' methods which eliminated even more highland rainforest than the expansion of the plantation economy in Victorian times.[14] With the disappearance of forest cover and soil, the land around Loolecondera is now 'unproductive', although efforts are underway to rehabilitate it, drawing on knowledge of the woodland that previously existed there.[15]

Besides cutting down and removing trees with his Sinhalese work-force, Taylor supervised road building on the estate. The roads were cut in zigzags along the side of the hill or, as Taylor described it further, 'along the sides of the brae winding about with a slope on them so as to get to the top of the estate and to the different parts of it'.[16] Indeed, there was not a level piece of ground to be found on the rugged terrain except some paddy fields.[17] He described with awe the 'hills rising in terraces of very steep faces' and perpendicular rocks climbing 200 to 500 feet, with level land on top (Figure 5.1).[18] The rocks were

5.1 The magnificent scenery of Loolecondera.

'extremely hard and sharp pointed and contains many pieces of white quartz and is regularly stratified'.[19]

Using compass directions, Taylor further described the surroundings in detail to his father, including the neighbouring estates of Gonavy and Wal Oya and the magnificent Loolecondera rock which still impresses visitors to the area today (Figure 5.2): 'you see a rock which would make you stop and look facing you. The ridge there ends in a perpendicular bare cliff of very great height and not very broad so it resembles the stern of some large war ship in shape and turns back a little in a cliff at the other side when it joins the highest part of the Naranghena hill.'[20] The stone walls he had constructed without mortar followed the building practices of his native Scotland and can still be seen at Loolecondera. Taylor admitted that he might be thought obsessive about his new surroundings: 'You will think I write lots about the scenery but if you saw it you would not think I said too much all the time.'[21] His admiration for and portrayal of his environs differed significantly from his contemporary William Boyd, who claimed that planters 'have little sympathy with either the sublime or the romantic in scenery'.[22]

Central to some of Taylor's commentary about the environment of Ceylon were comparisons with nostalgic recollections of 'home', a familiar reaction of migrants in the new lands. Many large and small brooks ran through the estate, but, he noted evocatively, they 'are not like our streams at home. They are just a quantity of water tumbling about amidst large rocks and deep holes in the bottom of a deep cut about as much water runs in each of the two largest of these as in the "Luther" at Denmill after a shower of rain and our ears are continually feasted by the noise of it.'[23] Five years later, Taylor returned to allusions from home. Most of the stars he saw in the sky at night were familiar: 'The greater part of those I see are the same as you see at home … Those that you look southward to I see over head and all or nearly all farther north than the pole star I never see.' He reckoned that a nearby hill resembled 'Ben Macdui the highest in Scotland', which was situated west of Auchenblae.[24] Indeed,

5.2 '[I]t resembles the stern of some large war ship in shape': Kondegalla Rock at Loolecondera.

wherever Scots went it seems that mountains 'conjured up Scotland' to them.[25] These reference points also helped his family in Scotland to imagine the new land where he had made his home.

These reminders of home meant that Taylor was not solely concerned with environmental transformations in Ceylon, but also in Auchenblae. In one poignant musing he reflected on the alterations taking place there:

> By your letter I understand that changes are making there so that although I be spared and enabled once more to see the place of my birth I fear that the joy will be mixed with reflections of what it once was for I suspect it will not then be in the same state as I left it. As yet I mind every thing as distinctly as though I had left it yesterday even every cut in the road and every large stone and all the blue hills and knows [*knolls*]. Be particular in letting me know all these small changes for they will be very interesting to me[.][26]

Some scholars have suggested that Scots took a distinctive approach to their new colonial environments. John MacKenzie, for instance, has argued that the writings of the Scottish Enlightenment may have aided them in responding to and understanding alien and exotic lands. But perhaps even more influential for those in Ceylon was the on-the-ground training that some migrants had received as gardeners.[27] Botany was also taught in some Scottish universities and Scots became central to the development of botanical science. The Scottish gardening tradition and garden design also proved influential elsewhere during the eighteenth and nineteenth centuries.[28] The Calcutta botanical gardens, for instance, were dominated by Scots who had been trained at King's College, Aberdeen.[29] Nevertheless, there is no evidence that they had a similar influence on the botanical gardens of Ceylon.

A visitor to Loolecondera today can still see many of the changes Taylor and his workers made to the landscape of the estate. It is also possible to encounter much of the rich wildlife that featured in his letters home, including 'monkeys, birds and serpents'.[30] Poisonous cobras were, and still are, found in the area. On one occasion, Taylor

> saw the ugly head of one lying within an inch of my shoe. I lifted my foot pretty quickly and it stopped and looked at me for some time with its big eyes and slowly moved down a small bit when I passed by and just as I was going the same way again there was another smaller one which I just almost stept over. It got up on a branch and there it fissed and darted out its fork. I got a stick and gave it a touch when it vanished through the jungle[.][31]

To scare them, off Taylor and his workers thumped sticks on the ground or stoned the snakes to death.[32] Henry Stiven also wrote about them: 'There are very few obnoxious reptiles or the like of which we hear such wonders at home. I have only seen one serpent of any size it being about 12 feet in length.'[33] Various animals of the cat family roamed the estate, including 'chaeters'. Jackals prowled in the neighbourhood and on at least one occasion took Taylor's hens.[34] Wild elephants on Loolecondera were less common, due to the steep terrain, but Taylor knew that some could be found not far away because of the evidence of their tracks and dung.[35] Some planters had closer encounters with elephants. Taylor told how on one occasion one majestic beast entered 'a fellows Bungalow (or rather only the verandah) lately just over the hill from me chasing out his wife and children never minding any of the people about and soon after went quietly away'.[36]

Ceylon in the nineteenth century was a 'prime sporting paradise' and, as in India, hunters ruthlessly sought elephants, tigers, and wild boar.[37] Taylor reported on the hunting expedition of one Major Milman, with 'Tyndall a great Ceylon sportsman'. William Tindall, who also owned estates in Ceylon, was with Milman and allegedly killed an elephant that charged them. The bullet to halt the animal went through Milman's shoulder. Taylor admiringly noted, 'That was a good shot. There is only two shots when a bullet will kill an elephant. One in his forehead about the middle and well up the other somewhere behind his ears.'[38] Shooting an elephant was regarded as prime evidence of 'courageous hunting in the sub-continent' and Tindall gained a reputation in this regard.[39]

He even showed Robert Boyd Tytler evidence of a rogue elephant kill: the point of its tail.[40] These 'trophies' could earn hunters awards of between seven and ten shillings offered by the government in an effort to protect the island's crops.[41] This is ironic, given that tamed elephants were used on the construction of roads and railways and to carry and transport heavy objects.[42] By the late 1870s, however, elephants were legally protected, partly because the government was no longer willing to provide the payments for killing them. Indeed, the stock had become so depleted that the animals no longer posed much danger to crops.[43]

Sometimes the planters made fun of those who came to Ceylon to hunt. Taylor told his father one story of a rogue elephant who 'runs after all he sees even follows their foot marks along the roads after they have passed to get at them. All my neighbours on that side have had escapes from him.' On one occasion, in 1858, planters hatched a plot to convince some visitors from New Zealand that a dangerous beast was on their trail. A fellow planter 'imitated the trumpeting of the Elephant' while his friends shook bushes around the party. According to Taylor, 'The traveller said he was making a book of his travels and that this would be the best adventure in it perhaps of the kind. So we shall probably have the whole story in a book.'[44] The commercialisation of hunting proceeded apace in the interior alongside the expansion of the plantations.[45] Yet the widespread slaughter of wild animals soon brought devastating consequences. In 1859 Taylor noted, 'there is no hunting here now. Every thing worth hunting is hunted out in the district almost.'[46]

While there is no evidence that Taylor himself hunted elephants, he did go after wild boar, albeit rarely, with his neighbour Mr Bannerman, who shot one from a tree: 'It was a fine large beast and we got some coolies to carry it home for a leg of it'. Unlike beef, 'Wild pork I think is the best eating I know in Ceylon.' Dogs were crucial to the hunt and Taylor's general indifference to hunting was because he was 'not fond of the dog kind and would not be bothered with them'.[47]

Less threatening wildlife on the estate included the 'exceedingly beautiful birds', although 'they dont sing any. We have a sort of a bird which I suppose to be a humming bird which flies about in the gardens among the flowers.' Wild cocks, hens, and deer roamed in the vicinity. Taylor found a porcupine's quill in 1852, an experience still common on the estate today. Cattle, meanwhile, were predominantly kept to provide manure for the estates. They also produced milk, but not butter and cheese.[48]

Health

Just as rain, wind, and drought influenced Ceylon's diverse crops, so too did the country's tropical environment have a significant effect on the health of planters. Ceylon was a breeding ground for a range of ailments, and lethal diseases such as dysentery and 'fever' cut down many young men during their time on the island, as they did throughout India and Asia. William Boyd recalled in a memoir which looked back to the 1840s and 1850s that

> many hundreds of kindly Scots, who, cut off in the very prime and vigour of their manhood ... [lie] under the dank weeds and wiry grasses which cover their neglected graves ... Left to the care of native servants, many of these young men died friendless and neglected in some distant jungle bungalow, from fever, from cholera, diarrhoea, or dysentery ... So great has been the mortality amongst young men whom I knew, that out of 17 who lived twenty-seven years ago within a few miles of me in one district, only two, myself and another, now survive[.][49]

Cholera, with its symptoms of 'mental depression and internal distress, followed by vomiting, stomach cramps, and acute diarrhea', was a feared killer.[50] It could be transferred by water, food, and bodily fluids. Victims became weak and thirsty, cold and clammy, and suffered from cramp. Startlingly, as one description had it, 'The tips of their tongues and their lips turn blue, their eyes sink back into their sockets, and their skin hangs limply on their bodies.'[51] Victims usually died from dehydration within hours of contracting the disease.[52] Cholera's third pandemic in Asia occurred between 1841 and 1859.[53] All told, around 60 per cent of those who contracted cholera in the nineteenth century were likely to die from the disease.[54] Among its victims in 1857 was David Moir, a cousin of Peter Moir and a maternal relative of Taylor's. He had been in Ceylon just five years and was only thirty-one years of age when he contracted cholera. As the twenty-two-year-old Taylor grimly told it, 'He was seized with it about 8 O'Clock in the morning and died at 4 O'Clock in the afternoon was carried into Kandy that night and buried next day. Poor fellow he was very lively at a dinner party I believe the night before. David was a brother of Peter's wife; a son of the Bishop; and Peter's cousin.'[55] Henry Stiven and his wife were similarly struck down in their prime, with Taylor inscribing beside a photograph (Figure 5.3) that Stiven 'died at the Galle face Boarding House Colombo on the afternoon of Wednesday 24th May 1865, and was buried next morning, at Colombo.' His wife died less than two years later.[56]

While Moir and Stiven died in towns renowned for their heat, the Loolecondera climate, as with much of Ceylon's highlands, is generally temperate.[57] Even so, it could cause difficulties as Taylor outlined. This included an early threat to his health a few weeks after his arrival in Ceylon, possibly the result of infected food or water: 'I am in excellent health and have been so all along yet except a week that I was ill with a Diarhoea or Dysentery which I believe is the most common and fatal disease Europeans are liable to here along with fever.' After a period of recuperation, during which he took castor oil and other powders, he recovered.[58] A few months later, however, he wrote of 'a very severe attack of illness' as a result of which he spent a month in Kandy for treatment. The procedure undertaken to save his life involved applying three

5.3 Taylor records Henry Stiven's death in 1865 on a photograph taken two years earlier.

dozen leeches to his body. His colleagues, he wrote, 'thought I was dying but thanks to God I am yet alive and in good spirits'.[59]

In 1857, a few years after these events, Taylor thought himself 'a little stout about the shoulders' and 'the strongest man in the district European and native though no doubt many in Ceylon are stronger. I'm very healthy though I feel the climate taking affect in weakening me.'[60] An unhealthy season two years later, however, resulted in 'a great deal of sickness among Europeans. I am as well as usual but I'm tired of this heat and wish the wind and rain would begin and cool us that is if there is not too much wet weather.'[61] Writing at the end of May, Taylor was anticipating the south-west monsoon, which lasted from May to September.

If European settlers were vulnerable, even more so were the Tamils who migrated from southern India to work on the coffee plantations of Ceylon. Their mortality rates were horrendous. One contemporary made the extraordinary claim that 'you have buried in Ceylon over the last seventeen years a quarter of a million of immigrant coolies, or over 25 per cent of the total Immigrant coolies for the same period'.[62] It was not until 1872, however, that medical care for them started to improve. That year, the government investigated the provision of aid for workers, a policy supported by most planters.[63] A smallpox outbreak among Taylor's coolies the same year reminded him of his vaccination years earlier, 'but it did not take effect and I got the small-pox. Every year since I have mostly got all the coolies on the place who could not show marks of small-pox or satisfactory marks of vaccination, vaccinated. Many of them have thus been vaccinated a second time, but I have never seen any effects of that even so bad as I have seen from a first vaccination, and no case at all serious either from a first or second vaccination.'[64] Normally, Taylor seems to have been in good health, as he hardly commented on any illnesses again until 1886 when, aged fifty-one years, he mentioned that he had a touch of sciatica in his right hip joint.[65] Further, there is no evidence in the correspondence that he was ever troubled during his life in the tropics by the kind of mental or psychological disorders that afflicted some European migrants.[66]

Living conditions

When Taylor first arrived in Ceylon he lived with the superintendent of the estate at a cost of £48 a year, which included everything except his clothing. He also spent a short spell in fellow planter Mr Howie's lodgings.[67] It was from Naranghena that Taylor provided an account of the interior of the bungalow he shared. In it were a comfortable bed and a table with a drawer for writing, in addition to his books, pens, pencils, ink bottles and penknives 'as if I were a man of business', together with matches to light his lamp in the morning. A tumbler filled with flowers sat on the table 'to relieve the business like look'. The room held a washing and dressing table with glass, combs, brushes, shaving utensils, washing basin, and jug. At the foot of the bed was a clothes stand. He kept his crockery, saucepans, frying pans, and tumblers under the bed in boxes. Thin net curtains were hung to keep out mosquitos.[68] Despite Taylor's possessing shaving equipment, it did not take long for his physical features to alter as a result of the challenges of shaving in Ceylon:

> I've got a kind of a beard and moustache & Whiskers and all the paraphernalia of the hair line not any of them particularly luxurient but a fair average at least I generally shave all but the whisker once a month or going to Kandy and it is always half an inch long or more before the next time I go to Kandy. I sometimes feel inclined to let it grow as it likes as many here do but I find it gets very troublesome after a month's growth so off it comes again and I never brush or trim or train it but let it bristle or twist or turn as it likes till I be going to Kandy.[69]

His father was apparently horrified, as Taylor protested to him, 'I'm no "fright" at all with the beard. I only allow it to grow to a certain length not for fancy but to save trouble. I have not used a razor for 8 months or more and dont mean to do again' (Figure 5.4)[70]

5.4 'I'm no "fright" at all with the beard': James Taylor, 1863.

To the front of the bungalow, a verandah gave protection from the sun and rain. The sofa and chairs there enabled Taylor to sit in the fresh air and observe estate life. At one end of the bungalow were the cookhouse and stable, while at the other was a garden.[71] There is little to suggest that he had 'his house in great disorder', as claimed of other planters.[72]

When first on Loolecondera in 1852, Taylor shared 'a sort of Bungalow made of boards' with a Portuguese assistant superintendent. It was, he stated,

> a temporary affair constructed of a few posts about the corners with boards nailed up across overlapping each other like slates as open as well can be with about a foot of opening above between that and the thatch at which when ever the light is out at night a flock of rats from the jungle beside us come running in looking out for something to eat and then the wind of which we have plenty at this season of the year blows a perfect hurricane in the Bungalow sometimes so as to put out the lamp.

Facing south-east, the bungalow had two cairns of rocks in front of it and small caves nearby. At the end of the building, a fast stream of water fell twenty feet into a ravine. Between it and the bungalow was a small coolie line, a row of basic huts to house estate workers. Across the stream to the west was a 'steep ascent with a flat piece of Land on the top'.[73]

Four years later, Taylor wrote that his new bungalow at Loolecondera was nearly ready, and sent home a pencil drawing of it. It faced east south-east and Taylor considered it 'by no means a fine one but it is neat and I have made it very substantially and the situation is magnificent'. It was forty-three feet long, with a front door of glass, while the five-foot-wide windows of the main rooms opened in two halves on hinges. The floor was made of boards while the verandah was 'lime plaster smooth and hard'. There were banks on both sides, with a steep drop and retaining wall in front and a 'very steep hill' growing coffee rising behind the bungalow. The coolie lines were nearby, while small ravines with streams 'just tumble down among large boulders and stones'.[74]

Taylor believed his bungalow to be 'the envy and admiration of all the chaps in the district and if I had made it from the plan I got it would have been a most incommodious insignificant senseless thing'. In Pride's absence, Taylor had altered the original drawings and believed that his boss would approve, despite its expense.[75] Such extravagance, at least in the eyes of his proprietors, was not, then, simply confined to his estate expenditure as we saw in chapter 2. In both his residential and working life, however, Taylor believed in quality. With such a 'splendid house to live in and a horse to ride about upon', Taylor soon reckoned himself 'quite a *sh*entleman'.[76] He expressed pleasure in his building achievements several years later: 'On most places the thatching of a house for instance lasts only a year and few can make a roof without drops – except on their Bungalow they dont care much. I thatch a building and it always lasts five and six years and never has a single drop.'[77]

For Taylor and other Victorian men, domesticity was often central to their masculinity.[78] His house both reflected his achievements and connected his private and working life. Just as his father had practised as a wright on the family's croft at home, so Taylor's first attempts at processing tea in Ceylon took place on the verandah of his bungalow.

But, unlike for other planters who suggested plantation life was 'unintellectual',[79] Taylor's home was also a place to refresh the mind. Indeed, a striking feature of Taylor's life in Ceylon was the amount of time he devoted to cerebral matters. He spent his evenings in his early years learning the Malabar and Sinhala languages from one Seena Tamby who had been 'educated at the Madjura Seminary, an American mission station'.[80] American missionaries had come to Ceylon in 1813 after the London Missionary Society withdrew, and the seminary at Batticotta proved 'a powerful evangelising force' until its closure.[81] Taylor also studied maths, algebra, geometry, Latin, and Greek, and read often.[82] His father was asked to send him Humphrey Prideaux's

> Connection of the Old & New Testaments which you bought from the Book Binder and any thing else you like to send in that way will be most acceptable in this Lone Wilderness to spend an hour or two at night. As for Religious Books I dont suppose they are scarcely to be found in the Jungle. The Books I have got here with me I find very good companions. I am all impatience for a lot more. If I had those I want out I would be as happy as a King.[83]

In 1859 Taylor received other books 'of a very suitable sort and very readable especially the lectures'.[84] This quest for knowledge had clearly arisen from his schooling in Scotland and initial training as a teacher. Indeed, Taylor reckoned himself 'above most Planters … But of course as they are above me I hold my peace though they are sometimes talking the greatest nonsense on scientific subjects.'[85] The practical expertise he believe he held prompted a further reflection that he was 'the most learned of all Mr Pride's superintendents though I am sorry I cant say I am a learned man'.[86] Taylor, not yet twenty when making these comments, was clearly developing self-awareness of his capabilities. Even so, he remained cautious about his intellectual capacity: 'I know I was as learned at 14 as I am now though I can now think with twice the force and soon overcome difficulties that would have baffled me then; and now I'm not likely to become more learned.'[87]

Leisure reading on religious subjects took on great significance for him because the nearest church was about eighteen miles away, in Kandy. 'I think it would be a good thing if there were a few ministers to travel about visiting the estates stopping at one always on sunday or something of that sort', he remarked in 1852.[88] Later that year, recuperating at Kandy during a period of illness, Taylor received a visit from a Baptist minister in the absence of a Presbyterian one: 'I got from him some shingalee Tracts &c part of which

I have distributed in the village. I had some difficulty in find[*ing*] people that could read them. It is something to know that the word of God is now in the village if it was not before.'[89]

When not indoors, Taylor spent considerable time in the estate gardens. At Naranghena he had a flower garden and hedge of roses and intended to develop a vegetable garden.[90] At his bungalow on Loolecondera in 1857, he asked his father to send flower seeds from 'home' to place in 'the finest gardens in the district'. Previous seeds had done well, although some failed. The marigolds his uncle sent, he noted, were a weed on the roadsides, while his Tamil workers planted them around their altar. Especially desired from home were seeds for whins, broon, gowans, tansies, larkspurs, pansies, marigolds, hollyhocks, daisies, and 'innumerable other things' which he believed would grow well.[91] He asked his father to obtain these from the Monboddo estate gardener. Upon receipt, Taylor thought the African marigolds 'splendid' but 'others are not doing much good and a few varieties never sprung at all'.[92] 'As a source of amusement', Henry Stiven similarly 'commenced a Flower Garden and Kitchen Garden'. He reckoned, 'Ferns and climbers are the most interesting plants I see.'[93] Both men also commented on the island's fruit, including peaches, Egyptian oranges, bananas, and plantains.[94] For Stiven, 'the best are the pineapple – plantains Melon Orange Lime shaddok and Cocoanut. The second I have named is the best and safest for Europeans and is much used.'[95] Taylor attributed the success of his gardening enterprise to the absence of seasons: 'there are no seasons here. We can sow at all times.'[96]

In reflecting on food in Ceylon, he still recalled agricultural conditions at home. In June 1852, shortly after his arrival in Ceylon and towards the end of the potato blight which had ravaged Ireland and the Highlands of Scotland, he wished to know 'what sort the crops are if the Potatoes are diseased … if the cows have been eating all the corn and how many new cows we have got … The cripple Bird will be busy laying eggs and building nests now.' He further mused, 'You will be now thinking of cutting Hay but by the time you get it you will be thinking the corn nearly ready I am wondering how the turnips are doing if the flies have eaten lots as usual I hope you have not had to deeple in Swedes. The Potatoe leaves I hope are not blackning. Write soon before the throng of the harvest begin and let me know all about home again.'[97] His next letter, of December that same year, conveyed concern that the potatoes have 'gone wrong again. We have got some here but they are not so good as with you.'[98] By the end of the decade, he again sought news about the crops 'and how the potatoes have fared with regard to disease'.[99]

Unlike other British planters who were said to prefer a diet of meat and vegetables,[100] Taylor preferred Ceylonese food, although this was likely due to its ready availability rather than his immersion in Ceylonese life. He began his day at 5.30am with boiled sago and sugar, then set the labourers to work before returning to the bungalow at 10.30am for a breakfast of rice and curry made of 'cocoa nut milk and some corriander seed some several spicy sort of things and is boiled with sweet potatoes mixed or eggs, beef &c &c any thing mostly and is eaten mixed with Rice'. Between 11am and 4pm he supervised the labour force of between one hundred and two hundred labourers in their tasks of weeding, pruning, and gathering the crops. Dinner was usually around 7pm, 'shortly after the lamp is lighted', as he 'cant enjoy it with day light'. His evening meal usually consisted of 'sweet Potatoes and a small piece of cocoa nut and rice and currie. The cocoa-nut milk is made by scraping down the nut and pressing the scrapings amon[*g*]st water till all the juice is pressed out then this is the milk.' Taylor's milk came from his forty cows but it was 'not like milk at home nor near so good ... it does not get sour but quite tasteless and then stinks our butter .... [which] mostly always tastes like cheese'. Later, he preferred to use tinned milk for tea. Indeed, the cattle of the district were 'poor affairs compared with cattle in Scotland'. They were, he reported, small and 'mostly all belly ... their flesh is tough and tasteless like leather'.[101] This may have resulted from 'indiscriminate breeding'.[102] Sheep 'are as bad only their flesh is rather easier to chew'. If alone, Taylor would have a bottle of hot porter and sugar with a biscuit, then read a book or occasionally do some writing. 'I don't drink nor smoke nor snuff', he declared, but admitted to sometimes playing the accordion, although he confessed that he could barely tolerate it.[103] He normally retired to bed at 9.30 in the evenings, but in later years, following a nap after dinner, went to the tea house between 11pm and midnight to 'see the night work finished'.[104] He tended to linger an extra hour in bed on Sundays, except when the sun was 'feverishly hot', and spent the day reading, gardening, and distributing the weekly supply of rice to his workers.[105]

Taylor's living conditions contrasted dramatically with those of his workforce who lived in the coolie lines: 'they are just a large long building of sticks and mud divided into rooms on both sides each with a door or only a doorway for there is no door but just a thing made of grass and sticks'. These were closed at night, with seven to eight men sleeping in each room.[106] Although the cost of erecting his own lines is not recorded, in 1862 an estate at Hannagala built lines to house forty to sixty men at an outlay of £45.[107]

Money was a perennial concern for James Taylor throughout his life in Ceylon. In the early 1850s he claimed to be able to live on less than £4 a month by limiting his 'expenses for food to one shilling a day and I drink water only'. He further kept costs low by purchasing 'vegetables or fruits from the villagers'. Even so, he still made use of a worker who would travel each week to Kandy to acquire his supplies. All told, he calculated that his food expenses totalled thirty shillings a month, with an additional £1 paid to his servant. At this time, however, Taylor lived with a fellow planter and they made one servant cater for both their needs.[108] He seems to have regarded his servants with some contempt, as he wrote some years later:

> We get lots of money but every thing we buy costs in proportion nearly and we have servants but how much comfort is there in the attendance of these ignorant; dishonest; black fellows. Of course we must have them to cook for us and keep the house clean as we nor our wives if we had them could not work nor stand cooking at a fire and we cannot live here for ever. We must make some money and get out of this or our life is thrown away and no enjoyment got in it.[109]

Clothing also cost money. New shoes lasted only a month, with Taylor noting almost four months after his arrival that 'The last of the three pairs I brought from home are nearly done.'[110] Little had changed by 1869, when he advised that thick-soled shoes or boots were necessary 'to walk on strong roads and scramble amongst rocks and wet earth'.[111] Loose cotton outfits, such as white or blue striped cotton trousers, shirts, and waistcoats, generally lasted a year but this depended on the work of the servants. Taylor noted the damage caused to clothes by dhobies who 'soon make holes in all the things they get to work by thrashing them on the stones, and rocks in the stream. Washing in tubs is unknown.'[112] Planters therefore had to be adept at mending clothes. While James Moir proved 'a peculiarly good hand at house keeping', Taylor admitted that he could not 'look after my stockings'.[113] His sense of humour also emerged when writing of more formal attire such as dress suits or white jackets, which were generally only worn for church, balls, or dining with ladies.[114] Sometimes a woollen coat was required which was short, 'close to the body and button all the way down if wanted with no tails. Generally they are worn a little longer with very short attempts at a tail but as I'm not ashamed of my backside if covered only with a thin cotton trouser I have never any tails to mine.'[115]

Taylor's letters reveal a constant need to save in order to 'send something home'. Immediately after his arrival in Ceylon, he estimated he could retain £9 a quarter from his pay of £20 10s every four months.[116] In 1857, however, when he became manager of both the Loolecondera and Wal Oya estates, he received a combined salary of £275 but quickly told his family at home not to 'think of me as a rich man. I'll tell you when that takes place.'[117] By September, his salary had gone up again to £300.[118] He had hoped in 1858 to achieve £400 a year but heavy estate expenditure made that unlikely.[119] By the mid-1870s, Taylor stood 'at the top of their rates of salary for superintendents' but for a number of reasons was still dissatisfied.[120] A major concern was the cost of living in Ceylon. Aged thirty-seven, he explained the predicament this way:

> I live worse or at least cheaper than many others and I live worse than I understand many tradesmen do at home, and yet it is all I can afford. Everything mostly is dear here and a vast lot of clothes and everything wanted. The servants here

> destroy and steal everything. But a respectable style as Ceylon goes must be kept up and neighbours and visitors have to be entertained accordingly at any time, and frequently. But some superintendents do save money though they are precious few.[121]

Even so, he strove to save: 'an ordinarily economical person (like myself say!) can save about a £100, a year out of about £500. It will want steadier care than many can give to do it out of £400.' Indeed, he calculated that it would take six to seven years' residence in the island before being able to save £100 a year. That meant an average of fifteen years to save £2,000, the minimum Taylor thought necessary to secure an independent retirement at home. Moreover, his post as estate superintendent was unlikely to make him rich, as the 'great agency firms' dominated the economy. His early proprietors also prohibited their superintendents from investing in estate purchases.[122] As he elaborated further in 1873: 'Money is made or lost in Ceylon by speculating in coffee or becoming proprietor. I have never had the chance of that. No one would have ever lent me money on the top of £100, or £200, on any such terms as would have left me a fair chance of doing any good. Then under K.D. & Co we are prohibited from doing anything of the sort unless we leave the employ.' Additionally, Taylor did not want to run the risk of what little savings he had being lost through speculating in land.[123] Even so, for a time he did just that, investing in a share of a cinchona estate at Nuwara Eliya around 1879. That he was able to do so was presumably a result of the new owners, A.G. Milne, taking over the estates he managed. There was, though, a caveat. If the agents, Whittall & Co., who invested with him 'become bankrupt the estate has to be sold by auction. Perhaps I could get some other firm to back me in buying it up. But what we are all coming to is a mystery. There is no money scarcely in Ceylon and no one to buy properties.' He had just 'Rs. 4500, or £450, of our money in the Bank after paying my share of Lover's Leap land'.[124] He held the land for less than two years, as it then passed to mortgagees. Less than a decade later, little had changed, due to the crash of Ceylon's silver money. Had it retained its value, Taylor reckoned he would have been worth the princely sum of £2,400. Even so, he invested his funds in shares of the new company owning the estate, while the remainder was earning interest in the bank.[125]

A further factor likely to have been holding Taylor back was his generally reserved personality. In an instructive commentary on the repercussions of his devotion to work because of his reticence, he judged that the

> best and most forward talkers get on the best though sometimes they least deserve it. I daresay I am not behind others in self conceit but then I guess I have something more tangible than talk to back it with. It's a pity I cant act the swell more. If I could go to parties and dance at Balls, and so forth, I should have been in a better position now. Only then I doubt if I should have as good a claim, or

> merit so much. I doubt if I would have studied coffee as I have, or have [*erased:* able] happened to improve on its customary cultivation.[126]

In a revealing philosophical reflection, Taylor summarised his own character, admitting that he was

> better off and possibly happier than I might have been digging in a ditch or something of that sort at home. All I know is that life seems a mighty unsatisfactory kind of an arrangement. They say that its enjoyment depends not on circumstances but the nature of the man. But I don't believe that in my case. I think rather that I am wonderfully contented with little generally, though sometimes a rebellious spirit springs up.[127]

Social life

In his memoir of life in Ceylon, British planter William Boyd recalled how planters kept an 'open house … our house, our servants, our horses, our guns were all at the disposal of our neighbours or our visitors'.[128] But in contrast to many of his fellow planters who met regularly at social events and business meetings, Taylor lived a life of relative isolation from European society. This was especially the case in the early years in Ceylon. In June 1852, just weeks after his arrival, Taylor sat down to read the first of many missives from his father: 'I have just to-night received your Letter which has been the greatest comfort I have had since I came here.' It is hardly surprising therefore that he set great store by his regular correspondence with his kindred in Scotland: 'tell my Aunt at St Cyrus that I shall write to her next mail and also Grandfather in Arbroath … Their letters will be a great comfort to me in this lonely wilderness where I see not a white person scarcely ever.'[129] As Taylor stressed to his father, 'I think if you knew what a pleasure it is to get news from home here I would get more. When it comes near the time of the mail arriving I am on the outlook and sadly dis*s*apointed if nothing comes.'[130] On another occasion he tried a more belligerent tactic to cajole the family to maintain contact with him: 'I dont know what is ado about home now but this is worse than ever I was especially as through the whole long winter forenights you have never got time to write nor even send a newspaper … I dont know when I may get any words. Perhaps there is something on the way but I have so often hoped so and been dis*s*appointed that I have little faith in it.' Even when Taylor's father did write, his son was not satisfied: 'I wish you would write me a letter a long one not just a sheet of note paper scrawled over with a few lines of text.'[131] Henry Stiven also recorded his remote situation. Although he could see Peter Moir's bungalow nineteen miles away and his residence was only 1½ miles from his manager's, 'In such an out of the way sort of place I often feel very lonely.'[132] Planters like Taylor, however, were never completely cut off and maintained

5.5 James Taylor and unidentified male, c.1863.

regular contact with assistants on the estates. For Taylor in the 1850s, this included one born in Spain whose 'father was a scotchman of Fifeshire and his mother an Irish woman'.[133] On Wal Oya he was supported by an Irishman from Cork, while another of his assistants was lured away by his relative Peter Moir. Taylor dismissively considered it 'not much of a loss. I dont think him a very excellent hand nor very able.'[134]

Planters undertook to visit each other, and Taylor recorded in his letters those occasions when fellow planters would call on him.[135] In the 1850s, such visits were infrequent for, as he admitted, 'I never go to call on them and so none come here. Though a neighbour here has promised to give a call with some when he happens to be conveying them past this to his place. They have not come yet but if they do I will make them welcome.' When urged to call back, he admitted, 'I'd scarcely promise to return the visit. I would rather make a vague promise and be [*word illegible*] long in fulfilling it.' Taylor's relatives Peter Moir and Henry Stiven made occasional visits. Mostly, however, Taylor considered himself 'a stop at home customer', preferring planters calling to see him rather than paying a visit to them: 'I like to get visits but not so much to give them'. Such communions resulted in 'a talk, a walk, a typhin, or lunch, and part or very often a visitor stops till dinner or all night sometimes.'[136] He did note, however, that 'acquaintances are expensive concerns here besides several other evils they bring'.[137]

One wonders, however, whether Taylor was entirely honest with his claims. Certainly, he had a good knowledge of the drinking prowess of his fellow planters, as is evident from a letter sent to his father in 1860 about his neighbour, Bannerman, who proposed to call at Auchenblae during a sojourn in Scotland. Taylor recommended that if Bannerman and his associates did appear, his father should supply them with

> lots of Beer or Whiskey. They are all good at drinking without getting drunk and I daresay will not be comfortable unless they get as much as would make an ordinary person drunk. They are all proprietors and above my rank on a small scale besides being all old planters of long standing. Bannerman will drink about 8 bottles of 'pale India ale' a day or nearly two bottles of whiskey and tells the most astounding crammers of stories of his adventures and doings. ... He wont get drunk but will need more than you would probably suppose to please him. I hope he will be kindly treated that is all. Brandy and 'Pale India Ale' are our drinks most used here especially the latter. Bannerman uses I think about a daily allowance of 5, bottles or so and more when in company. My allowance is a bottle a day and with extra hard work some days two bottles. We use brandy principally in a medicinal way when anything is wrong or on coming in from work wet and when anything is wrong about the stomach and so on.[138]

Taylor himself was reputed to have had the peculiar habit of opening a bottle of beer 'which he did pretty often in the old days' and pouring a little on the

5.6 Two images of three unidentified planters, one of whom resembles James Taylor.

floor. 'This was a good plan of clearing any dust from the cork out of the neck of the bottle' and 'when he had a number of visitors at his hospitable bungalow, the floor would be very wet indeed'.[139]

James Duncan has characterised planter life in Ceylon as a life of fraternity, masculine camaraderie, and homoeroticism.[140] This 'society of bachelors',[141] as Taylor termed it, was inevitable because of the relative absence of white women. Another commentator on the planting community reckoned that such exclusion from female society meant 'the polish wears off his mind' and that he 'becomes selfish'.[142] Early on, Taylor declared himself a 'confirmed bachelor' due to a lack of contact with white women, claiming to have spoken only about four times to them during the previous four years.[143] The planter William Boyd, who worked in Ceylon in the 1840s and 1850s, saw even fewer, claiming in his memoirs that he 'had not seen a European lady during the whole of my stay in Ceylon'.[144] Taylor's minimal contact with white women provoked his disdain because he believed their intentions were to secure a husband of a higher status than that of a planter. They were, he branded them in 1857, 'a despicable set … as being women they wont look at us so long as they have a chance of getting some proprietor or government official of high standing in some military office and if all that fail then we get a chance'. Even so, the twenty-two-year-old nonchalantly brushed aside his disappointment and mused that the 'heat must have dried up or melted my bump of amativeness for I dont care a penny for ladies'.[145] Three months later, he wrote an extended explanation:

> Whether that is to be attributed to the fact that there is no marriageable people here at least not suitable for me and I'm not so fond of it as to get a wife on chance from home or purpose merely to get married. Were I in the land of ladies I might be smitten but I've completely forgot about them and in fact never knew about them having left a little too early. Though I must say I would like well to get hold of a suitable one for a wife but am so convinced of the impudence of my marrying here that if I were to find one I should have a fight between passion and principle to decide whether I was to take her or not and I have no idea where a suitable one might be found to please me. I can scarcely suppose from home for I have changed and been changed since I left having had as much to do with black people as ever I had with white and certainly I'll never marry a black and am not sure if a white would suit and half and half is worse than either so I being hardly either myself I fear the class for me to select from will be very small.[146]

The following year, he reiterated his intentions to 'become an old bachelor'.[147] Despite his protestations, however, he occasionally thought of taking a wife 'to help me to better myself' although he feared what marriage might bring: 'The stupid silly extravagant ladies here would ruin any man.' Despite these misgivings, in musing on the Moirs he wistfully noted: 'I wish I were in as good a position to get a wife.'[148] For Taylor, then, economics, rather than fears of tropical influences on European women's sexuality, was to the fore.[149]

A decade later, now well into his thirties, Taylor wrote again about his marital opportunities and acknowledged that he was ill equipped to engage with the opposite sex, since he avoided balls and dinners where ladies were present. But his comments continued to cast women – and the potential offspring – in a bad light:

> Of course if a man marries he is in a perfectly hopeless condition. The wife gets sick always, and may have to live in England. The brats if there are any can be made no good of here. They learn more of the native character than the European and generally turn out worthless weakly or unprincipled, unless sent home for education. This on £500, a year can hardly be done. The wife gets old and ugly in a very few years at best in this country, and the poor planter has no hope but to grind out a miserable existence in Ceylon, and it is seldom a long existence, either.[150]

Taylor echoed here the broader fears of degeneration throughout the British Empire relating to native contact with European children.[151] He may have been thinking specifically of the children of his deceased relative Henry Stiven, who, as Figure 5.7 shows, were cared for by Sinhalese servants.

By 1873, aged thirty-seven, Taylor wrote at even greater length about his limited marital prospects, declaring that 'there is no chance of that'. He

5.7 'They learn more of the native character than the European': two images of children with local servants. The group of three children are Charlie, Margaret and Peter Stiven. The identity of the solo child is unknown.

claimed, 'I can't talk to them, I can't dance with them, nor help them off and on to their horses, &c and so I have always avoided them as much as possible. A white woman with petticoats and talking my own language would frighten me out of my wits!' Nevertheless, European women were becoming more widespread within Ceylon or, as Taylor put it, 'getting uncomfortably numerous' to the point where it was 'difficult to avoid them'. Here, however, he again declared one reason for his ambivalence by returning to his familiar obsessions about money: 'I can't afford to keep a wife in Ceylon and never will be able to do so. I have enough to do to keep myself make some small provision for myself should I live to be unfit to work here.'[152] By the time of the 1881 Census, there were almost two hundred European women aged in their thirties and forties residing in the Kandy district, and 1,655 of all ages in Ceylon. There were two and a half times as many European men in the same age groups in Kandy and almost 3,200 of all ages in Ceylon.[153]

When his father tried to encourage him to come home to wed, Taylor protested: 'Marrying has all along been beyond my reach.' As far as Ceylon was concerned, he thought it 'a very bad place' to keep a wife and family and 'may be a ruinous expense'. According to Taylor, 'We are all apt to break down out here but wives especially. I should have liked very well to have a wife but it is beyond my reach and however fortunate I may be I shall be too old before it be within my reach if ever it should be my fortune to make the necessary money. Matrimony in a Sup^ts place is only for selfish or reckless fellows.'[154] Taylor's reasons for such sustained opposition to marriage are suggested in the following chapter.

If Taylor was diffident around women in Ceylon, not all men were. His boss, G.H. Dundas, for instance, was in his opinion a 'senseless foppish fellow who knows little and likes to interfere and nothing interests him; or at any rate he seems to understand little but about horses and dinners and intriguing among women'. He recounted Dundas and John Gavin visiting the house in Kandy of a European woman 'of bad character ... but she did not like them and barred the door when one of them I forget which got out to open the door and her ladyship emptied the pisspot upon him from an upper window'.[155] Taylor's relative James Moir, meanwhile, had returned to Scotland in 1859 to seek a wife.[156] Cheekily, Taylor commented:

> to tell the truth I would not like to be a wife of him if I was a woman and would not advise any ordinary woman to take him because he'll be ill to please and then will not be much satisfaction in trying to do for he is very particular about his household affairs and has managed them so long and well himself no woman could do better[.][157]

Even had Taylor wished to marry, the difficulty of attracting a white woman to live in Ceylon was encapsulated in Peter Ryan's quip from the St Clair estate in 1865: 'there is nothing that I think of that you can do for me at home, unless you can manage to send me out a bonnie Scotch lassie in a tocher!! I fancy however if there is anything going in that way it would be rather a hard job to get them to come to Ceylon.'[158]

We turn to consider in the next chapter another aspect of Taylor's planting life, his relations with his workers, impressions of native peoples, and probably the real reason why he had no interest in marrying a white woman.

Notes

1 James L.A. Webb, *Tropical Pioneers: Human Agency and Ecological Change in the Highlands of Sri Lanka, 1800–1900* (Athens, 2002).

2 Webb, *Tropical Pioneers*; James S. Duncan, *In the Shadows of the Tropics: Climate, Race and Biopower in Nineteenth Century Ceylon* (Aldershot, 2007). See also John Weatherstone, a former planter in the twentieth century, who provides an evocative overview of the pioneers' plantation life in the nineteenth century in India and Ceylon. John Weatherstone, *The Pioneers, 1825–1900: The Early British Tea and Coffee Planters and their Way of Life* (London, 1986).

3 Taylor letters, 13 March 1852.

4 Ibid., 23 June 1852. According to one worker on Loolecondera, 'condera' means

small stream. Russell ('Rusty') Tennekoon further suggested in conversation that 'condera' means stream and 'Loole' a type of small fish.

5 By the late nineteenth century, 90 per cent of Britain's timber was imported. See William Beinart and Lotte Hughes, *Environment and Empire* (Oxford, 2007), p. 11; John M. MacKenzie, *Empires of Nature and the Nature of Empires: Imperialism, Scotland and the Environment* (East Linton, 1997), p. 68.
6 Taylor letters, 9 March 1854.
7 Ibid., 17 September 1857.
8 Ibid., 9 March 1854.
9 Ibid., c. mid-1870s; MacKenzie, *Empires of Nature and the Nature of Empires*, p. 44.
10 Beinart and Hughes, *Environment and Empire*, p. 1.
11 Webb, *Tropical Pioneers*, p. 2.
12 Ibid., p. 103.
13 Ibid., p. 150.
14 Ibid., p. 2.
15 Kamal Melvani, Peter Duncan and Priyantha Kamburegama, 'Freeing the land of the tea legacy – The case of wildflower landholding in Sri Lanka', p. 1, private document provided by Peter Duncan.
16 Taylor letters, 13 March 1852, 23 June 1852.
17 Ibid., 23 June 1852.
18 Ibid., 13 June 1856, 13 March 1852.
19 Ibid., 13 March 1852.
20 Ibid., 13 June 1856.
21 Ibid., 23 January 1858.
22 William Boyd, 'Ceylon and its pioneers', *Ceylon Literary Register*, issue 30, 10 February 1888, p. 234.
23 Taylor letters, 23 June 1852.
24 Ibid., 3 December 1857.
25 MacKenzie, *Empires of Nature and the Nature of Empires*, p. 69.
26 Taylor letters, 23 June 1852.
27 John M. MacKenzie, 'Scots and the environment of Empire', in John M. MacKenzie and T.M. Devine (eds), *Scotland and the British Empire* (Oxford, 2011), pp. 148, 162.
28 Cairns Craig, *Intending Scotland: Explorations in Scottish Culture since the Enlightenment* (Edinburgh, 2009), p. 33–34.
29 John Hargreaves cited in MacKenzie, *Empires of Nature and the Nature of Empires*, p. 67.
30 Taylor letters, 13 March 1852.
31 Ibid., 23 June 1852.
32 Ibid., 13 March 1852.
33 NLS, Fettercairn Estate Papers, Acc 4796, No. 54, Letters to Sir John Stuart Forbes, 1833–1852, Henry Stiven (Ancoombra) to Sir John Stuart Forbes (Fettercairn), 5 April 1852.
34 Taylor letters, 12 December 1852.

35 Ibid., 13 March 1852, 12 December 1852, 23 January 1858.
36 Ibid., 23 January 1858.
37 John M. MacKenzie, *The Empire of Nature: Hunting, Conservation and British Imperialism* (Manchester, 1988), pp. 178–179.
38 Taylor letters, 23 January 1858.
39 MacKenzie, *Empire of Nature*, p. 183.
40 Taylor letters, 10 July 1858.
41 MacKenzie, *Empire of Nature*, p. 184.
42 Weatherstone, *The Pioneers*, p. 110.
43 MacKenzie, *Empire of Nature*, pp. 183–185.
44 Taylor letters, 10 July 1858.
45 See, for instance, Beinart and Hughes *Environment and Empire*, p. 62.
46 Taylor letters, 27 May 1859. This period was even earlier than Samuel Baker noted in the 1870s. See MacKenzie, *Empire of Nature*, p. 179.
47 Taylor letters, 23 January 1858. MacKenzie, *Empire of Nature*, p. 178.
48 Taylor letters, 23 June 1852, 12 December 1852.
49 The memoir dates from 1888. William Boyd, 'Ceylon and its pioneers', *Ceylon Literary Register*, 16 March 1888, p. 273.
50 Philip D. Curtin, *Death by Migration: Europe's Encounter with the Tropical World in the Nineteenth Century* (Cambridge, 1989), p. 71.
51 Duncan, *In the Shadows of the Tropics*, p. 115. He cites C.L. Briggs and C. Mantini-Briggs, *Stories in the Time of Cholera: Racial Profiling During a Medical Nightmare* (Berkeley, 2003), p. 1.
52 Curtin, *Death by Migration*, p. 71.
53 Duncan, *In the Shadows of the Tropics*, p. 116, fn 72.
54 Ibid., p. 114.
55 Taylor letters, 17 September 1857. David Moir (1826–1857) was a son of Bishop David Moir (1777–1847). David's uncle, the bishop's brother, was Robert Moir (1780–1859), Taylor's maternal grandfather. David's sister Margaret Moir (1826–1899) married Peter Moir (1821–1895), a son of George Moir, another brother to the bishop. See Appendix 2. David Moir was buried at the Garrison's cemetery, Kandy, where his headstone can still be seen.
56 Henry Stiven's burial place in Colombo has not been located, although some old headstones from Galle Face were transferred to the Colombo general cemetery at Kanatte (known as the Borella cemetery). Margaret Stiven's death in February 1867 is noted in Eileen Hewson, *Graveyards in Ceylon: Tea Country Volume 3* (Wem, 2009), p. 56. She was at that time on the 'Soudoogana' [Suduganga] estate, presumably cared for by Peter Moir's family, as Moir is noted as being there in the *CO*, 2 September 1871, p. 9.
57 Webb, *Tropical Pioneers*, p. 8, notes that for every one thousand feet in altitude temperatures decrease approximately 3 to 4 degrees.
58 Taylor letters, 23 June 1852.
59 Ibid., 12 December 1852.
60 Ibid., 17 September 1857.
61 Ibid., 27 May 1859.

62 'Mr C.J. Barter on Labor', in *Proceedings of the Planters' Association, Kandy, for the year ending 17th February, 1862* (Colombo, 1862), p. 87.
63 'The Planters' Association', *OCO*, 8 June 1872, p. 228.
64 Taylor letters, 18 March 1872.
65 Ibid., 7 November 1886.
66 Duncan, *In the Shadows of the Tropics*, p. 9.
67 Taylor letters, 23 June 1852.
68 Ibid., 9 January 1853.
69 Ibid., 17 September 1857.
70 Ibid., 27 May 1859.
71 Ibid., 9 January 1853.
72 C.R. Rigg, 'On coffee planting in Ceylon', *Journal of Indian Archipelago and Eastern Asia*, 6 (1852), p. 131.
73 Taylor letters, 23 June 1852.
74 Ibid., 13 June 1856. This is similar to his description on 23 June 1852 when he noted: a 'stream of water runs fast', with housing for his workers set between the bungalow and the stream. Behind the bungalow was a steep ascent. From Taylor's description, the bungalow was likely near the site of the current Loolecondera assistant's house. This location differs from the ruins of a cabin (just a chimney remains) deep inside the estate that Loolecondera now commemorates as Taylor's. For further discussion, see chapter 8.
75 Ibid., 17 September 1857.
76 Ibid., 27 January 1857.
77 Ibid., 9 September 1860.
78 John Tosh, *A Man's Place: Masculinity and the Middle-Class Home in Victorian England* (New Haven and London, 1999), p. 2.
79 Rigg, 'On coffee planting in Ceylon', p. 130.
80 Taylor letters, 13 March 1852.
81 Revd W. Henly, 'Ecclesiastical', in Arnold Wright (ed.), *Twentieth Century Impressions of Ceylon: Its History, People, Commerce Industries and Resources* (New Delhi, 1999), p. 281. Parts of the book are available online at: https://books.google.co.nz/books?id=eUF_rS8FEoIC&pg=PA233&lpg=PA233&dq=edgar+turner+labour+on+estates+arnold+wright&source=bl&ots=IjkGmRcZif&sig=N-pfOYQ8ivo89cWTKV6yKG5wkMDU&hl=en&sa=X&ved=0ahUKEw-iE1qH9tanRAhWQq5QKHX2lAGYQ6AEIGTAA#v=onepage&q=edgar%20turner%20labour%20on%20estates%20arnold%20wright&f=false.
82 Taylor letters, 23 June 1852.
83 Ibid., 9 January 1853. Prideaux's work is *The Old and New Testaments Connected In the History of the Jews and Neighbouring Nations, from the Declensions of the Kingdoms of Israel and Judah to the Time of Christ*, 3 vols (Boston, 1823).
84 Taylor letters, 11 November 1859.
85 Ibid., 9 January 1853.
86 Ibid., 9 March 1854.
87 Ibid., 17 September 1857.
88 Ibid., 23 June 1852.

89 Ibid., 12 December 1852. A Scots Kirk at Kandy was established in 1845. Notes on the committee founded to establish the Kirk are held in University of St Andrews Special Collections, MS 38419/1/1, Papers and photographs of John Faulds.
90 Taylor letters, 9 January 1853.
91 Ibid., 3 December 1857.
92 Ibid., 10 July 1858.
93 Stiven to Forbes, 5 April 1852.
94 Taylor letters, 3 December 1857.
95 Stiven to Forbes, 5 April 1852.
96 Taylor letters, 3 December 1857.
97 Ibid., 23 June 1852.
98 Ibid., 12 December 1852.
99 Ibid., 11 November 1859.
100 Webb, *Tropical Pioneers*, pp. 53, 55.
101 Taylor letters, 13 March 1852, 23 June 1852, 12 December 1852, 17 September 1857, 15 December 1884.
102 Duncan, *In the Shadows of the Tropics*, p. 147.
103 Taylor letters, 12 December 1852, 17 September 1857.
104 Ibid., 17 September 1857, 9 September 1878.
105 Ibid., 17 September 1857, 23 June 1852.
106 Ibid., 23 June 1852.
107 NLS, Seton and Bremner Papers, MS 1928, Letters concerning Hannagalla estate, Walter Agar (Hannagalla) to Dugald Bremner, 16 December 1862.
108 Taylor letters, 23 June 1852.
109 Ibid., 27 May 1859.
110 Ibid., 23 June 1852.
111 Ibid., 30 January 1869.
112 Ibid., 13 March 1852, 17 September 1857, 30 January 1869.
113 Ibid., 27 May 1859.
114 Ibid., 30 January 1869.
115 Ibid., 17 September 1857.
116 Ibid., 23 June 1852.
117 Ibid., 27 January 1857, 24 July 1857.
118 Ibid., 17 September 1857.
119 Ibid., undated, c.1858.
120 Ibid., c. mid-1870s.
121 Ibid., 25 January 1873.
122 Ibid., 30 January 1869.
123 Ibid., 25 January 1873.
124 Ibid., 1 November 1879.
125 Ibid., 30 June 1887.
126 Ibid., mid-1870s.
127 Ibid., 25 January 1873.
128 William Boyd, 'Ceylon and its pioneers', *Ceylon Literary Register*, issue 34, 9 March 1888, p. 266.

129 Taylor letters, 23 June 1852.
130 Ibid., 12 December 1852.
131 Ibid., 9 March 1854.
132 Stiven to Forbes, 5 April 1852.
133 Ibid., 23 June 1852.
134 Ibid., 21 February 1859, 17 September 1857.
135 Ibid., 23 January 1858.
136 Ibid., 17 September 1857.
137 Ibid., 23 June 1852.
138 Ibid., 9 September 1860.
139 *TA*, 2 July 1894, p. 2.
140 Duncan, *In the Shadows of the Tropics*, p. 53.
141 Taylor letters, 30 January 1869.
142 Rigg, 'On coffee planting in Ceylon', p. 131.
143 Taylor letters, 17 September 1857.
144 William Boyd, 'Ceylon and its pioneers', *Ceylon Literary Register*, 24 February 1888, p. 252.
145 Taylor letters, 17 September 1857.
146 Ibid., 3 December 1857.
147 Ibid., 10 July 1858.
148 Ibid., 27 May 1859.
149 Duncan, *In the Shadows of the Tropics*, p. 60, notes fears of menstrual problems and reproductive dysfunctions for middle-class women, while lower-class white women were considered to be eroticised by the tropics.
150 Taylor letters, 30 January 1869.
151 Kirsten McKenzie, *Scandal in the Colonies: Sydney and Cape Town, 1820–1850* (Melbourne, 2004), p. 137.
152 Taylor letters, 25 January 1873.
153 Lionel Lee, *Census of Ceylon 1881: General Report and Statements and Tables* (Colombo, 1882), p. 143, Table 10.
154 Taylor letters, undated, c.mid-1870s.
155 Ibid., 17 September 1857.
156 Seemingly his wife died leaving Moir with six children, because Taylor comments on 18 March 1872 that Moir may marry again.
157 Taylor letters, 21 February 1859.
158 NLS, Hunter of Glencarse papers, MS 19722, Letters to Andrew Hunter, Patrick Ryan, St Clair Estate, to Andrew Hunter, 16 November 1865, p. 350. 'Tocher' is a dowry.

6

Cross-cultural contact

When James Taylor first arrived in Ceylon, he declared that if his proprietor 'had not coolies that understood better than I do I could not do at all'.[1] This chapter examines his impressions of the work-force and of other peoples whom he encountered during his four decades in Ceylon. These primarily encompass his views of the Sinhalese and Tamil populations, whose identities and often troubled relations have dominated the study of Sri Lanka's ethnic history.[2] The inhabitants of the island also had other 'racial' origins, their customs and experiences being captured in reports from the periods of Portuguese (1505–1658), Dutch (1658–1796), and British rule (1796–1948).

The classification of 'racial' difference is one of the features that 'new' British imperial historians use to demonstrate that colonisation was a cultural as well as economic or political project. 'Race' shaped not only political frameworks but also assessment of the diverse peoples of empire and their social and cultural lives. A major shift, it is contended, occurred between the 1830s and 1850s, when an earlier humanitarian discourse became transformed into one of racial analysis.[3] Views of the East were now said to constitute a new framework in which European supremacy was showcased through the prisms of superiority in military force, governance, and economic organisation. Nonetheless, Western responses could be more complex and varied than that model suggests and might include affinities as well as differences and hostilities.[4]

A Scottish Orientalist school of thought in the eighteenth century had been in the vanguard of conceptualising the 'other' in Asia. Influenced in large part by the ideas of the Scottish Enlightenment, scholars, soldiers, and administrators, many of them connected to the University of Edinburgh, wrote both in sympathetic and in negative terms about Asian languages, society, and culture.[5] Some have suggested that empathetic Scottish attitudes to indigenous peoples were maintained in the 'white' British world of the nineteenth century. In particular, Highland Scots were said to have shared an affinity with other peoples across the empire who had lost land or who shared similar tribal kin structures to that of former clansmen.[6] Recent scholarship has mainly discounted this thesis and concluded instead that there seems to have been little difference between Scottish and British colonists generally in the often harsh treatment of the indigenous inhabitants in North America and Australasia.[7]

This is the context within which James Taylor's views of other peoples in Ceylon will be considered. He recognised the ethnic mix in the island and his thoughts on the diversity of peoples there help to complicate and nuance over-simplistic generalisations about the attitudes of the colonising class as a whole towards them. Moreover, unlike other studies, which tend to draw on single snapshots of evidence in order to represent broader attitudes towards ethnic difference, Taylor's correspondence over the many years of his working life in Ceylon allows the tracing of different responses to events and developments as they took place over time. His opinions are not treated in a vacuum but within the broader context of nineteenth-century racial thought.

Ethnic diversity

From his first arrival in Ceylon, James Taylor showed awareness of the ethnic diversity of the population. In particular, he initially referred to the employment of two distinctive groups of workers on his estate who, in his view, were each suited to different tasks. Although Taylor's main interactions were with plantation Tamils and local Sinhalese or, as he termed the latter, 'native' workers, Taylor's early awareness of ethnic diversity in Ceylon also took in other groups:

> there are I believe three races of cingalese. These are the Kandyans who live in middle of the island all around here then there is a race of stronger men between Colombo and Galle of a darker colour. All the tradesmen such as carpenters who go about the estates are of these men. And in the north of the island somewhere there is a race of savage sort of fellows who live in the woods and hunt wild animals and there are Moors and Malabars in many places on the coast.[8]

The extract demonstrates his awareness of Kandyans, Karavas, Veddahs, Moors, and Malabars in Ceylon, but he seems to be unaware of the majority Low Country Sinhalese.[9]

Taylor's reports of five separate 'racial' groups were reduced to four in a later official report from 1865, which linked ethnicity with religion. That report concluded that, of Ceylon's population, 1.4 million were Buddhist Sinhalese, 500,000 were Ceylon Hindu Tamils, 250,000 were migrant Hindu Tamils from India, and 130,000 were Moormen. The latter were all classified as Mohammedans (Muslim) who spoke Tamil and intermarried with Malayans.[10] In 1858, Taylor wrote of them: 'The Moormen as we call the Mohammedans we have here are a nasty set too and would soon have brought us into a scrape if they could.'[11] The existence of a distinctive Kandyan people, however, found resonance in other reports, albeit limited to their chiefs. In 1855 many Highlanders from Scotland attended a planters' dinner where 'they will drink the healths of the Highland Chiefs of the Kandyan country with highland honours'.[12]

The British ethnic classification of Ceylon's population is attributed partly to the decision made in the 1830s that caste was not to be recognised as a social category even if it remained a social reality.[13] In earlier years, such classification had encompassed not only caste groupings but occupations and broader ethnicities.[14] Taylor was certainly aware of caste divisions although his comments on them were brief. Soon after his arrival in 1852 he noted that no Tamil 'except the Pariahs would touch a piece of Beef nor will they bring us any from Kandy ... Mr Hoffman got some the other day brought out in a hat case so the coolie did not know. ... The man I get my things from in Kandy is a Mahometan called Abraham Saibo. If we send a Pariah or man that has lost caste he will bring beef.'[15] Unlike higher caste groups, the paraiyan caste were considered 'untouchable'.[16] Taylor also commented on Brahmins, the highest-ranking social class in Hindu India, but who for Buddhists in Ceylon 'had little social or economic authority'.[17] They did not impress him:

> I've seen some Brahmins here and certainly they are such an insolent looking set just the people to expect all sorts of evil from one here lately setting up a humbug and getting money from the coolies; of course they make them of lower cast do as they like: I saw passing and asked who he was he simply told me he 'was a Brahmin sir' but the very tone in which it was spoken and the insolent look of the fellow so roused me I told him I knew he was a villain but if I saw him on my place again and if he did not march off instantly he should not be a Brahmin ten minutes longer. ... these cruel bigotted mahomedans are as bad [.][18]

Henry Stiven, meanwhile, observed that the 'Chetiis' were of high caste and 'known by wearing sandals'. Shaven heads were another 'mark of cast'.[19]

Christian belief among the Ceylonese was also not uncommon and reflected conversions that had taken place during the era of Portuguese rule. 'Many of the coolies are Roman Catholics',[20] Taylor recorded, and he thought them similar in many respects to the Hindu workforce: 'I have got some hindoos here and I dont see any differences in their feelings or thought from the tamals. They have no education and so every one's mind is as like anothers as ones two hands.' He also told family at home that the marigold seeds they sent 'are now a weed in the Patnas and road sides and the coolies plant them round their altar on the estate'.[21]

Ceylon's ethnic diversity certainly intrigued James Taylor and included the Europeans he encountered. He confessed to liking a Portuguese assistant superintendent on his estate, while observing that the father of another plantation manager was Scots and his mother Irish.[22] Ethnicity also explained the capacities of superintendents. He claimed that proprietors favoured Scottish superintendents over English and Irish managers:

> When ever any estate is doing well it is a Scotchman that is on it. If we speak with a Scotchman it is about estate matters and wives if with an Englishman his whole heart and soul is in dogs and horses and I think the few Irish that I know seem generally to give themselves precious little trouble about anything. I see little of the wit they are famed for and terrible little practical sense.[23]

Plainly, he did not always think in terms of the overarching categories of British or European but was fully aware of the significance of national cultures within them. Pride in his own Scottish identity was paramount. Before sailing from London for Colombo he told his father, 'When the people here see me drinking water they say "Ah there's a Scotchman".'[24] More than two decades later he continued to extol his Scottish identity: 'I am glad to hear that matrimony flourishes in the old country to keep up the excellent breed of Scotchmen.'[25] 'There is no doubt the Scotch breed is a very good one', he further suggested in 1876.[26] Certainly, at the time of Sri Lanka's first detailed census in 1871 both 'race' and nationality were categories of identity, although the country's censuses throughout the nineteenth and early twentieth centuries would remain problematic.[27]

Taylor's awareness of ethnic distinctions in Asia intensified during his trip to Darjeeling in India in 1874 (see Figure 6.1). There, he collected photographs of a range of peoples, including Lepcha, Sikkim Bhutias, and Nepalese.[28] His interest in and thinking about different peoples had clearly developed from his early impressions when first arriving in Ceylon twenty-two years earlier. In particular, the variation in their physical features fascinated him:

> Lots of the people here are nearly white. Many of them have as white faces as mine though the rest of their skin is darker and they have as much red in their cheeks as I have with less in the nose and the rest of their faces. They have broad faces and flat noses and chinese eyes and some wear their hair in a tail. They are generally short and very thickly made with very thick legs. They seem very dirty. I had just been to see the collection of various nationalities in the market place Sunday being their great market day.[29]

Even before his departure for Ceylon, Taylor would almost certainly have known about the characteristics of different 'races' in the East from neighbours and relatives at home who already had personal experience there. He may also have been aware of Lord Monboddo's writings on human difference, especially that of linguistic diversity. Monboddo was the principal landowner in the neighbourhood where Taylor was born and some scholars see his thinking as a precursor to Charles Darwin's theory of evolution. Information from Ceylon had circulated in Scotland from the early period of British settlement, as evidenced in a letter from Robert Arbuthnot, Chief Secretary in Ceylon, of 1801.

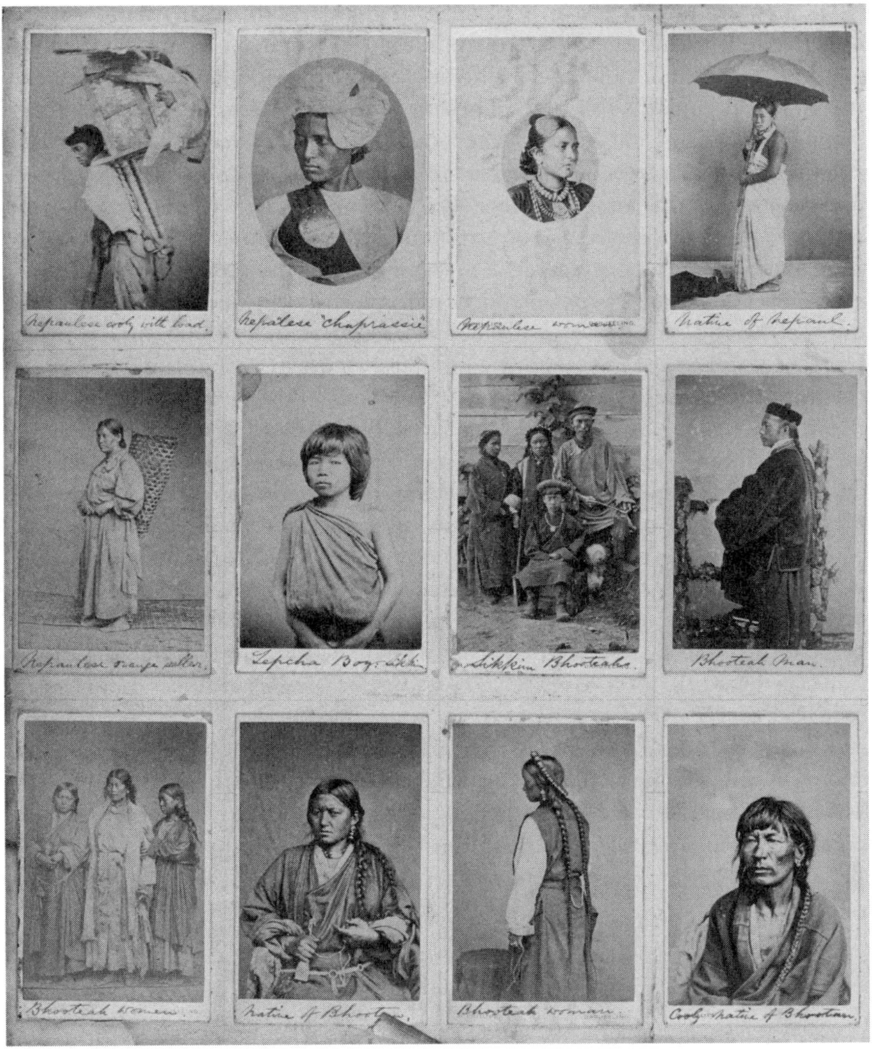

6.1 Taylor's captions about native peoples at Darjeeling, 1874.

Arbuthnot catalogued both the occupations and the ethnicity of his servants, a Frenchman, a Moor boy, and two Massalskes. He passed comment on the Dutch and considered the English 'the least sociable people in the world'. He further remarked that 'All Scotch friends are well.'[30] Taylor also sought out Humphrey Prideaux's writings, which reflected on Jewish connections to other nations.[31] This categorisation of other peoples was widespread throughout the British Empire as officials tried to order and control hugely diverse populations.

The efforts of officials in Sri Lanka to identify and calculate the population through various census returns would likewise have amplified Taylor's awareness of ethnic difference. This included, in particular, efforts to gauge the numbers and diversity of population on the estates. Estimates ranged from a total of 206,500 estate workers in 1881 to 262,000 a decade later. Such amounts are likely to be an under-estimate.[32] Indeed, planters often had little precise idea of the total numbers who actually resided there. In 1886, for instance, the Ceylon press drew attention to the number 'of the drones, or servants of servants, the hangers-on, the infirm, or the infants' living on their estates.[33] The same newspaper report reflected back on Taylor's actions at the time of the 1871 Census to try to determine the number living on the estate. It stated that he 'was not content with merely a muster of the coolies, but had the lines thoroughly cleaned out in his presence of every human being inside them. The result was that numerous faces, old and young, came to light, that he (old planter as he was) had never seen before and had no conception of as finding a home – and a permanent one – on the properties under his charge.'[34] Taylor's careful enumeration produced a remarkable result. His official list of workers contained 540 men, women, and children. But in addition there was a substantial group of 'non-productives', including 103 children under seven years of age and 165 'strangers to and unconnected with the Estate'.[35] Whichever total is correct, he oversaw a significantly larger population, three times as many, than the average slave-owner in Jamaica at the end of the previous century.[36]

Census data for 1911 marks the first attempt to record the ethnic breakdown of estate populations. On Loolecondera, indentured Tamils comprised the majority of 426 individuals. At neighbouring Naranghena, the recorded population was 500, including 362 who were indentured Tamils and 117 Ceylon Tamils. As at Loolecondera, only one European resided on the estate.[37]

Impressions of the Ceylonese

James Taylor valued the work carried out on his estates but was not impressed by the Tamil labour force. He termed them 'a set of the greatest cheaters that ever existed. They must be called back to every hole they make two or three times before it is large enough though each man has a measure stick with him.'[38] Henry Stiven likewise discerned a 'strong inclination they have got to cheating Europeans'.[39] Planters also found their Tamil labourers inadequate in other respects. When snow fell at Nuwara Eliya, Taylor claimed that they 'say they cant work for cold'.[40] His contemporary William Boyd similarly recalled in his memoirs that Tamils 'could not stand the cold, driving rain'.[41] Even more illuminating was Taylor's lengthy diatribe from 1859:

> I wish I could see our coolies hurt themselves from exertion in carrying sticks. If we wanted to carry a beam 12 inches square all the coolies that could get room to go near it would not carry it and if they were carrying one half that size they would require to be so close crammed under it that they could scarcely move their legs for each other and then they make such a noise blackguarding each other for not lifting enough and have to lay down the stick and have a rest every stone cast of about half an hour if they can get it. I often tell them if the log were cut into pieces one to each of them they would be able to cut it. They are very nimble at light work but a heavy job is quite beyond their ideas of working. They would provoke a saint to murder them when [*erased:* a] newly come from home among them but then if they think they are too hard dealt with they run away and we are generally glad to get all we can pick up so they think little in such a case of running away but if it were otherwise they'd die of starvation rather than work as people [*erased:* people] newly from home would expect them to do.[42]

Taylor was no different from other Europeans in seeing his Tamil labourers as being indolent and inadequate.[43] His criticism of the Sinhalese, however, concerned their reluctance to work on the estates as common labourers. As he put it in 1857, 'The Shingalese natives cant be got to work nor even to grow food enough for their own use. Even those who have paddy lands will not cultivate enough to have a bushel or two to sell and in bad seasons they half starve and all who are engaged otherwise depend on the supply from India.'[44] Stiven also reflected the traditional view of 'the Cingalese being too indolent to work'.[45] Their impressions echoed those in the press: 'The Cingalese have a terrible character for laziness, and there is a grain of truth in the charge, but they will work hard enough at their own little plots of rice. … They only want their own kind of work.'[46] Other contemporary claims suggested that they were unreliable and too wedded to the subsistence cultivation of their own patches of land.[47] A report in the *Proceedings of the Planters Association* for 1862 was equally scathing: 'If these natives (Cingalese) were not so inert, and would only work on the estates, there would be no occasion to be so dependent on India as we were, for labour.'[48] Tamil labour from India was therefore vital to weed, prune the plants, and harvest the crop.[49]

John Ferguson, however, did at least try to understand the attitudes of the local people. He took the view that the Sinhalese 'would feel insulted … were he or his sons asked to labour on a neighbouring plantation where a European acts as the Superintendent of a force of Tamil coolies, immigrants from the over-peopled plains of Southern India.' Ferguson also acknowledged that they were prepared to fell forests and that 'Low Country' Sinhalese would erect estate buildings and undertake crop work 'under the influence of offers of high remuneration'.[50]

In general, however, there was apparently little understanding in the minds of the managerial class, all of them born and bred within a system of agrarian capitalism and rigorous work ethic, that native peoples in Asia had been reared from birth within a radically different culture of subsistence agriculture and traditional cycles of labour. They were not easily lured into regular employment in order to maximise wage income at the expense of leisure and other activities. This was, in essence, a conflict between the ethic of capitalism and the traditionalism of a peasant society.

Yet Taylor's denunciation of the Sinhalese, or 'natives', did, at times, go beyond condemnation for poor work, and towards racial abuse. What follows, however, was written when lurid reports about native barbarity during the Indian 'Mutiny' disturbed many planters who lived in isolated areas, far from government protection, and who feared that they might be murdered in their beds:

> To see a native when he wishes to gain anything you would think there was not a more exemplary man alive he is so ready so willing to do you a service so humble and so flattering you would think he had a high opinion of you surely and he will fall at your feet and worship you calling you a god &c. and you naturally wont stand that but are so gained upon by him that you give him say a coat. Well he looks at it and will most likely say it is a bad one or ask you to give him a shirt too and then go away and have a joke and a laugh about you among his acquaintances. The place is give him a kick tell him to go and do his work and get his pay and then he *he* will respect you. People here have not the feeling of gratitude so we ought never to do a favour to them as such. They will feel the advantages of it but never thank you but think you are afraid of them and wish to gain favours from them and so raise their opinion of themselves and their contempt of you.[51]

This kind of thinking often legitimised the harsh treatment of non-European labour in the colonial empires. Slave-owners, for instance, justified the pitiless treatment of the enslaved because to them only brutal methods could compel greater effort.[52] But contemporaries pointed to other explanations for planter behaviour: 'The temper becomes soured by seclusion and the mind harassed by constant disappointments and the misconduct of others.'[53] Taylor certainly displayed anger and annoyance with his work-force and on occasion his treatment could be violent. He locked up some workers who had absconded from the estate and then their leader was 'tarred and feathered making the feathers stick in the tar and sent him off the place for trying to take some of my coolies to another estate trying to induce them to run away'.[54]

Resorting to violent punishment, however, seems to have been uncharacteristic of Taylor, as revealed in an official enquiry held in 1873 into 'the organized and systematic business' of coffee stealing. From the 133 submissions received in the course of the investigation it was apparent that theft was most prevalent in his own district of Hewaheta. He reckoned that his Tamil coolies engaged in 'smaller quantities' of theft while the Sinhalese 'natives' undertook 'extensive robberies'. The thieves then sold the stolen coffee to the 'owners of Coffee gardens in the villages', some of whom were Tamil. Several of Taylor's labourers were prepared, however, to identify the malefactors and appear in court to give evidence against them. Taylor's recommendation 'to check the evil', however, was special legislation, a stark contrast with the suggested penalties demanded by other planters, which included flogging, shooting, imprisonment, transportation, and even execution.[55]

Such punishments, however, rarely appear to have generated worker violence. Instead, most reported resistance tended to take the form of desertion or damage to crops and equipment rather than violence against the person. In 1862, for instance, 7 per cent of Tamil migrants were arrested for desertion from work.[56] The ability of planters to control their work-force, however, likely lies in the firm discipline they enacted, which could at times be violent. Even so, attacks on planters were not unknown. In the late 1870s Taylor was robbed and violently attacked in his own bungalow. Lurid headlines in the press trumpeted the news: 'The Attempt to Murder Mr. James Taylor'. Reports described the 'shooting at and wounding of Mr. James Taylor by a native'.[57] His own account of the assassination attempt was less dramatic and in keeping with his measured character. When he described the incident to his father, he recalled feeling a 'regular torrent' of blood coming from his ear. Initially, he tried to reassure his father that the attack was simply an attempt to 'plunder the Bungalow' rather than any act of revenge, as police enquiries on the estate and in the neighbourhood had shown that Taylor 'was so universally liked'. However, he revealed that in his opinion those responsible were his 'appoo (or servant)' and 'dholie (or washerwoman) whom I had dismissed a day or two before'. Since many bungalows in the district had been broken into and robbed, he added, 'The natives are constantly becoming greater & greater blackguards.'[58]

Despite a furore in the press, the alleged culprits were never prosecuted, due to a lack of evidence. Certainly, fellow planters suspected those living on the estate or close to it. The workers there claimed not to have been aware of any gunshot although a planter living a mile away heard it clearly. Another, in a letter to the *Ceylon Overland Observer*, asked the direct question, 'Does it not strike you that suspicion should rest on parties nearer home' – those up and working that night?[59] Whether the attack on Taylor's life was retribution for some act against his work-force must, however, remain a matter of speculation.

It is instructive to compare Taylor's treatment of his work-force with that of other planters. In comparison with the punishments levied by some of his peers, he does not seem to have been a severe taskmaster. Perhaps his solid, large physique (he was said to weigh 246 lbs) aided his authority among his work-force. They were, according to later accounts, 'in awe of him'.[60] His first boss, George Pride, by contrast, was a small, brutal master and in consequence 'there are a number of the coolies to go away because he made them do more work than they were able and they say he beat them because they did not do more'.[61] Taylor witnessed one of Pride's violent outbursts in June 1852:

> He is a little fellow and in his passions he is fearful and has no command of them. There he stands shaking his head, thumping his foot on the ground and cursing. The other day he thumped a coolie for nearly half an hour till the fellow was nearly dead and then kicked him of[*f*] the estate and some days before he was paying the Cingalese sitting before our Bungalow and he got in a passion at something and he had a tumbler of mine sitting on the table with water. He took it up and threw it at them. It passed through between two of their heads and was smashed to pieces. He has not given me another one and he is always in a mad passion giving and reversing them and giving contrary orders at an awful rate and flying about like a mad man or in a cold taunting ill natured humour[.][62]

But Pride was not alone. Taylor reported that another planter gave his workers 'a pounding' because they could not understand him since he only had one word of Tamil – 'po' (meaning 'go'). Another planter, Mr Williams, told 'some Shingalese to go away to work and they did not understand him and asked something when he got in a rage and told them to go they stood dumbfounded and did not know what to do'. According to Taylor, 'it was so ridiculous I was obliged to laugh in spite of all Williams' passion as the man moved a little out of Williams' way half afraid of a beating'. In the end, 'the appo had to be got to tell them what was wanted'.[63] Taylor's accounts might well suggest that William Knighton's vicious planter in the novel *Forest Life in Ceylon* (1854) could indeed have been based on someone from Ceylon rather than, as Patrick Peebles suggests, capitalising on the character Legree in *Uncle Tom's Cabin*.[64] The former planter William Boyd also pointed in his memoirs to 'men with low, brutal natures amongst the Ceylon coffee planters ... [who] used their coolies with disgraceful injustice and cruelty'.[65] One could speculate that significant planter migration from the West Indies to Ceylon in the wake of slave emancipation in 1833 may have been a factor. The Caribbean slavery regime was notorious for widespread brutality.[66]

If Taylor saw himself as a more sympathetic planter than Pride, he also did so in relation to his own kinsman, Henry Stiven. But he was realistic enough to recognise the likely consequences of too-kindly dealings with his labour force. Of Stiven he wrote: 'he is more forward and rough whereas I must be friendly. I cant be otherwise and much friendliness is certainly misplaced on a coolly. The feeling we call gratitude does not exist in their disposition and if they are well treated they only take advantage of that to despise you and take advantage of you. A Tamil any where is the same.'[67]

Similar comments were made about an Irishman whose 'coolies wont do near enough work and yet they complain of him being too hard on them. His disposition does not suit them at all. I had to go and turn them out to work the other day. They would not come out of their houses for him and I'm getting quite horrified at the slow progress of the work.'[68] Some planters, by contrast, argued that if workers suffered cruelty, it was at the hands of their kanganies:

> I do not believe that the Planters turned poor half starved wretches off the estates to die, but I have no doubt they were turned off by the Kanganies, and in my humble opinion the Kangani system is at the core of all the evil. No South American Slave, in the worst days of Slavery was more at the mercy of an inhuman master than the poor Tamil immigrant is under [*erased:* the] and dependant upon, the will of his cruel owner the Kangani. The Planter is a humane man, I have always said so. The Kangani is the worst of tyrants.[69]

By contrast with his firm treatment of his work-force, there is some evidence of Taylor's concern about their working and living conditions. In 1852 he noted of the rainy season, 'we have rain in abundance and cold too which I wonder how the naked fellows of coolies can stand at all. It does kill many of them at this season of the year. We had one died last sunday.'[70] The death rate for plantation labourers in Ceylon at this time has been estimated at a quarter of the total labour force on the plantations.[71] During these years, Taylor 'went to considerable expense and built a fine set of lines or houses for coolies'.[72] But he despaired of easily finding a remedy for the plight of some of the labourers. It is clear from some graphic testimony which he gave in 1857 that he thought human life was not valued highly among them:

> I've taken them from the road side half dead often lying on the bare ground sometimes with a handful of grass they have been able to collect lying beside them and if they are able they will try to get a fire kept up but they soon get unable to keep up that. I've passed them lying dead across the path in the mornings with a pool of blood that has come out at their mouth sometimes and in all this they dont seem to think themselves ill treated. Even some I've taken from the doors of their friends houses or rooms when 8 or 10 live in one room and put them into some place with fire and food and hired one of their friends to attend them which none will do without wages for it. They dont seem to like it. They would as soon be at the roadside and cry if I force them to take medicine sometimes thinking I am poisoning them and I know that on the way coming to Ceylon if any get sick and unable to come or they leave him to die by the way and on returning they will kill any sickly or weakly person and take his savings he is carrying home.[73]

Fifteen years later, during an official enquiry into medical aid on the estates, Taylor repeated his view about Tamil resistance to European medicine. He claimed that he did not 'hear of more than half the deaths on this place directly ... I believe that there are many more deaths than are reported on estates, and much more sickness than is known of.'[74] He attributed this to 'laziness or apathy on their own part and that of their friends, or the other coolies and canganies that keeps them from telling me of cases of illness'.[75] He went on to publicly support the appointment of a doctor in the Hewaheta district: 'A properly qualified

Doctor in this District would be a great blessing to many of the coolies and to myself. ... In cases when the best has not been done, and proper medical attendance not been procured, if the cooly dies, which is frequently the case, the result is very unsatisfactory for one's conscience.'[76] The *Overland Ceylon Observer* praised the 'sage of Hewahette' for 'telling "the whole truth"', although others were less supportive.[77] The high death rate among Tamil immigrants continued throughout the nineteenth century and in the years between 1883 and 1892 an estimated 21 per cent of immigrant labourers admitted to district hospitals eventually died.[78] While not all planters displayed indifference to the death of their workers, they, like West Indian planters, presumably interpreted it as part of the harsh realities of Ceylon plantation life.[79]

In assessing accounts similar to those of Taylor, one scholar has argued that the planter class blamed the cultural attitudes of the Tamils toward illness in order to justify that medical treatment should not be funded for them.[80] Some also took the view that, by their very racial nature, Tamils were exceedingly prone to experiencing serious ill health.[81] The evidence surveyed above suggests that James Taylor took a different view on sickness and death among his workers. In 1890 the *Tropical Agriculturalist* reported that 'One small fact will show how conscientiously careful Mr. Taylor is in his work. Strict cleanliness is of much importance in the preparation of tea; and when coolies are seen dressed in specially clean clothing, the remark made is, "Some of Taylor's tea coolies".'[82] While the comment focuses specifically on efficiency at work, it also suggests that Taylor did show some real concern for the people on his estate. The planter William Boyd, by contrast, referred to the attire of his coolies encompassing 'no better covering than old mat bags or tattered camblies'.[83]

But it is difficult to say how typical Taylor's attitude was, as relations between managers and workers undoubtedly varied from plantation to plantation and over time. Indeed, Taylor's correspondence falls largely silent on the Sinhalese and his Tamil workers after the 1870s, except in 1890 when he labelled the Sinhalese as 'scoundrels' and 'careless' when he sent home a box of tea.[84] His disinterest over time may have been due to both his and his Scottish family's growing familiarity with Ceylon's diverse population.

Nevertheless, the current scholarly consensus is that detached indifference about the condition of the labour force was the norm as long as it functioned to acceptable standards when at work.[85] In addition, Taylor, unlike the slave master Thomas Thistlewood in Jamaica, generally depicted his labour force in collective terms rather than as individuals.[86]

Explaining attitudes towards the Ceylonese

Judgements of other peoples in the Victorian empire can be attributed to racial theories which ranked human beings in hierarchies of value and worth ranging from the primitive to the civilised. These attitudes were commonplace in Britain and its empire and mainly derived from the innovative stadial theories of the eighteenth-century Scottish Enlightenment.[87] Just as James Taylor's deep sense of Scottishness helped to shape his awareness of ethnic diversity in Ceylon, so perhaps did his Scottish background help to fashion his understanding of the Ceylonese people among whom he lived and worked.

By the middle decades of the nineteenth century, Lowland opinion in Scotland had become deeply critical of aspects of Gaelic culture, especially during the great crisis of the potato famine after 1846. Resounding condemnation of the slothful and feckless Gaels who had fallen victim to such a disaster echoed throughout some of the press and pamphlet literature of the time. For those Scots who responded to this racist analysis, it was easy to accept that the evil of corrupt indolence had also infected other peoples whose labour cultures were based on a traditional pre-capitalist world.[88] In addition, Scottish writers such as George Combe and Robert Knox had a significant influence, through their best-selling publications, in the dissemination of racial analyses in the middle decades of the nineteenth century.[89] Knox, for instance, reckoned that Caledonian Celts held steady, productive labour 'in absolute horror and contempt' and they were 'the worst of agriculturalists'.[90]

Many of the ideas about racial differences and inferiorities also developed out of Britain's central engagement with slavery and the slave trade. Recent research has shown the very significant extent to which Scots were involved in the slave economies of the American and Caribbean colonies in the eighteenth and early nineteenth centuries.[91] Out of that connection black skin evolved as a marker of identity of the slave, and so also of the human inferiority of coloured peoples more generally. Long before the racist treatises of Victorian times were published, Edward Long's widely read *History of Jamaica* (1774) had set out the natural differences between black and white based on the distinctions between slave and slave-owner which were so fundamental to life on the sugar plantations of the West Indies. As Catherine Hall has argued, 'Ideas about racial difference that began with slavery were recalibrated across the centuries to encompass other colonised subjects – whether Indian, Aboriginal or east Asian. All were defined as racialised others, inferior to white Britons, and this process was central to imperial rule.'[92]

Whether Taylor's views were affected by these writings cannot be confirmed. Yet his attitudes must at least have been shaped by his position as superintendent of a work-force over which he had complete authority and on whose daily toil depended the processing of profitable commodities for sale throughout the empire. He was little different from the planters of both Assam and Ceylon who uncritically held to the conventional view that all their workers were lazy and feckless.[93]

However, when the Indian 'Mutiny' broke out in May 1857, Taylor's attitude to Asian peoples altered for the worse. He claimed that his response to what happened in India was determined by 'our private accounts by letters to friends here and people come over for safety are some thing sickening'. But he was also likely to have been affected by graphic articles in the press and published official reports of what had taken place.[94] His correspondence shows his feelings of horror at some of the reported excesses:

> The Ladies after having been prostituted and abused in all sorts of ways often before their husband's' eyes tied to a post and ravished by dozens of them and shamefully abused have been then cut open alive or skinned alive and burned alive and tortured with hot irons in the most cruel and indecent ways. Their breasts cut off and every one of them subjected to the most horrid cruelties till they were not exactly killed but tortured to death tortured slowly till they died from pain without being directly killed and then their husbands' and fathers' eyes put out his testicles cut off and put into the sockets and he also subjected to all sorts of torture and indignity. Children are put into boxes and burned alive have their hands and feet cut off an cut open and left to die.[95]

In 1857 the *Ceylon Times* had indeed described 'Children shut up in a box and burnt alive', while the *Bombay Times* had noted that 'they murdered ladies in the most brutal manner, burning them half and then cutting them up, and stripping them naked'.[96]

Accounts like these presented an image of India 'as a mysterious, barbaric land inhabited by fanatical religious devotees'.[97] But some argue that the more extreme depictions of violence against British women and children were groundless and that afterwards British magistrates found that women and children had not been subjected to mutilation and torture but, rather, had been wounded by bullets or had fallen victims of disease.[98] Yet Taylor's writings, inflated or otherwise, are in stark contrast with these modern interpretations, as well as their dismissal of claims that 'elaborate details concerning the torture of men' and 'mention of the male sexual organ being removed' were fictitious.[99] Whatever the revisionism of today's scholarship, Taylor and the British community in Ceylon clearly believed that gross atrocities had indeed taken place on a large scale and the most extreme penalties should therefore be exacted upon the criminal perpetrators of the outrages: 'Our soldiers are now finding fragments of European bodies and dresses in the villages finding arms and feet with shoes on and so forth. It may be immoral to hint even at things done but let it be known so that our vengeance may be fairly aroused and give a lesson sufficient to prevent such things in future.'[100]

The news from India served to harden Taylor's thinking on the non-European population of Ceylon. He further noted in July 1857 that the Ceylon regiment comprised 'Native Malays chiefly and Mahommedans' and that 'nothing would be easier than to kill every European in the Island in one night if they made their plans as well as they have done in India'. Malays, or Javanese, who were Muslims, came from Indonesia and Malaya and many had been recruited to Ceylon as soldiers during the periods of Dutch and British rule. Interestingly, however, this also reveals that Taylor's awareness of Ceylon's population had further developed during his five years in the country. A repressed mutiny at Colombo prompted Taylor to claim of the Malays that 'a more brave and bloodthirsty race does not exist nor a more revengeful'. His views on the majority Sinhalese, mainly Buddhist in belief, were likewise hostile: 'Cingalese are one of the cruelest races in existence ... However they are a cowardly pack.' He was also concerned about the problem of caste among Hindu soldiers and the possible threat which they posed:

> now the officers are afraid of their brahmin soldiers. They show disrespect to our officers and wont allow them to enter their apartments or do any thing but what they like because it would defile them and our officers and rulers have been pitying and tolerating such insolence for ten or twelve years and putting increased power into the hands of these people and our rulers and you at home reprimand us for not giving way to their predjudices and for doing anything or counterancing any effort to turn them from such a religion as they have ... They know no motive in themselves and believe none in us for any conduct in us save fear so the more impervious and overbearing we are the better for them and ourselves and though some things we may do seem harsh to people at home they are not so to natives here ... People here have not the feeling of gratitude so we ought never to do a favour to them as such. They will feel the advantages of it but never thank you but think you are afraid of them and wish to gain favours from them and so raise their opinion of themselves and their contempt of you ... They dont seem to fear death as we do[.][101]

Yet Taylor's opinions of non-European peoples were more complex than his immediate reactions to the 'Mutiny' would suggest. In her study of subaltern biographies, Clare Anderson shows that many scholars take moments of crisis as a starting point in their studies.[102] If this had been the approach in the case of James Taylor we could not have captured the full range of his views as a plantation manager. There is evidence, for instance, that he had earlier grappled with Ceylonese culture. On the one hand, he needed to learn the Tamil language in order to manage his workers, and one Seena Tamby instructed him in this regard. He confessed, however, that 'I have not got a great deal of it yet being so long with the Cingalese whose language is quite different. I have got a little of it too.' He undoubtedly learned such snippets of their language while surveying their cutting of trees on the estate. His supplies from Kandy, meanwhile, were usually acquired from 'a Mahometan called Abraham Saibo'.[103] Unlike other Europeans, he ate rice and curry in the mornings and sweet potatoes, coconut, and rice and curry in the evenings. Taylor seems to have followed what the *Tropical Agriculturalist* considered to be the ideal qualities of a worthy planter.

These included 'proper management of coloured labour ... including the learning to speak the coolies' language colloquially' and also the capacity to act as their physician.[104] As contemporary and later commentators have argued, the economic success of an estate ultimately depended on the fair treatment of the work-force by the planter/manager.[105]

A further factor to consider in Taylor's impressions of other peoples is his intimate relationships. On the one hand, as Ronald Hyam suggests, white men were more sympathetic to a community if they found its women attractive.[106] Certainly in Asia cross-cultural liaisons took place and could lead to transculturation. But such relationships created anxieties and did not necessarily extend to sympathy towards the wider community.[107] Taylor, for instance, was adamant in 1857 that 'I'll never marry a black and am not sure if a white would suit and half and half is worse than either'.[108] This statement was, of course, made at the time of the Indian 'Mutiny'. But British men like Taylor frequently kept their intimate liaisons with local women a secret, despite the frequency of such cross-cultural relationships. Early planters in Ceylon were said to have kept local women (Sinhalese rather than Tamil estate workers) in their bungalows, later maintaining them in nearby villages.[109] Such alliances, as Durba Ghosh argues, 'enabled European men to maximize not only their sexual opportunities but their economic ones as well'.[110] But all fleeting published accounts of Taylor's life to date state that his sole involvement was with tea.

While James Taylor did not have a marital relationship as recognised in British law, his will and his photograph albums suggest that he was not lacking in female companionship. The albums, for instance, contain several images of a young Tamil girl on the plantation, pictured initially in a sari (see Figure 6.2). There is no indication of who she was or when the photographs were taken, although it is likely it was around 1863.

A later photograph, however, shows her outfitted in what appears to be crinoline, suggestive of a European connection (Figure 6.3).[111] As other research has shown, Asian women could use such intimate liaisons to advance their and their family's position and interests.[112]

Taylor also wrote several cryptic messages inside one of the albums, including a note that 'Paarvathy's sister' was born in May 1865 and another, 'Paarvathy's sister P.M. in July 1880. Information got from Valiethime Cy of Stellenberg.' It is difficult not to speculate in light of this and the following information inscribed in the back cover of the album that Taylor was keeping track of menstrual cycles: 'Paar^y P.M. on 27th Novr 1864, subsequent dates 30th Dec^r; 27th Jany/65. Febr (not noted); 27th Mar. not in April; but twice in May, viz 3rd and 27th. Ran off Sep^t 25th 1872.'[113] Paarvathy, then, may have been Taylor's Tamil partner. Could her 'sister' have conceivably been Taylor's daughter reared at neighbouring Stellenberg and mentioned by the kangany there?

6.2 '[C]ertainly I'll never marry a black': two images of the Tamil girl believed to be Taylor's partner.

If Taylor was indeed intimate with the Tamil girl Paarvathy, then it appears that the relationship lasted less than a decade, for she 'Ran off' in 1872. Moreover, when Taylor died in 1892 his Sinhalese housekeeper emerged from 'the bungalow crying and waving her arms and would have gone to the funeral, but Mr Gordon prevented her'.[114] Whether this was a traditional Sinhalese expression of grief or an expression of more tender ties to Taylor is unknown.

What is incontrovertible, however, is that Taylor had children and a native partner. His will and codicil stipulated that funds were to be left to the 'mother of his children' and monies were also given to the Tamil Coolie Mission. If he desired this relationship to be kept secret, it no longer was after his death, its details made public in the press.[115] This information was shared in 2015 with Lalith Abeykoon, the superintendent of Loolecondera. His subsequent enquiries in the community suggested that Taylor's Sinhalese partner was

6.3 Two further images of Taylor's probable partner. Note the crinoline dress which suggests European contact.

from Gannewa, an adjoining village to Loolecondera. Her name was said to be Manika.[116] In addition, a Loolecondera estate worker, Inderkumar Kithnasami, whose great-grandfather and grandfather knew Taylor, reported in 2014 that Taylor may have been involved with more than one woman. Kithnasami also said that in 1992 some visitors who claimed to be grandchildren of Taylor's arrived at the estate and offered to buy the land but the government declined to sell.[117]

There are indeed some individuals based in Sri Lanka and overseas who claim descent from James Taylor but their genealogy indicates instead that they are connected to two other Taylor brothers in Ceylon at the time: John and William Taylor who worked on the Wanarajah and Darawella estates.[118] It is also important to note here that James Duncan's claim that Taylor referred to the children of mixed unions as 'striped' is wrong. Duncan has not only incorrectly cited the letter about Taylor's thoughts on such a union but has confused this with an earlier letter where he refers to his 'blue striped cotton trousers'.[119] Instead, as we saw in the previous chapter, Taylor's criticisms of children in Ceylon were confined to those born to European parents.

James Taylor's private life in Ceylon remains largely unknown and open to speculation. Based on his photographs, oral tradition from his great-great niece, and Forrest's book, the historian Tom Barron suggested in the 1970s that Taylor was intimate with both a Tamil and a Sinhalese woman. Barron learned during his visits to Sri Lanka in that same decade that Taylor left part of his life savings to his Sinhalese housekeeper.[120] What is clear is that James Taylor never admitted any such relationships to his family in Scotland. Instead, he consistently assured them of his intention to remain a bachelor. It is likely, however, that suspicions circulated around Auchenblae and were reinforced on receipt of Taylor's photograph albums following his death. His assertions to always remain a bachelor and the connections that he maintained with his Scottish family are discussed in the chapter which follows.

Notes

1 Taylor letters, 11 April 1852.

2 See, for instance, Nira Wickramasinghe, *Sri Lanka in the Modern Age: A History of Contested Identities* (London, 2006).

3 Stephen Howe, 'Empire and ideology', in Sarah Stockwell (ed.), *The British Empire: Themes and Perspectives* (Oxford, 2008), p. 166.

4 John MacKenzie, *Orientalism: History, Theory and the Arts* (Manchester and New York, 1995).

5 See Jane Rendall, 'Scottish Orientalism: From Robertson to James Mill', *Historical Journal*, 25:1 (1982), pp. 43–69; Martha McLaren, *British India and British Scotland, 1780–1830* (Akron, 2001).

6 See, for instance, Colin Calloway, *White People, Indians, and Highlanders: Tribal Peoples and Colonial Encounters in Scotland and America* (Oxford, 2008); Graeme Morton and David A. Wilson (eds), *Irish and Scottish Encounters with Indigenous Peoples* (Montreal and Kingston, 2013); Don Watson, *Caledonia Australis: Scottish Highlanders on the Frontier of Australia* (Sydney, 1997; first published 1984), esp. chs 4 and 8; Angela McCarthy, *Scottishness and Irishness in New Zealand since 1840* (Manchester, 2011), ch. 7.

7 See T.M. Devine, *To the Ends of the Earth: Scotland's Global Diaspora, 1750–2010* (London, 2011), ch. 8.

8 Taylor letters, 23 June 1852.

9 For discussion of Sri Lanka's ethnic groups see Wickramasinghe, *Sri Lanka in the Modern Age*.

10 ICS 86/4/9/7, Ferguson Papers, 'Report on Military Points connected with Ceylon', 31 December 1865. Patrick Peebles notes that Moors trace their ancestry to Arabia. See Patrick Peebles, *The Plantation Tamils of Ceylon* (London and New York, 2001), p. 4.

11 Taylor letters, 10 July 1858.

12 *Ceylon Times*, 23 February 1855, p. 126.

13 John D. Rogers, 'Caste as a social category and identity in colonial Lanka', *Indian Economic and Social History Review*, 41:1 (2004), p. 53. See also Kumari Jayawardena, *Nobodies to Somebodies: The Rise of the Colonial Bourgeoisie in Sri Lanka* (London and New York, 2002).

14 Wickramasinghe, *Sri Lanka in the Modern Age*, p. 47.

15 Taylor letters, 23 June 1852.
16 Raj Sekhar Basu, *Nandanar's Children: The Paraiyans' Tryst with Destiny, Tamil Nadu, 1850–1956* (New Delhi, 2011), p. 123.
17 Rogers, 'Caste as a social category', p. 52.
18 Taylor letters, 24 July 1857.
19 NLS, Fettercairn Estate Papers, Acc 4796, No. 54, Letters to Sir John Stuart Forbes, 1833–1852, Henry Stiven (Ancoombra) to Sir John Stuart Forbes (Fettercairn), 5 April 1852.
20 Taylor letters, 13 March 1852.
21 Ibid., 24 July 1857.
22 Ibid., 23 June 1852.
23 Ibid., 21 February 1859.
24 Ibid., 16 October 1851.
25 Ibid., 25 January 1873.
26 Ibid., 5 November 1876
27 Wickramasinghe, *Sri Lanka in the Modern Age*, p. 49. See also Anthony John Christopher, '"Ariane's thread": Sri Lankan census superintendents' reports as guides to identity data', *Asian Population Studies*, 11:3 (2015), pp. 1–19.
28 NMS, K2000.200, James Taylor photo album.
29 Taylor letters, 29 March 1874.
30 University of Aberdeen Special Collections, Charles Arbuthnot papers, MS 3029, Robert Arbuthnot (Colombo) to his mother, 22 September 1801, p. 115, and Robert Arbuthnot (Colombo) to his father, 16 November 1801, p. 138.
31 Taylor letters, 9 January 1853.
32 Roland Wenzlhuemer, *From Coffee to Tea Cultivation in Ceylon, 1880–1900* (Leiden and Boston, 2008), p. 118.
33 'Old labour supply', *WCO*, 11 June 1886, p. 584.
34 Ibid.
35 'The extra-labour population of coffee estates', *OCO*, 23 November 1872, p. 469.
36 Trevor Burnard, *Mastery, Tyranny and Desire: Thomas Thistlewood and his Slaves in the Anglo-Jamaican World* (Chapel Hill, 2004), p. 181.
37 E.B. Denham, *The Census of Ceylon 1911 Estate Statistics: The Estate Population* (Colombo, 1912), p. 12.
38 Taylor letters, 23 June 1852.
39 Stiven to Forbes, 5 April 1852.
40 Ibid., 17 September 1857.
41 William Boyd, 'Ceylon and its pioneers', *Ceylon Literary Register*, 24 February 1888, p. 251.
42 Taylor letters, 27 May 1859.
43 Peebles, *Plantation Tamils*, p. 57; Donovan Moldrich, *Bitter Berry Bondage: The Nineteenth Century Coffee Workers of Sri Lanka* (Kandy, 1989), p. 12.
44 Taylor letters, 17 September 1857.
45 Stiven to Forbes, 5 April 1852.
46 ICS86/9/5/46, Ferguson Papers, General correspondence and news cuttings, *The Times*, 'Ceylon under British rule'.

47 Peebles, *Plantation Tamils*; ICS86/4/9/9, Ferguson Papers, Report of the Labour Commission (September 1908); Roberts, 'Indian estate labour in Ceylon', Part I, esp. pp. 1–2.
48 *Proceedings of the Planters' Association, Kandy, for the year ending 17th February 1862* (Colombo, 1862), p. 11.
49 Taylor letters, 13 March 1852.
50 ICS86/9/1/3, Ferguson Papers, Correspondence and other papers of or relating to A. M. Ferguson, John Ferguson (Colombo), 25 October 1872.
51 Taylor letters, 24 July 1857.
52 Burnard, *Mastery, Tyranny and Desire*.
53 C.R. Rigg, 'On coffee planting in Ceylon', *Journal of Indian Archipelago and Eastern Asia*, 6 (1852), p. 131.
54 Taylor letters, 3 December 1857.
55 'Correspondence: Coffee stealing', *Proceedings of the Planters' Association of Ceylon for year ending February 17, 1874* (Colombo, 1874), pp. 54–185. Taylor's response can be found on pp. 111–115.
56 James Duncan, *In the Shadows of the Tropics: Climate, Race and Biopower in Nineteenth Century Ceylon* (Aldershot, 2007), pp. 71, 93.
57 'Attempt to murder Mr. James Taylor of Loolondra', *OCO*, 3 July 1878, p. 452; 'Case of shooting', *OCO*, 2 July 1878, p. 446.
58 Taylor letters, 9 September 1878.
59 *OCO*, 1 August 1878, p. 529.
60 D.M. Forrest, *A Hundred Years of Ceylon Tea, 1867–1967* (London, 1967), p. 57.
61 Taylor letters, 11 April 1852.
62 Ibid., 23 June 1852.
63 Ibid., 17 September 1857.
64 Peebles, *Plantation Tamils*, pp. 11–13.
65 William Boyd, 'Ceylon and its pioneers', *Ceylon Literary Register*, 23 March 1888, p. 281.
66 For evidence of extensive planter brutality in Jamaica see Burnard, *Mastery, Tyranny and Desire*.
67 Taylor letters, 27 January 1857.
68 Ibid., 21 February 1859.
69 ICS86/3/1, Ferguson papers, Correspondence with planters, W.R. Ferguson to John Ferguson, 28 February 1878.
70 Taylor letters, 23 June 1852.
71 Duncan, *In the Shadows of the Tropics*, pp. 111–112.
72 Taylor letters, undated.
73 Ibid., 24 July 1857.
74 *OCO*, 10 October 1872, p. 401.
75 James Taylor response, 'Outdoor relief and district hospitals', *Proceedings of the Planters Association, Kandy, for the year ending 17th February 1872* (Colombo, 1872), p. 263.
76 *OCO*, 10 June 1872, p. 233.
77 Ibid., 23 November 1872, p. 469.

78 Duncan, *In the Shadows of the Tropics*, p. 141.
79 Burnard, *Mastery, Tyranny, and Desire*, p. 129.
80 Peebles, *Plantation Tamils*, p. 95.
81 Duncan, *In the Shadows of the Tropics*, p. 107.
82 *TA*, 1 August 1890, p. 79.
83 William Boyd, 'Ceylon and its pioneers', *Ceylon Literary Register*, 24 February 1888, p. 251.
84 Taylor letters, 23 October 1890.
85 M.W. Roberts, 'Indian estate labour in Ceylon during the coffee period (1830–1880)', Part II, *Indian Economic and Social History Review*, 3:1 (1966), p. 109.
86 Burnard, *Master, Tyranny, and Desire*, p. 130.
87 Alexander Broadie, 'The rise (and fall?) of the Scottish Enlightenment', in T.M. Devine and Jenny Wormald (eds), *The Oxford Handbook of Modern Scottish History* (Oxford, 2012), pp. 370–385.
88 T.M. Devine, *The Great Highland Famine: Hunger, Emigration and the Scottish Highlands in the Nineteenth Century* (Edinburgh, 1988), pp. 111–145, and Devine, *To the Ends of the Earth*, pp. 107–124.
89 Colin Kidd, 'Race, empire and the limits of nineteenth century nationhood', *Historical Journal*, 46:4 (2003), pp. 873–892.
90 Robert Knox, *The Races of Men: A Fragment* (Philadelphia, 1850), p. 214.
91 T.M. Devine (ed.), *Recovering Scotland's Slavery Past: The Caribbean Connection* (Edinburgh, 2015).
92 Catherine Hall, 'The racist ideas of slave owners are still with us today', *Guardian*, 26 September 2016, online at: www.theguardian.com/commentisfree/2016/sep/26/racist-ideas-slavery-slave-owners-hate-crime-brexit-vote
93 Jayeeta Sharma, '"Lazy" natives, coolie labour, and the Assam tea industry', *Modern Asian Studies*, 43:6 (2009), pp. 1287–1324; Rana P. Behal, 'Coolie drivers or benevolent paternalists? British tea planters in Assam and the indenture labour system', *Modern Asian Studies*, 44:1 (2010), p. 36.
94 Taylor letters, 24 July 1857.
95 Ibid., 17 September 1857.
96 Peter Putnis includes these extracts in 'International press and the Indian uprising', in Marina Carter and Crispin Bates (eds), *Mutiny at the Margins: New Perspectives on the Indian Uprising of 1857. Volume 3: Global Perspectives* (New Delhi, 2013), pp. 5–6.
97 Rebecca Merritt, 'Public perceptions of 1857: An overview of British press responses to the Indian uprising', in Andrea Major and Crispin Bates (eds), *Mutiny at the Margins: New Perspectives on the Indian Uprising of 1857. Volume 2: Britain and the Indian Uprising* (New Delhi, 2013), p. 3.
98 Ibid., p. 13; Jenny Sharpe, 'The unspeakable limits of rape: Colonial violence and counter-insurgency', *Genders*, 10 (1991), pp. 31–32.
99 Sharpe, 'Unspeakable limits', pp. 33–34.
100 Taylor letters, 24 July 1857.
101 Ibid., 24 July 1857.

102 Clare Anderson, *Subaltern Lives: Biographies of Colonialism in the Indian Ocean World, 1790–1920* (Cambridge, 2012), p. 6.
103 Taylor letters, 23 June 1852.
104 *TA*, 1 November 1892, p. 337.
105 See Roberts, 'Indian estate labour in Ceylon', Part II, pp. 114–115.
106 Ronald Hyam, *Empire and Sexuality: The British Experience* (Manchester, 1990), p. 202.
107 See Durba Ghosh, *Sex and the Family in Colonial India: The Making of Empire* (Cambridge, 2006) and William Dalrymple, *White Mughals: Love and Betrayal in Eighteenth Century India* (London, 2003), p. 35.
108 Taylor letters, 3 December 1857. Duncan in his *In the Shadows of the Tropics* does not transcribe this – or several other quotes from Taylor – properly.
109 John Weatherstone, *The Early British Tea and Coffee Planters and their Way of Life, 1825–1900: The Pioneers* (London, 1986), pp. 180–182.
110 Ghosh, *Sex and the Family*, p. 29.
111 These two photographs appear with his letters in NLS, Papers of James Taylor, MS 15908.
112 Dalrymple, *White Mughals*, p. 182.
113 NLS, MS 15909, Photograph album of James Taylor.
114 Forrest, *A Hundred Years of Ceylon Tea*, p. 57.
115 Taylor's original will has not been located. Details from his last will and codicil, published in the press, state that 'One-fourth of the estate is bequeathed to the mother of Mr. Taylor's children'. By the codicil the mother was to receive R5,000 more. The will was dated 15 September 1855 and the codicil 26 March 1886. See *OCO*, 11 June 1892, p. 634. For further discussion, see chapter 8.
116 Conversation with Lalith Abeykoon, January 2016.
117 Conversation with Inderkumar Kithnasami, as translated by Kapila Ranathunga, 3 February 2014.
118 The children were placed in the Good Shepherd convent at Kandy by J. Taylor and were left shares in the Wanarajah tea estate to cover the cost of their education. John Taylor then moved to New Zealand, where he died in November 1892. Both John and William were born in Scotland, at Cruden, Aberdeenshire. There are also claims that former tea planter Andrew Gordon Taylor, who died suddenly in 2015, was descended from James Taylor. However, during my phone conversation with Andrew in February 2014 he claimed descent from Sir William Taylor.
119 Duncan claims that Taylor's comment about marriage is found in a letter dated 3 October 1857. The date is, however, 3 December 1857. Taylor's comment about his 'striped cotton trousers' appears in a letter dated 17 September 1857. Part of Duncan's confusion may be due to the incorrect sequencing of the letters in the Taylor archive, but that does not excuse the reference to 'striped' children. See Duncan, *In the Shadows of the Tropics*, p. 60.
120 T.J. Barron, 'British coffee planters in 19th century Ceylon', paper presented to Institute of Commonwealth Studies, University of London, 22 November, p. 4; e-mail communication to Angela McCarthy, 28 August 2013.

7

Ties to home

For the most part, the majority of Scots, as with the British in general who were drawn to Asia over much of the eighteenth and early nineteenth centuries, were young, single men who went out to make money, hopefully as quickly as possible, and then return home with their gains. Part of the explanation for this sojourning was that the climate and environment of Asia were not suited to mass European settler emigration. The chances of becoming rich were counterbalanced by the very real possibility of succumbing to disease soon after arrival. Yet for those who secured some means or even wealth, profits seeped home through a number of channels, not only via direct investment from returnees but also as remittances from expatriates to their families in Scotland.[1] In other cases, migrants sometimes had to depend on their kinfolk in Britain to provide financial succour while in distant lands, although connections between home and overseas extended well beyond a purely economic context.

Some migrants to the East like James Taylor, however, did spend their lives in the tropics while remaining deeply and intimately connected to their homeland. For those like Taylor, personal letters could function as a 'token of solidarity' and consolation with family in an environment radically different from the society they had left behind.[2] Yet, in their relatively rare discussions of the transnational exchange of migrant correspondence in the Scottish diaspora, historians have largely emphasised the practical – and positive – components of these ties.[3] Less consideration is given to the ways in which sentiments were 'designed to influence and sometimes manipulate readers',[4] or to the sometimes negative consequences of maintaining ties to home. Studies of more formal networking, such as the creation of ethnic associations in the new lands, likewise tend to focus on their importance for the provision of patronage and material support.[5]

When Taylor left Britain for Ceylon in 1851, he experienced a sense of loss and in his early years there often described his isolation and need for contact with his loved ones. Correspondence with family was a predictable way of alleviating these feelings while helping to sustain ties to home. Taylor undeniably relished contact with his family in Scotland. In examining these emotional and practical connections, we will draw attention not only to the deliberate deployment of feelings to achieve practical outcomes, but also to the more fractious component of these encounters. In particular, we consider evidence that sentimental ties to the old country were sometimes based on 'power relations'.[6] What follows, therefore, relates to studies of the history of the emotions as we trace the circumstances in which many of Taylor's inner feelings emerged through his interactions with home. This emotional side to his personality comes through despite his claim in 1859, when writing about a dispute over money, that 'I know I am of a cool and distant disposition and detest and despise all displays of feeling'.[7] The comment implies that he might be an exemplar of the stereotypical emotional reticence of the Victorian male.[8] But there are real doubts whether Taylor was quite as disconnected from his feelings as he claimed. His letters to his family suggest a different interpretation.

We begin by examining Taylor remitting funds and sending photographs to his relatives, before considering issues of health, death, and neighbourhood ties. Crucially, we do not focus on one particular emotion but show the range of his feelings in a number of different periods and circumstances.[9] Further, we assess whether Taylor's sometimes testy connections with home contributed to his decision to remain in Ceylon for the whole of his working life. Just as Taylor had established himself as patriarchal among his workers, so too did this extend to his family in Scotland.

Remitting money and sending objects

A study of northeast Scotland's links to Ceylon in the period before 1875 has shown the investment of planter profits at home and the commissioning of engineering firms to supply equipment for the coffee plantations. All this 'had important repercussions for the economy of the area'.[10] It is also well known that in the eighteenth century sojourning Scots employed by the East India Company had sent back significant funds to purchase landed estates and invest in farms.[11] But little information has survived on the more modest but continuous supply of family support of the kind described throughout Taylor's letters.

The first sums that James Taylor remitted to his family, at least according to his surviving letters, were sent in 1857 and were described as 'a little help to Robert and the rest May & Marg[t] to get some clothes. I have been rather neglectful but hoping to be excused for all faults and hoping a continuance of the respect of you all I shall be glad to do a little for your comfort.'[12] Taylor was clearly an exemplar of the dutiful migrant son and brother. After that, money continued to be forwarded on a regular basis and was generally of reasonable value as 'small sums cant be sent all the way to you. People here wont transmit them and so I cant send them unless of a respectable amount. If a few pounds could be sent I would send more.'[13] In 1858, therefore, Taylor forwarded £20 for his siblings and for the purchase of books to be sent to him in Ceylon. He invited his father to use the rest to buy tobacco.[14] Further financial outlay followed, including £30 in 1859 meant partly for his grandfather and brother and sister, May and Robert.[15] These were not inconsiderable sums for the time and were approximately the same value as a single agricultural labourer's annual wage in 1860 in Kincardine.[16] In 1882, he sent £16 14s 4d to his father, about half a ploughman's annual wage in that region,[17] to 'spend it on comforts such as you can enjoy, and not think of saving money for my benefit in the future at-any-rate. I fancy very little money was saved during my mother's life time by you and what you have made since has been with the help of the mother of another family.'[18] Taylor also gave money to allow his father to subscribe to local newspapers.[19]

His generosity extended to nieces and nephews. Sister Margaret received money in April 1875, the same month that she remarried, to 'look after the children'. But there was a proviso as he made clear: 'I confess I feel no very particular interest in them and shall not take it kind if she forces them too much on my attention.'[20] Another £16 12s 3d was despatched in 1882 for Margaret's son, James Davie, to enable him to become an apprentice saddler.[21] For Taylor, clearly one way of cementing bonds with his family was to support them for a range of different purposes. However, his blunt comments about his sister's children suggest that there was a limit to his generosity.

Those beyond his immediate family were also recipients of Taylor's largesse. In 1860, following his grandfather Robert Moir's death, he asked about Moir's widow, his second wife, accepting that 'we must see her attended to for his sake'.[22] Ann Middleton, an acquaintance at Montrose, received £11, for which Taylor had 'much pleasure in being able to acknowledge a service done to my mother before I was born'.[23] Others to whom he felt an obligation included Henry Stiven's orphaned children after the death of their mother, Margaret, in February 1867 (Henry had died two years earlier). Taylor himself had been godfather to their eldest son.[24] Stiven's life was insured but Taylor informed his father, 'There was a long law-suit about it as he died greatly in debt and the creditors tried to get this money.' The principal legacy 'will be given to them when they become of age. I do not think there could have been much dispute as to who was to have charge of the children. Mrs. Farquhar I believe was an executor to the will; and in the will itself, I understand, the children were made over to her care.' There was an assumption that the children's uncles, Peter and Charles Moir, might also make provision for them. But according to Taylor, James Moir 'thinks he has enough to do with his own family of six children'. In any case, Taylor felt obliged to give some support, as Peter Moir had arranged for his own first appointment in Ceylon, 'and this is another reason why I should help in ... doing a good turn for any connections of the Moirs'.[25] The familial link with the Stivens and Moirs was especially strong, as Taylor was directly related to them through his maternal grandparents. Another who received his assistance, according to a tribute after Taylor's death, was the widow of his brother Robert Moir Taylor.[26] Scottish families overseas, then, were just as broadly conceptualised as at home, consisting not just of the nuclear family but of wider blood and marriage ties.[27]

All told, at least in terms of the known evidence, Taylor sent a minimum of £270 to Scotland during his four decades in Ceylon. During the late 1850s he sent home £80, while in the 1870s he remitted £74 and in the early 1880s £116.[28] These were considerable amounts in relation to his income, given that he claimed in 1869 to be able to save only £100 from his £500 salary, and a decade later had just £450 saved in the bank.[29] Moreover, given the absence of his correspondence for the 1860s and his mention at other times of money sent without stipulating the value, the recorded monies are an under-estimate of his total remittances.

The ways in which migrant remittances were sent and their emotional repercussions have received little scholarly attention in studies of Scotland's diaspora.[30] Taylor's correspondence, however, shows how they could give rise to misunderstandings and disagreements. In 1859 he told his father that he felt 'quite ashamed' and wished to 'have nothing further to do with it' because of the 'squabbling' over monies he had sent, although he added that his comments were not 'angry nor meant to vex or abuse you'. The problem arose because he sometimes sent funds independently of his father directly to his siblings and his grandfather, Robert Moir. The father appears to have thought that this implied distrust of him as an intermediary with the rest of the family, a claim which Taylor flatly denied: 'My ideas were these that if I sent money to my sisters & brother through you it would not be so appreciated by them as if they were getting it into their own hands directly ... in sending money to Grandfather will it not be more gratifying ... and will it not be more comfortable for him to get it freely than that any one should supervise his expenditure and his private affairs?'[31] Taylor was deferential in communications with his father, but firm at the same time.

Taylor must, however, have sent his father more money intended for his brother and sister because Michael revealed later that he had refused to give it to Robert, claiming that the boy would 'be at horse delling [*dealing*] or something foolish'. Michael also placed May's share in the savings bank 'so that she will not require to call on you again'. Interfering, yet grateful at the same time, the father hoped that 'God will prosper and bless you in your temprel [*temporal*] and spiritual entrests [*interests*]'. He also told his son that he intended to buy a house in the village which 'will be a home to you when I am gone. It will repay you some measure for your kindness and if you dont require you will se who is most needing it'.[32] Taylor's help for his father, at least, did not go unappreciated.

James Taylor's relatives likewise sought financial help for specific purposes. In 1882 Margaret and her second husband, George Nairn, sought his support to buy a farm. Taylor's initial response was one of irritation. In paternal – and patriarchal – mode, he criticised their 'unbusiness sort of style' request in 'giving me no idea of the sum required'. Instead, he asked for a statement to show the outlay for the farm, rent, and probable returns, and how they intended to raise the money. He continued at length in exasperated fashion:

> It is far too much to suppose that I will go into a speculation I know nothing about in that off hand style and with no mention of security or interest beyond Maggie's assertion that 'my money will not grow any less with you'! How can any one be 'sure of that'? It is my belief that it is utter folly in the present state of the world to tie one's self down to a fixed rent for 19, years to come in any farm at home. It is quite possible that one might buy the farm outright by the end of that time for not more than several years of its present rent. Anyhow as far as I can judge rents will be much less [*erased:* by nine] before nineteen years than they are at present.
>
> ... I am willing, as I have been, to give you a little help out of my pay as I think I can spare it, though it is not a time in Ceylon when I ought to spare anything I can help. But you are scheming now to make me give up the little money I have saved and which is all I have to look to if I should have to leave Ceylon or planting in it fail so far as to leave me without employment. However, I am not likely to do that, though I run some risk of losing it or part of it in the Bank. I wish I could get a better investment than that. But there is nothing safe that I understand or can get at in the present state of things here. Nevertheless I am not going to part with any of it; nor invest any of it; on the terms you have proposed. A 'Home of your own' does not mean profits nor interest; nor yet safety for the money invested in this instance.[33]

Quite clearly, Taylor's preoccupation with money, which had intensified with his life as a planter, extended to his family. His sister and brother-in-law appear to have proposed new terms for Taylor to consider, as in his next letter he sent them the substantial sum of £83 1s 5 d.[34] Margaret, George, and their family used it to help them move from East Braikie, where in the 1881 Census George was recorded as an overseer, to Newton of Parkhill at St Vigean's, where he was returned in the next census as a farmer. This evidence of upward mobility prompted their benefactor to give voice to some anxiety, including observations about 'a bad season of drought' in 1884 and high rents in 1890 which he reckoned made leasing a farm not 'a safe speculation'. Taylor expressed preference for 'the English style of yearly lease', despite recognising that 'the old Scotch nineteen years was I suppose more satisfactory in the old steady going times'. Dumbstruck, he continued: 'It astonishes me how you can carry on at all with prices of produce so much reduced and the old fashioned rents still to pay.'[35]

We do not know how common the habit of sending home remittances was in north-east Scotland. But if other migrants behaved in the same way as Taylor then it might be suggested that a form of 'dependency culture' developed of the kind identified for the region of Cornwall in this period.[36]

If money sometimes generated tense exchanges, other items sent between Ceylon and Scotland were more likely to produce positive feelings, which enabled relationships to endure over long periods.[37] Among these, photographs were especially important. 'I'm most anxious to receive the photographic portraits you promise', Taylor wrote to his father in 1857.[38] 'Anxiety' in this context, however, did not imply fear but, rather, anticipation. A few months later, in January 1858, he promised to send his own picture: 'I hope to have a chance of getting a Photographic picture of myself to send you about the middle of next month and if I dont send it in this will send it soon after if I dont fail in getting it. I will try in order to show you that I am not a better looking cove than usual though not quite the same as when I left.'[39] The image was duly despatched and positively received. It was most likely the one reproduced in Figure 7.1, showing a strikingly handsome figure taken before the growth of his full beard in Ceylon:

> I'm glad you got my picture safe. I am now anxiously waiting for yours per Mr Blacklaw. ... You seem to be rather too highly pleased with it's appearance. Perhaps you must mind that it is not exactly like me and though it is said that a photograph never improves one's appearance I think it has at least done mine no harm and the general opinion here of those who saw it was that it looked better than myself.[40]

Taylor's surviving photographs are set in two albums, the first presented to him by his sister Margaret in October 1863 as a 'Weding Gift'. Mostly dating from 1863, the majority of images are not identified, although presumably one is that of Taylor's grandfather Robert Moir, which he received in 1859.[41] Another which can be recognised is that of brother Robert Moir Taylor, due to Taylor's recording his death in the United States in 1877 (Figure 7.2). For the most part the images appear to reflect more interest in kindred at home and less in friends and associates in Ceylon. This traffic in mementos was one way in which Taylor preserved memories of past times while helping also to nourish emotional connections with those from whom he was now physically separated across the seas. The pull of the old country and concern for the folk there remained with him until his death.[42] Nevertheless, there is little evidence that his mementoes stimulated the kind of memories of home to trigger nostalgic stories and homesickness as found in other studies of migration and material culture.[43]

7.1 'Better than myself': possibly the earliest photo of Taylor in existence. The original photograph (National Library of Scotland, MS 15908, f. 214) appears to have been printed in reverse. We have here corrected the photographer's error.

Health and death

Some historians of migrant correspondence have suggested that letters from home were often crafted in order to arouse guilt among those who had gone and encourage in them stronger feelings of obligation to the family that remained.[44] Unfortunately, however, apart from a few letters sent by his grandfather Robert Moir, other correspondence sent to Taylor in Ceylon does not seem to have survived. Robert's letters and Taylor's own, however, do show significant concern with the health and welfare of family in Scotland, even if Taylor's feelings were not always sympathetic, especially when discussing illness. In 1857, for instance, he scathingly dismissed his eighteen-year-old sister Margaret's alleged

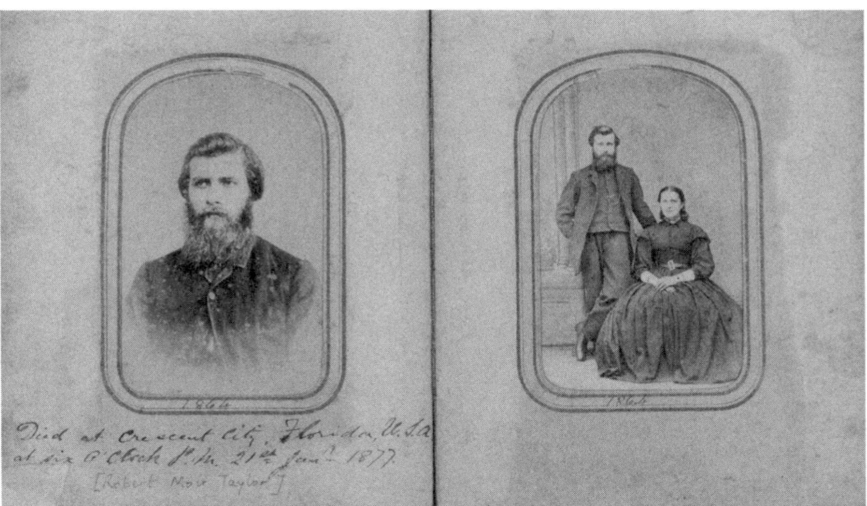

7.2 Taylor's brother, Robert Moir Taylor, who died in the USA in 1877. He is pictured here alone and with his wife in 1864. Taylor would later send money to Robert's widow.

bout of rheumatic fever: 'tell her to go and look out for a lad and dont let herself think about the possibility of being sick. It must be half imagination. Why does she not send me a letter if she is off work. She cannot be very busy. I dont think Rheumatic fever is a serious complaint though old people I mind used to declare all sorts of Rheumatism a painful one.'[45] During the nineteenth century rheumatism was characterised by several symptoms which could include swollen, inflamed, and painful joints, rashes, and fevers. By the time of Margaret's illness, heart damage had emerged as the 'most significant clinical manifestation of the disease'.[46] Taylor's complaints were highly gendered, as he considered women to be vulnerable to illness simply because of the very nature of their sex: 'I'm sorry to hear of my Aunts ill health but it is natural for women at home to be ill.'[47] He commented on his twenty-one-year-old sister May (Figure 7.3) in similar vein, drawing attention to the apparent physical repercussions of her emotions, but also their impact on her intimate relationships:

> she makes herself worse than she is. She always writes in a gloomy strain … She is of a terrible gloomy disposition surely. I daresay she is religious but half of it seems low spirits. She'll come to be a complaining uncomfortable wife by & bye if she dont brighten up. She must make herself ill with such a gloomy nature. I'd be ill in a day and would not live long here if I let my spirits get so low. Nothing will keep on well here so much as good spirits and diversion anything here but gloominess and low spirits that is the worst thing possible and must not be a good thing any where so get her roused up.[48]

7.3 'She must make herself ill with such a gloomy nature': May Taylor, James's sister.

In Taylor's mind, as suggested above, low spirits were linked not only to poor health but to difficult marital relations. Here he reflected the growing medical opinion in the nineteenth century that mental states had physical consequences, with extreme passions posing a threat to health and life.[49] A positive outlook, he reckoned, was critical in order to cope with the travails of life. His condescending views may also reflect a broader portrayal of women in Scotland 'as having many failings of biology and character'.[50]

Robert Moir's letters also discuss multiple maladies. Sent in the late 1850s, when Taylor's grandfather was aged 76, they are full of complaints about his poor health, business losses, and reluctance to live in his old age with the widow of his brother, John. In 1859 he lamented, 'it cost me many a troubled thought after misfortin [*misfortune*] followed one after another how I was to live out the ramander of my deays'.[51] Certainly, in at least some strata of Scottish society, those who left for careers abroad were expected to have a sense of responsibility and obligation to needy members of family at home. When Taylor sent back £10, 'a verrey seasonable gift', Moir replied, 'I neglected to menshon to you that with your kind allowance and an anuity of ten pound she has from the leat [*late*] Dr Fordyce after paying hous[*e*] rent we can live comfortably on her anuity'.[52] Moir hoped that in response to Taylor's generosity 'Almighty God may reward you in this World and in the world to com.'[53]

His grandfather also provided Taylor with information about other relatives, including members of the extended family living in Aberdeen and Liverpool. Moir admitted that he was not fit enough to visit Taylor's father, Michael, but said that contemplation of the journey brought to mind his deceased daughter and Taylor's mother, Margaret Moir.[54] Such memories, fraught with feeling, clearly struck a nerve with Taylor, as he asked his grandfather for a token of remembrance of his mother. In response, Moir regretted having lost his daughter's letters but enclosed a lock of her hair and also promised to send 'half a dozen of silver tea spones which belonged to your grand Mother. They wer a present she got from hir Mother, have ben carfuly kipt ever sins. I wil sind them by James Moir when he returns.'[55] Taylor's grandfather was as good as his word. In August 1859 he wrote, 'I send you by James Moir my portrait an half a dozen of silver tea spons which belonged to your Grand Mother Margrat Steven which I hop you wil *d*eep [*keep*] as a memarandoun of your Grand Father and grand Mother.'[56]

The items presumably took on great significance for Taylor, as four months later, in December 1859, Taylor's father wrote to tell his son of Robert Moir's death due to a 'bowell complant'. Michael Taylor had visited Moir and found him 'very poorly and much spent'. The doctor revealed that 'he thought him dieing'. Seeking comfort for Moir, Michael arranged for the minister to pray with him, 'which he did and gave him the sacrement and he was twice prayed for publickly in the Chaple the day before he died'. On a subsequent visit, Taylor's ailing grandfather learned that the prognosis was poor but he was 'in the hands of a Grashous God' to 'guide him thro the the dark Valey and his rod and his staf ould comfort him and I left the Dear old man not expecting again to se him in the Body, intill we meet at the judgement seat of Christ'. Robert Moir was buried in a covered coffin and a dinner was held 'after the funeral with various sorts of bread and beaf steak', attended by a range of relatives and friends including numerous Moirs and Stivens. Michael had made enquiries about the funeral of Moir's first wife, Margaret, and 'determined that equel respect should be shown to hir husbands remains'.[57] The cost associated with this clearly troubled Michael, for he sought his son's approval. In response, Taylor expressed appreciation: 'I have no criticisms to make on the funeral. The more honour that was paid to his remains the more satisfaction was given to me. You did not tell me where he is buried.'[58] Taylor would presumably learn that Moir, aged seventy-seven, was buried on 22 December 1859 at the Laurencekirk Episcopalian cemetery.[59]

Three decades later, death struck closer to Michael Taylor. Taylor's consolation on the loss of his father's second wife overlooked his testy past with her: 'I am very sorry for him being left alone without his wife and companion and at his age no one can make up for her loss to him but I hope "Bety" as you call her, my niece, may be able to keep him so far comfortable and his house in comfortable order for him. I have no doubt he will be kind to her.'[60] At this time, June 1890, these extended ties proved important for seventy-nine-year-old Michael Taylor. With his eldest son, James, in Ceylon, the youngest son, William, probably in India, daughters Margaret and Lizzie living elsewhere, and two further children (May and Robert) dead, wider family ties offered him important practical and emotional support. Reliance on family connections was not simply because folk were living longer,[61] but was a result of the dispersal and death of younger generations.

Concerns about their widowed father's plans continued to preoccupy Taylor and his siblings. In 1891 there was uncertainty surrounding Michael's intentions about whether he would live with a cousin at Montrose or remain in Auchenblae. Either option, Taylor considered, was beneficial compared to the old home at Mosspark which Michael had left sometime between the 1871 and 1881 censuses. The ageing of Michael Taylor, or perhaps that of Taylor himself (he was now fifty-six), appears to have caused a shift in the son's feelings towards his father:

> Then, on the other hand if our father is going to live with them in Montrose why shouldn't he? I can suppose life in a big town is more comfortable for an old man, or even life in the village of Auchenblae, than life in a country farm house with its washing days and the smells of feeds being boiled for pigs and cattle and people coming in wet and muddy, and steaming in front of a smoky fire. Then think of the gude wife's everlasting scolding at everything and everyone and no way to get out of all these discomforts except going out in the rain or to the cold barn, or byre to look at the cows.
>
> Anyhow our father is his own master and must be allowed to do as he likes. Any interference with his plans or any dislike shown towards them will not tend to gain more of his favour nor make him more comfortable.[62]

The 1891 Census shows James Taylor's niece, twenty-two-year-old 'Betsy Davie', daughter of his sister Margaret and her first husband, Stuart Davie, living with eighty-year-old Michael at Inverurie Street in Auchenblae. Michael eventually died there in September 1894, just a couple of weeks before his eighty-fourth birthday. He was buried in the Presbyterian kirkyard and the headstone over the grave, erected by his daughter Margaret in 1895, commemorates Michael and his first wife, Margaret Moir. The grave of his second wife, Isobel Anderson Taylor, is in the same cemetery and her stone records

7.4 Michael Taylor, aged in his early sixties, taken at Arbroath, c.1875–1876.

the death in 1894 of their son, William, at Jeypore, India.[63] Michael left an estate worth £286 12s 2d,[64] or £33,176 at 2016 values.[65] Taylor had shown surprise seven years earlier at 'how you have made it. If all I have were put into English money it would be very little more.'[66] Although it was a relatively modest sum, Michael Taylor had inevitably benefited from his son's generosity in sending funds home.

Neighbours

Unlike many Scottish migrants to Ceylon, Taylor never returned home, either permanently or even for a visit. One reason was his attitudes to the wider neighbourhood connections at home. As with migrant correspondence from Ireland to Australia, Taylor's letters show 'energetic social interaction'.[67] Strikingly, however, these associations were often recalled in acrimonious terms. Taylor's recollections reveal that emotions were shaped not just by direct contact with home but by memories which in his case oscillated between good and bad:[68]

> I'm glad Mr Taylor of Cushnie is getting better. I really will say he was the only one of all the leading men about us when I was at home that was well liked by us coves that is perhaps properly that was more liked than feared and so he is the one I like best to hear about yet. Him and Mr Souter I like to remember about more than any others, and next to them Mr Phillip. I like them because they were free and easy and not stuck up demanding reverence when they did not excite it. I like to see a man holding his position because he is really fit to hold it and giving himself no apparent concern about it and making himself free to all without assuming a dignity.[69]

These blunt comments on some Fordoun folk may perhaps provide one reason why Taylor remained in Ceylon. In another letter he went further, expressing disappointment at a community unwilling to defend itself against seemingly false accusations:

> Are the people in the parish of Forduan so ignorant and prejudiced as to regard that matter of opening or dissecting a person's dead body with the feelings attributed to them by Dr Henderson's opponents? Do they feel so in the matter? The people of the place ought to regard such proceedings as an insult especially in the face of the letters produced from other doctors of other places where the intelligence of the people seems in advance of what is supposed to belong to you auld fashioned bodies. I'd get up a remonstrance and see who would sign it. I dont think Dr Henderson is a very amiable character. I did not like him at any rate when a boy at school and perhaps his opponents and some of his supporters may possibly have the same feeling but that is no reason why they should set against him and turn him out of a job[.][70]

Here he was referring to Joseph Henderson, a native of Fife and 'skilful surgeon', who died on 3 June 1875.[71] In a later letter, Taylor remembered a particular episode with Dr Henderson which still rankled years after:

> Dr Henderson I think got [*?only*] justice but I dont like the man and scarcely wonder at people not considering themselves tied to him by connexion with the same church or something else trying to get rid of him. I myself have not forgot a depreciating remark he was pleased to make about me in a scolding he thought fit to give me at one time and if I had anything to say to him again I should most likely make a return[.][72]

This comment tells us about the type of man Taylor had become. He was not one to forget prior hurts and was prepared to confront those who had caused him offence.

In his views about religion, Taylor also targeted the broader community. When he arrived in Ceylon in 1852 he rued the absence of a Presbyterian church on the island. He still felt fondness for the faith of his fathers almost a decade later, but then became disturbed on learning of the rapturous emotions accompanying the religious revival of the early 1860s in Scotland: 'I am glad to hear of the good it does. I'm rather of a peculiar disposition perhaps but I should be terribly disgusted at any one "groaning" in the church and would feel terribly inclined to kick him out. I have no doubt however that there must be a great deal more in it than silliness & hypocrisy and hope it will not fall away. It would be a grand reformation if it went on till it became universal!'[73] The revival had reached the north-east of Scotland from New York via Ireland.[74] Contemporaries considered it the first 'great revival that stirred the life of Victorian Scotland', although later commentators have argued that its impact has been exaggerated.[75]

Generating an even more adverse response from Taylor in the mid-1870s was the *Times of Blessing*, a religious periodical published in Edinburgh, which contained information about 'Moody & Sankey's doings'. He supposed the composer Ira Sankey and evangelist Dwight Moody's 'influence was less from what they said than from the influence a strong mind has over other people and the novelty of hearing old doctrine in a new lingo'.[76] Taylor focused more on Moody's preaching, which incorporated 'Yankee phrases' and New England speech in his biblical accounts, than on Sankey's popularisation of familiar tunes.[77] He then launched into a bitter attack on the periodical, which he considered was 'not up to the mark':

> The empty brainless 'goody-goody' and auld wife claptrap of Times of Blessing is as different as verses in a valentine from the Song of Solomon. It seems to me a common and a great mistake to suppose that any writing is valuable if religious, whither it has the silliness of a good sunday-school boy or the empty dryness of a wooden headed officer of the church. People of auld wife and 'minister' worshipping dispositions I think must sour all good and proper religious feeling & appreciation out of themselves grunting and groaning over such trash. Even the Bible is made a senseless dry book to people by their having been kept reading it as children before they could appreciate it or properly understand it.[78]

Taylor was reaffirming his own sense of self as measured and rational in contrast to those who wallowed in religious emotionalism. His religious views foreshadow the writings of Lewis Grassic Gibbon's 'Sunset Song', part of *A Scots Quair* trilogy, set in the Mearns.[79] Perhaps reflecting on his own upbringing, Taylor continued with a robust condemnation of the conduct of clerics:

> The bible and testament adapt themselves and clearly refer to circumstances unprovided for by the church, and were clearly written by wiser men than 'ministers', who have nevertheless gone beyond their province. Hence the general wish among the padre classes for 'denominational education' in order that they may build up their particular church dogmas on their teaching of the bible to children

> who might not find them in the bible after growing up to be men & women. It is odd that the padre classes have no confidence in pure morality and whatever else they find in the Bible as a sure guide to keep mankind in order. They must all have church rules and influences and special interpretations and beliefs besides. But for this there would only be our Christian Church and that not a church as we understand churches.[80]

We have no record of how his father, a church elder, might have responded to the son's diatribe. It is important to remember, however, that Taylor had been reared in a country where differences over ecclesiastical issues were commonplace and dissent from the established order was extensive. In 1843, during the Disruption, the Church of Scotland itself split apart into two congregations with the foundation of the Free Church after many decades of acrimonious dispute over patronage and appointment of ministers.[81] Robust exchanges were also part of family life. A comment from Taylor on what his father had said about him when visiting his Stiven relatives at Laurencekirk must have prompted a gruff retort from his father. As Taylor explained:

> about what you said at Stivens never mind only I dont wish it to be supposed that I have an eye after Miss Stiven because such is not the case and if you speak much at all of such matters then she may be misrepresented and I would not like it to [*be*] thought that you were scheming to give an opportunity for any such thing being proposed and also I would not like you to express high opinion of me. What I was told was that you had said among other things that you were glad I had broken off correspondence with Janet Ross as she was not worthy of me. But never mind. It is all a piece of nonsense and only served for a talk here. If any were perhaps misled they must be led right again by now and anything else must be set down to the feeling of veneration or vanity people at home regard friends abroad with especially a parent always willing to believe anything good of his family. So let it be so. I should not have mentioned it at all but just having been told about it I wrote a piece on the subject not angry I dont mean that by a harsh style but only expressive of low opinions of your caution and thoughtfulness on that occasion that was all. So dont suppose that I meant I was ill pleased by saying I had written in a harsh style. I consider I have more sense than get angry at such things or any piece of botheration of the kind[.][82]

The episode shows Taylor in control of his disappointment and possible resentment at his father's behaviour but at the same time not afraid to express his opinions frankly.

He was again annoyed about this type of gossip in September 1878: 'Does Mr. Bisset tell you of other things he may see about me in Ceylon papers? You might very often hear of me and my doings that way. If not he should not have troubled you with that bit of news.'[83] Taylor's irritation was caused by the fact that the incident Bissett had spoken of was the notorious attempt on his life two months earlier (discussed in chapter 6).

His letters, however, do reveal that among his multiple attachments to home some connections were viewed positively. One of the key families about whom Taylor sought information were the Burnetts of Monboddo, the major landowners of the parish. Taylor sombrely wrote in 1857, 'I never hear of old Capt Burnett now. Is he at Monboddo or in Aberdeen or where? I hope he is still in good health and vigour. J. Burnett will have his courage by now. Remember me to all old friends and say I remember them all.'[84] Taylor's comments referred to both James Burnett Burnett ('the Captain') and his son James Cumine Burnett ('Jim'). Taylor's father obviously provided the information which he wanted and he later wrote, 'Tell Capt Burnett I'm well and getting on well enough and I often remember about him and his lots of curious ways or what we used to think curious although no doubt rational to him and we used to consider him a good man. I hope he is still as well and lively and life like as before. I hope Jim Burnett may have occasion to smell powder about this affair and that he may escape more frightened than hurt the less of either the better.'[85] This referred to 'Jim' Burnett's role in the 37th Regiment of Bengal Native Infantry which took part in putting down the Indian 'Mutiny', further evidence of the number of people from a small community who had ventured abroad to India, Ceylon, the United States, and elsewhere. It was indeed the Scottish diaspora in local microcosm. In a further letter, Taylor continued to show interest in his fellow expatriate who came from a quite different social background to himself:

> I'm glad to hear of the Captain being still well and strong and I'm very glad of the information about James Burnett. I have frequently been wondering what part of the Indian affair he was engaged in. I shall now be able to trace his movements a bit since I know the regiment … When away from home we seem to have a particular feeling of interest in those from the same place even though there be great difference in circumstances and but little knowledge of the person before leaving home.[86]

This last remark is instructive, as it shows that even if class distinctions were not as prevalent in Ceylon as in Britain, Taylor was fully aware of ongoing status divisions in the local community which he had left behind. Nevertheless, he continued to seek information about the Burnetts, including Arthur, another of the Captain's sons, who was travelling to the East. All the while, however, Taylor remained alert to class distinctions:

> If he were to come I should certainly be happy to see him and consider it an honour to have the opportunity of giving him the best treatment possible in the jungle but you need not suppose that I should have much chance of treating him well or ill. Were he coming up to have a look at the coffee estates he would take up his quarters with some of the Kandy gentry probably Harper [*erased:* and as] which would be but right and proper and as he has no places in this district I should not likely see him unless it were in Kandy.[87]

A particular theme of interest in Taylor's writings to home relates to his father's repeated requests that Taylor return to marry. In this, Michael Taylor was not unlike many aged parents at home who sought the return of their migrant offspring.[88] Indeed, familial duties were one of the reasons why many Scottish migrants went back home during the nineteenth and twentieth centuries.[89] Around one-third of Scots, for instance, returned to their country of origin in the 1890s.[90]

As we saw earlier, before Taylor left Auchenblae in 1851 he had apparently developed a relationship with a local girl, Janet Ross, who might have been his intended match. Although that relationship may have partly prompted his migration from Scotland, the correspondence from home about his own bachelor state had not put matters to rest. In 1856, aged twenty-one, he wrote, 'I should be glad to hear of her being married for anything farther than a sort of concern I cannot have any feeling in the matter and I suppose that would scarcely have lasted so long had there been others here of a kind fit to replace her. But I am interested to know what is becoming of her and should like to hear that she was better.'[91] The following year he expressed relief to 'hear Janet Ross is still doing well poor woman. It is about time she was getting married now but you see I was right. I'm not prepared to take her although I certainly could do it now at a very short notice.'[92] Even so, she appears to have retained a place in his heart: 'I got Janet Ross's likeness and have it here carefully preserved. It lies on my dressing table. I sometimes take a peep at it and think of younger days. So I have not forgot her but cant marry her. I'm glad she is well again and hope she will soon get a husband to look after her beauty.'[93]

Marital opportunities for other women in the district also featured in Taylor's letters: 'Misses Jolly and others seem long in getting married at home. Is Miss Taylor of Cushnie not off yet? People are so slow about it that I begin to have hopes that if ever I come home I may find some one unmarried even then.'[94] He did not, though, appear to be in any particular rush: 'I suspect Janet Ross and all the lasses will have to wait a while before I be ready for a wife and I'd advise them not to expect me to trouble myself seeking their favour.'[95] An undated letter seemed to resolve the issue for Taylor, although it may have been a tactic in response to one from his father to draw him back to Scotland:

> I'm glad to hear that 'My Jessie' as you call her is likely to get married. I shall then be clear of her instead of feeling as if I had wronged her and were still doing so by not courting faster. I long ago settled that matter that I could not marry and she might look out elsewhere. If ever I came home and she still in the market I might have struck a bargain but ten to one I should not now be pleased with what pleased me before. Not that I'm too big but my fancy may be changed and it would be absurd of her to wait for me coming home which I may never do or may only come when too old to marry or may not then be inclined and then if I did ten to one if I should choose her though I confess she would have had the best chance

unless I found something very superior so I hope she'll be pleased with the man at Goukmoor and that he will have luck of her[.][96]

In his admitting that what pleased him before would not satisfy him now, Taylor's new life in Ceylon, an environment overwhelmingly dominated by men, presumably influenced his ideas about women:

> Remember me to old friends and say I'm very busy and very well and to the young ladies that I'm not very happy but very forlorn alone here without them and no one to speak to. They have need to pity me. But it cant be helped as they cant get at me. I must just do without them and they had better look out else where. If ever I see one again I shall be afraid at them and run away I think. I'm sure I'd be frightened at them now I've been told by some that they felt afraid of the ladies and nervous when brought into their company after a residence in the jungle. How much worse am I to be that may say I never was in their company. I verily believe if I ever come home I shall run to the hills to be out of sight of them or hide in the barn till the coast be clear. So you may tell them if I ever come home it will not be to see them unless I get desperate and screw up the courage to have a sight of such a curiosity for once in my life even at the risk of hysterics or something.[97]

His jocular arguments relating to his misgivings about marriage, replete with emotional terminology, have an air of rehearsed opposition, presumably because his father persisted on returning to the vexed subject of future marriage for his son. These protestations, however, likely precede his involvement with a local woman whereas later rebuffs, outlined in chapter 5, were inevitably a consequence of the intimate relationships he established in Ceylon.

If Taylor regularly declared his own unwillingness to wed, he did not have the same reservations about marriage for his brother and sister. Writing home about Margaret (Figure 7.5) in 1860 he even linked marriage to her emotional state:

> What is the object in Maggie's marriage being postponed? I have a suspicion about delays. I should have been happy to hear of that matter being settled and am sorry to hear that it is not. It will however allow May a chance of taking the lead yet and brighten her spirits. Three years is a long time I suppose in a young woman's life. I shall be glad to have a letter from Maggie and am now beginning to weary for one again.[98]

Margaret appears to have waited three years until 1863, when she married Stuart Davie. By the time of the 1871 Census, however, she was widowed, living at Forfar with three children, all under four years of age. Taylor commented on the situation in 1872, stating a willingness to assist financially:

> I imagine it is likely that she will get another husband before long; at least I should suppose it likely that she would wish to, and I do not see any reason why

7.5 James Taylor's sister, Margaret, before her wedding in 1863.

she should not. I only hope that in that case the man may be a respectable and intelligent person with whom we would have no hesitation in being familiar, and who would treat her with more consideration than any coarse-minded vulgar fellow. I should not stop doing something to help her to maintain Davies' children though she got another husband. In fact I would like to hear of her getting another good husband.[99]

Margaret married her second husband, George Nairn, in April 1875 at St Cyrus. The following year, in November, Taylor wrote to Margaret and George, presumably about the birth of their son:

I see by your last letter that you have been increasing the population. It is well for one who has not got the chance of propagating it himself to see that the breed is not to become extinct. There is no doubt the Scotch breed is a very good one and Maggie seems very proud of her success in this instance, so I have no doubt this particular son must be a good specimen.[100]

Despite his oft-stated opposition to marry and to return home, there were times in his first years in Ceylon when Taylor saw the future differently, as he had admitted in January 1858: 'I have a wish to come home which I have got into my head lately. I think it is in great part however only to be able to get a wife. But really I dont know what I might do. I might take a farm but would soon go to nonsense. What do I know of*f* farming?'[101]

Yet the cost of travel when he was still making his way in Ceylon made returning home, even for a visit, a difficult option. His own shortage of money, at least in his early years in Ceylon, also prevented this. As he explained in May 1859: 'I wish they would give us cheap passages home in any cabin so that a person might hope to be able to visit home. I should not be too proud to go in it whither it was 2nd or 3rd class. There is a great deal of that stupid pride in most coffee planters and it is very ill suited for their circumstances.'[102] Taylor certainly thought seriously about going back to Scotland, although rarely with any sense of homesickness, but in the end it never happened.

Despite Taylor's physical separation from his family for four decades, he still remained intimately connected to them and the wider community at Auchenblae over that long period. These connections entailed a range of responsibilities and obligations that typified the Scottish family.[103] Did this huge gulf across the oceans encourage the verbal expression of an inner emotional life that would not have been possible had he remained at home? This is unlikely, given that he purposefully and consciously made use of emotional language from his new home in Ceylon for practical purposes, just as his kinsfolk did in writing to him. By his expression of pleasure, disappointment, and impatience, his feelings were often tactically deployed to ensure that reciprocal action was taken by his correspondents in order to maintain the close family bonds which he valued so much. He also would modify his writing style to suit his recipients and particular issues. This meant that he could be both deferential and strong minded with his father, and playful and parental with his siblings.

While some scholars might argue that the emotional life as viewed through the prism of one person is less satisfying than that of several voices, the duration of Taylor's correspondence offers valuable insights which can helpfully be compared with research results on groups of individuals.[104] The Taylor story also provides a valuable perspective from beyond the middle and upper classes, who thus far have attracted most attention in studies of the history of emotions.[105] More focus in migration scholarship on the feelings of people might, in addition, provide an important corrective and a degree of balance to the current dominance of 'economic rationalist' approaches to the study of human mobility.[106]

Notes

1 T.M. Devine and Angela McCarthy, 'The Scottish experience in Asia, c.1700 to the present: Settlers and sojourners', in T.M. Devine and Angela McCarthy (eds), *The Scottish Experience in Asia, c.1700 to the Present: Settlers and Sojourners* (Cham, 2017), pp. 4–8.

2 David Fitzpatrick, *Oceans of Consolation: Personal Accounts of Irish Migration to Australia* (Cork, 1995), p. 20.

3 Angela McCarthy (ed.), *A Global Clan: Scottish Migrant Networks and Identities since the Eighteenth Century* (London and New York, 2006).

4 Fitzpatrick, *Oceans of Consolation*, pp. 20, 24.

5 See, for instance, Tanja Bueltmann, *Clubbing Together: Ethnicity, Civility and Formal Sociability in the Scottish Diaspora to 1930* (Liverpool, 2014).

6 Joanna Bourke, 'Fear and anxiety: Writing about emotion in modern history', *History Workshop Journal*, 55 (2003), p. 124.

7 Taylor letters, 21 February 1859.

8 Eva Illouz, *Cold Intimacies: The Making of Emotional Capitalism* (Cambridge, 2007), pp. 40–41; Peter N. Stearns and Carol Z. Stearns, 'Emotionology: Clarifying the history of emotions and emotional standards', *American Historical Review*, 90:4 (1985), p. 820.

9 Susan J. Matt, 'Current emotion research in history: Or, doing history from the inside out', *Emotion Review*, 3:1 (2011), pp. 117–124; Barbara H. Rosenwein, 'Problems and methods in the history of emotions', *Passions in Context: International Journal for the History and Theory of Emotions*, 1 (2010), online at www.passionsincontext.de; Barbara H. Rosenwein, 'Worrying about emotions in history', *American Historical Review*, 107:3 (2002), pp. 821–845.

10 Ranald C. Michie, 'Aberdeen and Ceylon: Economic links in the nineteenth century', *Northern Scotland*, 4 (1981), pp. 74–75.

11 For examples see T.M. Devine, *Scotland's Empire, 1600–1815* (London, 2003), pp. 339–343; George K. McGilvary, *East India Patronage and the British State: The Scottish Elite and Politics in the Eighteenth Century* (London, 2008); and Andrew Mackillop, 'The Highlands and the returning nabob: Sir Hector Munro of Novar, 1760–1807', in Marjory Harper (ed.), *Emigrant Homecomings: The Return Movement of Emigrants, 1600–2000* (Manchester, 2005), pp. 233–261.

12 Taylor letters, 17 September 1857.

13 Ibid., 3 December 1857.

14 Ibid., 23 January 1858.

15 Ibid., 11 November 1859.

16 The yearly wage for an agricultural labourer in Kincardine in 1860 was £27 6s. See Frederick Purdy, 'On the earnings of agricultural labourers in Scotland and Ireland', *Journal of the Statistical Society*, 25:4 (1862), Table IV, p. 470.

17 James Macdonald, 'On the agriculture of the counties of Forfar and Kincardine', *Transactions of the Highland and Agricultural Society of Scotland for 1881* (online at www.electricscotland.com/agriculture/page51.htm).
18 Taylor letters, 2 September 1882.
19 Ibid., 3 December 1857; 18 March 1872.
20 Ibid., 11 April 1875.
21 Ibid., 27 March 1882.
22 Ibid., 28 January 1860.
23 Ibid., 11 April 1875.
24 Margaret's death is recorded in Eileen Hewson, *Graveyards in Ceylon: Tea Country. Volume 3* (Wern, 2009), p. 56.
25 Taylor letters, 18 March 1872. The 1871 Census for Scotland reveals 8-year-old Charles and 7-year-old Peter Stiven living with Mary and Alexander Farquhar at Dumfriesshire. By the time of the 1901 Census, Charles was a commercial clerk in Govan and Peter was a railway clerk at Gretna.
26 *TA*, 4 July 1894, p. 4.
27 Eleanor Gordon, 'The family', in Lynn Abrams, Eleanor Gordon, Deborah Simonton and Eileen Janes Yeo (eds), *Gender in Scottish History Since 1700* (Edinburgh, 2006), p. 245.
28 This included £42 8s 11d in 1876 and £20 19s 3d in 1879 to spend 'on your enjoyment'. See Taylor letters, 5 November 1876 and 1 November 1879.
29 Taylor letters, 30 January 1869, 1 November 1879.
30 Paolo Boccagni and Loretta Baldassar, 'Emotions on the move: Mapping the emergent field of emotion and migration', *Emotion, Space and Society*, 16 (2015), p. 5.
31 Taylor letters, 21 February 1859.
32 Ibid., 23 December 1859.
33 Ibid., 15 April 1882.
34 Ibid., 18 July 1882.
35 Ibid., 15 December 1884, 24 October 1890.
36 Andrew Thompson, *The Empire Strikes Back? The Impact of Imperialism on Britain from the mid-Nineteenth Century* (Harlow, 2005), p. 64, citing Philip Payton's work on Cornish migration.
37 Maruška Svašek, 'Affective moves: Transit, transition and transformation', in Maruška Svašek (ed.), *Moving Subjects, Moving Objects: Transnationalism, Cultural Production and Emotions* (New York and Oxford, 2012), p. 17.
38 Taylor letters, 17 September 1857.
39 Ibid., 23 January 1858.
40 Ibid., 10 July 1858.
41 Ibid., 11 November 1859.
42 Even so, several photographs were taken in Ceylon, where three significant photographers maintained studios during Taylor's lifetime. William Skeen was the first government printer in 1849 in Colombo while Joseph Lawton opened a studio at Kandy in 1866. Charles T. Scowen also operated out of Kandy from 1876 before establishing a branch at Colombo. R.K. de Silva, *19th Century Newspaper Engravings of Ceylon – Sri Lanka* (London, 1998), p. 20.

43 Svašek, 'Affective moves', p. 17.
44 Fitzpatrick, *Oceans of Consolation*, p. 504.
45 Taylor letters, 3 December 1857.
46 See Peter C. English, 'Emergence of rheumatic fever in the nineteenth century', in Charles E. Rosenberg and Janet Golden (eds), *Framing Disease: Studies in Cultural History* (New Brunswick, 1997), p. 26.
47 Taylor letters, 3 December 1857.
48 Ibid., 23 January 1858.
49 Thomas Dixon, '"Emotion": The history of a keyword in crisis', *Emotion Review*, 4:4 (2012), pp. 341, 343.
50 Callum G. Brown, 'Religion', in Lynn Abrams, Eleanor Gordon, Deborah Simonton and Eileen Janes Yeo (eds), *Gender in Scottish History Since 1700* (Edinburgh, 2006), p. 86.
51 Taylor letters, 27 June 1859.
52 Ibid., 27 October 1858, 27 June 1859. James Fordyce was the medical practitioner at Laurencekirk. With a 'grotesque appearance', due to his habit of powdering the front of his head, Fordyce had 'a brusque and somewhat uncouth manner'. He died in 1833 and left a substantial fund to 'certain legatees', of whom Moir's second wife was one. See William Buxton Fraser, *History of the Parish and Burgh of Laurencekirk* (Edinburgh and London, 1880), pp. 197–203.
53 Taylor letters, 27 October 1858.
54 Ibid., 10 July 1858.
55 Ibid., 27 October 1858.
56 Ibid., 1 August 1859.
57 Ibid., 23 December 1859.
58 Ibid., 28 January 1860.
59 We are grateful to the Revd Michael Turner of the Episcopalian church at Laurencekirk for this information.
60 Taylor letters, 12 June 1890. Isabella Anderson Taylor's estate of £105 5s was granted intestate to Michael. Ancestry.com. *Scotland, National Probate Index (Calendar of Confirmations and Inventories), 1876–1936* [database online]. Provo, UT, USA: Ancestry Operations Inc., 2015, 1890, p. 806.
61 Gordon, 'The family', p. 246.
62 Taylor letters, 28 July 1891.
63 Ancestry.com lists William Taylor's death at age 39 at Tezpur, Bengal: Ancestry.com. *India, Select Deaths and Burials, 1719–1948* [database online]. David Air advises that Taylor was buried at Tezpur cemetery and that many of the original graves have subsequently been moved to Pertabghur Tea Estate Cemetery. Records for Tezpur cemetery, initially known as the European and Indian cemetery but named the Christian cemetery since 1974, verify this. The tombstones were resited in 1987 though the physical remains are still at Tezpur. Neither map for Pertabghur or Tezpur shows William Taylor's grave. See the records for Pertabghur and Tezpur in the British Library, Mss Eur 370/61, 66, Archives of the British Association for Cemeteries in South Asia and personal correspondence with Angela McCarthy, 12 March 2015. William Taylor was an engineer who died

on board the SS *Cashmere* at Tezpore. The volume of his estate – £233 2s – was granted to his sister Elisabeth. See Ancestry.com. *Scotland National Probate Index (Calendar of Confirmations and Inventories), 1876–1936* [database online], William Taylor, 1895, p. 482.

64 Ancestry.com. *Scotland, National Probate Index (Calendar of Confirmations and Inventories), 1876–1936* [database online], Michael Taylor, 1894, p. 919.

65 Based on Historical UK Inflation Calculator at http://inflation.stephenmorley.org/.

66 Taylor letters, 30 June 1887.

67 Fitzpatrick, *Oceans of Consolation*, p. 551.

68 Maruška Svašek, 'On the move: Emotions and human mobility', *Journal of Ethnic and Migration Studies*, 36:6 (2010), p. 868.

69 Taylor letters, 3 December 1857.

70 Ibid., undated, c.1858.

71 Charles A. Mollyson, *The Parish of Fordoun: Chapters in its History or Reminiscences of Place and Character* (Aberdeen, 1893), p. 128.

72 Taylor letters, 21 February 1859.

73 Ibid., 28 January 1860. Most research on the emotions and religion, by contrast with Taylor's emphasis on weeping and rapture, focuses on religious fear. See R. Marie Griffith, '"Joy unspeakable and full of glory": The vocabulary of pious emotion in the narratives of American Pentecostal women, 1910–1945', in Jan Lewis and Peter N. Stearns (eds), *An Emotional History of the United States* (New York, 1998), p. 221.

74 See Callum G. Brown, *The Social History of Religion in Scotland since 1730* (London and New York, 1987), pp. 147, 159.

75 Clifford James Marrs, 'The 1859 Religious Revival in Scotland: A Review and Critique of the Movement with particular reference to the City of Glasgow' (PhD, University of Glasgow, 1995), pp. 2, 342.

76 Taylor letters, 11 April 1875.

77 James F. Findlay, *Dwight L. Moody: American Evangelist, 1837–1899* (Eugene, OR, 1969), pp. 222–224, 216.

78 Taylor letters, 11 April 1875.

79 One of the book's characters, Rob, claims that 'he'd rather be a thorn than a sucker any day, for he didn't believe in ministers or kirks'.

80 Taylor letters, 11 April 1875.

81 See Callum G. Brown, 'Religion and social change', in T.M. Devine and Rosalind Mitchison (eds), *People and Society in Scotland, I: 1760–1830* (Edinburgh, 1988), pp. 143–162.

82 Taylor letters, 3 December 1857.

83 Ibid., 9 September 1878.

84 Ibid., 24 July 1857.

85 Ibid., 3 December 1857.

86 Ibid., 10 July 1858.

87 Ibid., 28 January 1860.

88 For comparison with Irish examples see Angela McCarthy, *Irish Migrants in New Zealand, 1840–1937: 'The Desired Haven'* (Woodbridge, 2005), ch. 7.

89 For studies of return migration to Scotland see Marjory Harper (ed.), *Emigrant Homecomings: The Return Movement of Emigrants, 1600–2000* (Manchester, 2005) and Mario Varricchio (ed.), *Back to Caledonia: Scottish Homecomings from the Seventeenth Century to the Present* (Edinburgh, 2012).
90 M. Anderson and D.J. Morse, 'The people', in W. Hamish Fraser and R.J. Morris (eds), *People and Society in Scotland, II: 1830–1914* (Edinburgh, 1990), p. 16.
91 Taylor letters, 13 June 1856.
92 Ibid., 17 September 1857.
93 Ibid., 3 December 1857. See chapter 1 for Taylor's connection to Janet Ross.
94 Ibid., 23 January 1858.
95 Ibid., 21 February 1859.
96 Ibid., undated c.1858.
97 Ibid., 3 December 1857.
98 Ibid., 28 January 1860.
99 Ibid., 18 March 1872.
100 Ibid., 5 November 1876.
101 Ibid., 23 January 1858.
102 Ibid., 27 May 1859.
103 Gordon, 'The family', p. 248.
104 Rosenwein, 'Problems and methods in the history of emotions', pp. 12, 21.
105 Matt, 'Current emotion research', p. 122.
106 Boccagni and Baldassar, 'Emotions on the move', p. 2.

8

Triumph and tears: last years and legacy

In February 1889 the *Overland Ceylon Observer* reported on the Annual General Meeting of the Planters' Association of Ceylon, self-styled as 'the island's most influential and enterprising public body'.[1] The former chairman of the Association, George Wall, had proposed that the planters recognise James Taylor's efforts as pioneer of the tea enterprise. Wall emphasised the quality and 'fine flavor' of Taylor's Loolecondera tea besides specifying, 'It is impossible for me to estimate the value of that service, or the value of the success which attended Mr. Taylor's first efforts, because if that experiment had failed, it is impossible to know to what extent the discouragement so caused would have gone. It is impossible to say how many persons would have been deterred from attempting the cultivation of Tea, if they had known, for instance, that the experiment made by so practical a man as Mr. Taylor had failed.'[2] Wall's proposal was taken up in June 1890 by L.H. Kelly, the Association's Chairman, who asserted that a 'suitable and appropriate mention' be made to Taylor 'for his indefatigable perseverance in the successful production of a fine tea, which first made Ceylon tea known'.[3] Taylor, Kelly emphasised, 'was the original pusher and maker of the first teas which found their ways into the Colombo markets and sold as Ceylon tea'. In summary, he claimed, 'There was no denying the fact that he originally proved in this Island that Ceylon could make good tea.'[4]

During the intervening months, between February 1889 and June 1890, key figures in Ceylon were in communication with the Executive Committee of the Ceylon Association in London to obtain their 'hearty support' in providing a testimonial to Taylor. To further buttress the renewed proposal, which was made in June, the Association's Chairman read a letter from Wall testifying to Taylor's achievements. Wall acknowledged that there had indeed been earlier attempts by others to cultivate tea in Ceylon, but these had all failed. Taylor was the first to deliver an innovative commercial success:

> This great service was achieved single-handed, in the face of difficulties that are now forgotten even by most of those of the present day who knew them, and of

> discouragements of a formidable nature from highly influential quarters. Even after he had produced the finest tea, and had made a name for it in the London circle of experts; planters were warned that tea was an extra-tropical product unsuited to our tropical climate; they were alarmed by assurance that it could not possibly be produced without heavy loss, and that our soils were unsuitable. These ideas were freely disseminated in the country, but, in the face of them all, Mr. Taylor achieved a great success, and thus refuted all objections, and cleared the way for the great work which has since been done.[5]

Taylor's major contribution had impressed many. Among his supporters was Daniel Morris, assistant director of the Royal Botanical Gardens at Kew, who likewise testified:

> Mr. Taylor, in his plodding, careful way, worked out unaided, the details of tea manufacture, and certainly he deserves to be held in the highest estimation as a pioneer of the industry. The sudden transformation which took place in Ceylon in a few years from a large and flourishing coffee industry to the tea industry is one of the most wonderful instances of well-directed energy and perseverance that has ever been known in the history of any British colony. Having made a special study of colonial industries, I may say I do not know of another instance of such a transformation. The island was almost in a state of ruin after the collapse of the coffee industry, but the spirits of the Ceylon planters never sank. They have had difficulties that others have not had to contend with, but they have surmounted them all.[6]

Taylor's employer, William Martin Leake, also spoke, emphasising Taylor's personal qualities which encompassed hard work, competence, and modesty:

> Without James Taylor we could have done nothing. He is a man who, of all whom I have known, is the most entirely devoted to his work. Self-advancement has been, I believe as nothing in his eyes. He has cared for his work, and for that only. Here lies the root of the wonderful success attained. I would add that though Loolcondura had been selected as the estate most suitable for cinchona cultivation, it was not so in the case of tea. Mr. Taylor had shown what he was capable of in the matter of the cinchona. And it was therefore without hesitation that we entrusted the tea experiment to his care.[7]

With such sustained backing, Wall suggested the need for a permanent symbol 'to tell the story of his achievement to future generations both for the sake of his memory and as a stimulus to other workers and pioneers whose work may confer benefits of a lasting nature. Indeed, long after Mr. Taylor shall have passed away future planters should know and recognize his work.' This, Wall considered important, as 'without a *permanent* testimonial bearing its eternal record, who of the next generation of planters will know who Mr. Taylor was, or what he did?' To acknowledge Taylor's achievements, Wall recommended the gift of a silver tea service, although he recognised 'how useless, in a practical point of view, a silver tea service would be to the gentleman whose simple life and quiet habits would afford no use for it ... [but] Should it happen that Mr. Taylor has no heirs directly interested in his work, the testimonial will still stand for all time to commemorate his work whether it find a place in the rooms of the Planters' Association, or in the museum of his native town, or in any other public place.' Wall further argued that an annuity or gift of land be made to Taylor.[8]

George Wall's letter and the additional encouraging comments from other key figures in the tea industry had come about because an earlier proposal had been received with little enthusiasm, due to widespread ignorance at the time about the precise details of Taylor's past achievements. This was apparently the case despite the fact that he informed his kinsfolk at home in the mid-1870s that 'having started and taken the lead of these two cultivations in Ceylon you see I have got somewhat celebrated in the country'.[9] But, as one contemporary noted in 1890, 'It was a great work that Mr. Taylor had done: there were few men now living who knew what a work it was.' W. Mackenzie likewise observed that Taylor 'had been long connected with Ceylon, but no man, perhaps, had been less heard of or known except by his actions'. As such, Chairman Kelly remarked that the districts initially providing 'scanty support' ought to receive the subscription lists again and Taylor's name 'would now be so thoroughly understood that there would not be the slightest excuse for anyone to say they did not know Mr. Taylor and did not know the object for which this subscription list was being circulated'.[10]

The result was the creation of a sub-committee in London, comprising J. Whittall, H.K. Rutherford, J.L. Shand, and Leake, whose role was to collect funds for the Taylor memorial. These gentlemen all donated significant sums as did Sir Alfred Dent, Jardine, Matheson and Co, Baring Bros and Co, Anderson Brothers, and John Hamilton.[11] Sir William Gregory, the former Governor of Ceylon, subscribed £5, declaring that Ceylon tea was 'superior to all other tea', and hailed 'the movement to do honour to one who has conferred such signal benefit on the Colony'.[12] Thomas Lipton contributed 25 rupees.[13]

After receiving this recognition, Taylor, as described in chapter 3, outlined his own recollections of the contribution he had made to the tea industry and in so doing gave much credit to his employers. His self-deprecation extended to George Wall, who he felt deserved a memorial, as 'He has been by far its most conspicuous and leading member from the first.'[14] In response, the *Ceylon Observer* saluted Taylor's gratitude towards others as being 'creditable to him' and emphasised 'his own bashfulness, which he describes as of even more than ordinarily Scotch intensity'. The writer, presumably John Ferguson, did, however, go on to seek credit for his newspaper:

> others have done their part, amongst whom Mr. James Taylor, if he had not exhausted the English language in glorifying his special idol, might have

> mentioned the conductors of the *Ceylon Observer*, but for whom Mr. Taylor's merits would not have been so well-known to the world as is the case. But returning from this digression, necessary in the interests of impartial history, let us express the hope that Mr. James Taylor may live long to enjoy the well deserved honours conferred on him by his brother planters, not for introducing either tea or cinchona, but for the service rendered to the colony by a series of intelligent, careful and successful experiments in the cultivation and preparation of both.[15]

Ferguson was correct that the *Ceylon Observer* had praised Taylor's work. In 1884, for instance, the paper reckoned that it 'must be a proud day to Mr. James Taylor when his merits as pioneer tea planter were deservedly recognized. Loolecondura will ever be eminent in what is destined to be the long array of Ceylon tea estates.'[16] This referred to Governor Gregory's declaration that 'the colony owes a great deal of gratitude to James Taylor of Loolecondura who I look upon as the founder of the tea enterprize. The man was deterred by no difficulties; he was determined to accept nothing as satisfactory that was not perfect and he made his tea a household word throughout the island.'[17] Ferguson's *Ceylon Directory* also regularly acknowledged 'the great debt which this Colony owes to the proprietors and managers of Loole Condura, in connection with the tea and cinchona planting industries', and recommended they be given free grants of land.[18]

Most planters were in favour of a testimonial to Taylor but some argued that the contribution of others, such as Taylor's pupils C.S. Armstrong and P.R. Shand, should not be overlooked. After Taylor, it was contended, they 'were undoubtedly the pioneers in the new enterprise. They each boldly opened large plantations, the growth of which did much, perhaps everything, to dispel the general gloom, and light up men's minds to what has proved to be the case, that there was still a future for Ceylon in tea.'[19] Others asserted that Taylor himself had not been responsible for the introduction of tea to the island. But, as his supporters pointed out, he had never claimed to do so. Rather, his achievement was to have 'manufactured good tea on a considerable scale in Ceylon'. In their view, had his employers Messrs Harrison and Leake 'not had "a man in a thousand" as a Superintendent, it is doubtful if their experiment in tea would not have ended as those of others in *failure*'.[20]

Press coverage soon made Taylor aware of what was afoot. He was quick, however, to tell his family that the acclaim would not bring great riches:

> I see by the newspapers that some sort of honorary testimonial is being got up by planters and people at Home connected with Ceylon to be given to me as a memento of my successful starting of Tea and Cinchona cultivation or Tea manufacture in Ceylon. I have no particular knowledge of the matter. It has been kept hidden from me and I ask no questions. But you must not suppose it is anything to make me much richer. It is and can be only honorary and that is all

that is intended. I think it is specially in connection with the Tea industry though our Cinchona experiments have been also mentioned by people in connection with the matter. But there are few planters in Ceylon now who remember or can remember our first beginnings in these cultivations and of those who can recollect I suppose most have pretty much forgotten the experiments that gave them confidence in the after bustle and labour extending the cultivation over all the estates and erecting factories and machinery to deal with it. I have very largely forgotten about them myself.[21]

The revamped proposal met with strong support in both Ceylon and London. By early 1891, around 1,961 rupees and £108 had been subscribed to the Taylor memorial fund. The planters adopted Wall's suggestion of a silver tea service, as Taylor had approved such a gift. They agreed to spend

8.1 '[S]ure to be appreciated both for its intrinsic value and its beauty': the Taylor tea service and commemorative pot.

no more than £40 on it.[22] Procured from Mappin and Webb at Sheffield, the tea service was fashioned in the Queen Anne pattern, and exhibited at Mappin and Webb in London before shipment to Ceylon. A press reporter noted, 'Not having had as yet opportunity for viewing this testimonial, my own opinion of it cannot now be passed; but those who have seen it speak highly of it in every respect, and as a gift sure to be appreciated both for its intrinsic value and its beauty.'[23] A salver, tea-pot, coffee-pot, milk-jug, sugar-basin, and blue cloth were shipped to Ceylon in a fitted wooden box (Figure 8.1). The salver had the following inscription engraved: 'To James Taylor, Loole Condura, in grateful appreciation of his successful efforts which laid the foundation of the tea and Cinchona Industries of Ceylon 1891.'[24] The Planters' Association offered Taylor the opportunity to receive the gift in public, but he declined, as he was not keen on giving a public address of thanks. 'It would be my first attempt at "public speaking" for which I am certainly not fitted', he claimed.[25] Since only part of the fund was used for the purchase of the silver service, the Association sent him a cheque for the balance of 2867.11 rupees.[26] The elation and quiet satisfaction which Taylor must have felt, however, did not last for long.

Dismissal and death

James Taylor died six months after this public honour was bestowed. He passed away at approximately 10am on Monday 2 May 1892 on the Loolecondera estate after suffering from dysentery. Those closest to him, however, were utterly convinced that other factors explained his untimely death. C.E. Bonner, assistant superintendent at Naranghena and his neighbour and friend for seventeen years, provided an intimate account of immediate events. He told how the Oriental Bank Estates Company had instructed Taylor to take six months' leave of absence from the estate. Taylor, however, 'resented being ordered away', believing that the estate intended to 'get rid' of him, and so he defied the directive. The Company then demanded that he should resign. Bonner had been visiting his friend when the firm's instructions arrived and recalled Taylor's confusion and utter despair at the accusations levied against him: 'he seemed completely dum[*b*]founded at receiving such a letter & I may say from that day to the day of his death he never held up his head his one cry was what have I done? & why dont the Coy give me a reason for getting rid of me? He refused to resign & then was summarily dismissed.' In Bonner's version of events, 'the disgrace of dismissal without a reason was too much for [*erased:* him] one of his sensitive nature & he simply pined away & died of a broken heart at being turned away like a dog after 40 years of service on our Estate'. Although Taylor had indeed suffered from dysentery, Bonner suggested that the illness had almost gone by 1 May.[27] A press report confirmed that Taylor had rallied, 'getting up, and giving his orders about the work, just as usual, and made every enquiry as to how the work went on; how much tea of each grade was packed and ready; and all that sort of thing which had become a sort of second nature to him'.[28] What comes through from Bonner's narrative is the pain and distress Taylor felt, which was in contrast to the stereotyped gendered expectations of 'masculine emotional strength' of the Victorian era.[29]

Bonner's inconsolable wife, Emily, similarly attributed Taylor's death to anguish arising from the Company's behaviour. She wrote desolately of the darkness that surrounded Taylor's last days, declaring that 'it was not dysentery that killed Mr. James Taylor of Loolecondura, but grief at the idea of leaving the old place, where he had lived for 40 years. He received notice to quit a fortnight before he died, and he never held up his head afterwards; then dysentery attacked him, and he pined away. I can speak from personal experience as I frequently went up to see him. He was a dear and respected old friend of mine, and it grieved me bitterly to see him in this heart-broken condition.'[30]

Other friends and acquaintances likewise felt the need to publicly reveal their deep sorrow and astonishment at Taylor's untimely death. 'H.A.C' from 'Madulkelu' was among those who echoed Emily Bonner's viewpoint. He wrote a lengthy account for publication in the Ceylon press:

> It is certainly the universal opinion upcountry of those who knew him well that poor James Taylor died of a broken heart at the idea of having to leave the estate he loved so much and cared for so well and for so long. I am one of the few left in the island who intimately knew all the proprietors of Loolecondura since it was sold by Messrs. Pryde until it passed into the hands of the present company, and I know they, one and all, had the highest esteem and regard for the deceased, both as a planter and superintendent. It is many years ago since I made the late James Taylor's acquaintance and at one time I was closely connected with him in business, being visiting agent for the group of estates under his charge, so had every opportunity of fully realizing his great merits; and a more faithful conscientious worker I never met.

H.A.C continued:

> The old proprietors were *practical* men, and gave Taylor to a great extent a free hand in the cultivation of the estates in his charge, and the great success attending all his endeavours showed their wisdom as, when the collapse of coffee came, the resources of these properties were such that large dividends from cinchona and tea were available when the majority of estates could not meet their upkeep expenditure. It is well-known that it was the crowning success attained by the late Mr. Taylor which stimulated others to follow in his steps. Poor Taylor ! he deserved a better end than to die a broken-hearted man, after having achieved the longest service on record of any superintendent on one estate – upwards of forty years I believe. I know not why the directors of his company thought it necessary to part with his services, and far be it from me to question that right. At the same time, I find it hard to believe that it was from any shortcomings on

> his part, as I have good reason for saying his character had not changed in recent years.[31]

Another, 'Amicus', took a similar view:

> Those who knew the late Mr. James Taylor thoroughly, as the writer did, will not hesitate to accept Mrs. Bonner's statement as being literally true. To a man of Mr. Taylor's extremely sensitive nature notice to quit a place he had, by virtue of good and faithful service, been able to make his home for a period of forty years, would be, presumably equivalent to a sentence of death. And such it was in Mr. Taylor's case, I feel pretty certain, although you seem to doubt it ... There is, however, no gainsaying the fact that Mr. Taylor was, apparently, in good health when he got the 'sack', and that death followed that disturbing event in a fortnight. Surely there was more than a mere coincidence here.[32]

The possibility that in his stricken condition Taylor may have taken his own life cannot be entirely dismissed out of hand, although there is not a shred of evidence in the contemporary record that after his untimely death suicide was even suspected. But those who knew him well were in no doubt that his unexplained dismissal had shaken him to the core. He faced the certain prospect of leaving his Ceylonese family and returning to Scotland in disgrace. This would have been intolerable for a man of his character and personality. In Sri Lanka today, the yellow oleander flower is increasingly used as a method of self-harm. Bloody diarrhoea and cardiac abnormalities are among the symptoms when it is taken.[33] Its poisoning capacities were also known during Taylor's time.[34] Nevertheless, in the absence even of suspicion or rumour, suicide remains an unlikely cause of death. More probable is that he died of acute stress on his heart brought on by the shock and pain of dismissal, as some friends at the time suggested. Recent medical research, for instance, indicates that physical damage to the heart can arise from severe grief and result in broken heart syndrome (stress cardiomyopathy).[35] A broken heart was also occasionally linked in the nineteenth century with dysentery.[36] Whatever the method of death, Taylor's dismissal under a cloud of public shame echoes studies of scandal in the British imperial world, and particularly the use of the press to defend male reputations.[37]

This tragic turn of events begs the question of the reasons for Taylor's dismissal but, regrettably, the extant sources do not permit a conclusive explanation. We have been unable to locate the Company's relevant archives, while other sources, which do provide some insight, may be biased. According to one anonymous correspondent, 'it is generally understood that poor James Taylor died broken-hearted because he was, in his old age and after devoted service, dismissed for the reason that Loole Condera teas had ceased to command high prices'.[38] That the Company was clearly concerned with maintaining high profits was acknowledged by Taylor in October 1890: 'Our tea has been selling generally a little lighter than it was some time ago but for very much less than it used to years ago when the Company was formed, and I fear they will be more cantankerous and unreasonable than ever presently.' Only half of his cultivated land could provide crop and on two-thirds of that half it was only a partial crop, as the tea fields were 'still only young'. He bemoaned, 'Were the cultivated land all in full cropping things would be vastly different.' What the Company failed to fully appreciate, he contended, was that there was an inevitable gap of several years from seeding to harvesting during which funding was continually required to support the enterprise: 'Our London Directors seem to be a lot of Bankers who cannot understand this but think that money laid out should immediately begin to give a return of 10, or 12, percent.'[39]

Further clues to Taylor's dismissal emerge from his correspondence. Changes were taking place in the ranks of his employers. He recorded in 1886 that his proprietors, Keir, Dundas and Co., had sold the estate to the London firm of A.G. Milne and Co. before they in turn were taken over by the Oriental Bank Corporation.[40] That bank failed and valuation attempts were required for the liquidator, all of which required Taylor's time and attention.[41] He was regularly called upon to provide 'estimates valuation and statements and reports and accounts of all sorts. We have had a terrible time of this sort of trouble for many years now.' Each change of ownership entailed detailed information which meant 'The workings of the properties had to suffer.' All this was required, he recalled, 'to make out that they were in a sound position'.[42]

These developments damaged Taylor's relations with the company's agent, whom he termed 'a useless hanger on of the Oriental Bank in Colombo'. Taylor had always been caustic in his opinions of those in the industry whom he considered feckless, but now his letters became increasingly inflammatory. Disillusioned, he wrote damningly in 1887 about what he perceived as the agent's interference in the workings of Loolecondera. His letter is worth quoting at length:

> The man can't or won't do anything right and everything he does gives us a lot of trouble, sometimes a fearful lot of trouble and worry and anxiety to get things right or keep them so. He does not understand accounts and knows no more about matters on the estates than you do. His instructions; or his passing on to us of orders on purpose to carry out the instructions he gets from the people in London; are consequently impracticable, or unnecessarily troublesome and occasionally impossible. Sometimes they are unintelligible or he writes something which is not what he means; or there are exceptions to it that he does not mention; and when we think we have carried out our instructions it is all wrong. I had a great fight with him about an item in an account some months ago. He was totally wrong but could not or would not see it, and wanted me to pocket twice the amount in dispute to which I had no right. It was a small sum but I would not give in and it would soon have been a case of my resigning or being dismissed

> had not the Visiting Agent come to the rescue. I had no difficulty in showing him how the matter should be. He went to Colombo and got the agent to make out a correct account which was sent to me to sign. He told me that I was not the only one who had got trouble and that there were other superintendents who had worse troubles with our Colombo agent. I have had a few more myself since then and some of them very troublesome. I have several times thought seriously of resigning. This visiting agent resigned some months ago, shortly after that, owing to the troubles given him by the people in London. They want to manage and they know nothing about Ceylon affairs and give us all any amount of trouble. Some fresh instructions from them come by every mail. Some of them only show their utter ignorance but are never-the-less irritating. Others are unnecessarily troublesome or not suited to the circumstances. Instead of Visiting Agent who resigned we have got one from India who knows nothing of Ceylon and he seems likely to be a dictatorial troublesome curse.[43]

Given the situation, Taylor bemoaned his recent acquisition of shares worth £105 in the new company.[44] The situation continued to escalate, as did Taylor's disgust, frustration, and discontent. By June 1890, now fifty-five years of age, he deemed the Directors in London responsible for ruining the estates: 'They are a terrible trouble in all sorts of things and all their superintendents that I know or have met or heard about complain of them just as I do and their Head managing man in Ceylon complains of them even more bitterly.' Such was his despair and contempt that he admitted to having become increasingly defiant:

> I have two or three times been thinking seriously of resigning. I should not wonder if I may have to do so for I have been kicking back at them somewhat lately. They will not let us work the estate nor attend to anything we should be doing. They keep us constantly making up elaborate statements and calculations and seem to think if they get plenty of them that they must know all about things. They dictate nevertheless in utter ignorance and don't understand what we write to them and misunderstand it in most extraordinary ways. Then they are such an insolent and insulting lot of brutes, and so absurdly dictatorial. Their character seems to me what I might expect in a lot of low bred ill brought up [*illegible word erased*] ragamuffins who had fallen into money and power by some fluke. At any rate they treat us as if we were of that class but without the money and power and without any intelligence or knowledge of our business.[45]

It seems very likely that the Company was not impressed either with falling profits or with Taylor's determination to confront them in public. He spoke out and questioned the intention of an advertisement in the press surrounding the liquidation of the Oriental Banking Corporation.[46] When Taylor fell foul of their criticism in return, another correspondent wrote in his defence: 'Mr Taylor's letter referred to an advertisement which no fellah can understand.'[47] Worth considering also is that Taylor was the highest-paid superintendent on the

Company's estates, although part of his salary was used to pay for a conductor and another helper.[48]

Nevertheless, Taylor did acknowledge in 1884, a few months before he turned fifty, being perhaps 'too old and lazy and dilapidated to go in for professional visiting'.[49] In a later letter, when he was fifty-five years of age, he confessed to his sister, 'We are all getting old and I cannot do the walking I used to do by a long way. In fact I do not go about so much as I would need to to see what is doing on other estates.'[50] Whether the Company knew this is uncertain. Yet, even if he struggled to visit other estates, at no time did Taylor's comments, or those of others, suggest neglect of Loolecondera. Rather, he continued to be regarded as reliable, trustworthy, and dutiful.

What we do know for sure is that the Company was contrite and remorseful about their actions after his death. In July 1892, the Ceylon press revealed that the London correspondent for the local *Times* had met with the managing director of the Oriental Bank Estates Company, Robert Turner Rohde. According to Rohde, they sought Taylor's leave of absence 'in the belief that such a change was needed, not only for his health, but that he required rousing from a condition of lethargy engendered by too long a residence on the estate without change'. Taylor's refusal to take the leave, they claimed, left them with no option but to dispense with his services. In retrospect, 'They very much deplore the sad ending of this episode, as they would gladly have been parties to an amicable settlement of the matter pending between them.'[51]

This malicious public characterisation of Taylor as a lethargic manager provoked further outrage in Ceylon. In a forceful defence of Taylor, an incensed supporter stated that it could be proved that Taylor was not dismissed because of any personal problems but because he took a stand against his proprietors. As the 'Friend' put it, Taylor

> spoke too plainly about the interference of the Managing Director in the management of Loolecondura in which he had for nearly forty years given others satisfaction. It is a fact that up to within a week of his death Mr. Taylor was in good health and untiring in his zealous work in the interests of Loolecondura and that the disgrace of being ordered off the estate, after forty years of hard and unremitting work, was too much for his sensitive nature. Never was an old faithful and competent servant treated in a worse manner, and there are no extenuating circumstances in favour of the Oriental Bank Estates Company.

The writer further put the Company's actions under additional scrutiny, reiterating previous reports that they had tried to question Taylor's ability to make tea:

> It is indeed a sad reflection that this respected and honoured old planter, just after receiving a spontaneous testimonial from the whole body of Ceylon planters,

> should have been dismissed by a body of London Directors on whose board there is neither a practical planter nor a Ceylon man. Mr. Taylor was ordered to go on so-called leave with the express purpose of, if possible, discrediting his work during his absence and particularly that pertaining to his capacity as a tea maker. Further the so-called leave was not coupled with an offer of adequate remuneration to enable him to visit Europe.[52]

Other correspondents similarly challenged attempts to discredit Taylor as 'lethargic', including one who wrote:

> The many references in the press about Mr. Taylor show how much respected he was, and not without cause. I made his acquaintance in 1865, and during all those years I have never heard a word said against him, but many a score of favourable opinions. When Mr. Rhode [sic], Managing Director of the O.B. Estates Company, gave out that the reason for dispensing with Mr. Taylor's services was because of his 'lethargy,' I am sure that many an old Ceylon man must have smiled at the grimness of the joke. Fancy Taylor and lethargy combined![53]

Whatever the circumstances surrounding Taylor's dismissal, laudatory obituaries and posthumous recollections soon testified to his character and standing. Their testimony is fascinating for the robust and moving portrayal they gave of Taylor's character and reputation. Bonner assessed that Taylor 'was a man generally looked up to & respected by a great number of men out here, his end was I consider a very sad one'.[54] 'Amicus' declared that 'Mr. Taylor was the freest from *sham* of any man I ever knew. There was no sham amity, sham sincerity, sham philanthropy, sham politeness, sham virtue about him, and therefore he did not shine in what is called "society".'[55] According to a report in the *Ceylon Observer*, Taylor was 'A slave to his work and a careful guardian of his employers' interest, his high sense of duty commending him as a true and faithful servant to those for whom he worked so long. The indomitable determination which this fine specimen of a Scotch Colonial displayed in fathering the tea enterprise of this colony calls for something more than an ordinary stone to mark his resting place.'[56] He was further praised for his life of 'unceasing labour … restless energy in seeking out facts, and his telling of them to his fellow-planters, freely, and to the best of his knowledge'. In sum, Taylor was remembered as 'the noblest of men. The kindest of friends, the gentlest, the wisest, and the most experienced of planters … simple, lovable, charitable, and possessed of extreme modesty – such was the Father of the Ceylon Tea enterprise; a man whose kindnesses will live in many a planter's memory, and whose name will stand high in the archives of this Colony for ever'.[57] All the comments revealed that James Taylor was much respected by his peers in Ceylon, not only for his acknowledged achievements and character, but because he represented a key link to the early days of tea planting.

Legacy

On Tuesday 3 May 1892, a day after his death, Taylor's body was taken from Loolecondera for burial at Mahiayawa cemetery near Kandy. His brother William seemingly purchased the plot.[58] Reputedly, two gangs of twelve estate workers carried Taylor's large body (he is said to have weighed 246 pounds) to his final resting place, alternating every four miles during the eighteen-mile journey.[59] Among neighbours and friends attending the burial were C.E. Bonner, W.J. Scott, Stopford Sackville, Alexander Philip, Archibald Borron, and several others who had subscribed to Taylor's silver tea service.[60] The Revd Mr Watt read the funeral service. Such was the planting community's esteem for Taylor that they planned a subscription to acquire a monument for his grave. W.H. Walters of Gonavy suggested 'placing a granite slab and headstone with the inscription:- "To the memory of James Taylor of Loolecondura, the originator of the tea and cinchona enterprise, in Ceylon, who died May 2nd, 1892. This stone is erected by his friends in token of their high respect and esteem".'[61] E. Hamlin of the Oriental Bank Estates Company similarly wrote to the press stating his intention to provide funds for the erection of a tombstone and recommending that a memorial tablet 'be placed in the church at Kandy'.[62]

A Memorial Fund for a headstone was established and, by October 1893, fifty-two individuals had donated money, including Taylor's sister, Margaret Nairn. She gave the largest sum (410 rupees and 26 cents) out of the grand total of 1,135 rupees and 86 cents. The funds were all spent on a stone (costing £44 1s 0d), its delivery from the UK, and charges for landing, rail, cart and coolie hire, and chains and pillars around the headstone together with photographs of Taylor and his grave site to be sent to relatives in Scotland.[63] W.H. Walters, who managed the nearby Gonavy estate, sent the press a photograph of the tombstone and described how 'At one end of the marble-enclosed grave, rises a tasteful pedestal surmounted by a granite and flower-carved cross.'[64] It was most likely the same image reproduced in Figure 8.2, which is preserved within the *Views of Ceylon* album at National Museums Scotland. Its granite construction reflects Taylor's origins in the north-east of Scotland, while the vegetation seems to depict a passion flower, symbolising the passion of Jesus Christ. At the centre of the cross is engraved IHS, also redolent of Christ. Taylor's tombstone, then, did not simply illustrate secular respectability and the affection of his friends but had important Christian connotations.[65]

However, the photograph taken at the time of his burial reveals an unfortunate contrast with the deteriorating condition of the grave site today, although in 1977 a plaque was added to the headstone by a visiting group of leading tea figures from Japan to commemorate the 110th anniversary of Taylor's first cultivation of Ceylon tea. On one visit, a Japanese delegation is said to have cracked open a miniature bottle of whisky on the grave. More recently, tea

8.2 'This stone is erected by his friends in token of their high respect and esteem': Taylor's headstone at Mahiayawa cemetery.

trees have been planted in recognition of Taylor's importance to the country's tea economy.

No trace of Taylor's last will and testament has been located, but details from it were published in the Ceylon press. It was signed in September 1855, with a codicil added in March 1886. His assets, largely comprising fixed deposits in the Oriental Bank Corporation and CMB (Chartered Mercantile Bank), were valued at under 40,000 rupees. He left one half to his sister, Margaret Nairn, while the remainder was shared by his half-siblings Lizzie (May had died) and William (Robert was also deceased), and, significantly, 'the mother of Mr. James Taylor's children'. She received an additional 5,000 rupees (approximately £400). The will further specified that in the event of the mother's death her share was to be divided between the Tamil Coolie Mission and the Friend-in-Need Society. Taylor's executors were Alexander Philip, secretary to the Planters' Association, and Mr Traill, possibly a relative living in Ceylon. The estate included the silver tea service 'consisting of silver salver, tea pot, coffee pot, milk jug, and sugar basin' which had been awarded to Taylor shortly before his death.[66]

Some further information about Taylor's property can be found among his papers at the National Library of Scotland. They show that a total amount of £391 14s was to be shared among his family in Scotland. After deduction of fees, £364 8s 9d was divided among them. The following relatives, all children of his sister Margaret, received £72 17s 9d each: James S. Davie, Margaret M, Davie, George Nairn, Ellen Robb, and William T. Nairn.[67] If this sum represented the half share to his sister, Margaret, it is likely that he therefore left total assets to the value of £1,200. This equates to a purchasing power in 2016 of around £138,000. Clearly, Taylor's obsessions with saving and reducing costs had paid off, if not for himself, at least for his closest kin after his death. The sum totalled more than his father's estate, which was valued at £286 12s 2d in 1894, with a purchasing power in 2016 of £33,176. Both amounts, however, fell far short of the assets of Taylor's relative Peter Moir who, when he died in 1895, left a small fortune with a purchasing power in 2016 of £1,431,812.[68]

Occasional references were made to Taylor's significance in the history of Ceylon in the years after his death. But it was only with the centenary of Ceylon tea in 1967 that substantial efforts were made to assess his contribution to the tea enterprise. Denys Forrest's work remains important in this regard. A journalist and former tea worker, Forrest was commissioned to write the official 100th-anniversary history. He visited Loolecondera with his wife, Molly, on 15 November 1965, and then again between 18 and 21 November 1965, meeting with the then superintendent, Roy Cameron.[69] During his time there Forrest heard some of the local memories of Taylor. In addition, May Greig, Taylor's niece, contacted him and provided him with copies of her uncle's letters. Some of these fed into Forrest's chapter on the 'Loolecondera Story' in the anniversary publication.

Surprisingly, evidence of Taylor's legacy also appears in bestselling popular fiction. Barbara Cartland's romance novel *Moon Over Eden*, published in 1976, draws on Forrest's account of Taylor. Her key character, Chilton Hawk, had gone to Ceylon in 1870 as a coffee planter and 'had the luck almost as soon as he arrived of being introduced by his Oxford friend to an experienced, thirty-five-year-old Scottish planter named James Taylor'. Cartland then has Taylor inform Hawk where to buy land, how to obtain a labour force and build a cottage, as well as providing advice on clearing and planting. Such was his friendship with the fictional Hawk that he persuaded the character to plant nineteen acres of tea, which saved him from ruin when the leaf disease decimated the coffee crop. Cartland incorporated other aspects from Forrest's book, including details of Taylor's physique and his building of a tea house with a rolling machine. Intriguingly, Cartland has Taylor confront Hawk about Hawk's nephew, Gerald

Warren, who 'has broken the rules where a native girl is concerned'. She had Taylor declare, 'it is quite usual and in no way reprehensible for a young man to take a mistress from a nearby village or another plantation'. In Warren's case, however, the young woman was one of his employees but he had kicked her out and refused to pay her, having accused her of stealing a signet ring. Cartland wrote that the custom was for a planter to take a local girl who would visit his house but live nearby, rather than 'openly with him'.[70] Cartland visited Ceylon and may therefore have been privy to tales of Taylor's intimacy with someone in the district.[71] In common with much historical fiction, Taylor's name and reputation were clearly used as a device to give credibility to the setting of Cartland's novel. Nevertheless, while Cartland drew on Forrest's book to note that Taylor was a 'young giant of a man', not all her facts were accurate. She records, for instance, that he had signed a three-year contract at eighteen years of age, although he was in fact two years younger.[72]

James Taylor spent many years at Loolecondera, so it is not surprising that he is remembered there and in the neighbourhood. In 1992, one hundred years after his death, the estate created a small museum to commemorate him, although the contents were transferred in 2001 to the Ceylon Tea Museum at Hantana.[73] There, visitors can today see a bust, display, photographs, and possessions that allegedly belonged to Taylor, including a grinding stone, the wheel of his rickshaw, and his tobacco pipe.[74] The original museum at Loolecondera is no more and the superintendent's office simply features a few small framed drawings of Taylor on the wall.

Visitors to the estate can also inspect the remains of what is believed to be his cabin, a well dating from his times, and his granite seat, which affords stunning vistas across the beautiful interior highlands of Sri Lanka where he spent most of his life.[75] The ruin of the cabin was discovered only after the publication of Forrest's book. When Forrest visited the estate, he situated Taylor's bungalow where the assistant superintendent of Loolecondera now lives. He also suggested during his investigations that Taylor's first tea house was where the dhoby (laundryman) stayed. If so, that building no longer exists and the land on which it stood is now used to cultivate vegetables. The earliest known photograph of what appears to be Taylor's cabin and the tea factory (see Figure 3.2) also supports this theory, as do photographs of Roy Cameron's time at Loolecondera in the mid-twentieth century.[76]

If Taylor did indeed have a bungalow as remote as the one now thought to have been owned by him, it may have been constructed with the extension of coffee planting during the 1860s. Information at the ruin claims that the cabin was built in 1865 (Figure 8.3). That, alas, is the period of the gap in Taylor's correspondence. The chimney remains of the cabin, however, contain a clue. When the Lawson family visited Loolecondera in 2016 they noted that the fireplace resembled a style of construction which is unique to the Mearns

8.3 Memorial garden to Taylor at Loolecondera estate.

region of Scotland where Taylor was born and lived until he left for Ceylon. The tradition there was to have the hearth raised about one foot above floor level.[77] Certainly the former planter John Weatherstone was shown the site in 1982 when he was carrying out research on the early Ceylon pioneers.[78] Regardless of whether or not Taylor did reside there at some stage, it is not the bungalow described in his letters or the one that appears in the photograph of the early tea house. An alternative explanation is that it was his 'secret cabin', as one estate worker described it in 2015.[79] The early images of the Tamil girl in his photograph albums date from the 1860s, so this suggestion could well be plausible. Alternatively, it could have been one of many planter bungalows established throughout the estate.

A further attraction at Loolecondera is five acres of Taylor's original twenty acres of planted tea. They continued to generate interest in the years immediately after Taylor's death. John Ferguson had regularly sought information on the progress of the initial plantings, noting that 'Time after time, it was our pleasing duty to inquire of worthy James Taylor as to the condition of his oldest tea fields planted between 1866 and 1869 and his reports were uniformly satisfactory.' A report after Taylor's death from G.F. Deane, the new superintendent, revealed the field 'full of vigour shewing no signs of decay'.[80]

The most recent memorial on the estate is a monument commissioned by the current superintendent of Loolecondera, Lalith Abeykoon. A local, Milton Perera, built it at a cost of 150,000 rupees. Unveiled on 29 November 2013, it depicts Taylor with a tea-pot and tea-cup and a garland around his neck as a visible token of respect.[81] A plaque, regrettably with some errors, outlines details of his life.

8.4 Statue of James Taylor and information board at Loolecondera estate.

Taylor's name has also become associated with Sri Lanka's blossoming tea tourism and hotel industry. On the road from Deltota to Loolecondera is the luxurious boutique hotel Taylors Hill, the closest hotel to the estate. Formerly a planter's bungalow, both it and one of the bedrooms are named after James Taylor, while another bedroom is called Loolecondera. Other hotels also draw on Taylor's legacy. At the St Andrew's Jetwing Hotel at Nuwara Eliya a bust of Taylor is on display.[82] Meanwhile, bungalow guests at the Ceylon Tea Trails accommodation can avail themselves of a visit to the Dunkeld estate tea factory, which has a small tribute to Taylor.

Taylor's legacy is also recorded by the introduction of a 10 rupees postal stamp in 1992 to commemorate the 125th anniversary of Sri Lanka's tea industry. It depicts an artist's head portrait of Taylor set among lush tea fields. Most dramatically, in 2013 the British High Commissioner in Sri Lanka at the time, John Rankin, unveiled a plaque and a remarkable 13-foot-high monument to Taylor at the Mlesna Tea Castle at Talawakelle (Figure 8.5), in the presence of around five hundred invited guests.[83] This imposing bust, created by a Russian sculptor, sits at the entrance to a mock-Scottish baronial castle, made of Sri Lankan granite. The building, which opened in 2008 and cost 100 million rupees (c.£500,000) to build, drew its inspiration from the owner's fascination with books on Scottish castles. Both the castle and monument are a remarkable physical testament to Taylor's legacy and were funded by Anselm Perera, the managing director of the Mlesna tea company. As Perera explains:

> From the beginning we all knew that James Taylor was the father of Ceylon tea and I always realised that we don't give enough prominence to the man who gave

> us a business, the man who gave us a livelihood. This country has two million people working in the tea trade and all of us in the new generation are forgetting the fact that one man was responsible for creating this trade in this country. And that made me think of doing a castle here because the Scottish love this area of mountains and highlands[.][84]

Perera also acknowledges Taylor's achievements at his tea 'fortress' in Kandy and on a plaque at his tea shop at the Majestic City Shopping Centre in Colombo. So too does Taylor feature on several Mlesna tea tins and packages, one of which is marketed as Loolecondera tea, although it does not contain tea from the estate. Tea companies and the hospitality industry, then, not only are aware of Taylor's contribution but are alert to the financial benefits of publicising his name.

In stark contrast to how he is remembered and revered in Sri Lanka, James Taylor was virtually unknown until very recently in his native Scotland. By the

8.5 Bust of James Taylor at the Mlesna Tea Castle at Talawakelle, Sri Lanka.

later twentieth century, however, some efforts were beginning to be made to promote his legacy in the land of his birth. Initially, the impetus came from the family of his sister Margaret. In 1971 May Greig, Margaret's granddaughter, donated Taylor's letters and two photograph albums to the National Library of Scotland. We do not know, however, what happened to the letters which were sent to him from Scotland. His neighbour, C.E. Bonner, recalled how, at the time of Taylor's death, he regretted not being able to obtain a lock of Taylor's hair and that all his other possessions were sent to his executors. However, he had discovered 'a large number of letters in a desk' when visiting the bungalow.[85] These may have been Taylor's letters from the 1860s which were returned to him to help construct his account of the early development of tea and to challenge his employers. Or they may have been letters from his family.

In 2000, Frances Humphries, Margaret's great-granddaughter and Taylor's great-great niece, donated Taylor's tea service, which had been left to her by her aunt, May Greig, to the National Museum of Scotland (NMS). The service had featured in a Scotland and the World exhibition at the NMS between May and the end of July 1999. Frances also presented a commemorative ceramic tea-pot and lid made by Wedgwood, Staffordshire, in 1967 as a souvenir to mark the centenary of Ceylon tea. It is decorated with a black and white drawing of Taylor which, according to the legend on the base of the tea-pot, shows him supervising the planting of the first seedlings at Loolecondera (see Figure 8.1).

At Auchenblae, however, it was only the visit to the area in May 1995 of Takeshi Isobuchi, a Japanese tea importer and wholesaler, which started to make the local people aware of the international reputation of a long-forgotten son of the village. As Jenny Thomson, local historian at Auchenblae, remembers: 'I noticed a Japanese tourist taking photographs of the barometer on the wall of the village hall next door to my house and stopped to speak to him. He said that he had just arrived in Edinburgh that morning. I gave him directions to get to Mosspark but other than that I knew nothing about James Taylor whatsoever! It was just a ruin at that time.'[86] Takeshi's fascination with James Taylor led him to visit Mosspark, purchased the year before by the Lawson family. They had bought the croft from Anne and Jim Donnelly, who had acquired it in 1991 and who had set about restoring it. The Donnellys obtained planning permission to rebuild Mosspark, which stipulated that they must retain the gable and the traditional Mearns fireplace, as few examples had survived by then. Rebuilding began around the middle of 1993 and included the knocking down and reconstruction of the chimney to make it more stable. Yet, with just 20 per cent of the work to complete, the Donnellys' funding dried up and they elected to sell.[87]

It is not entirely certain, however, whether the renovated cottage at Mosspark is exactly the same building in which Taylor was reared. Certainly Forrest was shown a ruined croft in the 1960s that was alleged to be Mosspark (Figure 8.6), but its location differs from that of the original building believed to be Taylor's birthplace (see Figure 1.1). The 1960s ruined croft may, then, have been a later construction on the Mosspark croft. Buttressing this possibility are Taylor's wistful, pensive thoughts about building changes at Auchenblae in the 1870s:

> And so the old houses are being demolished and the home I came from being obliterated. Well, of course changes must go on and improvements. Are any new houses to be built on the site? Is the whole lot, old shop and all, coming down? After you leave the place it will not be worth my while going to see the old locality except to look at the old outline of the hills which I suppose will remain the same.[88]

Regardless, living at Mosspark prompted the Lawsons' daughter Jane, aged 9, to complete in 2010 a primer 4 school assignment about Taylor. The class were instructed to 'find about and describe any famous Scottish person, preferably someone historical, and explain why they are important'.[89] Whereas other pupils chose famous Scots, such as William Wallace, Jane focused her research on James Taylor. Her teachers knew nothing about him, and when the three judges of the Auchenblae History Society assessed the projects Jane's essay won first prize. Sri Lankan friends also started to visit Mosspark and the father of one family was so moved when he saw the fireplace that, on placing his hands on it, in awe said, 'He touched this, he lived here!'[90]

Further progress in heralding Taylor in Scotland followed when Marion Robson of the Dickson Hall decided to organise a tea event in Laurencekirk. The announcement, in mid-October 2013, coincided with a talk given by Angela McCarthy to the Howe o' the Mearns Heritage Club. Three months later, with

8.6 'And so the old houses are being demolished': Taylor's birthplace at Mosspark in the early 1960s.

Marion at the helm, a group of locals from Auchenblae and Laurencekirk met to plan Scotland's first ever tea festival. Held in August 2014, the Festival was planned 'to share with others the quite amazing story of a local unsung Victorian entrepreneur, James Taylor'.[91] A range of talks were organised, including from the authors of this book and tea experts, while McCarthy worked with Jenny Thomson and Malcolm McCoig from the Auchenblae Heritage Society on an exhibition of Taylor's life. Auchenblae also 'set up our teas using embroidered tea cloths, china cups and cake stand and lovely afternoon tea fare. We also contributed to a display of tea pots and kettles and other memorabilia of the time.'[92] Tea tastings, a church service, and a memorable dinner also featured. But the event did more than bring Taylor to life. As Marion Robson explained, the Festival highlighted a number of people from north-east Scotland who spent their entire lives in India and Sri Lanka involved in tea.[93] The commemoration also included the unveiling of a traditional one-foot-diameter blue heritage plaque at Taylor's childhood home of Mosspark. The owners, the Lawson family, commissioned JRC Contracts of Leicester to supply this and Taylor's great-great niece Frances Humphries attended the unveiling.

The most recent physical additions to Taylor's commemoration in Scotland is the construction of two smaller versions of the thirteen-foot bust at Talawakelle. Commissioned by Anselm Perera after the Lawson family visited Sri Lanka in 2016, they are 38 inches in height, 51 inches in length, and 18 inches wide. Weighing 100kg, the statues arrived at Auchenblae in mid 2017. Indeed, the year 2017 commemorates many Taylor anniversaries: 150 years after Taylor cleared the first tea field; 125 years since his death; and 165 years after his arrival in Sri Lanka. Unrecognised and unhonoured for so long in his homeland, 'the father of the Ceylon tea enterprise' is beginning to be remembered at last.

Notes

1 *OCO*, 18 February 1889; *Jubilee of the Planters' Association of Ceylon, 1854–1904: Illustrated Souvenir of the 'Times of Ceylon'* (Colombo, 1904), p. 1.

2 'The pioneer tea planter Mr. James Taylor's services recognized', *Proceedings of the Planters' Association of Ceylon for year ending 16th February, 1890* (Colombo, 1890), p. 4.

3 'Proposed testimonial to Mr. James Taylor, pioneer tea planter', *Proceedings of the Planters' Association of Ceylon for year ending February 17th, 1891. Kandy* (Colombo, 1891), p. 38.

4 Ibid.

5 *Times of Ceylon Weekly Summary*, 17 June 1890.

6 'The tea industry of Ceylon', *TA*, 1 March 1888, p. 601.

7 Ibid.

8 'Proposed testimonial to Mr. James Taylor, pioneer tea planter', pp. 39–41.

9 Taylor letters, undated, c.mid-1870s.
10 'Proposed testimonial to Mr. James Taylor, pioneer tea planter', pp. 42–43.
11 *Local Government Gazette*, 30 October 1890, p. 7, online www.newspapers.com/newspage/35661569/.
12 'The tea fund', *Proceedings of the Planters' Association of Ceylon for year ending February 17th, 1891. Kandy* (Colombo, 1891), p. 96.
13 *TA*, 1 September 1890, p. 198. The names of other subscribers can be found in 'The Jas. Taylor testimonial fund.' See *OCO*, 26 November 1890, p. 1251, and *OCO*, 15 January 1891, p. 61.
14 'The Taylor testimonial', letter from Taylor dated 28 September 1891, *TA*, 2 November 1891, p. 340.
15 *TA*, 2 November 1891, p. 339.
16 *WCO*, 1 April 1884, p. 296.
17 *Supplement to the CO*, 31 March 1884.
18 'The oldest regularly cropped tea in Ceylon still thoroughly vigorous', *OCO*, 16 May 1890, p. 503.
19 'Mr. James Taylor and Ceylon tea', *OCO*, 18 June 1890, p. 640.
20 'Honour to whom honour is due', *OCO*, 30 June 1890, p. 678.
21 Taylor letters, 23 October 1890.
22 *Proceedings of the Planters' Association of Ceylon for year ending February 17th, 1891. Kandy* (Colombo, 1891), p. xxxvii
23 *OCO*, 22 April 1891, p. 445. Its Sheffield origins are noted in the Taylor file at NMS.
24 *OCO*, 17 August 1891, p. 862. A description is also noted in the Taylor file at NMS. The NMS does not record a coffee pot but a hot-water jug.
25 *TA*, 2 November 1891, p. 339.
26 Taylor letters, 17 December 1891; *OCO*, 17 June 1891, p. 658. This amount equated at the time to approximately £250. [Taylor noted in 1882 that 200 rupees equalled £16 12s 3d.]
27 Taylor letters, 13 July 1892.
28 *Overland Times of Ceylon*, 4 May 1892, p. 592.
29 Julie-Marie Strange, *Death, Grief and Poverty in Britain, 1870–1914* (Cambridge, 2005), p. 212.
30 *Overland Times of Ceylon*, 9 May 1892, p. 611. A similar letter from her was published in the *Ceylon Observer*. See *CO*, 9 May 1892, p. 3.
31 *Overland Times of Ceylon*, 14 May 1892, p. 640.
32 Ibid.
33 Shobitha Puvaneswaralingam, 'Yellow oleander poisoning and suicide in Sri Lanka', *Scottish Universities Medical Journal, Dundee* (2012), http://sumj.dundee.ac.uk/data/uploads/epub-article/002-sumj.epub.pdf.
34 *TA*, 1 September 1881, p. 292. Also see accounts of the poisoning capacity of plants in Ceylon in William Knighton, *The History of Ceylon from the Earliest Period to the Present Time* (Colombo, 1845), p. 220.
35 https://en.wikipedia.org/wiki/Takotsubo_cardiomyopathy.
36 'Sir Henry Halford's *Essays and Orations*', *Edinburgh Medical and Surgical Journal*, 47 (1837), p. 197.

37 Kirsten McKenzie, *Scandal in the Colonies: Sydney and Cape Town, 1820–1850* (Melbourne, 2004), pp. 69, 90.
38 *OCO*, 16 May 1892, p. 534.
39 Taylor letters, 23 October 1890.
40 Ibid., 7 November 1886. Ferguson's Ceylon Directories suggest that A.G. Milne and Co. were the proprietors by the early 1880s, while later in that decade the Oriental Bank Estates were the owners.
41 Taylor letters, 15 December 1884.
42 Ibid., 7 November 1886.
43 Ibid., 30 June 1887.
44 Ibid., 30 June 1887. These were new shares, and so differ from his earlier stake in the Lover's Leap holding.
45 Ibid., 12 June 1890.
46 'The meaning of an advertisement', *WCO*, 8 August 1884, p. 29.
47 Ibid.; 'Claims on the O.B.C.', *WCO*, 21 August 1884, p. 8.
48 Taylor letters, 30 June 1887.
49 Ibid., 15 December 1884.
50 Ibid., 24 October 1890.
51 *OCO*, 26 July 1892, p. 801.
52 Ibid., 4 August 1892, p. 821.
53 Ibid., 29 October 1892, p. 1165.
54 Taylor letters, 13 July 1892.
55 *Overland Times of Ceylon*, 14 May 1892, p. 640.
56 'The late Mr. James Taylor', *CO*, 4 May 1892, p. 3. A similar report appears in *Overland Times of Ceylon*, 4 May 1892, p. 592.
57 *OCO*, online edition dated 12 May 1892, p. 8; NLS, Papers of James Taylor, planter in Ceylon, MS 15908, Anonymous, 'The late Mr James Taylor of Looleconderа', 4 May 1892.
58 The cost of the plot is unknown but it is listed in Register of Plots Purchased in the General Cemetery, Mahaiyawa, Kandy, p. 6. I am grateful to Dr Asoka Senarath, Chief Medical Officer, Municipal Council, Kandy, for this information.
59 D.M. Forrest, *A Hundred Years of Ceylon Tea, 1867–1967* (London, 1967), p. 57.
60 *Overland Times of Ceylon*, 4 May 1892, p. 592. Archibald Borron's attendance is noted in *OCO*, 25 May 1892, p. 2. He was said to have got a touch of sun at the funeral and shortly thereafter died.
61 *Overland Times of Ceylon*, 23 May 1892, p. 678.
62 Ibid., 25 May 1892, p. 694. There is no plaque at the Scots Kirk at Kandy.
63 *OCO*, 27 October 1893, p. 1206.
64 Ibid., 25 November 1893, p. 1323.
65 Strange, *Death, Grief and Poverty*, pp. 100–101.
66 'The will of the late Mr. James Taylor', *Overland Times of Ceylon*, 13 June 1892, p. 789.
67 NLS, Papers of James Taylor, planter in Ceylon, MS 15908, Taylor estate.
68 Ancestry.com. *England & Wales, National Probate Calendar (Index of Wills and Administrations), 1858–1966, 1973–1995* [database online]. Provo, UT, USA: Ancestry.com Operations, Inc., 2010, Peter Moir, 1895, p. 288. These amounts were

calculated in September 2016 using a historical UK inflation calculator: http://inflation.stephenmorley.org/.

69 The dates of Forrest's visits to Loolecondera are noted in Roy Cameron's Visitors Book held by his daughter, Catriona Warner.

70 Barbara Cartland, *Moon Over Eden* (London, 1976), ch. 1. Many thanks to Tom Barron for bringing this novel to our attention.

71 Ibid., author's note. Ian McCorquodale advised that Cartland travelled to Sri Lanka with his brother Glen, but that no notes of the trip exist.

72 Ibid., pp. 11–12.

73 D. Madugalle, *Ceylon Tea Pride of Our Nation* (2010), magazine in Ceylon Tea Museum Archives; *James Taylor, Tea Pioneer of Ceylon: 100th Death Anniversary, 2nd May 1892–1992* (commemoration day souvenir), Tea Institute.

74 www.ceylonteamuseum.com; www.sundaytimes.lk/070513/TV/tv_1.html.

75 http://trips.lakdasun.org/lulkandura-loolecondera-few-hours-with-the-pioneer-of-tea-planters-in-sri-lanka.htm#pictures.

76 Kindly revealed by Cameron's daughter, Catriona Warner, 13 February 2016.

77 E-mail from the Lawsons, 2 May 2016. That the bungalow is not written about in Taylor's surviving letters is further suggested in his letter of 15 December 1884, when he writes, 'I have no fire nor fireplace in my Bungalow here and do not need to warm my toes and hands. It is very wet outside, though just now, and we had great rain a few days ago.'

78 John Weatherstone, *The Pioneers, 1825–1900: The Early British Tea and Coffee Planters and their Way of Life* (London, 1986), p. 160.

79 Information provided by M.S. Sunderaj, Field Officer, Loolecondera.

80 *TA*, 2 October 1893, p. 244.

81 Discussion between Angela McCarthy and Lalith Abeykoon, 25 January 2015.

82 In addition, Peter Duncan, the late New Zealand owner of Windloft Retreat, redesigned the hotel's website following Angela McCarthy's visit to the area in 2015 to showcase its proximity to Loolecondera.

83 http://collect.ceylanka.net/itempage.asp?olditm=v92022; www.sundayobserver.lk/2013/01/27/new40.asp. See also http://exploresrilanka.lk/2013/03/tribute-to-the-father-of-ceylon-tea/.

84 Interview with Anselm Perera, 4 February 2014.

85 Taylor letters, 3 January 1892 [sic].

86 E-mail from Jenny Thomson, 5 January 2017.

87 E-mail from the Lawsons, 2 May 2016, and interview with them, 12 June 2016. During the 1960s and 1970s the house had an added mezzanine floor and was used as a holiday home, but thereafter had fallen into disrepair.

88 Taylor letters, 25 January 1873.

89 Letter from class teachers of Auchenblae School to parents, 26 February 2010. Letter kindly provided by the Lawsons.

90 Interview with the Lawsons, 12 June 2016.

91 Programme for Scotland's Tea Festival Opening Dinner.

92 E-mail from Jenny Thomson, 5 January 2017.

93 Interview with Marion and Mike Robson, 22 June 2016.

9

A Scottish effect?

James Taylor, of his fellow countrymen, had the most impact on the history of Sri Lanka, but he was by no means the only Scot to make his mark there. Indeed, a tradition emerged within the British community that Scots, especially those from the north-east Lowlands, had been the master builders par excellence of the coffee economy until its final collapse in the 1880s.[1] The accolade was also repeated during the period of tea cultivation, which has thus far been mainly overlooked by scholars in assessments of the Scottish contribution to Sri Lanka.

Praise was lavished on Scots from many quarters and they themselves predictably embroidered the acclaim with self-admiring tributes presented at Burns Suppers, at St Andrews dinners, and in glowing articles in the press. The Scottish-born publisher and journalist John Ferguson, for instance, alleged in the 1890s that no less than two-thirds of all Ceylon coffee planters in earlier times had hailed from his native land.[2] A decade earlier, he claimed that 'the hills and valleys of Ceylon had echoed to the accents of the tongues spoken and the classic songs sung on the banks of the Spey and the Ness as well as on the shores of the Dee, the Deveron and the Tay, while that night the souls of all of them had been cheered by the sounds of the Highland bagpipe'.[3] In 1884 he had eulogised the 'hard-headed Scots' for 'The rough work [they did] in the early days before there were district roads, villages, supplies, doctors, or other comforts of civilization.'[4] Essentially, he argued, Ceylon was a 'Scotch colony!'[5] Governors of the country also felt compelled to testify to its Scottish connections. At the St Andrew's Day dinner in Colombo in 1888, Governor Arthur Hamilton-Gordon, himself of Scottish ancestry, waxed lyrical:

> There is nobody sitting here who is not well aware that the great industrial enterprize, which has made Ceylon what it is, owes its present position in a very great degree to the exertions of Scotchmen. (Applause.) There is not a district in the country where you do not see familiar Scottish names as the names of the estates; there is not a district in the country where we do not find familiar Scottish names among those who are carrying on the work[.][6]

A modern writer on Sri Lanka, S.N. Breckenridge, presented an even more gushing appraisal of the Scots pioneers:

> The Scottish immigrants to the coffee enterprise in Ceylon brought with them their frugality, their work ethic and above all their love of the Highlands. They terraced the highlands of Ceylon like their beloved sheep country. The term estate was a Scottish term which became implanted during the period. The roads, the landscape and the bungalows that became distinctive of the plantations reflected their culture.[7]

It is indeed striking that Scottish plantation place names were so widespread in Ceylon, including, for instance, Caledonia, Glen Alpine, Fassifern, Ettrick, Lochnagar, Craigie Lea, Devon, Glencairn, Holyrood, Eildon, and Dunsinane.[8] Ceylon, therefore, was similar to other parts of the world where Scots migrants settled and named areas, towns, streets, and properties after their homeland districts.[9] Regional maps and Ferguson's Ceylon Directories confirm that Scottish estate names were most prevalent in the Dickoya, Dimbula, and Maskeliya districts in Kandy. The *Tropical Agriculturalist* noted, 'It is a pleasant characteristic of the British race, Celtic as well as Saxon, to revive, in the far-off scenes of their migration and sojourn, names associated with pleasant remembrances of the old country.'[10] While Scots were not alone in naming their Ceylon estates after areas at home, they seem to have done so more often than their English and Irish counterparts.[11]

Nonetheless, the Scots-born were far from alone in eulogising their influence on the island. Earlier, in 1870, a Lancashire man, George Wall, then Chairman of the Planters' Association, claimed at a St Andrews gathering, that 'The prosperity in the island was due … to Scotch enterprise and Scotch labour.'[12] G.D.B. Harrison, Taylor's English-born employer and Chairman of the Planters' Association, likewise noted that coffee's success

> was owing to Scotchmen, and those who had been trained in Scotland, more particularly in agricultural pursuits [who] had brought with them to the country a knowledge of what must be done to maintain the fertility of the soil. Whereas in previous years planters had been accustomed to take what they could out of the soil and give very little to it, they now brought home teaching and home practice to bear on the subject and were adopting a system of manuring in order to maintain the fertility of the land.[13]

By the time of tea's ascendancy, yet another Englishman, Clement Scott, travel writer and theatre critic, echoed these earlier comments:

> The best colonists all the world over are Scotchmen, and it is needless to say that half the success of Ceylon tea planting is due to the thrift, energy, and resistless determination of the Scotch character. You cannot go a mile in Ceylon without finding what a Buchanan, a Morrison, or a Stuart has done for this magnificently prosperous industry.[14]

Two years later, in 1895, Giles F. Walker spoke at a St Andrew's Day dinner at Hatton and declared 'that the planting community owed such a very large share of its prosperity to Scotchmen because it was mostly men of that race who initiated the enterprise of tea-planting and had the hardest work when the planting enterprise was started in this Colony'. He claimed to have been the only Englishman of around eighteen folk at breakfast when he first arrived in Ceylon; all the rest were Scots.[15]

Not surprisingly, Scots likewise attested to their role in tea and other industries. In 1888 a 'patriotic Scot' claimed that Ceylon's leading newspaper, lawyers, manufacturers, brokers, storekeepers, banks, tea estates, tobacco enterprise, and cacao cultivation were all run by Scots. The writer, clearly biased, concluded, 'Our railway will never be properly managed until a Scotchman is at its head!'[16] In the following decade, Arthur Sinclair similarly emphasised the critical role of Scots in the planting economy, presumably influenced by his own close ties to John Ferguson:

> Justly famous for agricultural enterprise at home, under conditions not the most favourable to success, the patient, plodding Aberdonian has certainly shown well to the front in the tropics. Indeed, it may be safely enough said of Aberdeen, that no county in Great Britain had contributed more to the success of tropical agriculture generally, and, in particular, to making Ceylon what it is[.][17]

Indeed, while Scotland, as a whole, attracted praise, so also did particular regions and districts of the country. Ferguson alleged that some considered Ceylon 'an outlying dependency of Aberdeenshire', so many were the migrants from that particular county working in the coffee plantations.[18] Another wrote in 1889 that

> Scotchmen, as is usual in all colonies, preponderate in numbers, and Aberdeenshire 'takes the cake', so much so that our present Governor, Sir Arthur Gordon, once remarked at a public gathering, that he saw so many familiar faces from his own county around him, that he looked upon Ceylon as an outlying district of Aberdeen[.][19]

Many of these remarks, of course, were designed to appeal to the patriotism and nostalgia at Scottish social events when considerable quantities of drink had doubtless been consumed. But how far was all this simply a potent mix of hyperbole, ethnic conceit, and anecdotal rambling? Certainly a word of caution should be entered at this point. It is now historical orthodoxy that the Scots had an immense influence on the development of the British Empire.[20] This was certainly more profound than that of the Welsh or Irish and, in terms of the relative size of the two countries, was probably even more significant than the impact of the English when the question is considered on a per capita basis of comparative size of national populations.[21]

But evaluating the specific Scottish role in any imperial territory is never easy. There is much historical baggage to remember. Scotland was an ancient nation with origins stretching back to early medieval times when most of Europe was still governed by small principalities and aristocratic jurisdictions. But after 1707 it came into a close political and economic union with a much larger and more powerful country. One response to the potential danger of anglicised assimilation or marginalisation was the vigorous assertion of Scottish achievement within the union state. By the Victorian era, many Scots were glorying in the role they played in partnership with the English in building and ruling the greatest territorial empire the world had ever seen. The empire was always British and never English. This was the time when Scottish heroes such as Robert Burns, William Wallace, and John Knox were publicly lionised in print, song, and statuary as the historical symbols of a remarkable people. Scottish education was praised as at least a match for any other system globally and the nation's outstanding success in manufacturing was proudly showcased to the world in the great International Exhibition in Glasgow in 1901.[22] But all this boosterism did not always reflect the reality of the impact of the Scots in every corner of the empire.

Fortunately, some recent research allows us to see part of the way through the prevailing Scotch mist in terms of the historiography of Victorian Ceylon.[23] Careful analysis of the first problematic Ceylon censuses for 1871 and 1881, when coffee was dominant, reveals that Scots were 23 per cent of the British community, and 25 per cent if only men are included.[24] These figures, of course, represent all British residents, not simply those engaged in planting. When the population of the Central Provinces is considered, where most planters were based, the Scottish figure for men rose to 28 per cent. Clearly, then, the Scots were not in a majority, even in the key coffee-planting areas at the time, although there is some anecdotal evidence that their representation might have been greater in the earlier pioneering decades of the 1830s and 1840s. However, even in the 1870s their proportion was substantially larger than their share of UK domestic population, where Scots numbered around 10 per cent of the total in the late nineteenth century. In Ceylon, by contrast, Scots were usually one in four of the UK-born inhabitants. This over-representation meant that Ceylon was indeed one of the most Scottish of British colonial territories at the time.[25]

Indeed, such was the perceived Scottish influence in Ceylon that the publication of the 1891 Census drew a surprised comment: 'That English should outnumber the Scotch nearly three to one is rather unexpected, seeing that Ceylon was once called a Scotch colony.'[26]

The significant Scottish presence in Ceylon can also be identified through the foundation of churches for Scots Presbyterians in both Colombo and Kandy and their over-representation in some years among the office bearers of the Planters'

Table 9.1 'Nationality/race/birthplace' of British and Irish migrants in Ceylon, 1871–1911

	Scotland	*Ireland*	*England*	*Total Ceylon*
1871	667	260	1,776	2,400,380
1881	930	375	1,747	2,759,738
1891	613	254	1,609	3,007,789
1901	728	272	2,199	3,565,954
1911	767	333	3,183	4,106,350

Sources: Figures extracted from Anthony John Christopher, '"Ariane's Thread: Sri Lankan census superintendents' reports as guides to identity data', *Asian Population Studies*, 11:3 (2015), p. 8; *Times of Ceylon Weekly Summary*, p. 1130, British Library microfilm, July–December 1892; *Census of the British Empire, 1901: Report with Summary* (London, 1906), Table 7, p. 119 (online at https://archive.org/stream/cu31924030396067#page/n3/mode/2up); S.N. Breckenridge, *The Hills of Paradise: British Enterprise and the Story of Plantation Growth in Sri Lanka* (Colombo, 2012), pp. 95, 128. The statistics exclude military, shipping, and prisoners of war populations.

Association.[27] Many of the largest coffee estates were also Scottish owned. The Caledonian presence was not, however, confined to planting but also included high-profile activity in banking, journalism, the law, and shipping. The Bank of Western India, established in Bombay in 1842, opened branches in Ceylon a year later. Its original directors were all Scots. Changing the name to the Oriental Bank Corporation, after amalgamating with the Bank of Ceylon in 1851, it had become Asia's premier bank by the early 1860s. Tom Barron asserts that its role in the 1850s and 1860s in extending the coffee industry was immense, 'though not unique'.[28] Equally, Scottish-born engineers were to the fore in setting up small workshops throughout the planting region, often with close links to specialist firms in Scotland itself. From these connections came a stream of innovations: coffee pulpers, turbines and sluices for irrigation, and wire 'shoots' built down the hillsides to convey the berries to the processing plants.[29]

The conclusion, therefore, is that some may have exaggerated the Scottish contribution to Ceylon, but its relative significance cannot be denied when the hard evidence is considered in detail. In that sense, the disproportionate Scottish impact on Ceylon in Victorian times mirrored that in both imperial and non-imperial territories in North America, Africa, Asia, and Australasia.[30] To a large extent this effect reflected factors deep within the social and economic history of Scotland itself. In few countries in Europe had the consequences of the Protestant Reformation been so far reaching. By the early seventeenth century, the new Calvinist ideology was triumphant across the land, with only a few pockets of loyalty to the old faith remaining in some parts of the western Highlands, the Outer Hebrides, and the north-east Lowlands. When censuses of the people were first published in the eighteenth century, Catholics accounted for a mere 2 per cent of the national population.[31] The reformers had a highly ambitious programme for spiritual revolution. At its heart was the universal dissemination of elementary schooling so that not only the clergy but the laity as well could have direct access to the sacred texts. Implementation of this aspiration took time, but by the later seventeenth century reading literacy at least had become very widespread in the Lowlands.

Some commentators might have been over-impressed by the progress that had been made. Writing in 1826, the noted Scottish writer on agrarian affairs, Sir John Sinclair, recorded that 'the commons of Scotland were considered to be the most enlightened people of that rank in Europe'. More than a century later, the distinguished English historian Sir George Clark went even further by describing them as 'the most enlightened peasantry in the world'.[32] These assertions can easily be dismissed as hyperbole but it is the case that over the long term the new church developed a remarkable influence over Scottish society. Through its local courts, the kirk sessions, Protestantism exerted a powerful control over the allocation of poor relief and the moral behaviour of the population. In their long weekly sermons on the Sabbath, the clergy insisted that industriousness, commitment to duty, and honesty in all transactions were the necessary steps to godliness and eternal salvation. By the early nineteenth century, this message had been an unrelenting theme in the public message of Scottish Protestantism, delivered systematically to many generations of its followers.[33]

Thus, by accident rather than by design, the educational and moral improvements which were designed to enhance Christian spirituality also, ironically, shaped a society with considerable potential in the secular sphere. A relatively poor country had become very rich in the development of human capital even before the experience of economic revolution from the later eighteenth century. This was one reason why some Scots seem to have done relatively well in the age of empire across the globe.

Another was the rapid modernisation of the Scottish economy in the late eighteenth and early nineteenth centuries. Both in manufacturing and in agriculture there was a decisive break with the past from the 1760s. Scotland rapidly emerged as the second industrial nation on earth after England with leading-edge sectors, firstly in textile production and then, from the 1830s, in iron, steel, coal, engineering, and shipbuilding. According to the UK census of 1851, the proportion of men engaged in mining and manufacturing pursuits by that time was actually marginally higher than in England. In parallel, Scottish agriculture was transformed over the same period in organisation, cultivation methods, and market orientation. By the mid-Victorian era the country was regarded internationally as a leading centre of excellence in agrarian capitalism whose reputation attracted visitors from elsewhere and whose precepts were often copied by other European economies. The transformation generated state-of-the-art skills in technology, farming, management, banking, accounting, and a host of other specialisations, several of which were relevant to imperial careers.[34]

It was perhaps predictable that there would be a substantial Scottish presence in Ceylon. As we have seen, early planters came from Jamaica, where one diarist pointed to their unacceptable prevalence: 'a Scotchman, like a Fly was in every one's dish, like a Rat to be found in every hole and Corner, and like a Fart never return'd to whence they came'.[35] Scots in the Caribbean had always tended to employ as overseers and managers their relatives from home, in a tradition of post-Culloden neo-clanship.[36] When coffee planting began to take root in Ceylon from the 1830s, Scots sojourners were also already very well established in geographical proximity to the island in the administration, army, and marine of the East India Company, within the private trade and shipping companies of Asia, as well as in the lucrative commerce in opium and tea to and from China.[37] One estimate, for instance, suggests that no less than 214 agency houses in the East were Scottish owned or controlled between 1765 and 1834.[38] Several of them became sources of capital, credit, and marketing facilities for the Ceylon coffee plantations. The most notable and influential company before 1850 was Ackland and Boyd, which grew out of the coastal trade between the Indian presidencies and Ceylon. This firm, which had strong family connections to north-east Scotland, soon acquired vast areas of land for coffee planting on the island and went on to recruit many potential planters from the north-east of Scotland.[39]

Scots had been also involved in the colonial administration of Ceylon in the pre-coffee era. They were among the Crown civil servants whom the government encouraged to invest in the nascent coffee industry by buying into land for plantation development from 1833 until the practice was prohibited in 1844. Even after that, however, they were allowed to transfer title to members of their own families.[40] Another important Scottish link was through the military. As in the case of the civil service, many army officers came to have a big stake in the coffee plantations. The colonial government saw them not simply as a source of investment but as a means of keeping good order as the huge increase in land sales in Kandy stoked increased tensions among local peasant communities. Significantly, between 1826 and 1842 the garrison in Ceylon was partially drawn from the 78th Highland Regiment, and the 90th Light Infantry, which was mainly recruited in Perthshire in the period 1835 to 1846.[41]

Migration from Scotland for work as managers in the coffee industry often came through personal connections, family and friendship networks, and recommendations. It was well known that the management of estates in distant lands was a perennial challenge for plantation owners. Sir James Tennent, in 1859, highlighted the problems:

> where the capitalist is helplessly reliant on the honour and services of a representative on his distant possessions; under circumstances in which few have the resolution to resist stimulants and the usual devices for diversifying monotony and overcoming the ennui attendant on isolation and solitude; property of this kind is accompanied by inextricable risks and anxieties[.][42]

There was a strong incentive, therefore, to recruit as superintendents and other responsible staff only family members and those personally supported and vouched for by relatives and close friends. These connections also confirm the significance of the Scottish 'brand'. In 1838, for instance, Governor James Alexander Stewart Mackenzie wrote to an acquaintance in London to seek two good road overseers and added, 'shall I say I would prefer Scotch people?'[43] Two years later he approached Alexander Bannermann in Aberdeen, asking: 'Can you send me out a good ploughman (who can milk cows – is that quite out of the question?) build Dikes, bring out with him, and work a pair of Aberdeenshire Oxen – a plough & Harrow, such as he is in habit of using?'[44] And in 1844, William Leslie contacted his father from his estate in Ceylon:

> I shall want a good honest, well brought up, educated young Scot for a superintendent on my Estate and I wish that my dear father would have an eye to any lad of the above description … not very stout as the heat may disagree with him. A man who understood something of surveying and road making and all that kind of work would be preferable … I should like one from near home whose honesty and general character would be known to you – one of Robert Singer's boys if grown up would just be the person I want.[45]

This very personal form of recruitment not only strengthened the ethnic connection between Scotland and Ceylon but also ensured that through chain migration enduring associations became established between some localities at home and the coffee plantations abroad. Villages in east Aberdeenshire and in the Mearns, focused on Crimond and Laurencekirk respectively, generated large numbers of recruits for the estates, including James Taylor himself. In both cases, the key figures were two prominent planters, Robert Boyd Tytler and Peter Moir, who had settled earlier in Ceylon and subsequently became the focal points for further recruitment from their parishes at home.[46] These ties were also important in bringing to Ceylon migrants equipped with essential skills. The planter William Boyd was especially effusive in this regard:

> It seems to me something little short of marvellous how speedily young Scotchmen, when they found that they had to execute work of this kind, acquired a thorough knowledge of matters, which is seldom attained at home by any but professional engineers. They not only erected stately buildings, but they traced and cut water-courses, put up intricate machinery, opened up new districts by means of roads traced and formed through most difficult and mountainous tracts of country, built bridges, and performed marvels of engineering skill which at home would not be entrusted to any but professional men of first-class eminence.[47]

This social environment helped to fashion the distinctive Scottish presence and impact in Ceylon. Indeed, Michie and McCarthy go so far as to argue that the particular backgrounds of some Scots suited them especially for planting life in Ceylon. Not only their agricultural skills but their ability to write and deal with numbers and accounts made them sought after.[48] Whatever views James Taylor had of his fellow Scots at home, they gained traction in Ceylon. As he described to his father in a letter written in 1859:

> Really neither the English nor Irish in this part of the world are nearly so good as Scotchmen with few exceptions. Even English proprietors try to get Scotch superintendents as for example Pride my old master and his brother says he thinks them the most useful people in the world and the Messrs Hadden proprietors of Moirs' places have found scotchmen serves them better than any other manager in the country perhaps of any class would have done.[49]

Even a contemporary in 1870 noted that 'The now numerous colony of Scotchmen in Ceylon are year by year introducing Scotch practices into the remoter districts of the Island'.[50]

It should be noted, however, that close ties of kin and neighbourhood did not always result in migration. When Taylor learned that his brother Robert was thinking of joining him, he urged that a job at home would be a better option because of the special qualities needed for success in Ceylon:

> I daresay he might come out here but if he could get forward pretty well at home it would be better in my opinion. I know he is not of a sharp observing habit which is the quality wanted here to get on well. Besides it is decidedly a bad place to live in and rather doubtful. I think the job is bad enough now but the enormous swarms of new hands coming out keep it down and if the trade was getting a check as it did a few years before we came out the job would be intolerable and all could scarcely live.[51]

A lengthy letter in May 1859 continued to discuss his brother's possible emigration but in a softer tone. Taylor now accepted that he would benefit from having 'a friend in the country' and that Robert would do well as he would not be 'liable to very great temptation to ruin himself but if he is not cautious he will not make a penny living here'. Taylor again stressed the need for 'self denial ... steadiness and perseverance and the application of considerable intelligence and vigilance'. All this implied that Taylor had those virtues. But in an indictment of planter life he added, 'We are not such gentlemen here as you at home think.'[52]

The point of Taylor's advice in the 1850s was to emphasise the difficulty in securing a position in Ceylon when the coffee enterprise might be experiencing relative decline, with limited opportunities; the four hundred coffee estates required only 'one European in charge and many of them are in the hands of Burghers and Natives. I dont suppose that over 150 of them require assistants.' As Taylor put it grimly, 'the country is swarming just now with people out of employment of all sorts and this is not a country when they can do anything for themselves if unemployed and it is too expensive living here for them to stop long if they are not getting salary'.[53] That same year, he again wrote home gloomily: 'There are only three hundred superintendents wanted for all the coffee estates and perhaps half as many assistants and there are upwards of sixty known to be applying for situations just now and all places are full. The country is swarming with idle fellows just now.' He speculated that many would move on to Australia or be forced to return to the UK.[54] In the end, Robert Taylor did not join his older brother in Ceylon, but emigrated instead to the United States.

Another man from the parish of Fordoun sought Taylor out in the late 1860s but, now aged thirty-three, Taylor was more forthright in his opposition, stating that he did not 'like the responsibility of inducing any one to come'. The boy in question, the son of a Mr Clark, was, he felt, too young. Taylor pointed to the changing nature of management since the early 1850s, with no superintendents now employed on three-year contracts. Instead, the country was 'flooded with young fellows who come out of their own accord, mostly with some money at their command to invest in coffee after they have learned something about it'. This backing was vital, Taylor thought, because new arrivals were not able to survive on an annual salary to the same extent as when he had first arrived. Clark's son would therefore have to travel with a considerable sum of money in order to stay out of debt for the first couple of years; his family would also have to pay his passage and outfit. If he could stay the course for three years, however, Taylor estimated that the lad might well go on to earn between £200 and £300 a year.

Even so, Taylor remained unsupportive, stressing that 'a boy from a country place as Fordoun' would likely be considered inferior, as others arriving 'are mostly all smart young gentlemen from public schools, accustomed to society, which gives them a wonderful advantage at first over slow going awkward loons such as I was'. Equipped with the wisdom gained from sixteen years in Ceylon, he added that 'any one like what I was would be dismissed from the employ within a few months as unfit for his business, especially if he were put under one of these swells'. But this did not mean that the 'swells' were up to the job: 'They have never learned to work and have no idea of it'; 'Their whole mind seems to be taken up with visiting, parties, dogs, & horses &c, and no one can be successful unless his chief interest is about his work. Every thing goes wrong in innumerable ways unless managed with a constant attention and consideration which no one not thoroughly interested can give.' Here Taylor's comments implicitly accentuated his own personal qualities. While he may have cast himself as an 'awkward loon' in earlier years, he now had the capacity to prioritise work at the expense of frivolity. In sum, Taylor declared of the young Clark, 'At all events let him be a man before he comes to Ceylon. If he then chooses to come let him do so and in the meantime put him into an office to learn business and sharpen his wits or to something at which he will learn work and at the same time keep his mental faculties on the stretch. If he is then honest with a good head and tolerable health and strength he will do well in Ceylon.' Even if a considerable sum was at the disposal of Clark's son, Taylor described how most of those with considerable support 'make a mess of this and lose their money' by investing too soon before gaining knowledge. There was no romance in coffee; instead it was a 'hard anxious struggle to make it pay'. Taylor also noted the probable debilitating consequences:

> When all this is considered and the chances of the man dying long before he makes an independence, as almost all do; and the chances of his becoming fast or taking to drink as is, I may say, so universally the case with old planters where is the inducement to come to Ceylon. There is the risk, to[*o*], of the climate not suiting him and of his having to return home again very soon after he comes out. There are other considerations I cannot mention here that but must leave them to be understood.

Perhaps conscious of his own straitened financial position, he bleakly concluded:

> No one under 20 or 21, ought to come out. The life of a Supt to one a few years used to it and doing well may be a rather pleasant one for the time but when he gets older and finds he has made no provision for getting out of it; as almost none have; and begins to think of things beyond present enjoyment he will feel the hopelessness of his case.[55]

Taylor's carefully crafted 'rhetoric of discouragement' echoes some migrant letters more broadly which deployed persuasive moral as well as economic arguments to dissuade potential new arrivals.[56] He may, partly, have been attempting to prevent job competition or to ensure that he would not be burdened with the responsibility of taking care of new arrivals. But, equally, he was probably influenced by the fact of his own intimate relationship with a Tamil woman which he was determined to keep secret from people at home (discussed in chapters 6 and 7).

Regardless of Taylor's motivations, by the 1870s and 1880s the nature of planter recruitment was indeed changing.[57] Personal connections were still important, but now a 'different class of men' were coming into the colony. In 1873 Taylor observed, 'No one of my class comes to Ceylon now. All are out with money or means of getting money and engage themselves as Superintendents for a time till they get trained to coffee & coolies and find a chance of investing for themselves. By such people the coffee cultivation of Ceylon has been doubled within a few years past.'[58] Press coverage echoed Taylor's thoughts, stating that newcomers comprised 'Younger sons with a capital, present or prospective, of a few thousand pounds, educated at public schools, and many of them University men, [who] found an opening in life on Ceylon plantations far more congenial than that of the Australian bush or the backwoods of Canada.'[59] They were contrasted in trenchant terms with the practical men of Taylor's generation, for many of the newcomers were English and were alleged to know 'absolutely nothing of agriculture ... They knew nothing of manuring and draining, roading and planting ... There was no preparation in England, either at school or at home, for the colonist's life in Ceylon, and everything had to be learnt from the beginning.'[60]

Even James Shank Burnett, the son of Taylor's laird at Monboddo, contemplated a move to Ceylon, a scenario that troubled Taylor: 'I think he had better not. People of that class almost never do well here.' To support his assertion, he cited a newspaper article that claimed those who had succeeded in Ceylon 'were men who had come here with no capital but their brains and a good constitution'. As Taylor bluntly put it:

> The Laird's son living with me in my little Bungalow would not suit at all. During the bad times I have had a number of old acquaintances living with me for two or three months at a time, and have refused several. I am terribly tired of that arrangement although these were men of something like my own age. To have a young gent like the Laird's son living with me permanently would not do at all. We would not suit each other in such confined space. I fancy the house would not be large enough to hold him and his gear and I want it all for mine and for estate books & papers.[61]

Presumably, Taylor did not see Burnett, from a rural landed family, as of the same social class as new English arrivals, who came largely from urban, public school-educated backgrounds, a contrast with the pioneering cohort of Taylor's generation who were primarily from rural, parish-school origins.[62] In the event, Burnett did not join Taylor in Ceylon but he did spend time India, where he was killed by an elephant.

In light of the changing dynamic of migration to Ceylon, it has been argued that 'North-east Scotland's "special relationship" with Ceylon ... disappeared with the collapse of the coffee economy' around 1875.[63] Certainly, the nature of migration did alter, but there is substantial evidence that Scotland's 'special relationship' with Ceylon extended beyond that time period and well into the era of the tea economy. As was seen in chapter 3, Taylor himself acknowledged the help he received from several fellow Scots in developing his abilities as a tea maker, including one William Cameron from Mull. Confirmation of a continuing Scottish presence in the tea economy also emerged from the names of planters whom Taylor is credited with instructing. Among them were George Maitland of Edinburgh[64] and Gilbert Francis Traill from Orkney.[65] Hugh Blacklaw from Laurencekirk, close to Taylor's own birthplace, came to Loolecondera in the 1880s to learn tea making from him.[66] Others whom he mentored included John Scott, J.H. Campbell, J.M. Purdon, E.S. Anderson,

9.1 Photograph taken at the time of James Taylor's first tea planting in 1867: Taylor with J.L. Purdon, Dougal McMaster, and D.W. Traill.

W.G. Mackilligin, Hugh Fraser Dunbar, George E. Bowby, A.L. Scott, Frank Evan Waring, Herbert Bressey, Hugh Miller, A.C. Bonner, C.H.T. Wilkinson, and J.G. Forsyth. Several of these names are redolent of Scottish origins.[67]

Among the other key figures in Ceylon's tea enterprise who were Scots, either through birth or descent, were David Reid (Kinross-shire), Sir Graeme H.D. Elphinstone (Aberdeenshire), and William Jackson (Aberdeen).[68] Henry Kerr Rutherford from the Mariawatte plantation was another Scot who paved 'the way for Ceylon to be known as the home of the best of all tea'.[69] He wrote an acclaimed publication on the subject which prompted one commentator to observe that 'although Englishmen have doubtless done their part, the author of the most generally useful and comprehensive book on tea and the greatest and most successful tea machinery engineers are Scotchmen!'[70] John Loudoun Shand was yet another Caledonian, his father apparently hailing

9.2 Mr. David Reid, Sir W. Johnstone, and Mr. Shand enjoy their tea!

from Edinburgh.[71] He, together with David Reid and Sir William Johnstone, dominated the Ceylon Tea Plantations Company (Figure 9.2): 'The directors are all Scotch, the chairman is a Scotchman, the secretary – a real live baronet, by the way – is a Scotchman, and the shareholders look Scotch to a man. It is queer to find Scotchmen combining together to vaunt the virtues of tea ... in view of the insult which the fact offers to whisky.'[72]

Peter Rolland Shand was likewise identified as a significant figure in the development of tea and he also trained under Taylor. According to one contemporary, 'I do not think the great impetus given to the same industry by Mr. Taylor's pupils, Mr. C.S. Armstrong and Mr. P.R. Shand, should be overlooked. At the very least, it ought to be publicly acknowledged, that, after Mr. Taylor, they were undoubtedly the pioneers in the new enterprise.'[73] Although Charles Spearman Armstrong originated from England, Shand was likely connected to the three generations of Shands of Scots descent with Liverpool connections.[74] Perhaps the most significant name of all is that of Sir Thomas Lipton. He considered himself a 'Glasgow Irishman' but in fact he had been born in the city of Irish immigrant parents.[75]

These few names, however, do not in themselves provide any rigorous statistical confirmation[76] of all those who were recognised as influential in Ceylon's tea enterprise. But, as with coffee, broad assessments still point to Scots playing a key part in it. What they do confirm is the perceived significance to contemporaries of ethnic background within the nineteenth-century British world. If some modern historians of emigration are sometimes less than sensitive to the importance of ethnicity within an undifferentiated mass of 'the British', there can be little doubt this was not the case among the migrant communities themselves. And it was certainly migrants from Scotland, equipped with relevant skill sets, who contributed substantially to the development of coffee and tea in Ceylon.

But, finally, what of Scotland's nineteenth-century legacy in Sri Lanka in 2017? As we have seen, echoes can be traced throughout the hill country where a plethora of estate names continue to testify to the early influence of Scots planters. Moreover, at Dambatenne a statue of Sir Thomas Lipton shows him taking tea while sitting on a seat overlooking his former estate. Known as 'Lipton's Seat', the vista affords 360° views across the countryside. Unilever, which now incorporates Lipton Tea, consulted Anselm Perera about his Taylor statue but, unlike that which took two years of planning and construction, the Lipton memorial of fibreglass was produced within a month.[77]

The graves of several Scottish planters can be seen at nearby St Andrews Church, Haputale, with place of birth often engraved on their headstones. Tombstones in other cemeteries, either overgrown or in good order, also confirm the Scottish presence in days gone by. Particularly noteworthy are the achingly beautiful Christ church at Warleigh (Dickoya), St John's church at Lindula, Holy Trinity church at Nuwara Eliya, and the Garrisons cemetery at Kandy where Taylor's relative David Moir is buried.[78]

The Scots churches at Colombo and Kandy are still active to this day, even though their congregations are now overwhelmingly Ceylonese. Indeed, the St Andrew's Scots Kirk at Colombo remains a congregation of the Church of Scotland, with Scottish ministers appointed to oversee it. An expatriate Scot, Gordon Kenny, meanwhile, is the current chief of the Caledonian Society of Sri Lanka, which has existed for at least a century. The Scots-born, however, make up only 10 per cent of the membership today although the Society's annual Burns night ball attracts more than two hundred people, most of whom are Tamil and Sinhalese.[79]

Many former tea bungalows of Scottish planters in Sri Lanka have been converted into tourist accommodation, including several near Nuwara Eliya.[80] Stafford bungalow, for instance, was once owned by Sir G.H.D. Elphinstone, while the former bungalow of a Scots planter at Glendevon has rooms named Macnaughton, Crawford, Steuart, and Farquharson after leading planters from Scotland who once worked in the district. The 'Planter's Bungalow' at Ella, meanwhile, was constructed in the late nineteenth century by the Scottish tea planter Malcolm George. Perhaps the most luxurious of these bungalow conversions is the Ceylon Tea Trails accommodation, Sri Lanka's first Relais and Chateaux resort, around Castlereagh Lake, close to Hatton. These developments fulfil John Still's prediction in 1930 that 'antiquaries will unearth the ancient bungalows of the British period, or even of the Scottish which will lie beneath it, and classify the different kinds of bottles found among the ruins, and arrange them in museums'.[81]

The most recent legacy of Scottish influence in Ceylon is the opening of a new hotel in Colombo, The Steuart by Citrus, in the former premises of Steuart House, the headquarters of Sri Lanka's oldest mercantile enterprise, the George Steuart Group. The hotel bedrooms take their names from Scottish cities (Edinburgh, Glasgow, Aberdeen, and Dundee), clan shields adorn the walls, the interiors are tartan, and Scottish fare features in the Scottish-themed pub.[82]

Not all the memorials of the age of Scottish planter pre-eminence can be considered authentic or grounded in serious historical evidence. Nonetheless, taken together, they effectively convey how the modern nation of Sri Lanka continues to remember aspects of its Scottish influence in the era of empire, coffee, and tea.

Notes

1 Ranald C. Michie, 'Aberdeen and Ceylon: Economic links in the nineteenth century', *Northern Scotland*, 4 (1981), pp. 69–82.
2 John Ferguson, *Ceylon in 1893* (Colombo, 1893), p. 230.
3 *WCO*, 6 December 1884, p. 1009a.
4 *Ceylon Observer New Year Supplement*, 31 December 1883, pp. 1–2.
5 *OCO*, 1 December, 1887, pp. 1064–1067.
6 Ibid., 1 December 1888, p. 1150.
7 S.N. Breckenridge, *The Hills of Paradise: British Enterprise and the Story of Plantation Growth in Sri Lanka* (Colombo, 2012), 42.
8 *OCO*, 4 December 1869, pp. 478–480. Devon is typically associated with England but may refer to the River Devon in Scotland. A computer print-out of plantations in Sri Lanka with a Scottish connection can be found in University of Aberdeen Library, Special Collections and Archives, MS 3813/4.
9 See, for instance, Leigh S.L. Straw, *A Semblance of Scotland: Scottish Identity in Colonial Western Australia* (Glasgow, 2006), ch. 4.
10 *TA*, 1 February 1887, p. 531.
11 Among Irish examples was the New Galway district to honour the governor Sir William Gregory while a 'Cornish boy' opened 'New Cornwall' in the Ambawella Valley. Welsh estate names included Aadneven and Cymru and English Devon, St. George, and Langdale. See *TA*, 1 February 1887, p. 531.
12 *OCO*, 3 December 1870, p. 428.
13 'The St Andrew's dinner', *OCO*, 3 December 1870, p. 428.
14 Clement Scott, 'A cup of tea' *TA*, 1 May 1893, p. 694.
15 *OCO*, 3 December 1895, pp. 1289–1293.
16 'Scotchmen lead Ceylon!', *OCO*, 11 December 1888, p. 1166.
17 Sinclair's book, *In Tropical Lands: Recent Travels to the Sources of the Amazon, the West Indian Islands, and Ceylon* (Aberdeen, 1895), p. 160, is online at: https://archive.org/details/intropicallandsr00sincrich.

18 *WCO*, 6 December 1884, p. 1009a. Ferguson estimated that two-thirds of all Scottish planters in Ceylon were from the north-east of Scotland. See Ferguson, *Ceylon in 1893*, p. 230.
19 Centre of South Asian Studies, University of Cambridge, Major J.A. Forsythe Papers, 1860–1933, Box 1, 'Ceylon tea planter's life', by Old Sydney College Boy, letter to the editor of *Bath Chronicle*, 15 March 1889.
20 The most recent treatment is John M. MacKenzie and T.M. Devine (eds), *Scotland and the British Empire* (Oxford, 2011).
21 T.M. Devine, *To the Ends of the Earth: Scotland's Global Diaspora, 1750–2010* (London, 2011), pp. 1–31, 158–172.
22 T.M. Devine and Angela McCarthy, 'The Scottish experience in Asia, c.1700 to the present: Settlers and sojourners', in T.M. Devine and Angela McCarthy (eds), *The Scottish Experience in Asia, c.1700 to the Present* (Cham, 2017), pp. 12–14.
23 T.J. Barron, 'Scots and the coffee industry in nineteenth century Ceylon', pp. 163–185, and Angela McCarthy, 'Ceylon: A Scottish colony?', in Devine and McCarthy (eds), *The Scottish Experience in Asia, c.1700 to the Present*, pp. 187–211.
24 Barron, 'Scots and the coffee industry', pp. 174–175.
25 David Fitzpatrick, 'What Scottish diaspora?', in Angela McCarthy and John M. MacKenzie (eds), *Global Migrations: The Scottish Diaspora since 1600* (Edinburgh, 2016), p. 249.
26 Census, *Times of Ceylon Weekly Summary*, 25 August 1891, p. 1130.
27 McCarthy, 'Ceylon: A Scottish colony?', p. 192; Barron, 'Scots and the coffee industry', p. 175.
28 Barron, 'Scots and the coffee industry', pp. 170–171,
29 Ibid., pp. 166–167.
30 Devine, *To The Ends of the Earth*.
31 For a recent analysis see Jenny Wormald, 'Reformed and Godly Scotland?', in T.M. Devine and Jenny Wormald (eds), *The Oxford Handbook of Modern Scottish History* (Oxford, 2012), pp. 204–219.
32 Cited in T.M. Devine, *The Scottish Nation: A Modern History* (London, 2012), p. 91.
33 Richard Saville and Paul Auerbach, 'Education and social capital in the development of Scotland to 1750', presented to the Annual Conference of the Economic History Society Annual Conference, University of Reading, 31 March–2 April 2006.
34 T.M. Devine, 'Industrialisation', pp. 34–70, and 'The Transformation of agriculture: Cultivation and clearance', pp. 71–99, in T.M. Devine, C.H. Lee, and G.C. Peden (eds), *The Transformation of Scotland: The Economy since 1700* (Edinburgh, 2005), pp. 34–99.
35 Quoted in Trevor Burnard, *Mastery, Tyranny, and Desire: Thomas Thistlewood and His Slaves in the Anglo-Jamaican World* (Chapel Hill, NC and London, 2004), p. 89.
36 Douglas J. Hamilton, *Scotland, the Caribbean and the Atlantic World, 1750–1820* (Manchester, 2005), p. 55.

37 T.M. Devine, 'A Scottish empire of enterprise in the East, c.1695–1914', in Devine and McCarthy (eds), *Scottish Experience in Asia, c.1700 to the Present*, pp. 23–49.
38 George McGilvary, 'Scottish agency houses in South-East Asia, c.1760–1813', in Devine and McCarthy, *Scottish Experience in Asia, c.1700 to the Present*, pp. 75–96, at p. 82.
39 Barron, 'Scots and the coffee industry', p. 169.
40 Ibid., p. 168.
41 Ibid., pp. 168–169.
42 Sir James Emerson Tennent, *Ceylon: An Account of the Island, Physical, Historical and Topographical* (London, 1859), II, p. 236.
43 National Records of Scotland, Papers of the Mackenzie Family, Earls of Seaforth, GD46/9/6, No. 99, James Alexander Stewart Mackenzie (Colombo) to James McAdam (London), 28 March 1838.
44 James Alexander Stewart Mackenzie (Galle) to Alexander Bannerman (Aberdeen), 7 July 1840, in ibid., No. 11.
45 Quoted in Michie, 'Aberdeen and Ceylon', p. 72.
46 Barron, 'Scots and the coffee industry', p. 172.
47 William Boyd, 'Ceylon and its pioneers', *Ceylon Literary Register*, 2 March 1888, p. 258.
48 Michie, 'Aberdeen and Ceylon', p. 73; McCarthy, 'The importance of Scottish origins', p. 124; McCarthy, 'Ceylon: A Scottish colony', pp. 199–202.
49 Taylor letters, 21 February, 1859.
50 Cited in Michie, 'Aberdeen and Ceylon', p. 73.
51 Taylor letters, 13 June 1856.
52 Ibid., 27 May 1859.
53 Ibid., 21 February 1859.
54 Ibid., 27 May 1859.
55 Ibid., 30 January 1869.
56 David Fitzpatrick, *Oceans of Consolation: Personal Accounts of Irish Migration to Australia* (Cork, 1995), p. 520.
57 See Barron, 'Scots and the coffee industry', p. 176.
58 Taylor letters, 25 January 1873.
59 *Ceylon Observer New Year Supplement*, 31 December 1883, p. 1.
60 FEFP [Fanny Emily Farr Penny], *Fickle Fortune in Ceylon* (Madras, 1887), p. 36.
61 Taylor letters, 7 November 1886. James Shank Burnett (1868–1910) was the eldest son of James Cumine Burnett.
62 Barron, 'Scots and the coffee industry'.
63 Michie, 'Aberdeen and Ceylon', p. 82.
64 http://ghgraham.org/georgemaitland1854.html.
65 www.thepeerage.com/p52845.htm.
66 'Another Ceylon planter retiring', *CO* (Weekly Edition), 9 April 1915, p. 651; *CO* (Weekly Edition), 24 October 1917, p. 1638.
67 'Pioneers of the planting enterprise in Ceylon', *TA*, 2 July 1894, p. 1. Some surnames have been corrected from those that appear in this list.

68 www.gracesguide.co.uk/David_Reid_(1841–1892); www.gracesguide.co.uk/William_Jackson_(1849–1915).

69 'Tea for America', *OCO*, 23 April 1888, p. 382. Rutherford also wrote an acclaimed tea publication. Henry K. Rutherford and John Hill, *Ceylon Tea Planters' Note Book of Useful Memoranda*, 4th edn. (Colombo, 1902–3). Online at http://storage.lib.uchicago.edu/pres/2014/pres2014–1196.pdf.

70 'Some thoughts about tea', *TA*, 2 May 1892, p. 845. Rutherford's birthplace is unknown but his father was born at Kelso. See: www.geni.com/people/Henry-Rutherford/6000000023953083125.

71 https://en.wikipedia.org/wiki/Stewart_Loudoun-Shand. See also https://en.wikipedia.org/wiki/Eric_Loudoun-Shand.

72 'The Ceylon Plantations Tea Company', *TA*, 1 April 1892, p. 742.

73 'Mr. James Taylor and Ceylon tea', *OCO*, 18 June 1890, p. 640.

74 The biography of Charles Shand (b. 1819) reveals that he was born in Liverpool to an Edinburgh-born father and Aberdonian mother. He had a brother Thomas Livingstone Reid Shand also in Ceylon. See *TA*, 1 December 1897, p. 371. Charles' partner was J.L.R Shand and he had a son Francis Livingstone Shand (b. c.1855). Francis Shand had estates in Antigua. Family information taken from: www.genes-reunited.co.uk/boards/board/general_topics/thread/542812.

75 Sir Thomas J. Lipton, *Leaves from the Lipton Logs* (London, n.d.), p. 180. Lipton had been born of Ulster Scots parents who had migrated to Glasgow.

76 There is no reliable statistical data for the number of planters who worked in Ceylon, let alone their ethnicity. A prosopographical study in this respect would therefore be enlightening.

77 Opened in 2015, the memorial is not, however, located at the exact spot that Lipton frequented, which is instead lower down. Information provided by Avi de Silva, Unilever, 25 January 2016.

78 The caretaker of the Garrisons cemetery, Charles Carmichael, is very knowledgeable and has a Scottish grandfather.

79 Interview with Gordon and Michelle Kenny, 10 February 2014. No early records exist to confirm the establishment of the Society, but its earliest item is a cup that Sir Hugh Clifford, the Colonial Secretary of Ceylon, presented to the Society in 1907.

80 On Sri Lanka's tea lodgings see M.S.M. Aslam and Lee Jolliffe, 'Repurposing colonial tea heritage through historic lodging', *Journal of Heritage Tourism*, 10:2 (2015), pp. 111–128; and Lee Jolliffe and Mohamed S.M. Aslam, 'Tea heritage tourism: Evidence from Sri Lanka', *Journal of Heritage Tourism*, 4:4 (2009), pp. 331–344.

81 John Still, *The Jungle Tide* (Edinburgh and London, 1930), pp. 77–78. Thanks to Tom Barron for this quote.

82 All of this is supposedly redolent of the Scottish ancestry of James and George Steuart. The Steuarts were, however, born in England and no mention of a Scottish ancestry is made in George Steuart & Co Ltd, *The George Steuart Story* (Colombo, 1985).

Afterword

When Denys Forrest wrote his commemorative book on the 100th anniversary of Ceylon tea, he remarked that James Taylor's legend was 'a tangle of myth and history'.[1] We hope that this book has helped to unravel some of those misconceptions about Taylor. But just as crucially we hope that the importance of James Taylor's surviving correspondence for a number of issues in imperial, Asian, Scottish, and Sri Lankan historical writing has been demonstrated throughout this book. His series of letters is by far the richest source for both a nineteenth-century migrant of his social position from Scotland and the life of a British planter in Asia during the Victorian empire. Of central significance was his relatively modest social position and one, might add, his sheer ordinariness, a man with little ambition for material riches and public acclaim, but who nevertheless left a deep mark on the country where he lived most of his life. As an instructive tribute to him recorded, 'He would have been the last to seek or desire public notice' and was 'the very ideal of a faithful, hard-working, intelligent Superintendent and a more devoted, reliable Manager an absent estate proprietor never had in Ceylon'. In the early days, it was said, there was also little 'to mark him off from his fellows', but 'it is for the service rendered to the colony by a series of intelligent, careful, and successful experiments in the cultivation and preparation of both Cinchona and Tea that the name of James Taylor of Loole Condera will always be had in remembrance and esteem among the planting community of Ceylon'.[2] After his death one letter writer noted sympathetically, 'A kinder hearted man never breathed; and it was in a great measure owing to his forethought, dogged perseverance, and cheerful example, that Ceylon owes her agricultural prosperity at the present day.'[3]

But, unlike many 'great Scots' of the time whose deeds remain familiar to this day, Taylor is hardly known in the land of his birth. Several reasons might account for this. He did not, for instance, ever return to his homeland. Nor did his progeny, if they survived to adulthood, maintain links with their father's country after he died. Their mother, of either Sinhalese or Tamil descent, would probably have raised them within her own ethnic family. Perhaps, as sometimes happened in India, the children were removed from the estate and raised in an institution for the 'hybrid' offspring of British planters.[4] The public scandal surrounding Taylor's dismissal from his position as superintendent at Loolecoondera, followed by his mysterious death, may also have played a part in ensuring that any surviving family members would maintain a low profile about both him and his achievements. Perhaps even more relevant, however, were Taylor's self-effacing persona and his determination to avoid playing any significant public role in colonial affairs.

The legacy and reputation of another Scot with famous connections to nineteenth-century Ceylon, the world-renowned Thomas Lipton, could also have ensured that Taylor's name remained in the shadows. Taylor had a diametrically opposite personality to that of the charismatic and energetic Scottish grocer. Lipton relentlessly promoted Ceylon tea and his own name from the local high street to the global market-place. During his lifetime and beyond, Lipton and Ceylon tea almost became synonymous.[5] He was the marketing man par excellence who instinctively knew how to catch the headlines and boost the interest of the general public in his many enterprises. The riches he garnered eventually enabled him to move in the highest circles of the land and he was eventually created Knight Commander of the Royal Victorian Order by King Edward VII in 1901. Taylor, by contrast, shunned the limelight and was so unassuming that 'few were aware of his high intellectual attainments' in 'almost every department of Natural Science'.[6]

Nevertheless, despite his limited public standing, and indeed perhaps for that reason, the life of James Taylor is eminently worthy of academic study. This book has shown that he made major contributions to Ceylon's plantation economy, primarily in tea, but also in coffee cultivation and cinchona production. That impact marries well with the new interest in the history of global commodities. Whether tracing the production, consumption, and transformation of sugar, chocolate, and tobacco, historians have drawn attention to the widespread ecological changes that were triggered by the vast expansion of these crops.[7] Tea itself has also attracted significant historical scholarship.[8] But no study, to our knowledge, has researched a global commodity through a wide-ranging biographical study based on the long and detailed correspondence of a single planter working in the tropics.[9] Moreover, Taylor was in many ways similar to several of his planting peers and his life can provide insights into migrant experiences beyond his own.

Taylor's story and the focus on Ceylon tea have also enabled engagement with the important debate on whether the British people en masse were aware of or interested in the imperial project during the nineteenth century.[10] The evidence presented here concerning Britain's favourite drink shows that Ceylon tea was overtly and systematically marketed as a product of empire, primarily in order to clearly distinguish it from the long-established favourite from China. This is apparent in both its packaging and advertising in the press. The series of international exhibitions, described earlier in the book, were intended to present a strong sense of exotic allure to the millions who attended the displays. Ceylon tea was presented there in unambiguously patriotic terms as supplied from the farthest reaches of the British Empire. But it was not simply consumed in the mother country; it eventually had a global reach and infused the everyday lives of Britons, both at home and abroad, as much as it filled their tea-cups. As Andrew Thompson has put it, 'Histories of commodities – and their impact on people's lives – social, political and aesthetic – have been one way of moving imaginatively in and out of the British Isles and traversing metropolitan and colonial spaces.'[11]

Our approach also seeks to bring economic factors back into play without omitting the 'new' imperial history's interest in empire as a cultural project with a particular focus on 'race' and representation. Indeed, we have been at pains to show the human as well as environmental and economic costs of Britain's colonisation and exploitation of Ceylon's territory, resources, and people. These transformations were enacted by subalterns like James Taylor as much as by governors, generals, high officials, and business leaders. But Taylor's life story shows that the imperial experience was not simply about conquest and subordination but could also involve both human contacts across the cultures and sometimes a degree of cooperation between them.

The book has also sought to engage with the range of identities associated with Taylor. He certainly saw himself as a Scot, but he remained deeply conscious of his north-east origins all his life. Moreover, when he died others noted that he was from the Mearns. His particular origins also gave him the entrée to life in Ceylon and skillsets that would facilitate his achievement abroad. Ongoing analysis of ethnic identities is likely to generate continuing refinement of 'the nation' as scholars search for the diversities which exist below the concept at the level of the region or locality and drill down to the sub-national experience. Taking that route is predictable, given the concentric nature of human identities encompassing, inter alia, nation, region, locality, faith, and family.[12] Whether uncoupling and refining these distinctions from the greater whole can provide analytical value will probably depend on the circumstances under scrutiny and the questions being considered.

In addition, we have tried to consider some new approaches to the history of diaspora studies by using James Taylor's life experiences as the evidential anchor. Migration histories have usually 'shied away from the realm of the emotional and have hesitated to explore the feelings immigrants endured and the meanings they invested in their experiences'.[13] That negligence is surprising, since migration is a very emotional undertaking often framed by exile, loneliness, and loss, but also by adventure and excitement. While emotions do appear tangentially in studies of migration and empire, they have rarely been analysed *explicitly* in connection with international mobility. The omission is perhaps understandable, since 'the turn' to the emotions is a recent development in the wider historiography and has been mainly influenced by studies of human mobility in the work of social scientists.[14] Few can doubt that demographic, economic, and political approaches to the history of migration have long been dominant.[15] If a fresh perspective is to be adopted, Hasia Diner suggests that 'it would be precisely in the realm of biography that we might learn more about the range of emotional reactions to these movements'.[16]

Taylor's correspondence has allowed us to bring out various aspects of his emotional life. These include considering the mingled sorrow and anticipation when he left home at the age of sixteen to journey across the globe to a different world, the anxiety and enthusiasm that he felt in cultivating various Ceylon commodities, the strain and exhilaration of planter life, the contempt he often demonstrated towards other peoples in Ceylon, the positive and negative feelings about his tight-knit community back in Scotland, and the frustration and torment of his last years when quarrels over transformations to the tea industry sparked his hostility and discontent. We have tried to identify these responses and when and why they found expression through the prism of his emotions. They, as much as self-interest, motivate human actions and without some focus on them this biographical study of James Taylor would have been incomplete.

We have likewise endeavoured to bring to life his character and personality. As a sixteen-year-old in London before leaving for Ceylon, he demonstrated a confidence and assurance beyond his years. The attention to detail and emphasis on frugality that he showed during his brief time in the city never left him; nor did his self-discipline. He also possessed, during his entire life, a strong sense of personal duty and responsibility. He placed great store on doing his job as a superintendent as conscientiously as possible but, on the other hand, appears not to have been overly ambitious. He was a modest man but at the same time fully confident in his abilities. The warm accolades which later came his way confirm that he was a popular figure among his peers. He had an enquiring mind which showed especially on practical and technical matters and which helps to explain the series of successful innovations he made as a planter. He shared this 'restless energy in seeking out facts' with his fellow planters and 'was ever ready to help any one who earnestly sought information from him'.[17] But he had much broader intellectual interests, which is confirmed by the range of books he read. The love of learning which was inculcated during his schooldays never left him. Taylor took solace in his own company but that did not prevent him enjoying that of his fellow planters from time to time. He also maintained ties – strong, tender, and truculent – to his family and provided for them financially during his many years in Ceylon.

If he was jocular, cautious, and reliable, James Taylor could be stubborn, impatient, and irascible. While we see signs of a bright youth, he was also sulky, sensitive to criticism, and seemed to be in real need of his father's approbation. A sense of frustration at the way things could and should be done better was a feature of his personality and came to dominate his final years. This exasperation, however, emerged from his perfectionism and his contempt of those who lacked first-hand practical experience of planting life in Ceylon, to which he had devoted his lifetime's work. He certainly did not suffer fools gladly. He likewise occasionally showed exasperation with his family, for whom he became a paternal benefactor, and could be cutting in his comments about Fordoun folk. These private thoughts, it seems, rarely came into public view, for after his death he was recalled as someone 'who was never heard to speak an unjust word of any human being.' His enemies, according to this recollection, were those who 'failed to recognise his real merits' and envied him his success. His height, towering above all, 'like the giant that he was ... made [him] a conspicuous figure to be aimed at'.[18] In his opinions of both Sinhalese and Tamils he comes across as very much a man of his time, and his attitudes towards them hardened further after he read about the reported atrocities associated with the Indian 'Mutiny'. Nonetheless, his letters suggest that he treated the labour force on his estates better than some of his fellow planters.

In sum, therefore, we would argue that this study makes a contribution at several levels to historical understanding: the British commercial empire in Asia; the story of tea as a global commodity; Sri Lanka's economic development in the nineteenth century; the experience of British Asian planters in the Victorian era; the history of the Scottish diaspora; and last, but by no means least, in providing the first biography of James Taylor, the pioneer of Ceylon tea, based to a large extent on his own words, taken from the letters he wrote to his family in Scotland over a period of four decades. His life and achievements do indeed testify to his acclaim as the 'father of the Ceylon tea enterprise'.

Perhaps the last words should be with a contemporary admirer who after Taylor's death made the following observation:

> Those who have been fortunate enough to meet Mr James Taylor will never forget him. His tall, venerable, figure, with his large head set on slightly stooping shoulders, his forehead highly and broadly arched; his kindly mild eyes looking forth under the shadow of prominent brows; his amiable mouth surrounded by a long silver grey beard. The gentle, mild voice; the slow, deliberate utterance; the charming freshness and originality of his conversation; all must have inspired his most casual acquaintance with a feeling of deep respect and admiration.
>
> Honourable in the smallest things in life, ever thinking of others, and giving them assistance; simple, lovable, charitable, and possessed of extreme modesty – such was the Father of the Ceylon Tea enterprise; a man whose kindnesses will live in many a planter's memory, and whose name will stand high in the archives of this Colony for ever.[19]

Notes

1 D.M. Forrest, *A Hundred Years of Ceylon Tea, 1867–1967* (London, 1967), p. 57.
2 *TA*, 2 July 1894, pp. 1, 4.
3 'A memorial to the late Mr. James Taylor', *CO*, 21 May 1892, p. 3.
4 Jane McCabe, *Race, Tea and Colonial Resettlement: Imperial Families, Interrupted* (London, 2017).
5 Sir Thomas J. Lipton, *Leaves from the Lipton Logs* (London, 1931), p. 25; Forrest, *A Hundred Years of Ceylon Tea*, p. 152.
6 NLS, Papers of James Taylor, planter in Ceylon, MS 15908, no. 223, 'The Late Mr James Taylor of Loolecondera'.
7 Sidney W. Mintz, *Sweetness and Power: The Place of Sugar in Modern History* (New York, 1985); Emma Robertson, *Chocolate, Women and Empire: A Social and Cultural History* (Manchester and New York, 2009).
8 See, most recently, Markman Ellis, Richard Coulton and Matthew Mauger, *Empire of Tea: The Asian Leaf that Conquered the World* (London, 2015).
9 Sarah Rose's study of Robert Fortune comes close but gives little consideration to his wider life beyond tea. See *For All the Tea in China: How England Stole the World's Favorite Drink and Changed History* (New York, 2011).
10 A key debate within British imperial historiography is the extent to which Britons were shaped by their empire. Bernard Porter's view, that empire's significance is exaggerated, has been robustly challenged by, among others, John M. MacKenzie and Antoinette Burton and, for Scotland, by T.M. Devine.
11 Andrew Thompson, 'Introduction', in Andrew Thompson (ed.), *Writing Imperial Histories* (Manchester and New York, 2013), p. 17.
12 T.C. Smout, 'Perspectives on the Scottish identity', *Scottish Affairs*, 6:1 (1994), pp. 101–113.
13 Hasia R. Diner, 'Ethnicity and emotions in America: Dimensions of the unexplored', in Peter N. Stearns and Jan Lewis (eds), *An Emotional History of the United States* (New York and London, 1998), pp. 197–217.
14 Ann Brooks and Ruth Simpson (eds), *Emotions in Transmigration: Transformation, Movement and Identity* (London and New York, 2012); Maruška Svašek, 'Affective moves: Transit, transition and transformation', in Maruška Svašek (ed.), *Moving Subjects, Moving Objects: Transnationalism, Cultural Production and Emotions* (New York and Oxford, 2012), pp. 1–40; Maruška Svašek, 'On the move: Emotions and human mobility', *Journal of Ethnic and Migration Studies*, 36:6 (2010), pp. 867–880.
15 Paolo Boccagni and Loretta Baldassar, 'Emotions on the move: Mapping the emergent field of emotion and migration', *Emotion, Space and Society* (2015), p. 1. Sarah Tarlow, 'The archaeology of emotion and affect', *Annual Review of Anthropology*, 41 (2012), p. 172.
16 Diner, 'Ethnicity and emotions in America', p. 203.
17 'The Late Mr James Taylor of Loolecondera'.
18 Ibid.
19 Ibid.

Appendix 1

Dates of James Taylor correspondence

The correspondence is held by NLS, MS 15908, Papers of James Taylor, planter in Ceylon.

James Taylor (London) to his father Michael Taylor (Mosspark), 13 October 1851.

James Taylor (London) to his father, Michael Taylor (Mosspark), 16 October 1851.

James Taylor (London) to his father, Michael Taylor (Mosspark), 18 October 1851.

James Taylor (Sydney) to his father, Michael Taylor (Mosspark), 23 October 1851.

James Taylor (Sydney) to his father, Michael Taylor (Mosspark), 24 October 1851.

James Taylor (Naranghena) to his father, Michael Taylor (Mosspark), 13 March 1852.

James Taylor (Naranghena) to his father, Michael Taylor (Mosspark), 11 April 1852.

James Taylor, Notes from Voyage.

James Taylor (Loolecondera) to his father, Michael Taylor (Mosspark), 23 June 1852.

James Taylor (Naranghena) to his father, Michael Taylor (Mosspark), 12 December 1852.

James Taylor (Naranghena) to his father, Michael Taylor (Mosspark), 9 January 1853 [this letter is a continuation of his letter dated 12 December 1852].

James Taylor (Loolecondera) to his father, Michael Taylor (Mosspark), 9 March 1854.

James Taylor (Loolecondera) to his father, Michael Taylor (Mosspark), 13 June 1856.

James Taylor (Loolecondera) to his father, Michael Taylor (Mosspark), 27 January 1857.

James Taylor (Loolecondera) to his father, Michael Taylor (Mosspark), 24 July 1857.

James Taylor (Loolecondera) to his father, Michael Taylor (Mosspark), 17 September 1857.

James Taylor (Loolecondera) to his father, Michael Taylor (Mosspark), 3 December 1857.

James Taylor (Loolecondera) to his father, Michael Taylor (Mosspark), 23 January 1858.

James Taylor to his father, Michael Taylor (Mosspark), envelope with a scrawl from Taylor dated 10 May 1858.

James Taylor (Loolecondera) to his father, Michael Taylor (Mosspark), 10 July 1858.

Robert Moir (Laurencekirk) to his grandson James Taylor (Loolecondera), 27 October 1858.

Robert Moir (Laurencekirk) to his grandson James Taylor (Loolecondera), 31 January 1859.

James Taylor (Loolecondera) to his father, Michael Taylor (Mosspark), 21 February 1859.

Robert Moir (Laurencekirk) to his grandson James Taylor (Loolecondera), 12 April 1859.

James Taylor (Loolecondera) to his father, Michael Taylor (Mosspark), 27 May 1859.

Robert Moir (Laurencekirk) to his grandson James Taylor (Loolecondera), 27 June 1859.

Robert Moir (Laurencekirk) to his grandson James Taylor (Loolecondera), 1 August 1859.

Robert Moir (Laurencekirk) to his grandson James Taylor (Loolecondera), 3 September 1859.

James Taylor (Loolecondera) to his father, Michael Taylor (Mosspark), 11 November 1859.

Michael Taylor (Mosspark) to his son James Taylor (Loolecondera), 23 December 1859.

James Taylor (Loolecondera) to his father, Michael Taylor (Mosspark), 28 January 1860.

James Taylor (Loolecondera) to his father, Michael Taylor (Mosspark), 18 June 1860.

James Taylor (Loolecondera) to his father, Michael Taylor (Mosspark), 9 September 1860.

James Taylor (Loolecondera) to his father, Michael Taylor (Mosspark), 30 January 1869.

James Taylor (Loolecondera) to his father, Michael Taylor (Mosspark), 18 March 1872.

Valuations of Keir Dundas and Co Tea, 21 August 1872.

James Taylor (Loolecondera) to his father, Michael Taylor (Mosspark), 25 January 1873.

James Taylor (Darjeeling) to his father, Michael Taylor, 29 March 1874.

James Taylor (Loolecondera) to his father, Michael Taylor, 11 April 1875.

James Taylor (Loolecondera) to his sister and brother [probably Margaret and George Nairn], 5 November 1876.

James Taylor (Loolecondera) to his father, Michael Taylor, 9 September 1878.

James Taylor (Loolecondera) to his father, Michael Taylor, 1 November 1879.

James Taylor (Loolecondera) to his sister Margaret Nairn, 27 March 1882.

James Taylor (Loolecondera) to his sister Margaret and brother-in-law George Nairn, 15 April 1882.

James Taylor (Loolecondera) to his brother-in-law George Nairn (Brakie, Arbroath), 18 July 1882.

James Taylor (Loolecondera) to his father, Michael Taylor (Auchenblae), 2 September 1882.

James Taylor (Loolecondera) to his sister Margaret and brother-in-law George Nairn, 15 December 1884.

James Taylor (Loolecondera) to his father, Michael Taylor (Auchenblae), 7 November 1886.

James Taylor (Loolecondera) to his father, Michael Taylor (Auchenblae), 30 June 1887.

James Taylor (Loolecondera) to his father, Michael Taylor (Auchenblae), 18 July 1889.

James Taylor (Loolecondera) to his sister [Margaret] and brother-in-law [George Nairn], 12 June 1890.
James Taylor (Loolecondera) to his father, Michael Taylor (Auchenblae), 23 October 1890.
James Taylor (Loolecondera) to his brother-in-law [George Nairn] and sister [Margaret], 24 October 1890.
James Taylor (Loolecondera) to his brother-in-law [George Nairn] and sister [Margaret], 28 July 1891.
A. Philip (Kandy) to James Taylor (Loolecondera), 19 August 1891.
A. Philip (Kandy) to James Taylor (Loolecondera), 29 August 1891.
A. Philip (Kandy) to James Taylor (Loolecondera), 31 August 1891.
A. Philip (Kandy) to James Taylor (Loolecondera), 17 December 1891.
C.E. Bonner (Naranghena) to George Nairn, 13 July 1892.
C.E. Bonner (Naranghena) to George Nairn, 3 Jan 1892 [sic].
James Taylor [?Loolecondera] to [unknown], c.1858.
James Taylor [?Loolecondera] to [unknown], undated.
James Taylor [?Loolecondera] to [unknown], mid-1870s.
Robert Taylor to his brother James Taylor, c.1864.

Appendix 2

Family trees of Taylor, Moir and Stiven families

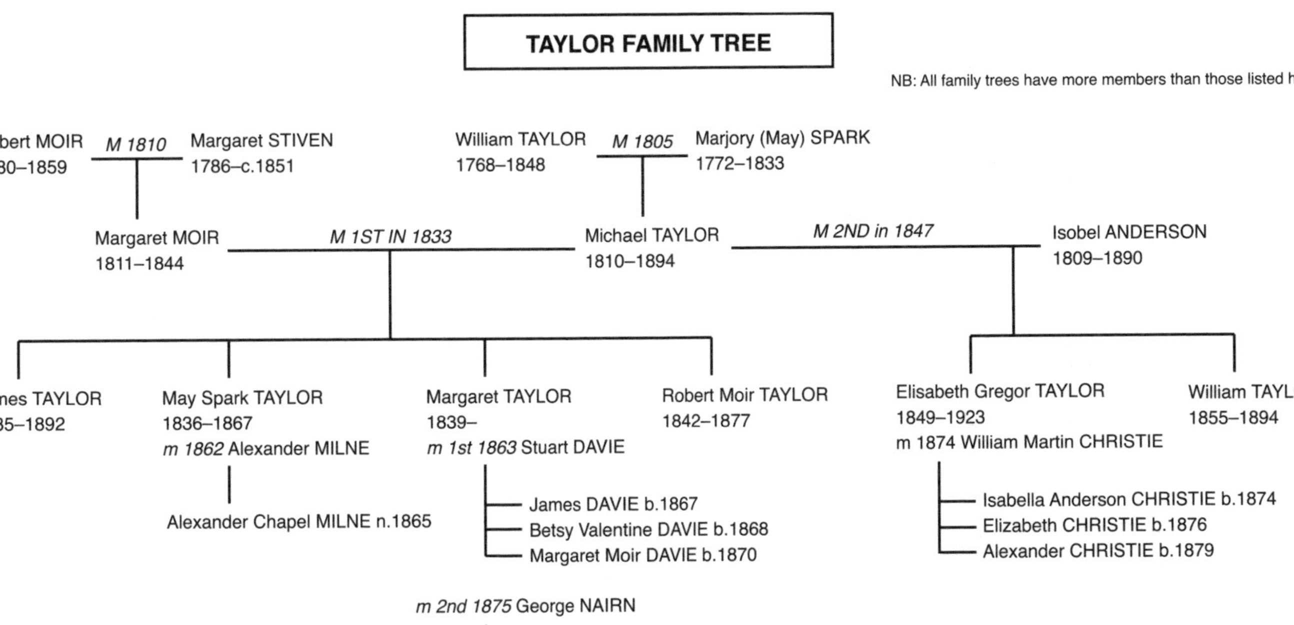

MOIR/STIVEN FAMILY TREE

NB: All family trees have more members than those listed here.

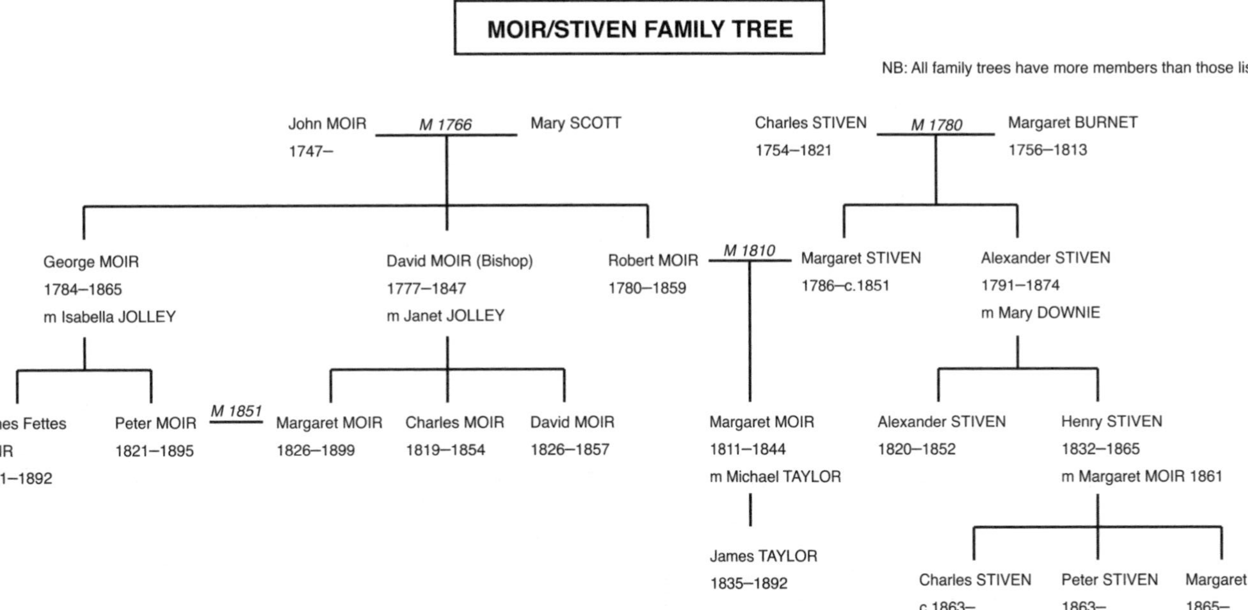

Bibliography

Primary sources

Archives of the Royal Botanic Gardens at Kew

Miscellaneous Reports Ceylon, 1847–1900, MR/284
Miscellaneous Reports Ceylon, 1861–1890, MR/285
Miscellaneous Reports Ceylon, 1891–1900, MR/286
Miscellaneous Reports – Cinchona, 1859–1890, MR/290
Miscellaneous Reports – Cultural Products, 1863–1916, MR/293

Bodleian Library at the Weston Library, University of Oxford

W.H. Gregory Papers, Correspondence concerning Ceylon, 1872–91
  Correspondence as Governor-General, 1872–77, Dep. c. 1282
  General correspondence concerning Ceylon, Aug. 1877–Dec. 1878, Dep. d. 979
  Correspondence concerning Ceylon, 1879, Dep. d. 978
  Correspondence concerning Ceylon, 1880–83, Dep. c. 1279
  Correspondence concerning Ceylon, 1884–91, Dep. c. 1280
  Correspondence concerning Ceylon, Dep. c. 1281
  Letters from the Governor-General, Sir Arthur Hamilton-Gordon, 1883–90, Dep. d. 980

British Library

Administration Reports Ceylon 1867 (Colombo, 1868), C531
Directory of Ceylon, 1863
Tropical Agriculturalist, 1882–1900
Newspapers on microfilm
  Ceylon Examiner, 27 July–31 December 1892, MC 1210
  Ceylon Overland Bi-Monthly Examiner, 1872, MC 1211
  Ceylon Times, January–June 1863, MC 1204
  Overland Examiner, 1875, MC 1211
  Overland Examiner, 7 January 1878–19 December 1879, MC 1211.
  The Examiner, 1865, MC 1210

Times of Ceylon Weekly Summary, January–June 1890, MC 1205
Times of Ceylon Weekly Summary, July–December 1891, MC 1205
Times of Ceylon Weekly Summary, January–June 1892
Times of Ceylon Weekly Summary, July–December 1892

Centre of South Asian Studies, University of Cambridge

Major J.A. Forsythe Papers, 1860–1933, Box 1

Ceylon Tea Museum Archives

Madugalle, D., *Ceylon Tea Pride of Our Nation* (2010)

Highland Council Archive

Ceylon estate – William Rule, Sir Alexander MacEwan Papers, D375/1/4
Springfield Estate Ceylon, 1848–1912, D339

Institute of Commonwealth Studies, University of London

Ferguson Papers, ICS86
Correspondence of Ferguson, as editor of the 'Ceylon Observer', 1/1–44
Correspondence of John Ferguson, mainly in his editorial capacity, and news cuttings regarding the 'Ceylon Observer' or its editors, 1/2/1–40
Publications of A.M. and J. Ferguson Ltd, 1/3/1–2
News cutting from the 'Overland Ceylon Observer', 2/1/2
Correspondence with planters regarding the compilation of reports and statistics, 3/1/1–26
Correspondence and papers regarding the planting industry, 3/2/1–42
News cuttings and other papers regarding the planting industry, 3/3/1–46
Lectures and papers given by Ferguson on the planting industry, 3/4/1–14
Correspondence between Ferguson and Sir Henry Mccallum, 4/2/1–8
Correspondence between W.H. Gregory and Ferguson, 4/3/1–6
News cuttings on the history and current affairs of Ceylon, 4/8/1–26
Publications and reports relating to the governance of Ceylon, 4/9/1–9
Supplement to the 'Ceylon Observer', 4/10/1
Correspondence and news cuttings relating to lectures given and exhibitions attended overseas by Ferguson, 7/1/1–53
News cutting relating to overseas tours by Ferguson to China, Japan, North America and Britain, 7/2/1–23
Draft of lecture by Ferguson entitled 'Leaves from a holiday notebook', 7/3/1
Menu and news cuttings regarding St Andrew's Dinners held in Ceylon, 8/1/1–3
Correspondence, list of guests, programmes, news cuttings and articles regarding the Annual Dinner of the Glasgow Ross and Cromarty Benevolent Association, 8/2/1–17

Letters from Ferguson to his mother[?-in-law], 8/4/1–35
Biographical notes on the life of John Ferguson, 8/6/1–36
Correspondence and other papers of or relating to A.M. Ferguson, 9/1/1–10
Correspondence and papers regarding the Royal Asiatic Society, 9/2/1–22
General correspondence, mainly personal and social, and news cuttings relating directly to Ferguson, 9/3/1–56
General correspondence, 9/4/1–6
General correspondence and news cuttings, 9/5/1–60
General correspondence, 9/6/1–51
General correspondence and cuttings, 9/7/1–53
General correspondence and papers, 9/8/1–40

Mitchell Library, Glasgow

Sir Thomas Lipton Collection
Ceylon, Indian and Foreign Notices, Vol. 6, May 1890–January 1898
General Press Notices, Vol. 1, April 1877–December 1891
General Press Notices, Vol. 2, January 1892–December 1894

National Library of Scotland

Andrew Hunter, Hunter of Glencarse, MS 19722–33
Ceylon: Letters of George and Robert Arbuthnot, 1801–2, MS 5208
Fettercairn Estate Papers, Acc 4796
Letters to Sir John Stuart Forbes, 1833–1852, no. 54
Letters to Sir John Stuart Forbes 1853–1864, no. 55
Letters to Sir John Stuart Forbes 1864–1866, no. 56
Fettercairn estate papers: Factor's letters 1837–1859, no. 149
Fettercairn estate papers: miscellaneous 1840–1850, no. 158
Fettercairn estate correspondence and other papers 1843–1864, no. 166
Monboddo Papers, Notebook of James B. Burnett, MS 24604
Monboddo Estate Accounts, MS 24608
Monboddo Estate Papers (1840–65), MS 24627
Papers concerning Hannagalla Coffee Plantation, Seton and Bremner Papers, MS 19227–32
Papers of James Taylor, planter in Ceylon, MS 15908
Photograph album of James Taylor, MS 15909
Photograph album of James Taylor, MS 15910
Robertson-MacDonald papers, MS 3970–1, 3979

National Museums Scotland

James Taylor photo album, K.2000.200

National Records of Scotland

Colonial Office correspondence relating to Australia, New Zealand, Canada, the West Indies and church matters in Ceylon, GD364/1/522/1–65

Correspondence of the Revd. John Mackall, CH1/11/2

Kabaragala estate correspondence, GD176/2576

Letters, Alex Macqueen, surgeon, Ceylon Rifles, GD23/6/634

Letters from H.I. Cameron, GD46/1/405

Letters from Hugh Cleghorn, GD26/13/859

Letters, with relative enclosures, from Hugh Cleghorn to Henry Dundas mainly on Ceylon and its government, GD51/3/83/1–9

Letters from Sancroft Holmes to Alfred Donald Mackintosh, GD176/2388

Letters from John Page, Madeira and Ceylon, GD364/1/1230

Papers of the Mackenzie Family, Earls of Seaforth (Seaforth Papers), GD46

- Copies of letters from Ceylon to England by J.A. Stewart Mackenzie, GD46/9/6
- Book of letters by the Hon Mrs Stewart Mackenzie to J.A. Stewart Mackenzie, GD46/9/9
- Personal letters by J.A. Stewart Mackenzie, Governor of Ceylon, to Mrs Stewart Mackenzie, GD46/9/11
- Volume of letters to J.A. Stewart Mackenzie as Governor of Ceylon and later Lord High Commissioner of the Ionian Islands, GD46/9/19
- Letter to Mrs Stewart Mackenzie relating to the libellous article in the Herald, her proposal to purchase estates in Ceylon and personal matters, GD46/9/21
- Letters from Mrs Stewart Mackenzie to the Governor on her leaving Ceylon, GD 46/9/23
- Letter by the Revd. E. Daniel, Colombo, to Mrs Stewart Mackenzie relating to Ceylon affairs, GD46/9/34
- Letter by J. Braybrooke from Kandy to Mrs Stewart Mackenzie, GD46/9/38

Personal letters to the Mackintosh: Colombo, GD176/2410

Public Record Office of Northern Ireland

Autobiographical and obituary material on Sir James Emerson Tennent, D2922/A/1

Colonial Office Correspondence, D2922/C/20

Letters and papers relating to particular aspects or phases of Emerson Tennent's political career, D2922/C/22

Travel, literary and personal papers of Emerson Tennent, D2922/D/11

Scrapbook about Tea, D3639/G/3

Sri Lanka Tea Board

James Taylor, Tea Pioneer of Ceylon: 100th Death Anniversary, 2nd May 1892–1992 (Hewaheta, 1992).

University of Aberdeen Library, Special Collections and Archives

Charles Arbuthnot Papers, MS 3029/3/1/26–49
Computer print-out of plantation in Sri Lanka marked with those of a Scottish connection, MS 3813/4
Moir Family of Stoneywood and Scotstown, Aberdeenshire: Papers, MS 2736/6, 7, 10
Printed booklet listing Sri Lankan estates, MS 3813/3
Records of Alexander Pirie & Sons, MS 2911

University of St Andrews Special Collections

Papers and photographs of John Faulds, MS 38419
Papers of Hugh Cleghorn of Strathivie and the Cleghorn family, MS dep 53, box 6–7

Contemporary publications

[Anon.], *The New Statistical Account of Scotland: Vol. 11. Forfar, Kincardine* (Edinburgh and London, 1845).
Baker, S.W., *Eight Years' Wanderings in Ceylon* (London, 1855).
Boyd, William, 'Ceylon and its pioneers', *Ceylon Literary Register*:
27 January 1888, pp. 217–220
3 February 1888, pp. 225–227
10 February 1888, pp. 233–235
17 February 1888, pp. 241–242
24 February 1888, pp. 251–252
2 March 1888, pp. 257–258
9 March 1888, pp. 265–267
16 March 1888, pp. 273–275
23 March 1888, pp. 281–284
Capper, John, *Handbook Ceylon Products and Industries with a Catalogue of the Exhibits in the Ceylon Court* (Edinburgh, 1888).
Cramond, W., *The Annals of Fordoun* (Montrose, 1894).
Denham, E.B., *Census of Ceylon 1911 Tables Showing the Population* (Colombo, 1912).
Denham, E.B., *The Census of Ceylon 1911 Estate Statistics. The Estate Population* (Colombo, 1912).
Donaldson, James, *General View of the Agriculture of the County of Kincardine; Or, The Mearns: With Observations on the Means of its Improvement* (London, 1795).
Exhibition of the Works of Industry of All Nations, 1851: Reports by the Juries on the Subjects in the Thirty Classes into which the Exhibition was Divided (London, 1852).
FEFP [Fanny Emily Farr Penny], *Fickle Fortune in Ceylon* (Madras, 1887).
[Ferguson, A.M.], *The Abbotsford Album: A Series of Twenty Views on and from a Mountain Plantation in the District of Dimbula, Ceylon, Illustrative of the Culture of Coffee, Tea, and Cinchona* (Colombo, c. 1875).

Ferguson, A.M., *The Ceylon Directory; Calendar and Compendium of Useful Information for 1871–72* (Colombo, 1872).

Ferguson, A.M. and J. Ferguson, *Planting Directory for India and Ceylon* (Colombo, 1878).

Ferguson, A.M. and J. Ferguson, *The Ceylon Directory; Calendar and Compendium of Useful Information, 1880–81* (Colombo, 1881).

Ferguson, A.M. and J. Ferguson, *The Ceylon Handbook & Directory; Calendar and Compendium of Useful Information, 1883–84* (Colombo, 1883).

Ferguson, A.M., and J. Ferguson, *The Ceylon Directory; Calendar, and Compendium of Useful Information (edition of 1883–84)* (Colombo, 1884).

Ferguson, A.M. and J. Ferguson, *The Ceylon Handbook & Directory; and Compendium of Useful Information, 1885–86* (Colombo, 1885).

Ferguson, A.M. and J. Ferguson, *The Ceylon Directory; Calendar, and Compendium of Useful Information, 1887–88* (Colombo, 1887).

Ferguson, A.M. and J. Ferguson, *The Ceylon Handbook & Directory and Compendium of Useful Information, 1890–91* (Colombo, 1890).

Ferguson, A.M. and J. Ferguson, *The Ceylon Handbook & Directory and Compendium of Useful Information, 1893* (Colombo, 1893).

Ferguson, A.M. and J. Ferguson, *The Ceylon Mercantile and Planting Directory; 1891–1892* (Colombo, 1891).

Ferguson, John, *Ceylon in 1893* (London, 1893).

Ferguson, John, *Ceylon in the "Jubilee Year"* (Colombo, 1887).

Ferguson, John, *The Rise of the Planting Enterprise and Trade in Ceylon Tea* (c. 1907).

Fraser, William Ruxton, *History of the Parish and Burgh of Laurencekirk* (Edinburgh and London, 1880).

Great Exhibition of the Works of Industry of All Nations, 1851, Official Descriptive and Illustrated Catalogue, vol. 2 (London, 1851).

Halford, Sir Henry, 'Essays and Orations, read and delivered at the Royal College of Physicians', *Edinburgh Medical and Surgical Journal*, 47 (1837), pp. 183–199.

Hamilton, V.M. and S.M. Fasson, *Scenes in Ceylon* (London, 1881).

Hull, E.C.P., *Coffee Planting in Southern India and Ceylon* (London, 1877).

Johnston, William, *A Genealogical Account of the Descendants of James Young, Merchant Burgess of Aberdeen and Rachel Cruickshank his wife, 1697–1893* (Aberdeen, 1894), https://archive.org/stream/agenealogicalac00johngoog#page/n60/mode/2up.

Jubilee of the Planters' Association of Ceylon, 1854–1904: Illustrated Souvenir of the 'Times of Ceylon' (Colombo, 1904).

Knighton, William, *The History of Ceylon from the Earliest Period to the Present Time* (Colombo, 1845).

Labourie, P.J., *The Coffee Planter of Saint Domingo* (London, 1798).

Lewis, Frederick, *Sixty-Four Years in Ceylon: Reminiscences of Life and Adventure* (Colombo, 1926).

Lewis, J. Perry, *A List of Inscriptions on Tombstones and Monuments in Ceylon* (Colombo, 1913), online at https://archive.org/stream/cu31924007648516#page/n0/mode/2up.

Lipton, Sir Thomas J., *Leaves from the Lipton Logs* (London, n.d.).

Macdonald, James, 'On the agriculture of the counties of Forfar and Kincardine', *Transactions of the Highland and Agricultural Society of Scotland for 1881* (online at www.electricscotland.com/agriculture/page51.htm).

Memoir of the Life and Work of Rev. John Brebner, MA., LL.D, late Superintendent of Education in the Orange Free State, South Africa (Edinburgh, 1903).

Millie, P.D. *Thirty Years Ago or Reminiscences of the Early Days of Coffee Planting in Ceylon* (Colombo, 1878).

Mollyson, Charles A., *The Parish of Fordoun: Chapters in its History, or Reminiscences of Place and Character* (Aberdeen, 1893).

Planters Association of Ceylon, *Report of the Proceedings of the Planters Association of Kandy with an Appendix* (Colombo, 1855).

Planters Association of Ceylon, *Annual Report of the Planters Association for the Year Ending 17th February 1857* (Colombo, 1857).

Planters Association of Ceylon, *Proceedings of the Planters' Association, Kandy, for the year ending 17th February 1862* (Colombo, 1862).

Planters Association of Ceylon, *Proceedings of the Planters Association for the Year Ending 17th February 1863* (Colombo, 1863).

Planters Association of Ceylon, *Proceedings of the Planters Association, Kandy, for the year ending 17th February 1864* (Colombo, 1864).

Planters Association of Ceylon, *Proceedings of the Planters Association, Kandy, for the year ending 17th February 1865* (Colombo, 1865).

Planters Association of Ceylon, *Proceedings of the Planters Association, Kandy, for the year ending 16th February 1867* (Colombo, 1867).

Planters Association of Ceylon, *Proceedings of the Planters Association, Kandy, for the year ending 17th February 1870* (Colombo, 1870).

Planters Association of Ceylon, *Proceedings of the Planters Association, Kandy, for the year ending 17th February 1871* (1871, Colombo).

Planters Association of Ceylon, *Proceedings of the Planters Association, Kandy, for the year ending 17th February 1872* (Colombo, 1872).

Planters Association of Ceylon, *Proceedings of the Planters' Association of Ceylon for year ending February 17, 1874* (Colombo, 1874).

Planters Association of Ceylon, *Proceedings of the Planters' Association of Ceylon for year ending February 17th, 1875* (Liverpool, 1875).

Planters Association of Ceylon, *Proceedings of the Planters' Association of Ceylon for year ending February 17th, 1876* (Liverpool, 1876).

Planters Association of Ceylon, *Proceedings of the Planters' Association of Ceylon for year ending February 17th, 1877* (Colombo, 1877).

Planters Association of Ceylon, *Proceedings of the Planters' Association of Ceylon for year ending February 17th, 1878* (Colombo, 1878).

Planters Association of Ceylon, *Proceedings of the Planters' association of Ceylon for year ending February 17th, 1879* (Colombo, 1879).

Planters Association of Ceylon, *Proceedings of the Planters Association, Kandy, for the year ending 17th February 1880* (Colombo, 1880).

Planters Association of Ceylon, *Proceedings of the Planters Association, Kandy, for the year ending 17th February 1881* (Colombo, 1881).

Planters Association of Ceylon, *Proceedings of the Planters Association, Kandy, for the year ending 17th February 1882* (Colombo, 1882).

Planters Association of Ceylon, *Proceedings of the Planters Association, Kandy, for the year ending 17th February 1883* (Colombo, 1883).

Planters Association of Ceylon, *Proceedings of the Planters Association, Kandy, for the year ending 17th February 1884* (Colombo, 1884).

Planters Association of Ceylon, *Proceedings of the Planters Association, Kandy, for the year ending 17th February 1885* (Colombo, 1885).

Planters Association of Ceylon, *Proceedings of the Planters Association of Ceylon for the year ending 17th February 1886* (Colombo, 1886).

Planters Association of Ceylon, *Proceedings of the Planters Association, Kandy, for the year ending 17th February 1887* (Colombo, 1887).

Planters Association of Ceylon, *Proceedings of the Planters' Association of Ceylon for year ending February 17th, 1888* (Colombo, 1888).

Planters Association of Ceylon, *Proceedings of the Planters' Association of Ceylon for year ending 16th February, 1889* (Colombo, 1889).

Planters Association of Ceylon, *Proceedings of the Planters' Association of Ceylon for year ending 16th February, 1890* (Colombo, 1890).

Planters Association of Ceylon, *Proceedings of the Planters' Association of Ceylon for year ending 17th February, 1891* (Colombo, 1891).

Purdy, Frederick, 'On the earnings of agricultural labourers in Scotland and Ireland', *Journal of the Statistical Society*, 25:4 (1862), pp. 425–490.

Rigg, C.R., 'On coffee planting in Ceylon', *Journal of Indian Archipelago and Eastern Asia*, 6 (1852), pp. 123–142.

Rutherford. Henry K. and John Hill, *Ceylon Tea Planters' Note Book of Useful Memoranda*, 4th edn (Colombo, 1902–3), online at: http://storage.lib.uchicago.edu/pres/2014/pres2014–1196.pdf.

Sabonadière, William, *The Coffee Planter of Ceylon* (Guernsey, 1866).

Sinclair, Arthur, *In Tropical Lands: Recent Travels to the Sources of the Amazon, the West Indian Islands, and Ceylon* (Aberdeen, 1895).

Strutt, J.G. (ed.), *Tallis's Description of the Crystal Palace, and the Exhibition of the World's Industry in 1851*, vol. 2 (London and New York, 1851).

Tallis, John, *Tallis's History and Description of the Crystal Palace and the Exhibition of the World's Industry in 1851*, vol. 1 (London and New York, 1852).

Tennent, Sir James Emerson, *Ceylon: An Account of the Island, Physical, Historical and Topographical* (London, 1859), II.

Ukers, William H., *All About Tea*, vol. 1 (New York, 1935).

Ukers, William H., *All About Tea*, vol. 2 (New York, 1935).

Villiers, Thomas Lister (ed.), *Recollections Personal and Official of James Steuart, 1817–1866* (Colombo, c.1935).

Villiers, Sir Thomas L., *Some Pioneers of the Tea Industry* (Colombo, 1951).

Online sources

125th anniversary of tea industry, http://collect.ceylanka.net/itempage.asp?olditm=v92022

Ancestry.com, *England & Wales, National Probate Calendar (Index of Wills and Administrations), 1858–1966, 1973–1995* [database online]. Provo, UT, USA: Ancestry.com Operations, Inc., 2010.

Ancestry.com, *India, Select Deaths and Burials, 1719–1948* [database online].

Ancestry.com. *Scotland, National Probate Index (Calendar of Confirmations and Inventories), 1876–1936* [database online]. Provo, UT, USA: Ancestry.com Operations, Inc., 2010.

Ceylon Tea Museum, www.ceylonteamuseum.com

Eric Loudoun-Shand biography, https://en.wikipedia.org/wiki/Eric_Loudoun-Shand

Father of Ceylon Tea, James Taylor Monument Unveiled, Sunday Observer, 27 January 2013, www.sundayobserver.lk/2013/01/27/new40.asp

Genes Reunited, Shand family, www.genesreunited.co.uk/boards/board/general_topics/thread/542812

George Keith Maitland genealogy, http://ghgraham.org/georgemaitland1854.html

Grace's Guide to British Industrial History, David Reid, www.gracesguide.co.uk/David_Reid_(1841–1892)

Grace's Guide to British Industrial History, William Jackson, www.gracesguide.co.uk/William_Jackson_(1849–1915)

Gray, Victor, and Ismeth Raheem, 'Cousins in Ceylon', www.rothschildarchive.org/materials/ar2004ceylon.pdf

Henry Kerr Rutherford genealogy, www.geni.com/people/Henry-Rutherford/6000000023953083125

Lakdasum Trips, http://trips.lakdasun.org/lulkandura-loolecondera-few-hours-with-the-pioneer-of-tea-planters-in-sri-lanka.htm#pictures

Puvaneswaralingam, Shobitha, 'Yellow oleander poisoning and suicide in Sri Lanka', *Scottish Universities Medical Journal, Dundee* (2012), http://sumj.dundee.ac.uk/data/uploads/epub-article/002-sumj.epub.pdf

Scotland, National Probate Index (Calendar of Confirmations and Inventories), 1876–1936 [database online], 1890, p. 806.

Stewart Loudoun-Shand biography, https://en.wikipedia.org/wiki/Stewart_Loudoun-Shand

The Peerage, www.thepeerage.com/p52845.htm

'The Tale of Ceylon Tea', 13 May 2007, www.sundaytimes.lk/070513/TV/tv_1.html

Tribute to the Father of Ceylon Tea, March 2013, http://exploresrilanka.lk/2013/03/tribute-to-the-father-of-ceylon-tea/

Digital collections

Ceylon Observer, South Asian newspapers, 1864–1922: A World Newspaper Archive Collection

Interviews

With Lalith Abeykoon, January 2016
With Anil Cooke, 26 January 2016
With Avi de Silva, 25 January 2016
With Lawson family, 12 June 2016
With Anselm Perera, 4 February 2014
With Mike and Marion Robson, 22 June 2016
With Catriona Warner, 13 February 2016

Secondary sources

Books

Amrith, Sunil S., *Migration and Diaspora in Modern Asia* (Cambridge, 2011).
Anderson, Clare, *Subaltern Lives: Biographies of Colonialism in the Indian Ocean World, 1790–1820* (Cambridge, 2012).
Anderson, R.D., *Education and the Scottish People, 1750–1918* (Oxford, 1995).
Baines, Dudley, *Emigration from Europe, 1815–1930* (London, 1991).
Ball, J. Dyer, *Things Chinese* (1903; reprinted Singapore, 1989).
Bandarage, Asoka, *Colonialism in Sri Lanka: The Political Economy of the Kandyan Highlands 1833–1886* (New York, 1983).
Basu, Raj Sekhar, *Nandanar's Children: The Paraiyans' Tryst with Destiny, Tamil Nadu, 1850–1956* (New Delhi, 2011).
Beinart, William and Lotte Hughes, *Environment and Empire* (Oxford, 2007).
Belich, James, *Replenishing the Earth: The Settler Revolution and the Rise of the Anglo-World, 1783–1939* (Oxford, 2009).
Breckenridge, S.N., *The Hills of Paradise: British Enterprise and the Story of Plantation Growth in Sri Lanka* (Colombo, 2012).
Brooks, Ann and Ruth Simpson (eds), *Emotions in Transmigration: Transformation, Movement and Identity* (London and New York, 2012).
Brown, Callum G., *The Social History of Religion in Scotland since 1730* (London and New York, 1987).
Bruce, Arthur, *Laurencekirk: Days Gone By* (Laurencekirk, 2004).
Bueltmann, Tanja, *Clubbing Together: Ethnicity, Civility and Formal Sociability in the Scottish Diaspora to 1930* (Liverpool, 2014).
Burnard, Trevor, *Mastery, Tyranny and Desire: Thomas Thistlewood and his Slaves in the Anglo-Jamaican World* (Chapel Hill, 2004).
Cain, P.J. and A.G. Hopkins, *British Imperialism: Innovation and Expansion, 1688–1914* (London and New York, 1993).
Calloway, Colin, *White People, Indians, and Highlanders: Tribal Peoples and Colonial Encounters in Scotland and America* (Oxford, 2008).
Cartland, Barbara, *Moon Over Eden* (London, 1976).
Cloyd, E.L., *James Burnett: Lord Monboddo* (Oxford, 1972).
Craig, Cairns, *Intending Scotland: Explorations in Scottish Culture since the Enlightenment* (Edinburgh, 2009).

Curtin, Philip D., *Death by Migration: Europe's Encounter with the Tropical World in the Nineteenth Century* (Cambridge, 1989).

Dalrymple, William, *White Mughals: Love and Betrayal in Eighteenth Century India* (London, 2003).

Darwin, John, *The Empire Project: The Rise and Fall of the British World-System 1830–1970* (Cambridge, 2009)

de Silva, K.M., *A History of Sri Lanka* (Colombo, 2005 edition).

de Silva, R.K., *19th Century Newspaper Engravings of Ceylon – Sri Lanka* (London, 1998).

Devine, T.M., *The Transformation of Rural Scotland: Social Change and the Agrarian Economy, 1660–1815* (Edinburgh, 1994).

Devine, T.M., *The Great Highland Famine: Hunger, Emigration and the Scottish Highlands in the Nineteenth Century* (Edinburgh, 1988).

Devine, T.M., *To the Ends of the Earth: Scotland's Global Diaspora, 1750–2010* (London, 2011).

Devine, T.M., *The Scottish Nation, 1700–2000* (London, 2000).

Devine, T.M., *Scotland's Empire, 1600–1815* (London, 2003).

Duncan, James, *In the Shadows of the Tropics: Climate, Race and Biopower in Nineteenth Century Ceylon* (Aldershot, 2007).

Ellis, Markman, Richard Coulton and Matthew Mauger, *Empire of Tea: The Asian Leaf that Conquered the World* (London, 2015).

Ellis, Royston, *The Growing Years: History of the Ceylon Planters' Association* (Colombo, 2014).

Fernando, Maxwell, *The Story of Ceylon Tea* (Colombo, 2000).

Findlay, James F., *Dwight L. Moody: American Evangelist, 1837–1899* (Eugene, OR, 1969).

Fitzpatrick, David, *Oceans of Consolation: Personal Accounts of Irish Migration to Australia* (Cork, 1995).

Forrest, D.M., *A Hundred Years of Ceylon Tea, 1867–1967* (London, 1967).

Gardiner, Michael, *At the Edge of Empire: The Life of Thomas Blake Glover* (Edinburgh, 2008).

George Steuart & Co Ltd, *The George Steuart Story* (Colombo, 1985).

Ghosh, Durba, *Sex and the Family in Colonial India* (Cambridge, 2006).

Gove, A., *The History of Auchenblae* (unpublished booklet entered in the Village History book competition under the auspices of the Scottish Women's Rural Institutes, 1967) held at NLS).

Greenhalgh, Paul, *Ephemeral Vistas: The* Expositions Universelles, *Great Exhibitions and World's Fairs, 1851–1939* (Manchester, 1988).

Griffiths, Sir Percival, *The History of the Indian Tea Industry* (London, 1967).

Hall, Catherine et al., *Legacies of British Slave-Ownership: Colonial Slavery and the Formation of Victorian Britain* (Cambridge, 2014).

Hamilton, Douglas J., *Scotland, the Caribbean and the Atlantic World, 1750–1820* (Manchester, 2005).

Harman, Claire, *Robert Louis Stevenson: A Biography* (London, 2005).

Harper, Marjory, *Emigration from North-East Scotland: Volume One. Willing Exiles* (Aberdeen, 1988).

Harper, Marjory, *Adventurers and Exiles: The Great Scottish Exodus* (London, 2003).

Harper, Marjory (ed.), *Emigrant Homecomings: The Return Movement of Emigrants, 1600–2000* (Manchester, 2005).
Heidemann, Frank, *Kanganies in Sri Lanka and Malaysia* (Munich, 1992).
Hewson, Eileen, *Graveyards in Ceylon: Tea Country. Volume 3* (Wem, 2009).
Hoffenberg, Peter H., *An Empire on Display: English, Indian, and Australian Exhibitions from the Crystal Palace to the Great War* (Berkeley and Los Angeles, 2001).
Illouz, Eva, *Cold Intimacies: The Making of Emotional Capitalism* (Cambridge, 2007).
Jayawardena, Kumari, *Nobodies to Somebodies: The Rise of the Colonial Bourgeoisie in Sri Lanka* (London and New York, 2002).
Kriegel, Lara, *Grand Designs: Labor, Empire, and the Museum in Victorian Culture* (Durham, NC and London, 2007).
Lambert, David and Alan Lester (eds), *Colonial Lives Across the British Empire: Imperial Careering in the Long Nineteenth Century* (Cambridge, 2006).
Macfarlane, Alan and Iris Macfarlane, *Green Gold: The Empire of Tea* (London, 2003).
Magee, Gary B. and Andrew S. Thompson, *Empire and Globalisation: Networks of People, Goods and Capital in the British World, c.1850–1914* (Cambridge, 2010).
McCabe, Jane, *Race, Tea and Colonial Resettlement: Imperial Families, Interrupted* (London, 2017).
McCarthy, Angela, *Personal Narratives of Irish and Scottish Migration, 1921–65: 'For Spirit and Adventure'* (Manchester, 2007).
McCarthy, Angela (ed.), *A Global Clan. Scottish Migrant Networks and Identities since the Eighteenth Century* (London and New York, 2006).
McCarthy, Angela, *Irish Migrants in New Zealand, 1840–1937: 'The Desired Haven'* (Woodbridge, 2005).
McCarthy, Angela, *Scottishness and Irishness in New Zealand since 1840* (Manchester, 2011).
McGilvary, George K., *East India Patronage and the British State: The Scottish Elite and Politics in the Eighteenth Century* (London, 2008).
Mackay, James A. (ed.), *The Complete Letters of Robert Burns* (Alloway, 1987).
MacKenzie, John, *Orientalism: History, Theory and the Arts* (Manchester and New York, 1995).
MacKenzie, John M., *Empires of Nature and the Nature of Empires: Imperialism, Scotland and the Environment* (East Linton, 1997).
MacKenzie, John M., *The Empire of Nature: Hunting, Conservation and British Imperialism* (Manchester, 1988).
MacKenzie, John M. with Nigel R. Dalziel, *The Scots in South Africa: Ethnicity, Identity, Gender and Race, 1772–1914* (Manchester, 2005).
MacKenzie, John M. and T.M. Devine (eds), *Scotland and the British Empire* (Oxford, 2011).
McKenzie, Kirsten, *Scandal in the Colonies: Sydney and Cape Town, 1820–1850* (Melbourne, 2004).
McLaren, Martha, *British India and British Scotland, 1780–1830* (Akron, 2001).
Mendis, G.C. (ed.), *The Colebrooke-Cameron Papers*, 2 vols (Oxford, 1959).
Mendis, G.C., *Ceylon Under the British* (Colombo, 1946).

Miller, Kerby A., *Emigrants and Exiles: Ireland and the Irish Exodus to North America* (New York, 1984).

Mills, Lennox A., *Ceylon under British Rule, 1795–1932* (London, 1933).

Mintz, Sidney W., *Sweetness and Power: The Place of Sugar in Modern History* (New York, 1985).

Mitchell, Beryl T., *Tea, Tytlers and Tribes: An Australian Woman's Memories of Tea Planting in Ceylon* (Henley Beach, 1996).

Moldrich, Donovan, *Bitter Berry Bondage: The Nineteenth Century Coffee Workers of Sri Lanka* (Kandy, 1989).

Morton, Graeme and David A. Wilson (eds), *Irish and Scottish Encounters with Indigenous Peoples* (Montreal and Kingston, 2013).

Moxham, Roy, *A Brief History of Tea: The Extraordinary Story of the World's Favourite Drink* (London, 2009).

Nasaw, David, *Andrew Carnegie* (New York, 2006).

O'Farrell, Patrick, *Letters from Irish Australia, 1825–1929* (Kensington, 1984).

Peebles, Patrick, *Sri Lanka: A Handbook of Historical Statistics* (Boston, 1982).

Peebles, Patrick, *Plantation Tamils of Ceylon* (London and New York, 2001).

Ramamurthy, Anandi, *Imperial Persuaders: Images of Africa and Asia in British Advertising* (Manchester, 2003).

Robertson, Emma, *Chocolate, Women and Empire: A Social and Cultural History* (Manchester and New York, 2009).

Rose, Sarah, *For All the Tea in China: How England Stole the World's Favorite Drink and Changed History* (New York, 2011).

Rothschild, Emma, *The Inner Life of Empires: An Eighteenth-Century History* (Princeton, 2011).

Saunders, Laurance James, *Scottish Democracy, 1815–1840: The Social and Intellectual Background* (Edinburgh, 1950).

Snodgrass, Donald R., *Ceylon: An Export Economy in Transition* (Homewood, IL, 1966).

Spiers, Sheila M., *The Kirkyard of Glenbervie* (Aberdeen, 1996).

Still, John, *The Jungle Tide* (Edinburgh and London, 1930).

Strange, Julie-Marie, *Death, Grief and Poverty in Britain, 1870–1914* (Cambridge, 2005).

Straw, Leigh S.L., *A Semblance of Scotland: Scottish Identity in Colonial Western Australia* (Glasgow, 2006).

Thompson, Andrew, *The Empire Strikes Back: The Impact of Imperialism on Britain from the Mid-Nineteenth Century* (Abingdon, 2014).

Tosh, John, *A Man's Place: Masculinity and the Middle-Class Home in Victorian England* (New Haven and London, 1999).

vanden Driesen, I.H., *The Long Walk: Indian Plantation Labour in Sri Lanka in the Nineteenth Century* (New Delhi, 1997).

Varricchio, Mario (ed.), *Back to Caledonia: Scottish Homecomings from the Seventeenth Century to the Present* (Edinburgh, 2012).

Watson, Don, *Caledonia Australis: Scottish Highlanders on the Frontier of Australia* (Sydney, 1997; first published 1984).

Waugh, Alex, *The Lipton Story: A Centennial Biography* (London, 2013).

Weatherstone, John, *The Early British Tea and Coffee Planters and their Way of Life, 1825–1900: The Pioneers* (London, 1986).
Webb, James, *Tropical Pioneers: Human Agency and Ecological Change in the Highlands of Sri Lanka, 1800–1900* (Athens, 2002).
Wenzlhuemer, Roland, *From Coffee to Tea Cultivation in Ceylon, 1880–1900* (Leiden and Boston, 2008).
Wesumperuma, D., *Indian Immigrant Plantation Workers in Sri Lanka, 1880–1910* (Nugegoga, 1986).
Wickramasinghe, Nira, *Sri Lanka in the Modern Age: A History of Contested Identities* (London, 2006).
Wright, Arnold (ed.), *Twentieth Century Impressions of Ceylon: Its History, People, Commerce Industries and Resources* (New Delhi, 1999).

Articles and chapters

Anderson, M. and D.J. Morse, 'The people', in W. Hamish Fraser and R.J. Morris (eds), *People and Society in Scotland, II: 1830–1914* (Edinburgh, 1990), pp. 8–45.
Armitage, David, 'The Scottish diaspora', in Jenny Wormald (ed.), *Scotland: A History* (Oxford, 2005), pp. 272–303.
Arunachalam, P., 'Population: The island's race, religions, languages, caste, and customs', in Arnold Wright (ed.), *Twentieth Century Impressions of Ceylon: Its History, People, Commerce, Industries and Resources* (New Delhi, 1999), pp. 323–354.
Aslam M.S.M. and Lee Jolliffe, 'Repurposing colonial tea heritage through historic lodging', *Journal of Heritage Tourism*, 10:2 (2015), pp. 111–128.
Bamber, M. Kelway, 'The tea industry', in Arnold Wright (ed.), *Twentieth Century Impressions of Ceylon: Its History, People, Commerce, Industries and Resources* (New Delhi, 1999), pp. 248–250.
Barron, T.J., 'Scots and the coffee industry in nineteenth century Ceylon', in T.M. Devine and Angela McCarthy (eds), *The Scottish Experience in Asia, c.1700 to the Present: Settlers and Sojourners* (Cham, 2017), pp. 163–185.
Barron, T.J., 'Science and the nineteenth-century Ceylon coffee planters', *Journal of Imperial and Commonwealth History*, 16:1 (1987), pp. 5–23.
Behal, Rana P., 'Coolie drivers or benevolent paternalists? British tea planters in Assam and the indenture labour system', *Modern Asian Studies*, 44:1 (2010), pp. 29–51.
Boccagni, Paolo and Loretta Baldassar, 'Emotions on the move: Mapping the emergent field of emotion and migration', *Emotion, Space and Society*, 16 (2015), pp. 73–80.
Bourke, Joanna, 'Fear and anxiety: Writing about emotion in modern history', *History Workshop Journal*, 55:1 (2003), pp. 111–133.
Broadie, Alexander, 'The rise (and fall?) of the Scottish Enlightenment', in T.M. Devine and Jenny Wormald (eds), *The Oxford Handbook of Modern Scottish History* (Oxford, 2012), pp. 370–385.
Brown, Callum G., 'Religion', in Lynn Abrams, Eleanor Gordon, Deborah Simonton and Eileen Janes Yeo (eds), *Gender in Scottish History Since 1700* (Edinburgh, 2006), pp. 84–110.

Brown, Callum G., 'Religion and social change', in T.M. Devine and Rosalind Mitchison (eds), *People and Society in Scotland, I: 1760–1830* (Edinburgh, 1988), pp. 143–162.

Burton, Antoinette, 'Who needs the nation? Interrogating "British" history', *Journal of Historical Sociology*, 10:3 (1997), pp. 227–248.

Christopher, Anthony John, '"Ariane's thread": Sri Lankan census superintendents' reports as guides to identity data', *Asian Population Studies*, 11:3 (2015), pp. 1–19.

De Groot, Joanna, 'Metropolitan desires and colonial connections: Reflections on consumption and empire', in Catherine Hall and Sonya Rose (eds), *At Home with Empire: Metropolitan Culture and the Imperial World* (Cambridge, 2006), pp. 166–191.

de Silva, K.M., 'Nineteenth century origins of nationalism in Ceylon', in K.M. de Silva (ed.), *University of Ceylon History of Ceylon vol. 3: From the Beginning of the Nineteenth Century to 1948* (Peradeniya, 1973), pp. 249–261.

Devine, T.M., 'Scottish farm service in the agricultural revolution', in T.M. Devine (ed.), *Farm Servants and Labour in Lowland Scotland, 1770–1914* (Edinburgh, 1984), pp. 1–8.

Devine, T.M., 'Industrialisation', in T.M. Devine, Clive Lee and George Peden (eds), *The Transformation of Scotland: The Economy since 1700* (Edinburgh, 2005), pp. 34–70.

Devine, T.M., 'The transformation of agriculture: Cultivation and clearance', in T.M. Devine, Clive Lee and George Peden (eds), *The Transformation of Scotland: The Economy since 1700* (Edinburgh, 2005), pp. 71–99.

Devine, T.M., 'History, Scotland and slavery', in T.M. Devine (ed.), *Recovering Scotland's Slavery Past: The Caribbean Connection* (Edinburgh, 2015), pp. 246–251.

Devine, T.M., 'A Scottish empire of enterprise in the East, c.1695–1914', in T.M. Devine and Angela McCarthy (eds), *Scottish Experience in Asia, c. 1700 to the Present* (Cham, 2017), pp. 22–49.

Devine, T.M. and Angela McCarthy, 'The Scottish experience in Asia, c.1700 to the present: Settlers and sojourners', in T.M. Devine and Angela McCarthy (eds), *The Scottish Experience in Asia, c. 1700 to the Present* (Cham, 2017), pp. 1–21.

Diner, Hasia R., 'Ethnicity and emotions in America: Dimensions of the unexplored', in Peter N. Stearns and Jan Lewis (eds), *An Emotional History of the United States* (New York and London, 1998), pp. 197–217.

English, Peter C., 'Emergence of rheumatic fever in the nineteenth century', in Charles E. Rosenberg and Janet Golden (eds), *Framing Disease: Studies in Cultural History* (New Brunswick, 1997), pp. 21–32.

Fitzpatrick, David, 'What Scottish diaspora?', in Angela McCarthy and John M. MacKenzie (eds), *Global Migrations: The Scottish Diaspora since 1600* (Edinburgh, 2016), pp. 240–271.

Gordon, Eleanor, 'The family', in Lynn Abrams, Eleanor Gordon, Deborah Simonton and Eileen Janes Yeo (eds), *Gender in Scottish History Since 1700* (Edinburgh, 2006), pp. 235–267.

Griffith, R. Marie, '"Joy unspeakable and full of glory": The vocabulary of pious emotion in the narratives of American Pentecostal women, 1910–1945', in Jan Lewis and Peter N. Stearns (eds), *An Emotional History of the United States* (New York, 1998), pp. 218–240.

Henly, Revd. W. 'Ecclesiastical', in Arnold Wright (ed.), *Twentieth Century Impressions of Ceylon: Its History, People, Commerce Industries and Resources* (New Delhi, 1999), pp. 268–290.

Howe, Stephen, 'Empire and ideology', in Sarah Stockwell (ed.), *The British Empire: Themes and Perspectives* (Oxford, 2008), pp. 157–176.

Jolliffe, Lee and Mohamed S.M. Aslam, 'Tea heritage tourism: Evidence from Sri Lanka', *Journal of Heritage Tourism*, 4:4 (2009), pp. 331–344.

Jones, Margaret, '"Permanent boarders": The British in Ceylon, 1815–1960', in Robert Bickers (ed.) *Settlers and Expatriates: Britons over the Seas* (Oxford, 2010), pp. 205–232.

Kershaw, Ian, 'Personality and power: The individual's role in the history of twentieth-century Europe', *Historian*, 83 (2004), pp. 7–19.

Kidd, Colin, 'Race, empire and the limits of nineteenth century nationhood', *Historical Journal*, 46:4 (2003), pp. 873–892.

McCarthy, Angela, 'The importance of Scottish origins in the nineteenth century: James Taylor and Ceylon tea', in Angela McCarthy and John M. MacKenzie (eds), *Global Migrations: The Scottish Diaspora since 1600* (Edinburgh, 2016), pp. 117–137.

McCarthy, Angela, 'Ceylon: A Scottish colony?', in T.M. Devine and Angela McCarthy (eds), *The Scottish Experience in Asia, c. 1700 to the Present* (Cham, 2017), pp. 187–211.

McGilvary, George, 'Scottish agency houses in South-East Asia, c.1760–1813', in T.M. Devine and Angela McCarthy (eds), *The Scottish Experience in Asia, c. 1700 to the Present* (Cham, 2017), pp. 75–96.

MacKenzie, John M., 'Scots and the environment of Empire', in John M. MacKenzie and T.M. Devine (eds), *Scotland and the British Empire* (Oxford, 2011), pp. 147–175.

MacKenzie, John M. and T.M. Devine, 'Introduction', in John M. MacKenzie and T.M. Devine (eds), *Scotland and the British Empire* (Oxford, 2011), pp. 1–29.

Mackillop, Andrew, 'Locality, nation, and empire: Scots and the empire in Asia, c.1695–c.1813', in John M. MacKenzie and T.M. Devine (eds), *Scotland and the British Empire* (Oxford, 2012), pp. 54–83.

Mackillop, Andrew, 'The Highlands and the returning nabob: Sir Hector Munro of Novar, 1760–1807', in Marjory Harper (ed.), *Emigrant Homecomings: The Return Movement of Emigrants, 1600–2000* (Manchester, 2005), pp. 233–261.

Marker, Willis B., 'Scottish teachers', in Heather Holmes (ed.), *Scottish Life and Society: Institutions of Scotland: Education* (East Linton, 2000), pp. 273–296.

Matt, Susan J., 'Current emotion research in history: Or, doing history from the inside out', *Emotion Review*, 3:1 (2011), pp. 117–124.

Merritt, Rebecca, 'Public perceptions of 1857: An overview of British press responses to the Indian uprising', in Andrea Major and Crispin Bates (eds), *Mutiny at the Margins: New Perspectives on the Indian Uprising of 1857. Volume 2: Britain and the Indian Uprising* (New Delhi, 2013), pp. 1–24.

Michie, Ranald C., 'Aberdeen and Ceylon: Economic links in the nineteenth century', *Northern Scotland*, 4 (1981), pp. 69–82.

Orr, Alastair, 'Farm servants and farm labour in the Forth Valley and south-east lowlands', in T.M. Devine (ed.), *Farm Servants and Labour in Lowland Scotland, 1770–1914* (Edinburgh, 1984), pp. 29–54.

Parris, John and A.G.L. Shaw, 'The Melbourne International Exhibition 1880–1881', *Victorian Historical Journal*, 51:4 (1980), pp. 237–254.

Paterson, Lindsay, 'Traditions of Scottish education', in Heather Holmes (ed.), *Scottish Life and Society: Institutions of Scotland: Education* (East Linton, 2000), pp. 21–43.

Putnis, Peter, 'International press and the Indian uprising', in Marina Carter and Crispin Bates (eds), *Mutiny at the Margins: New Perspectives on the Indian Uprising of 1857. Volume 3: Global Perspectives* (New Delhi, 2013), pp. 1–17.

Rajaratnum, S. 'Growth of plantation agriculture in Ceylon, 1886–1931', *Ceylon Journal of Historical and Social Studies*, 4:1 (1961), pp. 1–20.

Rajaratnam, S., 'The Ceylon tea industry 1886–1931', *Ceylon Journal of Historical and Social Studies*, 4:2 (1961), pp. 169–202.

Rendall, Jane, 'Scottish Orientalism: From Robertson to James Mill' *Historical Journal*, 25:1 (1982), pp. 43–69.

Roberts, Michael, 'Land problems and policies, c.1832–c.1900', in K.M. de Silva (ed.), *University of Ceylon History of Ceylon, vol. 3: From the Beginning of the Nineteenth Century to 1948* (Peradeniya, 1973), pp. 119–145.

Roberts, M.W., 'Indian estate labour in Ceylon during the coffee period (1830–1880), Part I', *Indian Economic and Social History Review*, 3:1 (1966), pp. 1–52.

Roberts, M.W., 'Indian estate labour in Ceylon during the coffee period (1830–1880), Part II', *Indian Economic and Social History Review*, 3:2 (1966), pp. 101–136.

Roberts, Michael and L.A. Wickremeratne, 'Export agriculture in the nineteenth century', in K.M. de Silva (ed.), *University of Ceylon History of Ceylon vol. 3: From the Beginning of the Nineteenth Century to 1948* (Peradeniya, 1973), pp. 89–118.

Rogers, John D., 'Caste as a social category and identity in colonial Lanka', *Indian Economic and Social History Review*, 41:1 (2004), pp. 51–77.

Rosenwein, Barbara H., 'Problems and methods in the history of emotions', *Passions in Context: International Journal for the History and Theory of Emotions*, 1 (2010), pp. 1–32, online at www.passionsincontext.de.

Rosenwein, Barbara H., 'Worrying about emotions in history', *American Historical Review*, 107:3 (2002), pp. 821–845.

Samaraweera, Vijaya, 'Economic and social developments under the British, 1796–1832', in K.M. de Silva (ed.), *University of Ceylon History of Ceylon vol. 3: From the Beginning of the Nineteenth Century to 1948* (Peradeniya, 1973), pp. 48–65.

Sharma, Jayeeta, '"Lazy" natives, coolie labour, and the Assam tea industry', *Modern Asian Studies*, 43:6 (2009), pp. 1287–1324.

Sharpe, Jenny, 'The unspeakable limits of rape: Colonial violence and counter-insurgency', *Genders*, 10 (1991), pp. 25–46.

Smout, T.C., 'Perspectives on the Scottish identity', *Scottish Affairs*, 6:1 (1994), pp. 101–113.

Sprott, Gavin, 'The country tradesman', in T.M. Devine (ed.), *Farm Servants and Labour in Lowland Scotland, 1700–1914* (Edinburgh, 1984), pp.143–155.

Stearns, Peter N. and Carol Z. Stearns, 'Emotionology: Clarifying the history of emotions and emotional standards', *American Historical Review*, 90:4 (1985), pp. 813–836.

Svašek, Maruška, 'Affective moves: Transit, transition and transformation', in Maruška Svašek (ed.), *Moving Subjects, Moving Objects: Transnationalism, Cultural Production and Emotions* (New York and Oxford, 2012), pp. 1–40.

Svašek, Maruška, 'On the move: Emotions and human mobility', *Journal of Ethnic and Migration Studies*, 36:6 (2010), pp. 867–880.

Tarlow, Sarah, 'The archaeology of emotion and affect', *Annual Review of Anthropology*, 41 (2012), pp. 169–185.

Thompson, Andrew, 'Introduction', in Andrew Thompson (ed.), *Writing Imperial Histories* (Manchester and New York, 2013), pp. 1–28.

Wickremeratne, L.A., 'The development of transportation in Ceylon c.1800–1947', in K.M. de Silva (ed.), *University of Ceylon History of Ceylon vol. 3: From the Beginning of the Nineteenth Century to 1948* (Peradeniya, 1973), pp. 303–316.

Wormald, Jenny, 'Reformed and Godly Scotland?', in T.M. Devine and Jenny Wormald (eds), *The Oxford Handbook of Modern Scottish History* (Oxford, 2012), pp. 204–219.

Theses

Haley, Jill, 'The Colonial Family Album: Photography and Identity in Otago, 1848–1890' (PhD, University of Otago, 2017).

Marrs, Clifford James, 'The 1859 Religious Revival in Scotland: A Review and Critique of the Movement with particular reference to the City of Glasgow' (PhD, University of Glasgow, 1995).

Unpublished articles

Barron, T.J., 'Sir James Emerson Tennent and the planting pioneers', unpublished paper presented to the Ceylon Studies seminar series 1970/72.

Barron, T.J. 'British coffee planters in 19th century Ceylon', presented to the postgraduate seminar at the Institute of Commonwealth Studies, University of London, 1973.

Melvani, Kamal, Peter Duncan, and Priyantha Kamburegama, 'Freeing the land of the tea legacy – The case of wildflower landholding in Sri Lanka', private document provided by Peter Duncan.

Saville, Richard and Paul Auerbach, 'Education and social capital in the development of Scotland to 1750', presented to the Annual Conference of the Economic History Society, University of Reading, 31 March–2 April 2006.

Index

Note: page numbers in *italic* refer to illustrations.